An Honest Calling

An Honest Calling

THE LAW PRACTICE OF
Abraham Lincoln

MARK E. STEINER

NORTHERN ILLINOIS UNIVERSITY PRESS / DEKALB

© 2006 by Northern Illinois University Press

Published by the Northern Illinois University Press, DeKalb, Illinois   60115

Manufactured in the United States using acid-free paper

All Rights Reserved

Design by Julia Fauci

Library of Congress Cataloging-in-Publication Data

Steiner, Mark E.

An honest calling : the law practice of Abraham Lincoln / Mark E. Steiner.

   p.   cm.

Includes bibliographical references and index.

ISBN-13: 978-0-87580-358-6 (clothbound : alk. paper)

ISBN-10: 0-87580-358-X (clothbound : alk. paper)

1. Lincoln, Abraham, 1809–1865—Career in law. 2. Lawyers—Illinois—Biography.

3. Presidents—United States—Biography. I. Title.

E457.2.S8 2006

340.092—dc22

2006001575

For Lee

Contents

Acknowledgments

Without the Lincoln Legal Papers project in Springfield, Illinois, this book would not have been possible. Cullom Davis allowed access to documents when I first started this project and later hired me as an associate editor. Past and present members of the Lincoln Legal Papers/Papers of Abraham Lincoln—Bill Beard, Marty Benner, Cullom Davis, John Lupton, Chris Schnell, and Daniel Stowell—were exceedingly patient and helpful.

For their support and encouragement, I would like to thank Scott Carpenter, Lynne Liberato, Robert C. Oliver, Ramon Rosales, Jr., and R. M. Sharpe, Jr., all members of the Texas bar, and Jim Alfini, John Bauman, Kathleen Bergin, David Goldstein, Dick Graving, Randy Kelso, Matthew Mirow, Shelby Moore, Phillip Page, Jim Paulsen, Tom Read, Jeff Rensberger, Cherie Taylor, Buford Terrell, Charles Weigel, Ursula Weigold, and John Worley, my colleagues, past and present, at South Texas College of Law. Lincoln scholars Michael Burlingame and Allen Guelzo each read an earlier version of the manuscript. I also appreciated kind words from legal historians Tom Russell and James W. Ely, Jr., on specific portions of the manuscript. My editors at Northern Illinois University Press, Martin Johnson and Melody Herr, exhibited almost saintly forbearance. I benefited greatly from the critical readings of the two anonymous referees who read the manuscript for the press. Near the end of a long process, when I really needed some help, James Lee double-checked the endnotes and Sharon Yin assisted with indexing

I am grateful for my teachers and mentors: John Germann, Arthur Rosenbaum, Gus A. Schill, Jr., James Kirby Martin, Steven Mintz, Joseph A. Glatthaar, Craig Joyce, and Robert C. Palmer. Jim Martin and Joe Glatthaar gave me the idea of writing on lawyer Lincoln; Bob Palmer got me through the early stages. I am indebted to librarians and archivists, including Keiko Horton at Interlibrary Loan in the Anderson Library, University of Houston; Thomas F. Schwartz, Illinois State Historian; Kim Bauer, Curator of the Henry Horner Lincoln Collection, and Kathryn Harris at the Abraham Lincoln Presidential Library & Museum, Springfield, Illinois; Mike Widener, Rare Books Librarian, Tarlton Law Library, The University of Texas; and Ann Puckett, David Cowan, and Monica Ortale at the South Texas College of Law Library.

I appreciate my family's support; I thank Mignon Steiner, Karen Hixon, Mike Steiner, Mary Ellen Steiner, M'Adele Carson, Anne Burnson, and Mindy Karr. My in-laws, Don and Ginny Helmers and Ray Helmers, have been great. My daughters, Hannah and Emma, have shown both interest and pride in this book, which I have appreciated enormously. My greatest debt is to my wife, Lee Helmers Steiner, for her support and patience.

Parts of chapter two appeared in the *Lincoln Herald* (used courtesy of the Abraham Library and Museum, Lincoln Memorial University, Harrogate, Tenn.) and in 18 *Legal Reference Services Quarterly* 47–122 (1999) (used with permission of The Haworth Press, Inc.). Portions of chapter three are an expanded version of an article that appeared in the *Journal of the Abraham Lincoln Association* (used courtesy of the Abraham Lincoln Association). Parts of chapter four were published in the *University of Detroit Mercy Law Review* and are used here with permission of the university. Portions of chapter five appeared in the *Illinois Historical Journal* and are used here with permission of the Illinois Historic Preservation Agency.

An Honest Calling

Introduction

There is a vague popular belief that lawyers are necessarily dishonest. I
say *vague,* because when we consider to what extent *confidence,* and *honors* are reposed in, and conferred upon lawyers by the people, it appears
improbable that their impression of dishonesty, is very distinct and
vivid. Yet the expression is common—almost universal. Let no young
man, choosing the law for a calling, for a moment yield to the popular
belief. Resolve to be honest at all events; and if, in your own judgment
you cannot be an honest lawyer, resolve to be honest without being a
lawyer. Choose some other occupation rather than one in the choosing
of which you do, in advance, consent to be a knave.

—Abraham Lincoln, Notes for a Law Lecture[1]

Like many other young men in antebellum America, Abraham
Lincoln chose law as a calling. He practiced law for almost
twenty-five years, handling thousands of cases. Throughout his
career, he displayed his resolve to be "honest at all times"—it
was as a lawyer that he earned the nickname "Honest Abe." Lincoln had a firm belief about the role lawyers were to play in resolving disputes, and he held fast to that role.

As a lawyer, Abraham Lincoln developed a distinctive Whiggish attitude toward law and the role of law in American society.
Politically, Whigs were modernizing conservatives who favored
internal improvements such as railroads to foster economic
growth. Whigs also believed that the rule of law provided a neutral means to resolve disputes. Lincoln was a Whig lawyer who
embodied the Whig reverence for law and order.

Lincoln's essentially political conception of a lawyer's role defined what an "honest lawyer" would do in his practice: represent clients faithfully. What unified his practice was a belief in

the importance of order and law. Contrary to what earlier scholars have said, Lincoln was neither a saint nor a consistent advocate for corporate interests, economic development, or even railroad interests. Lincoln instead possessed a service mentality; he was ready to represent any client. But Whig lawyers like Lincoln were more than mere legal technicians; they also stressed the importance of lawyers serving as guardians of community values. Lincoln was as interested in mediating and settling cases as he was in trying them.

Lincoln's early practice involved litigants who were primarily members of relatively small rural communities. He always enjoyed the lawyering style demanded by purely local lawsuits. Lincoln, like most lawyers in small communities, was keenly aware of the social context of these local disputes. Their community orientation favored mediation and compromise, and Lincoln thus tried to serve as a mediator or peacemaker.

As his practice changed during his career, Lincoln became less willing to serve any client or to mediate disputes. Lincoln began handling cases that typified the rise of a market economy that was national in scope. His corporate clients often stymied his efforts to mediate these disputes. The "market morality" that developed during this period required lawyers to represent only the narrow interests of their clients. This service mentality also led Lincoln, like many antebellum lawyers, to suspend his judgment on the justness of his clients' claims. Lincoln, despite holding principled antislavery beliefs, was able to represent a slaveholder in an unsuccessful attempt to regain custody of an African-American woman and four of her children. His willingness to subordinate his personal beliefs shows the moral failure of Whig lawyering.

Lincoln somewhat reluctantly represented corporate clients. He resented the quickened pace and the impersonal style of lawyering that his corporate clients demanded, and he disliked the loss of autonomy that came with the increased supervision by his corporate clients. Lincoln, at times, appeared to want things both ways: he wanted the freedom to exercise his discretion and judgment, and he wanted to represent only the interests of his clients. Nor was Lincoln in the later stages of his career free to represent anyone who desired his services. Lincoln accepted a retainer from the Illinois Central Railroad that prohibited him from suing the railroad. During the course of his career, Whig lawyering had become outmoded, suffering the strains of litigation arising from both slavery and market capitalism.

Lawyer Lincoln in American Memory

An opinion poll once revealed that Abraham Lincoln was one of the five most admired lawyers in America.[1] Such elevated status has more to do with how Americans view Lincoln the president than what they know about Lincoln the lawyer. The portrait that emerges from the literature on Lincoln's law practice is not that of the Whig lawyer willing to represent any side of a dispute. The literature on Lincoln's law career instead has been shaped largely by the positive cultural image of Lincoln and the negative cultural image of lawyers in American society. Early biographers, aware of the distrust and hostility toward lawyers, glossed over Lincoln's law practice. These writers were content with superficial depictions of Lincoln as a virtuous, heroic country lawyer. The treatment of Lincoln's law practice improved somewhat with the professionalization of history in the twentieth century yet remains insufficient. Historians' lack of interest in his law career, their apparent belief that their lack of legal training precluded study of Lincoln's law practice, and the inaccessibility of documents has stymied a thorough examination of his law practice. Lawyers have produced considerable writings on lawyer Lincoln. These attempts, however, are aimed not at understanding, but appropriation. Lawyers have wanted to use the image of Lincoln to refurbish their own.

All three types of writings on Lincoln's legal career show the impact of cultural stereotypes about both Lincoln and lawyers. The first group consists of memoirs by lawyers who practiced law with Lincoln. These works include *Herndon's Lincoln: The True Story of a Great Life* (1888) by William H. Herndon and *Jesse Weik and Life on the Circuit with Lincoln* (1892) by Henry Clay Whitney. The second group, Lincoln biographers, generally overlook Lincoln's law practice but do not dismiss it entirely. The third group consists of studies on Lincoln's law practice by lawyers, who generally claim too much for lawyer Lincoln.

Treatment of Lincoln's law practice has tended to be anecdotal, examining only the same four or five cases out of the thousands of cases Lincoln handled.[2] These cases serve to build Lincoln's image or to inflate his reputation as a nationally prominent lawyer. The best-known of this handful is the Duff Armstrong murder case, which is also known as the Almanac trial.[3] There, a witness had testified that he could see Armstrong strike the fatal blow because the moon was high overhead. Lincoln, who defended Armstrong, secured an acquittal for his client by producing an almanac for the year that showed the moon was near the horizon at that time of night. This case, which is hardly typical of Lincoln's practice, has been overemphasized for two reasons. First, it is a good story. Duff Armstrong was the son of Jack and Hannah Armstrong, friends of Lincoln from his early days in New Salem. The typical account tells how the widow Armstrong begged Lincoln to represent her son, how Lincoln emotionally argued Armstrong's innocence, and how Lincoln refused to charge a fee.[4] This 1858 case shows that Lincoln was still a man of the people. Second, the typical account of Lincoln's defense of Duff resonates with the positive cultural image of the heroic criminal defense lawyer winning, against the odds, the acquittal of an innocent person.[5]

Writers often note the Manny Reaper case for its ironic overtones. This 1855 case is mentioned because Lincoln's co-counsel, who included Edwin M. Stanton, snubbed Lincoln at the trial. For many writers this treatment foreshadows how Lincoln was often underestimated by members of his Cabinet during the Civil War.[6]

While the number of cases that are mentioned by most writers has not changed over time, the selection has. Lincoln once represented slaveowner Robert Matson in a habeas corpus hearing that determined the freedom of an African-American woman and four of her children. Many early biographers avoided mentioning the case while modern writers have struggled to explain it. More recent commentators have disagreed about Lincoln's motivation in taking the case and his effectiveness in handling it.

Writers include other cases for their economic importance. For example, the McLean County tax case is mentioned because Lincoln won an important victory for the Illinois Central Railroad that secured its exemption from county and local taxation, and he had to sue the railroad for his five-thousand-dollar fee for the victory that he believed "was worth half a million dollars" to the railroad. In the *Effie Afton* case, Lincoln again defended railroad interests. The *Effie Afton* collided with a Chicago, Rock Island, and Pacific Railroad Company bridge, which was the first to span the Mississippi. The vessel owners sued for damages, claiming the bridge was an obstruction to navigation. Historian Benjamin Thomas noted that the "case had significance far beyond the property loss involved—it was a conflict of sections, economies, and eras. It arrayed the east–west railroad axis against the north–south river axis; New Orleans and St. Louis against Chicago and New York; the steamboat age against the new era of railroads."[7] Lincoln argued to the jury about the importance of western expansion. The result was somewhat anticlimactic: the jury deadlocked.[8] The economic interests colliding here merged too strongly with national economic themes for historians to ignore this case.

The negative cultural image of lawyers and the positive cultural image of Lincoln were the two primary reasons that biographers generally have paid scant attention to lawyer Lincoln.[9] The image of lawyer Lincoln clashes with the images of Lincoln as frontier hero or great emancipator. Lincoln, more than any other president, is shrouded in mythology and symbolism. Lincoln biographer Stephen B. Oates explained how Lincoln "comes to us in the mists of legend as a homespun 'rail splitter' from the Illinois prairie" or as "Father Abraham, the Great Emancipator who led the North off to civil war to free the slaves and after the conflict ended offered the South a tender and forgiving hand."[10] Within these images, there is little room for a successful lawyer.

Early biographers emphasized how Lincoln symbolized the "heroic frontier." Other biographers wrote of the great emancipator, the martyred hero whose death "expiated the sins of his country." David Potter, in reviewing this literature, discovered a "national legend," where Lincoln emerged as "a figure born in a log cabin as lowly as any manger, growing up to bear the sorrows of the race and to suffer vicariously for all humanity." David Donald in his study of the "folklore Lincoln" found that the two conceptions of Lincoln—as mythological patron saint and as mythological frontier hero—began to blend by the turn of the century.[11] Lincoln, as Don Fehrenbacher suggested, has been "abstracted from history to serve as the representative American."[12]

Biographers, however, weaving a narrative of a saintly emancipator or robust frontiersman, faced a disconcerting problem: Lincoln's lengthy legal career. Americans seldom have considered lawyers particularly saintly or virile; in fact, Americans generally have disliked or distrusted lawyers. Legal historian James Willard Hurst concluded that "whether mistaken, unjust, or hypercritical, the unfavorable popular image of the lawyer was a reality throughout our social history."[13] Lawyers are disliked because instead of serving the public interest, they merely served their clients' self-interest.[14] This cultural animosity existed when popular biographies first crafted the Lincoln image. In nineteenth-century popular literature, the lawyer often appeared as a pettifogger who used lawsuits to create strife and line his own pockets. Lawyers were soulless technicians who manipulated legal rules.[15]

Law and Remembrance

The memoirs by lawyers who practiced with Lincoln provide much of the information we have about lawyer Lincoln that goes beyond formulaic court pleadings and mundane docket book entries. William H. Herndon, Lincoln's law partner, and Henry Clay Whitney, a lawyer who was associated with Lincoln on the circuit, provided the two most valuable sources about Lincoln's legal career.

Lincoln practiced law when there were no official court reporters transcribing trials; only two known transcripts of his trials have survived. One transcript is from the federal admiralty lawsuit by the owners of the steamboat *Effie Afton* against the Rock Island Bridge Company. During the 1857 trial, the *St. Louis Republican* published a number of articles containing a near-verbatim transcript of that day's court proceedings. A typescript that collects the entire transcript from the newspaper is located at the Abraham Lincoln Presidential Library and Museum and is reprinted in the *Law Practice of Abraham Lincoln: Complete Documentary Edition*. The other transcript surfaced more recently and is from the 1859 Peachy Quinn Harrison murder trial; it also appears in the *Law Practice of Abraham Lincoln: Complete Documentary Edition*.[16] Although there are a few contemporary newspaper accounts of Lincoln's court appearances, descriptions of Lincoln in court or on the circuit survive mainly in Herndon's and Whitney's accounts.

Herndon practiced law with Lincoln for sixteen years. He began collecting materials for a biography about Lincoln shortly after Lincoln's assassination, but he was not able to complete it until 1888. The lapse of time and Herndon's personal agenda make his work somewhat problematic. Herndon has long been a controversial figure, although there have been recent, largely successful attempts to rehabilitate his reputation.[17] David M. Potter may have typified the more traditional view of Herndon among Lincoln scholars when he wrote that Herndon "wrote with an obsessive passion for the whole truth, and a comprehensive lack of capacity to distinguish the truth from flimsy rumor and garbled reminiscence."[18] Similarly, John P. Frank, who studied Lincoln's law practice, believed that Herndon's "arrogance, his high-flown pretensions to great knowledge, wisdom, and insight, his occasional bouts with drunkenness, and his tendency to romanticize the Lincoln story, when the facts fell short of his necessities" impair Herndon's usefulness for scholars. Frank, nonetheless, concluded that "we learn more of value about Lincoln the lawyer from Herndon than from any other source but the documents themselves."[19]

Lincoln usually emerges from Herndon's work as a virtuous lawyer with a gift for communication but little technical expertise. According to David Donald, Herndon publicized the "folk pattern of Lincoln as frontier hero"; Herndon envisioned Lincoln as the "natural product of the soil of the West." David M. Potter agreed that Herndon "was deliberately striving to explain Lincoln as the product of frontier forces."[20] Herndon portrayed lawyer Lincoln as the legal equivalent of a frontier hero. Lincoln's opponents feared his "apparent disregard of custom or professional propriety in managing a case before a jury." Lincoln was "strikingly deficient in the technical rules of the law"; he "knew nothing of the rules of evidence, of pleading, or practice." Moreover, Lincoln could not represent any case that "seemed untrue." Lincoln would quit in the middle of a trial "if he believed he was espousing an unjust cause." Lincoln also "detested the mechanical work of the office. He wrote few papers—less perhaps than any other man at the bar."[21] Most of these particular comments by Herndon are inaccurate. Lincoln did understand the technical rules of law and used them to his client's advantage. David Donald has pointed out that the thousands of documents collected by the Lincoln Legal Papers refute the notion that Lincoln somehow failed to draft documents or was otherwise disengaged from all the quotidian activities of a law practice.[22]

Herndon also may have helped create an image of Lincoln as someone whose true calling was politics and who practiced law to pay the bills. Herndon thought that Lincoln's "restless ambition" was gratified only by politics. Law, for Lincoln, was used as "merely a stepping-stone to what he considered a more attractive condition in the political world." This crimped view of Lincoln's law practice has permeated subsequent biographies. It is in need of reexamination. Lincoln showed considerable ambition in his practice, maintained a heavy caseload, and maneuvered to be involved in high-profile cases. Although practicing law complemented his involvement in politics, law was more than just a stepping-stone to him. As Lincoln was leaving Congress in 1849, the patronage position of Commissioner of the General Land Office was available. He initially resisted pursuing the job because accepting it "would be a final surrender of the law."[23]

Despite his exaggerations and oversights, Herndon does provide a valuable perspective on Lincoln's legal career. His description of Lincoln's appellate work is enlightening. The biographer concluded that "it was in the Supreme Court of the State of Illinois that he was truly a great lawyer, and nowhere else." Appellate work gave Lincoln ample time "to read the record and gather up the facts of the case" and "to hunt up the law." Lincoln's advice to Herndon about jury argument—"Billy, don't shoot too high—aim lower and the common people will understand you"—rings true.[24]

Henry Clay Whitney, the second of Lincoln's former colleagues to leave us a record, contributed a rambling reminiscence of Lincoln's "unsteady, nomadic life" on the circuit. Whitney was an Urbana, Illinois, attorney who met Lincoln in 1854. Evidently, Lincoln thought well of Whitney and referred business to him.[25] Whitney served as Lincoln's co-counsel in seventy-one cases.[26] In 1892, Whitney published *Life on the Circuit with Lincoln.* Throughout his memoir, he digressed. Lincoln scholar Paul M. Angle aptly summarized Whitney's contribution as writing colorfully about what he remembered but, unfortunately, writing more than he remembered.[27] Some of Whitney's claims, like Herndon's, can be tested against the Lincoln Legal Papers database. Whitney wrote that he traveled with Lincoln to many of the counties of the circuit; however, the two lawyers were associated with only one case outside Champaign County, Whitney's home county. Because Herndon generally stayed in Springfield while Lincoln traveled the circuit, Whitney's book nonetheless is a sometimes valuable firsthand portrait of those experiences.[28]

Lincoln scholars have not ignored his circuit-riding. From 1839 until 1857, Lincoln's Sangamon County was a part of the Illinois Eighth Judicial Circuit. The composition of the circuit changed over time but from 1843 to 1853, fourteen counties comprised the circuit. Twice a year, Judge David Davis and a retinue of lawyers would ride the circuit for three months, "traveling by horse or buggy and stopping at the county seats for court terms of two days to one week." Lincoln usually was the only attorney who would ride the entire circuit for both terms.[29]

Whitney's book contains several anecdotes about Lincoln as a trial lawyer riding the circuit. Whitney, like Herndon, stressed Lincoln's "moral and intellectual honesty." Lincoln "would not do anything mean, or which savored of dishonesty or sharp practice, or which required absolute sophistry or chicanery in order to succeed." Whitney, however, criticized Lincoln's biographers who, in a "gush of enthusiasm," asserted that Lincoln would quit midtrial from "every case in which he found himself to be wrong." Lincoln would try the case "like any other lawyer, except that he absolutely abjured technicality, and went for justice and victory." Once Lincoln accepted a case, "he wanted to win as badly as any lawyer." Whitney also was impressed by Lincoln's "infallible and remorseless logic," his ability to analyze a problem and break it down into "simple elements."[30]

Both Herndon and Whitney are valuable sources, but both suffer deficiencies relating to their relationship to Lincoln or to the rapidly growing mythology of Lincoln. Herndon's experience as Lincoln's junior partner gave him only a partial insight into Lincoln's career, and one slanted understandably by Herndon's perspective. Whitney found himself heavily influenced by Lincoln's post-Illinois image.

Lincoln Biographers

Lincoln's biographers generally have paid very little attention to his law practice. Generally, biographers devote two chapters to lawyer Lincoln. One chapter usually describes his studying for the bar and his early partnerships with John T. Stuart and Stephen Trigg Logan. The second chapter, which generally follows the chapter on Lincoln in Congress, recounts his partnership with Herndon, his riding the circuit, and some notable cases.[31] Such treatment regards the legal career as only an unimportant prelude to the vital substance of Lincoln's life.

While the overall negative image of lawyers in American society explains the lack of attention paid to Lincoln's legal practice, a countervailing positive image of lawyers shaped the depiction of that practice in Lincoln biographies. The lawyer's image in American popular culture is ambivalent; a positive image of lawyers coexists with the negative image of the greedy shyster. Legal historian Maxwell Bloomfield discovered a "model attorney" in antebellum fiction—a self-made man who overcomes the adverse circumstances of his youth. The model attorney grows up on a farm or in a small country town where he learns the Protestant work ethic from his poor but virtuous parents. Once admitted to the bar, he protects the poor and defenseless. During his career he represents both rich and poor, although he doesn't charge to represent the poor. He is concerned about establishing justice and uses only just means to do so. The fictional model attorney's entry into politics was the culmination of his career.[32]

In this case, biography imitates art, and Lincoln appears as an idealized attorney in his early biographies. Biographers wanted to represent Lincoln as a model attorney; only the fictional model attorney was worthy of the folklore Lincoln. The "country lawyer" became a variant of the frontier hero. Lincoln thus emerges as a country attorney, who was uninterested in fees, who protected the poor and defenseless, who would not defend unjust causes, and who would not take advantage of legal technicalities. This portrayal simplifies and distorts Lincoln's law practice.

This simplistic and romanticized view of Lincoln's law practice first appeared in campaign biographies published in 1860 and 1864.[33] The "Honest Abe" image, according to Gabor Boritt, was central to Lincoln's election in 1860 and was created by the "sure political instincts of the Republican managers of 1860." While their candidate "had devoted a lifetime to the maneuverings of politics and lawyering," the Republicans "offered to a welcoming public the Honest Railsplitter of the West."[34] These campaign biographies set the tone for later ones. They devoted little space to Lincoln's law practice, and they barely concealed the attempt to combat the negative cultural stereotype about lawyers. The Duff Armstrong case surfaces in at least six biographies; Lincoln's association with the Illinois Central was not mentioned once.[35] The probable source for this depiction of Lincoln's practice was not the Republican managers, but Lincoln himself; Richard Hofstadter noted that "the first author of the Lincoln legend and the greatest of the Lincoln dramatists was Lincoln himself."[36]

While Republican literature framed Lincoln's law practice within the positive cultural image of lawyers, hostile cultural attitudes toward lawyers are evident in portraits of Lincoln in Democratic campaign literature. "He went across from Kentucky to Illinois on a flat boat to find one John Hanks, who taught him how to split rails," satirized an 1860 Democratic pamphlet. "After he left that business, he went into the law and practised splitting hairs."[37] An 1864 satire described how Lincoln began studying law by following the advice of a fellow Whig legislator, John T. Stuart:

> He once more entered the political arena, was twice elected to the legislature, fell into evil company, and became a lawyer! How many poor wretches, alas! have dated back to their fall, and the triumph of the fiend over them, to the time when they began to associate with bad companions.[38]

The image of Lincoln as the model attorney also appeared in one of the first biographies written after his assassination. Josiah Gilbert Holland, the editor of the Springfield, Massachusetts, *Republican,* consulted campaign biographies, studied published sources, and spent two days in Springfield talking to Herndon. Holland concluded that Lincoln "established his reputation as one of the best lawyers in Illinois, and in, some respects, the superior of any lawyer in the state." Lincoln, however, "was a very weak lawyer when engaged by the weak side." Holland depicted lawyer Lincoln as a model attorney who had a "genuine interest in the establishment of justice between man and man." Lincoln was "opposed to the success of villainy and the triumph of wrong, and he would not sell himself to purposes of injustice and immorality."[39]

Lincoln, according to Holland, was a powerful lawyer in front of a jury, but he did not manipulate the jury: "He had no interest in the establishment of anything but justice, and injustice, even if it favored him, could give him no satisfaction." Lincoln, like the model attorney, found it "very difficult" to charge expensive fees, and still more difficult for him to charge his friends anything at all for professional services. Holland did not mention Lincoln's association with the Illinois Central Railroad. Nor did Holland note Lincoln's extensive appellate practice.[40]

The cultural images of lawyers shaped the depiction of Lincoln's law practice in the first major biography of Lincoln, which was written by President Lincoln's private secretaries, John George Nicolay and John Hay. Lincoln was their hero. In their account of Lincoln's pre-presidential life, Nicolay and Hay glossed over conduct that might be considered unbecoming, and emphasized instead what was in keeping with the presidential Lincoln.[41] Despite the multivolume length of this biography, Nicolay and Hay paid little attention to Lincoln's law practice. The lawyer who does appear is wise, righteous, and heroic.

Nicolay and Hay also did not stray far from the stereotypical virtuous attorney. Their description of Lincoln's practice emphasized how Lincoln avoided using legal technicalities and refused to defend unjust causes. They wrote that Lincoln "never learned the technicalities, what some would call the tricks of the profession." Lincoln could only represent a just cause: "On the wrong side he was always weak. He knew this himself, and avoided such cases when he could consistently with the rules of his profession." In an effort to shield Lincoln's reputation from the negative cultural image of the greedy pettifogger, they specifically denied that Lincoln used "the sleight of plea and demurrer, the legerdemain by which justice is balked and a weak case is made to gain an unfair advantage."[42] (A demurrer is nothing more than an assertion that the opponent's pleading is defective in substance or in form.[43]) It's simply untrue that Lincoln was somehow above demurring to an opponent's pleading. Lincoln, after all, practiced in a court system based on common-law pleading; it's not surprising that at least eighty-one demurrers written by Lincoln survive.[44]

The apotheosis of the folklore Lincoln was reached in Carl Sandburg's 1926 biography. In Sandburg's *Prairie Years,* a rich portrait of a legendary Lincoln appears. This emphasis on the mythic, legendary Lincoln posed some problems for Sandburg's depiction of Lincoln's law practice.[45]

Sandburg was well aware of the negative image of lawyers. In a five-stanza poem published in 1920, he neatly summarized the popular critique of lawyers. In the first stanza Sandburg criticized lawyers for knowing "too much . . . what a dead hand wrote." In the next three stanzas Sandburg attacked lawyers for their mystifying language and their greed.

> In the heels of the higgling lawyers, Bob,
> Too many slippery ifs and buts and howevers,
> Too many hereinbefore provided whereas,
> Too many doors to go in and out of.
>
> When the lawyers are through
> What is there left, Bob?
> Can a mouse nibble at it
> And find enough to fasten a tooth in?
>
> Why is there always a secret singing
> When a lawyer cashes in?
> Why does a hearse horse snicker
> Hauling a lawyer away?

Sandburg ended his poem by contrasting lawyers unfavorably to brick-layers, masons, and farmers. Attorneys, so Sandburg argued, produce nothing of value for society, while laboring occupations perform socially useful tasks.[46]

To avoid any snickers about lawyer Lincoln, Sandburg portrayed him as a heroic, virtuous attorney. Other lawyers were greedy, Lincoln was selfless. He was careless and easygoing about fees. In the Duff Armstrong case, he "dropped all his big law cases, dropped all big political affairs then stirring, and threw himself with all he had into the defense of a young man charged with murder." Other lawyers used arcane, artificial language; Lincoln employed the vernacular of the people. "He spoke their language and stories," said Sandburg. Unlike other lawyers, Lincoln could not defend guilty clients. Nor could he use the "tricks and twists" that other lawyers used. Lincoln was unable to recommend the practice of law to those who wanted to live by the Golden Rule. Sandburg, who apparently accepted all recollections of Lincoln as truthful, recounted the story of Ralph Emerson. Emerson claimed that he decided not to become a lawyer after he asked Lincoln whether it was possible "for a man to practice law and always do by others as he would be done by," and Lincoln "had no answer."[47]

Lincoln scholar Mark E. Neely, Jr., has called Albert Beveridge's *Abraham Lincoln, 1809–1858* (1928) "the best single account of Lincoln's life before the Presidency." Beveridge's descriptions of lawyer Lincoln, however, did not advance beyond affirming that Lincoln fit the positive cultural image of lawyers and denying that he possessed any of the negative trappings. Beveridge, probably because he was trained as an attorney, portrayed Lincoln not so much as a model attorney (who is just and honest) but as a typical attorney (who is just and honest). Beveridge was a senator from Indiana who had written a biography of John Marshall in 1919. After finishing the biography of Marshall, Beveridge began a biography of Lincoln, whom he associated with the nationalistic Marshall. Although Beveridge privately confessed that Lincoln's "law cases, little and big, put together, do not, on their merits, deserve a line in history and not more than a paragraph in any biography," he, nonetheless, devoted more attention to Lincoln's law practice than had earlier biographers.[48]

Because of his legal training, Beveridge's depiction of the legal career improved somewhat upon previous biographies. Beveridge concluded that Lincoln was "no phenomenon of success" as a trial attorney and that he "showed little knowledge of decisions or textbooks" in jury trials. But Lincoln in trial "spoke the language of the jurymen, the speech of the people." Lincoln, according to Beveridge, withdrew from trials when he found that his client had deceived him, but this was "an experience not uncommon to scrupulous lawyers everywhere and in all times." Lincoln's treatment of clients and associate lawyers was "like that of most high-minded and honorable attorneys." Beveridge concluded that Lincoln was "no knight-errant of the law seeking out the poor and distressed in order to lift them up and relieve them." He "accepted what came to him, provided it was not morally bad, and did his best for his client."[49]

Beveridge believed that Lincoln appeared in only four "important cases": the Manny Reaper case, the Duff Armstrong murder case, the McLean County tax case, and the *Effie Afton* case. Beveridge's list became canonical; subsequent biographers (with the notable exception of David Donald) rarely have mentioned any other cases. Beveridge also discussed the Matson case where Lincoln unsuccessfully represented a slaveholder who was asserting his right of property to five human beings. Beveridge also described Lincoln's appellate work, which he stated was Lincoln's "most distinguished effort at the bar."[50]

The treatment of Lincoln's law practice improved with the increasing professionalism of Lincoln studies in the twentieth century.[51] One of the first professional historians associated with Lincoln scholarship was Benjamin P. Thomas. Thomas received his doctorate in history from Johns Hopkins University in 1929 and became executive secretary of the Abraham Lincoln Association in 1932. Four years later, the Association published Thomas's *Lincoln 1847–1853*, a calendar that described Lincoln's daily whereabouts and activities for those seven years. In researching that book, Thomas "discovered hundreds of Lincoln documents and references to Lincoln in grimy Illinois courthouses long thought to have been exhausted as repositories of Lincolniana." Thomas published several articles in the 1930s on aspects of Lincoln's law career, including Lincoln's practice in federal court. Thomas, not surprisingly, provided one of the best treatments of Lincoln's legal career in his 1952 biography.[52]

Thomas reflected the influence of Frederick Jackson Turner in his portrait of Lincoln as a product of the frontier. The frontier infused Lincoln with "qualities of courage, perseverance, and self-confidence, and a capacity and determination to order one's own destiny." Lincoln's training as a lawyer, however, served as a check on the unattractive qualities of the frontier. While Lincoln drew from "the raw, rich strength of the frontier," he avoided the frontier's faults when he "realized the value of law and tradition."[53]

Unlike Lincoln's earlier biographers, Thomas considered the effect of practicing law on Lincoln's development. Thomas described Lincoln riding the circuit and also described what Lincoln learned from that experience. According to Thomas, the law practice "was an educational process"—no other profession offered "such insights into human nature as does the law, while in the give-and-take of discussions in these rural forums." This was Lincoln's "training-ground on which he further developed his political astuteness, learning the thought-processes of the people." Thomas, unlike Lincoln's earlier biographers, described how the legal landscape changed during Lincoln's legal career. In Lincoln's early law practice, "cases were usually simple," "required little preparation," and "were usually decided according to fundamental precepts of right and wrong." Fifteen years later, however, Lincoln had to adapt to changing legal conditions brought by "revolutionary industrial developments." Science and invention altered the pattern of American life and changed the law by making more complex and demanding "broader and more expert knowledge of its practitioners."[54]

Thomas was also one of the first biographers to describe how the lawyer influenced the president. Thomas, for example, concluded that Lincoln's presidential speeches and writings were a product of his legal training. In Lincoln's state papers, he "manifested that capacity to understand an opponent's point of view, and to present his own case clearly and simply, which he had so painstakingly acquired as a circuit lawyer."[55]

Stephen B. Oates, who, like Thomas, was a professionally trained historian, wrote a popular one-volume biography of Lincoln that continued in Thomas's path. Oates's treatment of Lincoln's law practice might be fuller than Thomas's, but Oates benefited from several works on Lincoln's legal career published in the early 1960s. Oates emphasized Lincoln's appellate work, where "he did his most influential legal work in the prestigious Supreme Court of Illinois." There, Lincoln won most of his appeals and "earned his reputation as a lawyer's lawyer, adept at meticulous preparation and cogent argument." Oates discovered "contrary to myth, he took cases as they came to him regardless of the justice involved." Oates discussed the same handful of cases that appear in other biographies. Oates's treatment of the Matson case, however, is significantly different from that of other biographers. Oates concluded that Lincoln did not argue the case weakly for his slaveholder client; Lincoln argued "in the strongest possible terms" and with "cold and brutal logic" that Matson was entitled to the return of his slaves. Lincoln's handling of this case illustrated the "essentially pragmatic approach to the law" that Lincoln and other lawyers adopted.[56]

Oates, like Thomas, considered how practicing law influenced Lincoln's political career. Oates concluded that Lincoln "derived a lot more from the law than just a high income." The law gave him "rare insight into the foibles and complexities of human affairs," sharpened his literary talents, taught him how to structure arguments and use interrogatories, and made him realize "the merits of accuracy, precision, and painstaking thoroughness."[57]

The depiction of Lincoln's law practice in the biographies of Thomas and Oates did not rely on the cultural stereotype of a heroic lawyer. While the quality of the treatment of Lincoln's legal career improved, the space devoted to the law practice did not.[58] In one sense, Lincoln biographies are little different from any biography of a lawyer who is famous primarily for something other than practicing law. Legal historian Robert W. Gordon notes that "previous work on or by lawyers have talked about almost any aspect of their careers other than how they made a living." If a lawyer becomes a judge or politician, says Gordon, his biography "usually devotes only a perfunctory early chapter to his law practice, mentioning only his involvement in famous cases or notorious trials." Gordon's explanation for this inattention is that "the details of day-to-day practice often seem trivial, repetitious, and boring even to those whose living depends upon them." Lyman Butterfield, the editor-in-chief of the John Adams Papers, also noted that most biographies of lawyers and judges hurry past the legal careers in order to concentrate on the political one.[59]

The biographers' lack of legal training also has prevented more attention to Lincoln's law practice. Historian David Donald in his biography of William Herndon stated there was no definitive study of Lincoln's law career because "the terminology of the law itself is a sufficient barrier for most investigators." Donald explained how even "those obvious distinctions between traverses and demurrers, between mandamus and quo warranto, between real property and chattels can hardly be made in other than the formal legal language which is itself inexplicable to the layman." Donald also noted that the state of the documentary evidence presented problems for the study of Lincoln's law practice. Most of the court records were scattered throughout courthouses in Illinois. Many of the records are incomplete because of the destruction or theft of legal papers relating to Lincoln.[60]

The professionalization of Lincoln studies also has not overcome the lack of interest in Lincoln's law practice. When James G. Randall surveyed Lincoln scholarship in 1936 he complained that "the hand of the amateur has rested heavily upon Lincoln scholarship." Yet Randall failed to suggest that "historically trained scholars" might explore Lincoln's law practice or that the law practice was one area where "there is both spade work and re-fining work to be done."[61] In 1979 Mark E. Neely, Jr., examined Lincoln scholarship since the publication of Randall's article. Unlike Randall, Neely saw the need for "spade work" in legal history, an area "where professional-ism has been slow to command." He saw legal history as a promising route for a fresh understanding of Abraham Lincoln.[62] Interestingly, Neely almost completely neglects Lincoln's legal career in his 1993 biography of Lincoln; he spends only two paragraphs on lawyer Lincoln. According to Neely, Lin-coln's "professional life remains inaccessible to the historian"; he concludes that this problem is largely archival. He also complains that documents from Lincoln's law practice yield information grudgingly. First, Neely be-lieves that, without transcripts of trials, "it is impossible to know what hap-pened in the courtroom unless the trial was sensational enough to be cov-ered by newspapers." Second, the antebellum legal system used antique terms and obscure forms that since have been discarded.[63]

David Donald accurately noted in 1948 the documentary problems that faced scholars interested in Lincoln's law practice; however, the problem with lack of access to documents disappeared when the Law Practice of Abraham Lincoln: Complete Documentary Edition was published in 2000. This state-of-the-art electronic collection of over 100,000 legal documents culminated a decade-long project by the Illinois Historic Preservation Agency. The impact of this project on Lincoln studies was felt before the publication of the electronic edition. During the collection and accession stage, scholars associated with the project began publishing the fruits of their research and opened their files to such Lincoln scholars as Robert Bray and Paul H. Verduin.[64] In 2002, a collection of studies on family law in Lin-coln's Illinois based on the records from the Complete Documentary Edi-tion and written by researchers from the Lincoln Legal Papers appeared.[65] The scholarship that began appearing from the "Lincoln Legals" showed that the prior lack of interest and neglect of Lincoln's law practice by his bi-ographers now would be difficult to justify.

David Donald became the first Lincoln biographer to use the materials from the Lincoln Legal Papers project, which he hailed as "perhaps the most important archival investigation now under way in the United States." Although Donald finished his biography several years before the Lincoln Legal Papers project was complete, the book shows the influence of the project. One chapter on Lincoln "at the head of his profession in this state" was based on "the hundreds of [then] unpublished documents in the files of the Lincoln Legal Papers." Donald gave a fuller sense of the breadth of Lincoln's practice. Donald included cases that previous biographers had ignored; he gave examples of cases in circuit courts "of no great interest or consequence to anyone except the parties involved in the litigation." Donald also offered valuable insight into Lincoln's development as a lawyer. For example, he looked at how Lincoln changed how he drafted pleadings: "As he became more experienced, he pared legalisms and redundancies, and his declarations became models of simplicity and clarity."[66]

Other Lincoln scholars continue to devote scant attention to Lincoln's law practice. William E. Gienapp, for example, generally avoided the law practice in his Lincoln biography. Gienapp followed a familiar path; he briefly discussed or alluded to four of the usual suspects: the *Effie Afton* case, the Illinois Central tax case, the Duff Armstrong murder trial, and the Manny Reaper case. By ignoring the scholarship of the previous ten years on Lincoln's law practice, Gienapp highlighted the same cases that Beveridge had noted nearly seventy-five years earlier. Gienapp concluded that Lincoln's circuit-riding "heightened his political skills at the same time it enhanced his political reputation"; circuit-riding "offered him an unrivaled opportunity to meet people and study human nature."[67]

Even more puzzling has been the aversion of the law practice by Douglas L. Wilson, the foremost scholar of "Lincoln Before Washington."[68] In *Honor's Voice: The Transformation of Abraham Lincoln,* Wilson studied Lincoln's early years in Illinois from 1831 until 1841. He described in great detail Lincoln studying law before he became a lawyer, but he avoided any discussion of Lincoln's early partnerships with Stuart or Logan. The only mention of Lincoln as a lawyer is when Wilson describes Herndon informants who recalled that Lincoln was "notably ineffective when his client was obviously in the wrong." Wilson notes that Lincoln's "overall record of success" means that this could not have remained generally true, but his "ineffectiveness in certain cases must have been sufficiently evident to account for such testimony by close friends."[69] Wilson doesn't question that this particular portrait of Lincoln effectively answers the critique of lawyer as hired gun. Wilson also doesn't question why there is no record of anyone actually noticing this ineffectiveness while Lincoln was practicing law.

The Lawyers' Lincoln

Abraham Lincoln is one of the great heroes of the American legal profession. As the legal profession's public image sank to new depths in the 1980s and 1990s, lawyers attempted to appropriate Lincoln's image to rehabilitate their own.[70] By overemphasizing Lincoln's background in law, lawyers have sought to legitimize their own profession. In a television show on the poor public image of lawyers, Harvard Law School professor Alan Dershowitz significantly turned first to the image of Lincoln as a heroic lawyer to defend the profession.

Well, there certainly are some heroes. We have a long tradition, starting with Abraham Lincoln and even before that, of lawyers who have risked their lives—Thurgood Marshall was one of them—who have risked everything in order to bring about justice, not for themselves, but for the downtrodden, for the poor, for those who are unrepresented.[71]

Dershowitz didn't explain what lawyer Lincoln (as opposed to President Lincoln) exactly did in his law practice that was heroic.

Dershowitz isn't the only member of the legal profession who's tried to "get right with Lincoln."[72] The cover of the *ABA Journal* in March 1991 featured a portrait of Lincoln at work in a contemporary law office. It also contained an axiom often attributed to Lincoln, although there's no record that he ever said it: "A lawyer's time and advice are his stock and trade."[73] The cover was so popular with members of the American Bar Association that the ABA reproduced it as a poster.[74] Abraham Lincoln literally had become the poster boy of the American legal profession.

Philadelphia lawyer Jerome J. Shestack published five articles on lawyer Lincoln in legal periodicals and state bar journals before he was elected president of the ABA.[75] Shestack, unlike earlier bar leaders, was more modest in his claim for Lincoln; he concluded that "Lincoln's place in history derives not from his abilities as a lawyer but from his qualities as human being and his seminal achievements as president. Still, he was a lawyer of whom the bar could be proud."[76]

It's easy to understand the attraction to Lincoln. Lawyers have a lousy image; Lincoln has an almost saintly one. Lawyers rush to Lincoln because he was a lawyer before he was president and they hope some of his mojo will rub off on them. Lawyers thus are drawn to a particular image of lawyer Lincoln: the country lawyer who's above the fray, who seeks justice and not just a win for his client. With the advent of alternative dispute resolution, lawyers and law professors often turn to Lincoln's advice to lawyers to "discourage litigation": "As a peace-maker, the lawyer has a superior opportunity of being a good man. There will still be business enough."[77]

Modern critics of the "role morality"of American lawyers are also quite fond of Lincoln. Legal ethicist David Luban, for example, used Lincoln as an example of a lawyer who "rejected the lawyer's amoral ethical role." Luban pointed to a scene recounted in William Herndon's biography where Lincoln advised a would-be client that he wouldn't take the case and "set a whole neighborhood at loggerheads and distress a widowed mother and her six fatherless children" over a six-hundred-dollar debt. Lincoln, according to Herndon's informant James J. Lord, told the man, "You must remember that some things legally right are not morally right." Luban concluded that "Lincoln seems to have taken 'some things legally right are not morally right' to be an important truth. It shows that exercising one's legal rights is not always morally acceptable. From that, Lincoln evidently concluded that helping someone exercise their legal rights is not always morally acceptable."[78]

Luban's reliance upon a single dubious anecdote is telling. Historians Don E. Fehrenbacher and Virginia Fehrenbacher in their study of Lincoln's recollected words characterize this influential account by Lord—who they caustically note was listed in a Springfield directory as "Proprietor of Dr. Topping's Alterative Sirup"—as "intrinsically hard-to-believe" and of doubtful authenticity.[79]

While biographers have tended to hurry past Lincoln's law practice, lawyers have stopped to gaze proudly at lawyer Lincoln. Lincoln's law practice has been a favorite subject for legal authors. Although many presidents have been lawyers, no other lawyer-president has attracted as much devotion or attention from lawyers. Not only have lawyers written all five monographs on Lincoln's legal career, but there are innumerable articles in bar journals and countless speeches at bar association proceedings on lawyer Lincoln. While lawyers consistently have claimed that Lincoln was a typical lawyer, the reasons advanced for his typicality have changed.

Lawyers undoubtedly have been drawn to the mythic Lincoln, the frontier hero and great emancipator. Lawyers have claimed that Lincoln the great emancipator would not have been possible without Lincoln the country lawyer. Many articles and speeches by lawyers on lawyer Lincoln have linked Lincoln's greatness as president to his legal background. In 1925 Edward J. Fox told the Pennsylvania Bar Association that Lincoln's "pre-eminent ability as a lawyer" was "the foundation of his success as a statesman" and made Lincoln "one of the most beloved presidents."[80] Another speaker told the Minnesota Bar Association in 1927 that Lincoln was "the most striking instance of a lawyer president and a lawyer statesman."[81] In 1905 a former president of the Oklahoma State Bar Association concluded, "Lincoln, the President,—Lincoln, the Emancipator,—Lincoln, the Orator,—Lincoln, the Statesman, acquired his great power, wisdom and virtue of and from his training at the bar as LINCOLN, THE LAWYER." Lawyers also extolled the honesty and virtue of lawyer Lincoln as emblematic of the entire profession.[82]

In addition to this attempt at expropriating the positive cultural image of Lincoln, modern lawyers often have been drawn to Lincoln because of nostalgia for the simpler times of the circuit-riding country lawyer. This interest with lawyer Lincoln was especially pronounced at the turn of the century when the legal profession underwent a profound transformation.[83] The solo practitioner was supplanted by the development of large law firms; the courtroom advocate gave way to the boardroom counselor. During this period of unsettling change, the image of Lincoln the country lawyer had a reassuring, nostalgic function for lawyers.[84] Jerold Auerbach, in reviewing this literature, discovered that "lawyers cherished Lincoln's memory as fondly as school boys treasured tales of Old Hickory and Davey

Crockett." To lawyers, Lincoln represented the "self-reliant and persevering" country lawyer, the "common-man's lawyer in a pre-urban, pre-industrial society."[85] Throughout the twentieth century, lawyer Lincoln continued as a topic of bar association dinner speeches and bar journal articles.[86]

The lawyers' fascination with Lincoln is responsible for the five books on Lincoln's law practice. Each lawyer who has written a book about Lincoln's law practice has justified his endeavor by noting that Lincoln's biographers have overlooked Lincoln's legal career. Frederick Trevor Hill, who published the first full-length study of Lincoln's legal practice in 1906, noted that "no one has heretofore attempted a summing-up of the great President's legal career." John T. Richards, writing ten years later, observed how Lincoln's "biographers have said very little upon the subject of his career at the bar." In 1936, Albert A. Woldman complained that "Lincoln's biographers, with few exceptions, have seen fit to give his law career but passing comment." John J. Duff believed his book, *A. Lincoln, Prairie Lawyer* (1960), answered "a crying need in Lincoln literature." John P. Frank, a year later, emphasized how "the finest and most compendious of Lincoln's biographies devote only a chapter or two to his law practice."[87]

Lawyers have not been at a loss to assert great meaning and significance to Lincoln's law practice. Woldman claimed that "Lincoln's training at the bar prepared, molded, and qualified him for his mighty task and enabled him to meet the unprecedented constitutional questions created by the crisis." Richards contended that Lincoln's "greatness as a lawyer made him a great President." Hill thought that America was fortunate to have elected Lincoln president in 1860 because "the times demanded a lawyer." The lawyers who have written books on Lincoln's law practice all agree that "it is impossible to overestimate the value of these active professional years on Lincoln's subsequent career."[88]

Frederick Trevor Hill, a New York lawyer who was an authority on estate and business law, wrote the first book on Lincoln's law practice. Hill was a prolific author, publishing technical legal treatises such as *The Care of Estates* (1901) and novels with a legal background. Hill's book, *Lincoln the Lawyer* (1906), has been described as Hill's "outstanding contribution as an author."[89]

Hill, like most of Lincoln's biographers, believed there were moral lessons to be learned from a study of Lincoln's legal career. Lincoln did not defend unjust causes or manipulate legal technicalities. Lincoln was a "formidable opponent whenever he believed in a cause." Lincoln had "had the courage and the character to uphold the highest standards of the bar in daily practice" and he was "entitled to a place in the foremost rank of the profession." Lincoln "lived its ideals and showed them to be practical, and his example gives inspiration and encouragement to thousands of practitioners who believe that these things which detract from the character of the man detract from the character of the lawyer." Hill was aware of the stereotype of the greedy pettifogger; Lincoln, however, did not fit that mold. Lincoln was a great lawyer because he was a man of integrity.[90]

Hill also covered Lincoln's law practice in some detail. Hill concluded that Lincoln was the "best all-around jury lawyer of his day in Illinois" because of his "knowledge of human nature" and his "clearness and simplicity of statement." Hill also discussed Lincoln's appellate work. Hill, like all lawyers who have studied Lincoln, believed Lincoln's legal experience "guided his conduct in the political areas." Hill, again like all lawyers who have studied Lincoln, was vague on how lawyer Lincoln guided President Lincoln. Lincoln's simple and clear literary style, according to Hill, was also a product of the courtroom.[91]

John T. Richards was a Chicago lawyer who had been president of the Chicago Bar Association. In *Abraham Lincoln: The Lawyer-Statesman* (1916), Richards made many of the same points that Hill had made ten years before. Richards, however, made these points in a more pompous and bombastic manner. All great presidents had been lawyers; while president, "their experience and training as lawyers were of inestimable value." The only great president who was not a lawyer was George Washington, who "while not himself a member of the bar, availed himself continuously of the services of that great lawyer, Alexander Hamilton." Lincoln was one "of the truly great lawyers of his generation." Richards concluded, "In truth his greatness as a lawyer made him a great President."[92]

Albert A. Woldman wrote *Lawyer Lincoln* (1936) because 1937 was the centennial of Lincoln's admission to the bar, because "Lincoln was the law profession's greatest contribution to American civilization," and because "without his twenty-three years of experience at the bar, he might never have become President of the United States."[93] Woldman's book was researched adequately, and he made some balanced assessments of Lincoln's law practice. Woldman rejected the biographers' representations of Lincoln "as a lawyer disinclined to take advantage of any technical defense." Woldman concluded instead that "this contention is contrary to fact, and is amply refuted by available records." He similarly rejected Herndon's assertion that Lincoln was "strikingly deficient in the technical rules of the law." Woldman discovered that Lincoln resorted to every legal device and technical advantage to win his cases. Woldman agreed with earlier writers that Lincoln "could not enthusiastically and wholeheartedly argue cases which clashed with his moral sense" but disagreed that Lincoln was a "heavenly agent of justice and a knight-errant of law and equity." Lincoln was a "realist—shrewd, practical, and matter of fact."[94]

Woldman also reflected a differing conception of the attorney's professional role. Previous students of Lincoln's law practice had approved of Lincoln's alleged inability to defend or prosecute unjust causes. Woldman, however, criticized Lincoln's "inflexible and fastidious morality." Lincoln's "strict obedience to conscience weakened his usefulness to clients whenever their cause became incompatible with his sense of morals."[95]

Woldman believed that Lincoln was qualified "to assume his stupendous obligations because the problems which confronted him as President, in a general sense, were not unlike those he had tackled for nearly a quarter of a century as a lawyer—only on a scale far more vast." Lincoln's jury arguments were like his later presidential speeches—"clear, lucid, fair in statement, and marked by logic and accurate reasoning power." Lincoln's state papers resembled his appellate briefs in their "brevity, simplicity, and directness." The law taught Lincoln not only the technical knowledge of the rules of practice but "proved for him a study of human institutions and of history itself." No other profession could have given Lincoln "a better background of life and conditions and manners of mankind."[96]

The best book on Lincoln's law practice is John J. Duff's *A. Lincoln, Prairie Lawyer* (1960). Duff, a sole practitioner in New York City, wrote a fairly comprehensive account of Lincoln's law practice, including separate chapters on several of Lincoln's cases.[97] Duff believed that both the Lincoln biographers and Herndon were wrong about lawyer Lincoln. The biographers had a "stained glass concept" about Lincoln and went to "fantastic lengths" to propagate myths that presented attorney Lincoln as a "candidate for sainthood." Herndon, on the other hand, unfairly denigrated Lincoln's legal abilities. Herndon treated Lincoln's trial work superficially and did not understand the scope of Lincoln's achievements as a lawyer. Herndon had received "deserved condemnation as an ingrate and fluent liar" from Lincoln scholars.[98]

In addition to detailed chapters on various trials, Duff also emphasized Lincoln's appellate practice. It was in the supreme court, and not on the circuit, that Lincoln had his greatest impact as a lawyer. Duff ended his account of Lincoln's legal career with Lincoln's election in 1860. Duff did not consider the influence of the law career on Lincoln's presidency, except to note briefly that Lincoln, while he was a lawyer, developed his judgment, lucidity of expression, and unforgettable prose.[99] Duff's work nonetheless is marred by his lack of depth and ignorance of legal history.

Like other lawyers who previously had written about Lincoln's law practice, Duff claimed that Lincoln was a typical lawyer: an article he wrote about the law practice was entitled "This Was a Lawyer."[100] Unlike the other lawyers who had written about Lincoln's law practice, Duff did not claim that Lincoln only represented honest and just clients. Lincoln did represent unjust causes, and he did resort to hypertechnical defenses whenever it suited his clients' purposes. In the Matson case, Lincoln was not "halfhearted" on protecting the slaveowner's interests; Lincoln displayed "legal generalship of a high order." Previous writers had claimed that Lincoln fulfilled his moral obligations as a lawyer by refusing to represent unjust causes and that Lincoln was a typical lawyer when he did so. Previous writers had extolled Lincoln's "sense of moral responsibility that can always distinguish between duty to a client and duty to society and the truth."[101]

Duff now asserted that Lincoln fulfilled his legal obligations as a lawyer by zealously representing his clients regardless of the merits of their claims, and, in so doing, Lincoln was a typical attorney.[102] Duff, who practiced criminal law, resorted to what had become "the official view of most lawyers: the lawyer's morality is distinct from, and not implicated in, the client's." This dominant ethic for contemporary American lawyers is an adversary ethic based upon a unique claim of moral immunity for lawyers.[103]

One year after the publication of Duff's work, John P. Frank published *Lincoln as a Lawyer* (1961). Frank received his law degree from the University of Wisconsin in 1940 and served as law clerk to United States Supreme Court Justice Hugo Black. In 1954, Frank had noted that the recently published edition of Lincoln's works could be seen "by a lawyer with the eye of a fellow craftsman, which makes it look a little different than it does to others. If Lincoln is read with a professional eye, any lawyer can learn from his reading."[104] Frank's book received very different reactions. Willard King, the author of a study of David Davis, called the book a "new low in the Lincoln literature—a field that has not lacked for trash." King thought Frank knew little about Lincoln; Frank was "a person unacquainted with the Lincoln literature." A review in the *American Journal of Legal History*, however, praised the book as an outstanding biography.[105]

Frank, like Duff, sometimes failed to appreciate nineteenth-century legal culture. Frank often criticized Lincoln's actions as a lawyer based on the implied assumption that modern law is the same as Illinois law in the 1840s. In other respects, Frank's approach is also similar to Duff's. Frank dismissed Nicolay and Hay's image of Lincoln refusing to use the technical resources of the law as "foolishness." Lincoln did raise hypertechnical points. Frank also realized that it "would be cheap sentimentality for lawyers to claim any special credit for Lincoln." Nonetheless, Frank concluded that Lincoln was an "outstandingly able and successful lawyer for his time and place. He was one of the best products of a frontier legal system."[106]

Frank, unlike Duff, considered the effect of Lincoln's law practice on his public life as candidate for Senate in 1858 and as president. Frank believed that "the key to Lincoln's practice" was his "directness of thought. His mind worked in terms of basic ideas presented as fundamentals." Lawyer Lincoln's "way of thought" or "cast of mind" was used also by President Lincoln in analyzing problems. Frank also believed that Lincoln's "extraordinary success" as president was "the product of his simplicity, his capacity to reach the one essential element of his case," his talent for speaking squarely to the American people. Lincoln's years on the frontier circuit had perfected these capacities, but they were not an "inevitable by-product of that experience."[107]

The quality and quantity of literature on Lincoln's law practice suffers in comparison to the writing on other aspects of his life. This imbalance is a result of cultural stereotypes about Lincoln and about lawyers. Starting with Lincoln's campaign biographies, biographers have glossed over Lincoln's law practice. These writers were aware of the negative image of lawyers and were content to depict Lincoln superficially as a model attorney. This portrait corresponded with the model attorney depicted in antebellum fiction. With the professionalization of history in the twentieth century, the treatment of Lincoln's law practice has improved somewhat. Yet the treatment of the law practice remained insufficient because of the lack of interest in this aspect of Lincoln's pre-presidential career, the lack of legal training, and the lack of access to documents. Lawyers have devoted considerable attention to lawyer Lincoln, but this attention generally has been motivated by attempts to appropriate the image of Lincoln. The lawyers always have claimed that Lincoln was a typical lawyer, but their conception of a typical lawyer has changed over time.

CHAPTER TWO

The Education of a Whig Lawyer

In an age of lawyer-politicians, Lincoln's pursuit of twin careers in law and politics appears, on the surface, to be typical. But unlike most lawyer-politicians of his day, he became a lawyer after he had become a politician. Unlike most lawyers, he did not apprentice in a law office, although his reading for law was similar in breadth to the training that most antebellum lawyers received. His education and training were more unusual when compared to those of other prominent members of the Illinois bar, most of whom had attended college or law school. Lincoln's minimal preparation ensured that his legal education continued throughout his law practice. As a lawyer Lincoln only read law books when he had to; but he ably used available resources to find answers to legal problems. By the end of his legal career, Lincoln's initial preparation was unusual when compared to that of those then entering the profession, who were more likely to have attended law school or to apprentice. This did not stop Lincoln from advising would-be lawyers in the 1850s to train the same way he had in the 1830s.

Politics and Law

While discussing on the floor of the House an obscure measure concerning a postal contract, Abraham Lincoln mentioned a legal point about the construction of statutes. He paused to "ask the lawyers in this House (I suppose there are some)" whether he was right. The *Congressional Globe* recorded a laugh after Lincoln's aside.[1] There were, of course, "some" lawyers in the House: Lincoln served in Congress at a time when two-thirds of its members were lawyers. Lawyers also dominated the Senate; ninety-five percent of United States Senators in 1845 had legal training.[2] Lincoln was a lawyer-politician when lawyer-politicians dominated American politics.[3]

Many antebellum lawyers entered politics to advance their legal careers.[4] For most lawyers, political office gave them needed public exposure for their law practice. Springfield lawyer James C. Conkling, a Lincoln contemporary, recalled that for Illinois lawyers in the 1840s "a political contest gave them notoriety among the masses, and afforded them an opportunity to display their abilities. A reputation for eloquence and skill in debate was a recommendation as lawyers in the practice of their profession."[5] Sometimes not even an election contest was needed. As a young lawyer in Jacksonville, Illinois, Stephen A. Douglas discovered that a high profile in politics meant increased revenue for his law practice. After giving a political speech, he was attacked for "two or three weeks" by the opposition paper. Within a week, Douglas had received collection cases worth thousands of dollars from persons who would not have otherwise heard of him. Douglas later confessed, "So essential was the service thus rendered me by my opponents that I have sometimes doubted whether I was not morally bound to pay the editor for his abuse according to the usual prices of advertisements."[6] Other Illinois lawyers sought political office to supplement their "slender incomes."[7]

For other lawyers, according to one 1851 commentator, the legal profession was not the path to riches but "the highway to official distinction. Many enter it not to practice its duties, and win its honors, but because it affords facilities for obtaining public stations."[8] William H. Herndon, Lincoln's law partner, believed that "Lincoln's restless ambition found its gratification only in the field of politics. He used the law merely as a stepping-stone to what he considered a more attractive condition in the political world."[9]

Lincoln had begun reading law books shortly after moving to New Salem in 1831. He was soon doing more than reading law; Lincoln drafted legal documents for his neighbors and argued their cases before a justice of the peace. New Salem doctor Jason Duncan recalled that "as there were no Attorneys nearer than Springfield his services were sometimes sought in suits, at law, and he frequently consented to appear before Esq. Bowling Greens' court, to argue cases."[10] New Salem merchant Abner Y. Ellis remembered that Lincoln "had an old form Book from which he used in writing Deeds, Wills & Letters when desired to do so by his friends and neighbors."[11] Among those early legal documents that Lincoln wrote for his neighbors are an 1831 bond for title, an 1832 bill of sale for the "right and title" to the New Salem ferry, an 1833 summons for a suit on a $21.57 note (against Jason Duncan), and three deeds written in 1833 or 1834.[12] By 1832 Lincoln had thought about studying law but decided "he could not succeed at that without a better education."[13]

Lincoln decided on law as a profession during the 1834 election campaign, two years after his first try for political office. When Lincoln was running for the legislature, John T. Stuart, a Whig legislator from Sangamon County, encouraged Lincoln to study law. His fellow Whig later took Lincoln in as his partner. This was not uncommon in antebellum America. Of the twenty-five law students named in Chicago city directories, four became partners with one of their preceptors after finishing their law studies. A study of antebellum New Jersey found that many aspirants to political office would study with older lawyers who would serve as guides to both professions.[14] Stuart, in some ways, served this role for Lincoln.

Lawyer-politicians somehow flourished in a culture that was hostile toward lawyers.[15] Some of this antilawyer hostility was directed specifically toward lawyers in politics. John W. Pitts, a polemicist from Georgia, argued in 1843 that Americans should elect farmers, not lawyers, to the legislature. Lawyers, unfortunately, were "the law-making corps of the State." Lawyers made the rules that governed society "exceedingly prolix and difficult to be understood, so that no class can comprehend them, or attend to matters under their rules, but they themselves."[16] Frederick Robinson, a Democratic legislator in Massachusetts, similarly asserted in 1834 that the "trades union of lawyers" deliberately monopolized political office. Lawyers met regularly to "enter into social conversations and agreements as to what individuals among them would be most likely to succeed in any election for the principal officers of the government." "By means of this regularly organized combination of lawyers throughout the land," said Robinson, "the whole government of the nation has always been in their hands."[17]

Tennessee politician Andrew Johnson, Lincoln's future vice-president, attacked the domination of lawyers in government during his congressional race in 1851. Johnson claimed that all but twenty-three of 223 congressmen were lawyers: "The laboring man of America is ignored, he has no proportionate representation, though he constitutes a large majority of the voting population."[18] In an earlier speech, Johnson criticized how the legal profession had become the American aristocracy (a development that Tocqueville famously had praised). Johnson believed that lawyers were corrupted by their reading of English law books; they appreciated British government more than their own. Lawyers "might, indeed, talk about Democracy, but it was all theory; it was talk, and talk only. They had no sympathy with the man in the workshop or the field."[19]

The popular animosity toward lawyers did not prevent them from dominating politics. Lincoln pointed out in his notes for a law lecture that the popular belief that lawyers were dishonest was *"vague"* and noted "to what extent *confidence* and *honors* are reposed in and conferred upon lawyers by the people."[20] Moreover, while antilawyer sentiment was part of the Jacksonian attack on "privilege," the heavy participation of lawyers in both parties removed its partisan edge. The *Chicago Weekly Democrat* lamented that in the 1847 Illinois elections two Democrats lost "by the cry of 'Anti-lawyer'" while another lost "by the cry 'don't send a merchant, we must have a lawyer.'"[21]

In addition to the antilawyer bias in popular culture, lawyer-politicians also faced criticism from elite lawyers who cautioned against mixing law and politics.[22] Kentucky lawyer George Robertson in his *Scrap Book on Law and Politics, Men and Times* (1855), a book Lincoln owned, warned that a "young lawyer, attending properly to his profession, cannot be a very useful or distinguished statesman; nor can such a statesman easily or conveniently be a first rate practising lawyer." He advised lawyers to avoid the seductions of politics and warned that the twin sisters of law and politics couldn't live together in the same house.[23] Ohio judge Timothy Walker told his graduating students at the Cincinnati Law School that "to be successful lawyers, you must be nothing but lawyers." Walker conceded his warning against entry into politics was futile; "there is some unaccountable fascination in political life, to most persons, against which it is useless to reason."[24]

Lincoln chose a legal career after he had entered politics. Most public men, as Tocqueville noted, were legal practitioners.[25] Thus, Lincoln's decision undoubtedly was reinforced by the symbiotic relationship between law and politics in the antebellum period.[26] A law practice kept an aspiring politician in the public eye, and, for a man of ability such as Lincoln, ensured a steady income.[27]

Legal Training in Antebellum America

Most antebellum lawyers prepared for their career by reading in a lawyer's office; the remainder received at least some law school training. In Chicago, for example, of the forty-four lawyers who were admitted to practice from 1831 to 1850, thirty-nine (88%) had studied in a law office and five had attended law school. Twenty-six (59%) had at least some college education.[28] In Kentucky, most lawyers in the 1840s had received their law training as apprentices. In a sampling of thirty-one lawyers, eighteen (58%) read law with an established lawyer, four went to law school, six attended law school and studied in a law office, two read law under the guidance of a circuit clerk, and one read law on his own while working as a harness maker.[29]

Lincoln's contemporaries took well-trod paths to the bar—they attended college or law school and worked as apprentices.[30] John T. Stuart, his first law partner, graduated from Centre College in Danville, Kentucky, and studied law with Judge Daniel Breck in Richmond, Kentucky, for over a year. Stephen T. Logan, his second partner, studied law with his uncle, who was a judge in southern Kentucky. William Herndon, his third law partner, attended Illinois College for a year and clerked in Lincoln's law office. Judge David Davis attended Kenyon College, studied law in an office, and attended New Haven Law School. Orville H. Browning, a political associate and friend of Lincoln's, attended Augusta College in Ohio and read law in his uncle's law office. Elihu Washburne, who was associated with Lincoln in the Whig and Republican parties, studied in a law office in Hallowell, Maine, for one year, then attended Harvard Law School for fourteen months while studying in a law office in Boston. E. D. Baker, Lincoln's close associate in the Whig Party, read law with a lawyer in Carrollton, Illinois. John J. Hardin, another Whig, graduated from Transylvania University and read law with a supreme court justice in Kentucky. Richard Yates, Whig representative and president of the Tonica and Petersburg Railroad, attended Illinois College, studied in Hardin's law office, and attended the law department at Transylvania. Henry E. Dummer, Stuart's former partner and Lincoln's frequent co-counsel, was a graduate of Bowdoin and Harvard Law School. Leonard Swett, Lincoln's companion on the Eighth Circuit, attended Waterville College for three years and studied law in a Portland, Maine, law office for two years.[31]

New Haven Law School, where David Davis studied, required students to read Blackstone's *Commentaries on the Laws of England,* Kent's *Commentaries on American Law,* Chitty's *Pleadings,* and Cruise's *Digest of the Law of Real Property.* The required texts at Cincinnati Law School in 1844 included Timothy Walker's *Introduction to American Law,* Blackstone's *Commentaries, Chitty on Contracts, Stephen on Pleading,* Greenleaf's *Evidence,* and Story's *Equity Jurisprudence.* The law department at Indiana University had a two-year course in 1843 that required students to read ten treatises: Blackstone's *Commentaries,* Story's *Commentaries on the Constitution, Chitty on Contracts, Stephen on Pleading,* Kent's *Commentaries, Chitty on Bills,* Chitty's *Pleadings,* Starkie's *Evidence,* Story's *Equity Jurisprudence,* and Story's *Equity Pleading.*[32] Moreover, law schools also included lectures and moot courts.[33]

Few would-be lawyers, however, attended law school in the 1830s.[34] Only six law schools existed in 1830 in the United States. When Lincoln began his law studies in 1834, a seventh, located in Cincinnati, was operating. The combined enrollment of all seven schools was around 350 in 1840. In 1850, the total law school enrollment was 400 in a nation with almost 24,000 lawyers.[35] Lincoln wouldn't have been able to attend law school in Illinois: there were no law schools in Illinois in the 1830s. Legal education came to Illinois later; when Lincoln was studying to be a lawyer, the only two schools west of the Appalachians were in Cincinnati and Lexington.[36]

While the dominant form of antebellum legal education was law-office study, it is rare to find a nineteenth-century lawyer who had kinds words to say about this experience. Massachusetts lawyer Josiah Quincy in 1832 summarized law-office study as "regular instruction there was none; examination as to progress in acquaintance with the law,—none; occasional lectures,—none; oversight as to general attention and conduct,—none."[37] Maryland writer John Pendleton Kennedy described a character's law office study in his novel *Swallow Barn* (1832) as the "three years he smoked segars in a lawyer's office in Richmond, which enabled him to obtain a bird's-eye view of Blackstone and the Revised Code."[38] New York lawyer Thomas W. Clerke complained in 1840 that students in law offices did not receive any legal instruction: "The practitioners, to whose offices they are attached, do not pretend, generally speaking, to afford them this instruction. Receiving no compensation, and immersed in the cares and labors of practice, they have neither time nor inclination for the performance of this duty."[39]

Would-be lawyers prepared for the bar by reading treatises.[40] The proliferation of legal treatises had shaped antebellum legal education. Their increased publication made it easier for would-be lawyers to learn law and may have hindered the growth of law schools.[41] An Ohio lawyer in 1856 observed that "the multitude of treatises and commentaries upon every branch of the law, divided and subdivided as they are have perhaps furnished the means for a more popular mode of study, and a speedier accomplishment of the probation required of the student."[42]

Lincoln's Training

Most antebellum lawyers read in a law office where they also copied documents. Lincoln was entirely self-taught; as he proudly noted in 1860, he "studied with nobody." After the election in August 1834, "he borrowed books of Stuart, took them home with him, and went at it in good earnest."[43] Henry E. Dummer, Stuart's then partner, later remembered how Lincoln "used to come to our office . . . in Springfield from New Salem and borrow law books. He seemed to have little to say; seemed to feel timid, with a tinge of sadness visible in the countenance, but when he did talk all this disappeared for the time and demonstrated that he was both strong and acute. He surprised us more and more at every visit."[44] But Lincoln shared something in common with an apprentice in a law office: they both received little real training or instruction and read the same treatises.

Many of Lincoln's contemporaries in Sangamon County had some college education or had attended law school. Lincoln estimated that "the agregate of all his schooling did not amount to one year." Lincoln's friend Joshua Fry Speed distinguished Lincoln from his fellow Sangamon County lawyers, who "were all educated men." Speed contrasted those worthies who "had read many books, and studied law, many of them with able lawyers" with Lincoln, who "had read but few books, but had studied those." Lincoln read books at "his humble home on the banks of the Sangamon, without a preceptor or fellow student. With such preparation he came to the bar."[45]

While Lincoln borrowed books from Stuart and Dummer, he did not work in their office as a law clerk. Lincoln missed little by not copying documents in their office. In a purported interview published in 1864, Lincoln allegedly said that he "'read law,' as the phrase is; that is, I became a lawyer's clerk in Springfield, and copied tedious documents, and picked up what I could of law in the intervals of other work."[46] Herndon, however, later disputed this account. He flatly said, "Mr. Lincoln was never clerk for any man in the law business in Springfield or elsewhere, and never copied tedious documents for anyone."[47] Herndon's position is supported by the available evidence: the only other legal document written by Lincoln besides the pleadings in *Hawthorn v. Wooldridge* that survives from this period is a will written in August 1836.[48]

Lincoln, through his unusual path to the bar, uncannily received the advantages of the apprenticeship system while avoiding its disadvantages. Someone studying in a law office typically would have the benefits of access to law books and to a lawyer to direct his reading, as well as the ability to develop a relationship with an established attorney. For these benefits, an apprentice often paid a fee to the lawyer and was given mind-numbing tasks such as drafting documents from form books.[49] Without studying in an office, Lincoln was able to borrow law books from Stuart and Dummer, who undoubtedly also directed his reading, and Stuart later offered him a partnership when Lincoln gained his license. At the same time, Lincoln apparently avoided both performing the drudge work that was so familiar to law clerks and paying any fees for that privilege.

Lincoln's preparation for the bar largely consisted of reading borrowed treatises. Lincoln read more than Blackstone's *Commentaries,* but not much more. He later recommended five different legal treatises to law students in the 1850s. In 1858, he advised John H. Widmer to read "Blackstone's Commentaries, Chitty's Pleadings—Greenleaf's Evidence, Story's Equity, and Story's Equity Pleadings."[50] In 1860, he advised John M. Brockman "to get the books, and read, and study them carefully. Begin with Blackstone's Commentaries, and after reading it carefully through, say twice, take up Chitty's Pleadings, Greenleaf's Evidence & Story's Equity &c in succession."[51] Three of Lincoln's recommended treatises were available when he studied the law. These three were Blackstone, Story's *Equity Jurisprudence,*[52] and Chitty's *Pleadings.*[53] Story's *Equity Pleadings*[54] and Greenleaf's *Evidence*[55] were published too late to assist Lincoln in his studies. Except for Blackstone, Lincoln recommended treatises that he used heavily in his law practice. The four treatises that Lincoln cited most often in his appellate cases were Story's *Equity Pleadings* and *Equity Jurisprudence,* Chitty's *Pleadings,* and Greenleaf's *Evidence.* Blackstone's *Commentaries* and Chitty's *Pleadings* probably were the two most popular treatises found in antebellum law offices.[56] Lincoln cited Joseph Story's *Commentaries on Equity Pleadings* at least eleven times in five appellate cases.[57] Lincoln cited another treatise by Story, *Commentaries on Equity Jurisprudence,* at least eight times in six appellate cases.[58] He cited Simon Greenleaf's *Treatise on the Law of Evidence* at least eleven times in legal documents.[59] Lincoln cited Joseph Chitty's *Practical Treatise on Pleading* at least nine times in four appellate cases. He referred to Chitty in a letter to William Martin, where Lincoln told Martin that he would "find a very apt precedent for such a count in 2. Chitty's Pleading, 52."[60]

If Lincoln limited his reading to Blackstone, Story, and Chitty, then his legal studies were relatively superficial when compared with formal legal education. Lincoln recognized this. After nineteen-year-old Beardstown resident Isham Reavis asked if he could study law with him, Lincoln suggested that Reavis contact Henry Dummer, Stuart's old law partner and a resident of Beardstown. Dummer, a graduate of Bowdoin and Harvard Law School, was, according to Lincoln, "a very clever man and an excellent lawyer (much better than I, in law-learning)."[61]

Lincoln and Blackstone

Lincoln, as Robert A. Ferguson notes, was the last "Blackstone lawyer" to lead the country.[62] Sir William Blackstone's *Commentaries on the Laws of England* had a profound impact on Lincoln. Lincoln has been quoted as saying he "never read anything which so profoundly interested and thrilled me" and "never in my whole life was my mind so thoroughly absorbed."[63]

A large part of Lincoln's preparation for the bar was reading Blackstone's *Commentaries*. William Dean Howells in his 1860 campaign biography described the "peculiar manner" in which Lincoln "pursued his law studies." Lincoln bought an "old copy of Blackstone" at auction and began reading it with his "characteristic energy."

> His favorite place of study was a wooded knoll near New Salem, where he threw himself under a wide-spreading oak, and expansively made a reading desk of the hillside. Here he would pore over Blackstone day after day shifting his position as the sun rose and sank, so as to keep in the shade, and utterly unconscious of everything but the principles of common law.

Lincoln did not change this account in his corrected copy.[64] Another campaign biography reported that Lincoln, after purchasing Blackstone, "became for a time so absorbed in the study of law that his friends were fearful that he would injure his mind by too close application."[65] New Salem resident Henry McHenry had told campaign biographer James Quay Howard in 1860 that Lincoln had been so absorbed in Blackstone that "people said he was crazy."[66] Isaac Cogdal, another New Salem resident, recalled that Lincoln in 1832 already "was then reading Blackstone—read hard—day & night—terribly hard." Several of Lincoln's neighbors recall him reading Blackstone in 1831 and 1832.[67] Because Lincoln later stated he studied law "in good earnest" only after his election in August 1834, his 1831–1832 immersion in Blackstone appears to be what Lincoln biographer Douglas Wilson has called an "earlier exploratory reading in law."[68]

Lincoln at least twice recommended Blackstone's *Commentaries* to would-be lawyers.[69] Blackstone was the only work that he recommended that he did not regularly cite in his law practice; he cited the *Commentaries* only three times in appellate cases.[70] While Lincoln's heavy intellectual debt to Blackstone was typical of antebellum lawyers, he did not share the concerns of those lawyers sensitive of the differences between American and British principles of governance.

Blackstone profoundly influenced American law and legal institutions. Literary historian Robert A. Ferguson, for example, asserts that Blackstone's *Commentaries* ranks only behind the Bible as an intellectual influence on the development of American institutions.[71] Lincoln too was influenced by Blackstone. His unqualified admiration for Blackstone is related to how he must have reacted to first reading the *Commentaries*. The *Commentaries* had one quality with particular significance for Lincoln: Blackstone presented an orderly system in a comprehensible manner. This quality stemmed from Blackstone's intended audience.

Blackstone's *Commentaries*, as English writer Frederick Ritso pointed out in 1815, "were not designed for students at law, but for students at the University; they were not addressed to professional but to unprofessional readers."[72] Because Blackstone was addressing lay readers, he tried to present a scheme that was understandable to outsiders. Blackstone rejected the arrangement previously given the law by writers and organized his materials into four major concepts: the rights of persons, the rights of things, public wrongs, and private wrongs.[73] According to legal historian S. F. C. Milsom, Blackstone's achievement was that by trying to give lay readers "a view from above the procedural technicalities, he had given lawyers a new vision of the law."[74] Unlike earlier English treatise writers, Blackstone did not focus on the technical aspects of English procedure. (United States Supreme Court Justice Joseph Story in 1838 noted that "English law-treatises are, for the most part, mere formularies for practice."[75]) Blackstone instead presented a coherent system based on substantive law, not procedure.[76]

Story, who in addition to being a supreme court justice was a Harvard law professor and legal treatise writer, believed that "the publication of Blackstone's Commentaries (in 1765) constituted a new epoch in the annals of the common law." Story asserted that "the most incontestible proof of the excellence of the work is to be found in the striking effects which its publication produced in every department of the common law."[77] Story's student, Ohio judge Timothy Walker, wrote in his *Introduction to American Law* (1837) that with the publication of Blackstone's *Commentaries*, "the scene all at once changed; and from a repulsive mass of disjointed fragments, the law suddenly became a connected and methodical science." Walker concluded that this "transformation was effected by the comprehensive knowledge, luminous method, and beautiful style of Sir William Blackstone. There is probably no branch of knowledge, towards the perfecting of which, a single mind has accomplished more."[78]

While Lincoln's admiration for Blackstone apparently was without reservation, other lawyers were painfully aware of the problem that Blackstone presented republican America. While Blackstone was omnipresent in antebellum legal literature, his ideas often were attacked.[79] American independence prompted careful consideration of the concepts presented in the *Commentaries*. Thomas Jefferson in 1801 declared that "we can no longer say there is nothing new under the sun. For this whole chapter in the history of man is new."[80] The newness of the American nation posed difficult challenges for its courts and legislatures. American legal thinkers specifically rejected Blackstone's notion of individual rights.[81]

Nathaniel Chipman, a Vermont lawyer, supreme court justice and Federalist politician, in *Sketches of the Principles of Government* (1793), warned that the governments of "the several American states" were "of the democratic republican kind" but that Blackstone was a "British subject, highly in favor with the government. He was enamored with its principles." Blackstone was a writer "who has, in a masterly manner, delineated the laws and jurisprudence of a foreign nation, under a government very different from our own." Unfortunately, the *Commentaries* was the only treatise of law to which American law students had access. The American law student, according to Chipman, had to learn that many of the principles contained in the *Commentaries* "are not universal; that in a democratic republic, they are wholly inadmissible." The student needed to be led "through a system of laws applicable to our governments and a train of reasoning congenial to their principles. Such a system we yet want. Surely genius is not wanting in America."[82]

Timothy Walker's *Introduction to American Law* (1837), which was published the same year that Lincoln became a lawyer, was one of many books designed for Chipman's American law student. Walker himself was wary of students using Blackstone's *Commentaries*. The *Commentaries*, while admirable, were written for English students. An American student could fall into a trap for the unwary:

> The American student, who reads it without a guide, obtains many erroneous impressions, and much useless learning. We have innovated upon the institutions of our English ancestors, with an unsparing hand; and not merely in minute details, but also in fundamental principles. We cannot therefore find in Blackstone, an accurate outline of American law.[83]

Walker's *Introduction* was well received. An 1838 review in the *North American Review* stated "it is an admirable First book for students of Law. It is also thoroughly American." This reviewer found two principal objections in placing Blackstone in the hands of American law students. First, the *Commentaries* contained much that was "antiquated and obsolete, even in England, much that is irrelevant in this country, that has never been adopted among us at law, and that is entirely uncongenial with our existing institutions." Second, the *Commentaries* were written in an "apologetic and servile spirit," which was "entirely at variance with the whole tone of American institutions and character."[84] An 1844 review in the *Western Literary Journal and Monthly Review* stated it was "absurd to make the Commentaries of Blackstone the first book for American students, when we have so clear an exposition of our political and juridical system." The reviewer sarcastically noted that an American student after reading Blackstone's lengthy exposition of all things British would be "about as wise a lawyer as he would be, had he spent the same time upon the novels of Sir Walter Scott."[85]

Other treatise writers presented new works that could supplant American dependence on Blackstone. Kentucky lawyer Charles Humphreys, in his *Compendium of the Common Law in Force in Kentucky* (1822), proposed to go through Blackstone's *Commentaries* and "to select what appears to be in force in this country; without taking any notice of the observations of the authors as to what the law has been in times past." Humphreys was critical of Blackstone, who seldom lost "an opportunity of eulogizing the perfection of the body politic of his own country" and "divers other good things not exactly suited to the tastes of our republicans on this side of the Atlantic.[86] Similarly, Massachusetts lawyer and treatise writer Francis Hilliard in his *Elements of Law: Being A Comprehensive Summary of American Jurisprudence* (2d ed. 1848) stated that Blackstone's *Commentaries* "contain a large amount of matter, which is neither, in its nature not *legal,* but *historical,* and political, or has no applicability, and even to the professional reader is of little use, in this country."[87]

American law writers were intellectually enthralled but politically wary of Blackstone. This tension created an anxiety about Blackstone's influence. His enormous influence meant that there were at least sixteen American editions of the *Commentaries* by the time Lincoln read for the bar and twenty-five American editions by 1860.[88] The first American edition, published by Robert Bell in 1771–1772, was "Re-printed from the British copy, page for page with the last edition." After independence, a mere reprint was not enough. Thus, the most famous American edition of Blackstone was by St. George Tucker, which Robert M. Cover noted was "not only a publication of the Blackstone text but also an engagement of it in combat."[89] Tucker acknowledged that with "the appearance of the COMMENTARIES, the laws of England, from a rude chaos, instantly assumed the semblance of a regular system." But Tucker also realized that "the revolution which separated the present United States of America from Britain" produced "a corresponding revolution not only in the principles of our government, but in the laws which relate to property, and in a variety of these cases, equally contradictory to the law, and irreconcilable to the principles contained in the COMMENTARIES." Tucker's solution was to produce an edition of Blackstone that was supplemented by American precedents and republican annotations.[90]

Other American editors followed Tucker's lead. Hugh Henry Brackenridge planned a similar edition for Pennsylvania. Although he abandoned his plan, he did publish his notes on Blackstone's *Commentaries,* "pointing out variations in the law of Pennsylvania from the common and statute law of England." In 1831, John Reed, a court of common pleas judge in

Pennsylvania, published his *Pennsylvania Blackstone*, which was represented as a "modification of the Commentaries of Sir William Blackstone, with numerous alterations and additions." In 1852, John L. Wendell edited another edition of Blackstone's *Commentaries*, which included notes "adapting the work to the American student."[91]

But Lincoln did not share this concern about Blackstone. Blackstone's *Commentaries* presented Lincoln with a comprehensible, orderly system. Lincoln had decided against studying law in 1832 because he believed "he could not succeed at that without a better education." Lincoln believed that his education was "defective."[92] Thomas Jefferson complained that Blackstone's *Commentaries* allowed law students to pretend a mastery of the law; Blackstone must have been reassuring for Lincoln for that very reason.[93] Lincoln became convinced during his single-minded absorption of the *Commentaries* that, despite his earlier insecurity about his inferior education, he could succeed as a lawyer. Moreover, Lincoln, whose adult life was defined by a search for order, would have deeply appreciated Blackstone's orderly system.[94]

Admission to the Bar

Lincoln could become a lawyer after minimal preparation because few formal barriers prevented entry into the legal profession in Jacksonian America. Those Americans who envisioned a society of unlimited opportunity demanded access to the elite professions of law and medicine.[95] The suspicion of privilege and the distrust of elites led states to lower standards for admission to the bar.[96] In 1800, fourteen out of nineteen states required all lawyers to complete an apprenticeship; by 1840, only eleven out of thirty did so.[97] Jacksonian democracy intended to let the market, not the legal profession, regulate the number of lawyers.[98]

The Illinois statute that governed admission to the bar encouraged broad access to the legal profession by setting minimal entry requirements. The would-be lawyer had to fulfill three statutory requirements. First, he needed a "certificate of some county judge of his good moral character." Second, he had to obtain a license from two of the justices of the supreme court. At this stage, a perfunctory examination was given. Third, after taking an oath, he was enrolled by the clerk of the supreme court.[99]

Lincoln fulfilled the statutory requirements expeditiously. On March 24, 1836, Judge Stephen T. Logan entered a certification of Lincoln's good moral character into the records of the Sangamon Circuit Court.[100] Lincoln received his license on September 9, 1836, and was enrolled on March 1, 1837.[101] Enrollment was more than a merely technical requirement. In 1840 the Illinois Supreme Court refused to permit an attorney who was sworn in in 1837 but was not enrolled until 1840 to change his date of enrollment to the earlier date. The court also noted that this attorney could not recover for services as an attorney performed before his name was entered on the roll.[102] Apparently, the failure to conform to the statute was not uncommon for Illinois lawyers. John Dean Caton, an Illinois Supreme Court Justice in the 1840s, later recalled that he already was practicing law when he received his law license.[103]

Between receiving his license and being enrolled (from September 1836 to March 1837), Lincoln probably was doing some law work, but neither as a lawyer nor as an apprentice. No evidence exists that Lincoln held himself out as an attorney during this time. Perhaps the date of his formal entry should be October 5, 1836, when John T. Stuart filed several documents written in Lincoln's hand in two cases brought by James P. Hawthorn against David Wooldridge. Lincoln, however, did not sign these pleading nor did his name appear on them. Lincoln was not acting as a lawyer but as a scrivener. He did not formally appear in either Hawthorn case until March 14, 1837, almost two weeks after he was formally enrolled.[104] The first advertisement for the partnership of Stuart & Lincoln appeared in the April 15, 1837, *Sangamo Journal* and was dated April 12.[105]

There is no record of Lincoln's examination, but John D. Caton provides an excellent description of what must have been a typical bar examination in 1830s Illinois. Caton asked Samuel D. Lockwood, a justice on the Illinois Supreme Court, to examine him. Lockwood invited Caton for a walk after supper and then inquired generally about with whom Caton had apprenticed and what books he had read. Lockwood then asked more specific questions about the forms of action, criminal law, and the administration of estates. Caton recalled that he was "surprised and somewhat embarrassed to find myself so unexpectedly undergoing the examination, and bungled considerably at the first when he inquired about the different forms of action." After a thirty-minute examination, Lockwood told Caton he would give him a license, but warned him that he had much to learn and said he "had better adopt some other pursuit, unless I was determined to work hard, to read much and to think strongly of what I did read."[106]

The minimal examination for admission to the bar was not limited to Illinois. An Ohio lawyer in 1849 observed that "the examination of students" was "in most cases, but a farce; and friendship or partiality, haste or ignorance, allows to applicants an easy entrance."[107] After George Templeton Strong took his examination for the New York bar in 1841, he wrote in his diary that one of the examiners "examined as sharp as he knew, which wasn't much." He found the "richest part of the affair" to be the further examination of "some half-dozen of those who had flunked the most barefacedly on the preceding queries." Strong exclaimed "such a farce of an examination, such an asinine set of candidates, and such prodigiously uncomfortable timber benches I never met with before." The results were announced the next day: "All passed!"[108] The elitist Strong saw no value in ensuring broad access to the legal profession.

Sometimes even this cursory examination was skipped entirely. Lincoln's future general William Tecumseh Sherman recalled entering into a partnership with attorney T. E. Ewing in Leavenworth, Kansas, in 1858 and "accordingly the firm of Sherman & Ewing was duly announced, and our services to the public offered as attorneys-at-law." Because he wasn't actually a lawyer at the time, Sherman thought it best to obtain a license. When he mentioned this to the federal judge, the judge told him to get a license from the judge's clerk. Sherman asked about his examination, the judge told him there would be none; Sherman would be admitted based on his general intelligence.[109] War may be hell; but getting a law license wasn't.

Standards for admission to the bar remained low even when Illinois changed from an oral examination given by judges to an oral examination given by attorneys in 1850. The ease of the examination remained the same. Lincoln served as an examiner for at least eleven applicants for a law license; all eleven applicants passed their examinations.[110] Jonathan Birch, a candidate who was examined by Lincoln, later recalled his experience. Lincoln's first question was "What books have you read?" When Birch told him, he said, "Well, that is more than I had read before I was admitted to practice." Lincoln then told a story about trying a case against a "college-bred lawyer who apparently had studied all the books." While the judge and the other lawyers were impressed by his opponent's learning, the jury wasn't. "And they," said Lincoln, "were the fellows I was aiming at." Resuming his questioning, Lincoln rapidly asked Birch a series of questions that appeared to Birch to be but faintly related to the practice of law. Lincoln never indicated whether any of Birch's responses were correct. Lincoln abruptly stopped, declaring that he had asked Birch enough, and wrote the requisite certificate of recommendation. Lincoln also gave Birch advice about his future course of study, which Birch later realized "was about the first thing that had been said to indicate that the entire proceeding was, after all, an examination to test the applicant's ability to practice law."[111] After Lincoln and Herndon examined John T. Stuart's son-in-law, C. C. Brown, Brown and his examiners went to a restaurant and ate oysters and fried pickled pigs feet. Brown picked up the tab.[112]

Lincoln became a lawyer when there were few formal barriers to entry. This Illinois Whig ironically benefited from a Jacksonian policy that ensured broad access to the legal profession. As a result, his "defective" education, despite Lincoln's fears, did not impede his entry to the profession. He expeditiously fulfilled the minimal statutory requirements that Illinois placed on aspiring lawyers and formally began his legal career in March 1837.

Because of the minimal formal requirements, it is easy to overlook John T. Stuart's role in aiding Lincoln's entry into the legal profession. The antebellum legal profession was one of "sponsored mobility," and Stuart served as Lincoln's sponsor by loaning him books to study and later forming a partnership with him.[113] Lincoln probably was able to use Stuart's name when he needed the certificate of good moral character signed by the circuit judge and the license signed by two supreme court judges. A letter written by Judge David Davis to Lincoln in January 1860 reveals the importance of having a sponsor. Davis wrote Lincoln that he was "very solicitous about our mutual friend Albert Jones getting admitted to the bar." Davis wondered whether the court could "appoint a Committee to examine him out of Court—Say you & I." If the court wouldn't appoint such a committee, Davis asked Lincoln to "please try & get Mr. Peck to sign a license." Davis concluded by noting that Jones was a political ally and wouldn't embarrass himself as a lawyer: "Jones is working for us, very faithfully now & you know he would be a respectable acquisition to the bar—It strikes me that with Judge Treat's personal influence (the Judges being in Springfield) that you can solve this question."[114]

Other Illinois lawyers served as sponsors for would-be lawyers. Clifton Moore, who practiced law alongside Lincoln in De Witt County, wrote Lincoln about a young man named Green who had been studying in his office for ten months. Moore vouched for Green, saying he was "satisfied that there is something of him." He told Lincoln that he wanted "to send him down to you & you have him 'past through,'" adding that Green was "not afraid of a rigid examination."[115] Jacksonville lawyer Murray McConnel lent Stephen A. Douglas a helping hand at a critical juncture; he advised Douglas to go to Pekin and open a law office shortly after Douglas arrived in Illinois. When Douglas countered that he had never practiced law and had neither a license nor a library, McConnel furnished Douglas with some essential law books and suggested he practice before the justice of the court until he had a license, which McConnel assured him he could get any time.[116]

Lincoln's Continuing Legal Education

Abraham Lincoln was not a diligent student of the law, but when pressed by necessity, he was a sophisticated user of the available sources of legal information. His early legal training and the rapid changes in antebellum law ensured that his legal education continued throughout his law career. Although Lincoln advised would-be lawyers to "still keep reading" after becoming licensed, Lincoln's reading instead was directed toward the case before him.[117] Herndon believed that Lincoln "never studied law books unless a case was on hand for consideration." Judge David Davis, who regularly saw Lincoln on the circuit, similarly believed that Lincoln "read law books but little, except when the cause in hand made it necessary."[118] Lincoln, according to Herndon, "was in every respect a case lawyer, never cramming himself on any question till he had a case in which the question was involved." Herndon wrote that Lincoln "never followed up the decisions of the supreme courts, as other lawyers did."[119] Lincoln's second partner, Stephen T. Logan, later recalled that "Lincoln's knowledge of law was very small when I took him in." Logan explained that:

I don't think he studied very much. I think he learned his law more in the study of cases. He would work hard and learn all there was in a case he had in hand. He got to be a pretty good lawyer though his general knowledge of law was never very formidable. But he would study out his case and make about as much of it as anybody.[120]

Henry Clay Whitney, who traveled the Eighth Circuit with Lincoln, wrote that Lincoln was not "profoundly versed in black letter or yet case law."[121] Lincoln's approach to reading law books was typical for a lawyer. Although Herndon noted that "Lincoln never read much law, and never did I see him read a law book through," he completed the sentence by noting "and no one else ever did."[122] Lawyers read purposively; lawyers, as legal historian M. H. Hoeflich notes, "read to acquire knowledge with a specific end in sight. . . . They seek to find the specific nuggets of information they require for purposes wholly external to the text itself."[123] John H. Littlefield, who studied law in Lincoln & Herndon's office, later described Lincoln reading law books: "Lincoln's favorite position when unraveling some knotty law point was to stretch both of his legs at full length upon a chair in front of him. In this position, with books on the table near by and in his lap, he worked up his case."[124] Lincoln's approach can be seen in the actions that he took after he was mailed a catalogue of law books. Lincoln kept the catalogue, which listed over 1,100 English and American treatises by subject, but he also wrote "Too deep for me" on the outside of the envelope.[125]

Lincoln did not keep a commonplace book of reported decisions.[126] Commonplace books were notebooks kept by law students and lawyers that contained summaries of cases and statutes arranged by topic.[127] Thomas Jefferson in 1814 advised law students: "In reading the Reporters, enter in a Common-place book, every case of value, condensed into the narrowest compass possible which will admit of presenting distinctly the principles of the case." But common-placing was in decline in the nineteenth century. Joseph Story believed that lawyers' commonplace books were being replaced by the publication of case-finding aids such as digests and abridgments.[128]

Lincoln particularly relied on Herndon to find cases for him. Herndon, as the junior partner, did much of the legal research for the firm. Albert Taylor Bledsoe, who practiced law in Springfield in the 1840s, remembered Lincoln did his reading "as some men do their religion, by *proxy*, by his Good-Man-Friday, William H. Herndon, who, with creditable zeal and industry, would collect all sorts of cases and authorities for him."[129] Herndon, unlike Lincoln, kept commonplace books.[130] Herndon's research skills are apparent in supreme court cases like *St. Louis, Alton & Chicago Railroad v. Dalby.* There, Herndon successfully argued that the railroad could be held liable for its employees' actions in beating a passenger.[131] In other cases, Lincoln relied upon Herndon's research skills. Herndon later wrote that many people would flatter him by saying that he "made out the best briefs in the largest law cases, and that Lincoln would argue his case from these briefs and get the credit for them while I was the power behind them."[132] Herndon, however, understood the division of labor in the office. In a 1857 letter to abolitionist Wendell Phillips, he wrote that Lincoln was the "hoss" and he was the "runt" of the firm.[133]

Lincoln also relied on other lawyers for legal research. In a letter to Hezekiah M. Wead, a Lewistown attorney, Lincoln wrote, "Be sure to send the brief, with the authorities on it."[134] He wrote Newton Deming and George P. Strong "to prepare, on the question jurisdiction as well as you can."[135] Lincoln wrote a letter to his client, Charles Hoyt, after he learned that he had lost the appeal of Hoyt's case. He told Hoyt that he had "made every point, and used every authority sent me by yourself & by Mr. Goodrich; in addition, all the points I could think of, and all the authorities I could find myself."[136] In *Martin v. Dryden,* Lincoln and St. Louis lawyer John M. Krum (who later as a circuit court judge would hear Dred Scott's original freedom suit) represented the appellant, but it was Krum who presented the court with an extensive "printed argument" with legal authorities.[137]

But Lincoln didn't delegate all legal research to other lawyers; he also hunted up cases in the law books. Because Lincoln did not read legal reporters as they were published, Lincoln used treatises and digests to find relevant cases. Legal treatises and digests provided Lincoln and other antebellum lawyers an efficient means to "study out" a case. American legal treatises served the practical needs of American lawyers.

American lawyers had to determine whether English common law applied because English common law, as stated by Supreme Court Justice Joseph Story, was not "to be taken in all respects to be that of America."[138] Having broken away from England, American states had to define their own common law.[139] John Bouvier in his *Law Dictionary* (1839) admitted that "there is no general rule to ascertain what part of the English common law is valid and binding."[140] As Lincoln observed, "the decisions of our courts were conforming, as they should do, to the nature and wants of our country."[141] While American courts reevaluated English common-law rules, they didn't necessarily reject them; these courts only changed one-third of core common-law rules during the nineteenth century.[142] A firm theory of precedent also was developing during this period, which increased the importance of prior decisions. The increasing reliance on case law by antebellum lawyers reflected the triumph of technical knowledge about law over more general knowledge.[143]

Antebellum lawyers not only had to be familiar with the case law from their own state but also had to research decisions from other states and England. One commentator in 1848 noted that decisions from other states weren't technically binding (they were "persuasive authority" only), but they couldn't be ignored: they "weigh so powerfully upon all doubtful questions, that no well-read lawyer dares be ignorant of them."[144] That same commentator believed that "English decisions are of more weight than those of the sister states—partly through prestige, but more through merit: and they are more numerous than all the American decisions put together."[145] Lincoln reflected this reliance upon judicial opinions from other states and England—he routinely cited cases from those jurisdictions.[146]

Finding cases was burdensome. Every profession, an antebellum observer noted, has grievances "under which they groan without the sympathy, or even knowledge" of others. For antebellum lawyers, their grievance was the sheer number of books. Courts were primarily responsible for "the bewildering bulk, complexity, and multitude of law-books."[147] Legal treatises then performed a valuable function by collecting cases from the various jurisdictions, a task most lawyers could not perform from their own law libraries because of the scarcity of reporters. One commentator in 1847 thus explained the function of a treatise:

> We have now more than seven hundred volumes of American Reports, and they are rapidly increasing. Few have access to them all, or even to the more important. On doubtful or difficult questions, it is important to have a more full statement of the decisions that can well be embraced in an ordinary digest. The reasons for such decisions, and the degree of consideration given in making them, it is also important to know. These wants, an American treatise on any branch of law ought to supply.[148]

Most American legal treatises were practitioners' manuals whose primary virtues were providing summaries and citations of cases.[149]

Ward Hill Lamon, who practiced law with Lincoln on the circuit, noted that Lincoln "reasoned almost entirely to the court and jury from analogous causes previously decided and reported in the books, and not from the elementary principles of the law, or the great underlying reasons for its existence."[150] Lincoln, like most antebellum lawyers, relied heavily on legal treatises in his law practice.[151] Lincoln's court documents and legal correspondence attest to his frequent use of treatises. Lincoln cited thirty-six treatises in forty-seven trial and appellate cases.[152] Thirty authors were represented. Ten were American: Joseph K. Angell, Samuel Ames, John Bouvier, James Gould, Simon Greenleaf, James Kent, James T. Morehead, Tapping Reeve, Joseph Story, and William Wetmore Story (see Table 1). Lincoln cited four different treatises by Joseph Story.[153] All twenty-three English treatises that Lincoln cited had American editions (Table 2). In antebellum America, publishers routinely pirated books by English authors. When they did so, they added annotations to American precedents.[154]

Table 1—AMERICAN LEGAL TREATISES CITED BY LINCOLN

Joseph K. Angell, A Treatise on the Limitations of Actions at Law, 2d ed. (Boston: C. C. Little & J. Brown, 1846)

Argument, Dec. Term 1848 [917], *Lewis v. Lewis* [L02339] casefile, LPAL

Joseph K. Angell & Samuel Ames, A Treatise on the Law of Private Corporations Aggregate 6th ed. (Boston: Little, Brown & Co. 1858)

Authorities, Dec. Term 1859 [89349], *Clark & Morrison v. Page* [L00826] casefile, LPAL

John Bouvier, Law Dictionary, 2 vols. (Philadelphia: T. and J. W. Johnson, 1839)

Cook v. Hall, 6 Ill. (1 Gilm.) 575 (1844)

James Gould, Treatise on the Principles of Pleading in Civil Actions (Boston: Lilly & Wait, 1832)

Murphy v. Summerville, 7 Ill. (2 Gilm.) 360 (1845)

Simon Greenleaf, A Treatise on the Law of Evidence, 2 vols. (Boston: Charles C. Little & James Brown, 1842)

Kincaid v. Turner, 7 Ill. (2 Gilm.) 618 (1845)
Henderson v. Welch, 8 Ill. (3 Gilm.) 340 (1845)
Argument, [May 1, 1848] [5745], *Watson v. Gill* [L00733] casefile, LPAL
Pearl v. Wellman, 11 Ill. 352 (1849)
Penny v. Graves, 12 Ill. 287 (1850)
Whitecraft v. Vanderver, 12 Ill. 235 (1850)
Smith v. Dunlap, 12 Ill. 184 (1850)
Opinion on Land Titles, March 24, 1856 [4169], *Dillingham v. Fisher* [L02512] casefile, LPAL

James Kent, Commentaries on American Law, 4 vols. (New York: O. Halsted, 1826–1830)

Dorman v. Lane, 6 Ill. (1 Gilm.) 143 (1844)
Cook v. Hall, 6 Ill. (1 Gilm.) 575 (1844)
Webster v. French, 11 Ill. 173 (1844)
Brief, Dec. Term 1853 [3230], *Illinois Central RR Co. v. McLean County* [L01655] casefile, LPAL

James T. Morehead, The Practice in Civil Actions and Proceedings in Kentucky (Louisville: Derby, Anthony & Co., 1846)

People ex rel. Harris v. Browne, 8 Ill. (3 Gilm.) 87 (1846)

Tapping Reeve, The Law of Baron and Femme (New Haven: Oliver Steele, 1816)

Davis v. Harkness, 6 Ill. (1 Gilm.) 173 (1844)

Joseph Story, Commentaries on Equity Jurisprudence, 2 vols. (Boston: Hilliard, Gray & Co., 1836)

Abrams v. Camp, 4 Ill. (3 Scam.) 290 (1841)
Davis v. Harkness, 6 Ill. (1 Gilm.) 173 (1844)

Joseph Story, Commentaries on Equity Jurisprudence, 2 vols. (Boston: Hilliard, Gray & Co., 1836)	*Broadwell v. Broadwell*, 6 Ill. (1 Gilm.) 599 (1844) *Hall v. Irwin*, 7 Ill. (2 Gilm.) 176 (1845) *Trumbull v. Campbell*, 8 Ill. (3 Gilm.) 502 (1846) *Webster v. French*, 11 Ill. 254 (1849)
Joseph Story, Commentaries on Equity Pleadings (Boston: C. C. Little & J. Brown, 1838)	*Ballentine v. Beall*, 12 Ill 426 (1841) *Spear v. Campbell*, 5 Ill. (4 Scam.) 424 (1843) *McCall v. Lesher*, 7 Ill. (2 Gilm.) 46 (1845) Brief, Dec. Term 1849 [5364], *Lewis v. Moffett & Johnson* [L03866] casefile, LPAL
Joseph Story, Commentaries on the Law of Agency (Boston: C. C. Little & J. Brown, 1839)	*Chase v. DeBolt*, 7 Ill. (2 Gilm.) 371 (1845)
Joseph Story, Commentaries on the Law of Partnership (Boston: C. C. Little & J. Brown, 1841)	Brief, Dec. Term 1849 [5364], *Lewis v. Moffett & Johnson* [L03866] casefile, LPAL
William Wetmore Story, Treatise on the Law of Contracts Not Under Seal (Boston: C. C. Little & J. Brown, 1844)	*Chase v. DeBolt*, 7 Ill. (2 Gilm.) 371 (1845) *Adam v. County of Logan*, 11 Ill. 336 (1849) *Webster v. French*, 12 Ill. 302 (1849)

Lincoln & Herndon, in all likelihood, subscribed to the Law Library, a 104-volume series of American reprints of English legal treatises.[155] J. G. Marvin in his *Legal Bibliography* (1847) hailed this series as furnishing "at reduced price the best elementary legal Treatises of Great Britain."[156] A portion of a treatise was published as a pamphlet and mailed each month to subscribers. Four pamphlets would make up one volume. The pamphlet form allowed the treatises to be shipped through the mails and avoided the higher shipping charges on books, which had to be shipped as freight.[157] Lincoln cited Richard Babington's *Treatise on the Law of Auctions* and John Coryton's *Treatise on the Law of Letters-Patents* in appellate cases.[158] Herndon in his notes in the *St. Louis, Alton & Chicago R. R. Co. v. Dalby* appeal referred to *Smith on Master and Servant* and *Grant on Corporations*.[159] All four treatises were published in the Law Library series.

Lincoln did not necessarily own every treatise he cited. Only five of these treatises appear on Louis A. Warren's list of Lincoln's law

Table 2—ENGLISH LEGAL TREATISES CITED BY LINCOLN

Richard Babington, A Treatise on the Law of Auctions, With an Appendix of Precedents (Philadelphia: J. S. Littell, 1838) (Law Library, v. 19)	*Webster v. French*, 11 Ill. 254 (1849)
Matthew Bacon, A New Abridgement of the Law, 7 vols. (Philadelphia: Farrand & Nicholas, 1811–1813)	Brief, Dec. Term 1839 [4668], *Cannon v. Kinney* [L02875] case file, LPAL *England v. Clark*, 5 Ill. (4 Scam.) 486 (1843)
Sir William Blackstone, Commentaries on the Laws of England, 4 vols. (New York: Collins & Hannay, 1832)	*Watkins v. White*, 4 Ill. (3 Scam.). 549 (1842) *Cook v. Hall*, 6 Ill. (1 Gilm.) 575 (1844) *Whitecraft v. Vanderver*, 12 Ill. 335 (1850)
Joseph Chitty, A Treatise on the Parties to Actions, and on Pleading, 2 vols. (Springfield, Mass.: G. & C. Merriam, 1837)	Brief, Dec. Term 1839 [4668], *Cannon v. Kinney* [L02875] casefile, LPAL *Averill v. Field*, 4 Ill. (3 Scam.) 390 (1842) *Field v. Rawlings*, 6 Ill. (1 Gilm.) 581 (1844) *Murphy v. Summerville*, 7 Ill. (2 Gilm.) 360 (1845)
Joseph Chitty, Practical Treatise on the Law of Contracts Not Under Seal (Springfield, Mass.: G. & C. Merriam, 1842)	*Trumbull v. Campbell*, 8 Ill. (3 Gilm.) 502 (1846) *Webster v. French*, 11 Ill. 254 (1849) AL to William Martin, Feb. 19, 1851 [4887], *Alton & Sangamon R.R. v. Barret* [L02610] case file, LPAL
John Collyer, A Practical Treatise on the Law of Partnership (Boston: C. C. Little & J. Brown, 1848)	Brief, Dec. Term 1849 [5364], *Lewis v. Moffett & Johnson* [L03866] case file, LPAL
Samuel Comyn, A Treatise of the Law Relative to Contracts and Agreements Not Under Seal (New York: Collins & Hannay, 1831)	*Henderson v. Welch*, 8 Ill. (3 Gilm.) 502 (1846) *Trumbull v. Campbell*, 8 Ill. (3 Gilm.) 502 (1846)
George Cooper, A Treatise of Pleading on the Equity Side of the High Court of Chancery (New York: I. Riley, 1813)	*Hawks v. Lands*, 8 Ill. (3 Gilm.) 227 (1846)
John Coryton, A Treatise on the Law of Letters-Patent (Philadelphia: T & J.W. Johnson, 1855)	Brief, Dec. Term 1855 [3244], *Mayers & Mayers v. Turner* [L00960], LPAL
Edmund Robert Daniel, Pleading and Practice of the High Court of Chancery, 3 vols. (Boston: Charles C. Little & James Brown, 1851)	Authorities, June 15, 1853 [73497], *Enos v. Capps* [L02459] case file, LPAL

Murray Hoffman, A Treatise upon the Practice of the Court of Chancery (New York: J. S. Voorhies, 1843)

Stewart Kyd, A Treatise on the Law of Awards (Philadelphia: William P. Farrand & Co., 1808)

Patrick Brady Leigh, An Abridgement of the Law of Nisi Prius with Notes and References to the Latest American Cases, 2 vols. (Philadelphia: P. H. Nicklin & T. Johnson, 1838)

George Long, A Treatise on the Law Relative to Sales (Boston: Charles C. Little & James Brown, 1839)

Basil Montagu, A Summary of the Law of Lien (Exeter: G. Lamson, 1822)

John Joseph Powell, A Treatise on the Law of Mortgages (Boston: Wells & Lilly, 1828)

John Joseph Powell, Essay upon the Law of Contracts and Agreements (New York: G. Lamson, 1825)

Henry Roscoe, A Digest of the Law of Evidence on the Trial of Actions at Nisi Prius (Philadelphia: P. H. Nicklin & T. Johnson, 1832)

John Simon Saunders, The Law of Pleading and Evidence in Civil Actions, 2 vols. (Philadelphia: R. H. Small, 1844)

Thomas Starkie, A Practical Treatise on the Laws of Evidence and Digest of Proofs on Civil and Criminal Proceedings, 3 vols. (Philadelphia: P. H. Nicklin & T. Johnson, 1837)

Thomas Starkie, A Treatise on the Law of Slander and Libel, and Incidentally of Malicious Prosecutions, 2 vols. (Albany: C. Van Benthuysen & Co., 1843)

Samuel Toller, The Law of Executors and Administrators (Philadelphia: Grigg & Elliot, 1834)

Edward Williams, Treatise on the Law of Executors and Administrators (Philadelphia: Francis J. Troubat, 1832)

Authorities, June 15, 1853 [73497], *Enos v. Capps* [L02459] case file, LPAL

Kincaid v. Turner, 7 Ill. (2 Gilm.) 618 (1845)

England v. Clark, 5 Ill. (4 Scam.) 486 (1843)

Watkins v. White, 4 Ill. (3 Scam.) 549(1842)

Cannon v. Kinney, 4 Ill. (3 Scam.) 9 (1841)

Cook v. Hall, 6 Ill. (1 Gilm.) 575 (1844)

Field v. Rawlings, 6 Ill. (1 Gilm.) 581 (1844)

Mason v. Park, 4 Ill. (3 Scam.) 532 (1842)

Trumbull v. Campbell, 8 Ill. (3 Gilm.) 502 (1846)

Cannon v. Kinney, 4 Ill. (3 Scam.) 9 (1841)
Henderson v. Welch, 8 Ill. (3 Gilm.) 340 (1846)

Petition for Rehearing, [39617], *Patterson et ux. v. Edwards et ux.* [L00884] case file, LPAL

Davis v. Harkness, 6 Ill. (1 Gilm.) 173 (1844)

Davis v. Harkness, 6 Ill. (1 Gilm.) 173 (1844)

books.[160] John H. Littlefield, who studied in Lincoln's law office in 1858, later recalled that the office contained about 200 law books as well as other books.[161] By way of comparison, Judge David Davis owned fifty-four legal treatises in 1848.[162] Lincoln also used the Illinois Supreme Court library.[163]

Lincoln did not read law books until necessity forced him; however, when forced he effectively used what was available to him in his law office and at the supreme court library. In the motion for rehearing in *Patterson v. Edwards,* Lincoln offered to "furnish the court, if they desire, with a new edition, in two volumes of Starkie on Slander." Lincoln's offer meant that he knew that the judges did not have ready access to the "new edition" of this English treatise. Lincoln made a similar offer in an 1847 motion for rehearing that he wrote for another attorney. There, Lincoln relied on "one of the latest editions of Chitty's Pleadings," and then stated that the edition was "in the library of Mssrs Lincoln & Herndon which I hope they will allow use of to the court in the investigation of this petition."[164] Lincoln also frequently cited relatively new legal treatises. For example, in an 1849 appeal he referred to the second volume of *American Leading Cases,* which had been published the previous year.[165] He kept a mental inventory of the treatises in the supreme court library. In an 1857 letter to his co-counsel in an admiralty case, he wrote, "I understand they have some new Admiralty Books here, but I have not examined them."[166]

Lincoln's reliance on treatises is shown in his petition for rehearing in *Patterson v. Edwards.*[167] Ambrose Edwards and his wife sued William Patterson and his wife for slander because Mrs. Patterson allegedly said that Mrs. Edwards had "raised a family of children by a negro, and I can prove it." After the Edwards won a $220 judgment, the Pattersons appealed. Lincoln represented the Edwards on appeal. The Pattersons successfully argued on appeal that there was a variance between what was pleaded and what was proved and that the words sued upon were not slanderous.[168]

After the Illinois Supreme Court reversed on these two points and remanded for a new trial, Lincoln filed a petition for rehearing. In response to the court's holding on the variance between pleadings and proof, Lincoln asserted that the variance was not material and that it was unfair to reverse the judgment on a point not raised in the trial court. On the second point, the supreme court had held that the words in the declaration did not "necessarily amount to a charge of fornication and adultery."[169] Lincoln replied that they "*need* not *necessarily* to amount to such a charge. We say they need only be *capable* of the meaning attached to them by the declaration." He based his argument on a new American edition of the English treatise *Starkie on Slander*:

> In this we do not speak without the books. We will furnish the court, if they
> desire, with a new edition, in two volumes of Starkie on Slander and refer to
> volume 1—side pages 44 to 61 inclusive. The construction of words of doubt-

ful meaning is there fully discussed. It is there shown that there *was* an *old* and is a *new* rule on this subject; that the old rule was to construe words in *mitiori sensu*, or, in the most favourable sense for the defendant, which they were capable of bearing, never allowing a plaintiff to have a judgment, unless the words *necessarily* amounted to the charge he alleged in his declaration; that this old rule has been exploded nearly or quite a hundred years; and a new rule fully established. A train of decisions under each point is given.[170]

Lincoln then included a long quotation from the treatise, which was an American edition by John Wendell that included Wendell's notes of American and English cases.[171] It was three years old when Lincoln filed his motion. Lincoln's motion highlights the dependence by antebellum lawyers on treatises; he did not have complete access to the "train of decisions."

Lincoln, like other antebellum lawyers, also relied on published digests of reported decisions. Digests provided concise summaries of the various points of law found in reported decisions. The summaries would be arranged under a system of classified headings.[172] Norman L. Freeman, the author of the 1856 *Illinois Digest,* said that "digests have become almost a necessary evil in the practising lawyer's library." Freeman noted that "the rapidly increasing number of reports of adjudged cases had become a source of great inconvenience."[173] The availability of digests meant that lawyers did not have to read every published decision to stay abreast of legal developments. Digests thus served two purposes for antebellum lawyers. One was as a case-finding tool. In its review of the *United States Digest,* the *Western Law Journal* noted that "the chief use of all digests is to assist lawyers in the preparation of their cases. They are not of themselves *authorities,* but only guides to authorities."[174] Because of the paucity of reporters, however, digests often were used as a substitute for the reported cases. The *American Law Magazine* in 1846 pointed out that "such is the number of American reports, increasing too at the rate of between thirty and forty every year, that it is scarcely possible for the practising lawyer to possess them." The *United States Digest* "will be a little library in itself."[175]

Lincoln often used and cited digests in appellate cases (see Table 3). His favorite was the *United States Digest,* which was the first comprehensive American digest, providing summaries of cases from state and federal courts.[176] In *Risinger v. Cheney,* a contract case, Lincoln's clients had lost in the trial court. Lincoln argued that his clients' nonperformance of a contract was excused by an injunction against the plaintiff that affected the property that was the focus of the agreement. To support this argument, Lincoln gave but one citation: "1 U. S. Dig. 540, § 66."[177] The exact citation was to the following section under the topic "Condition."

He who prevents or dispenses with the performance of a condition cannot take advantage of the non-performance. *Majors v. Hickman,* 2 Bibb, 218. *Williams v. Bank of United States,* 2 Pet. 102. *Marshall v. Craig,* 1 Bibb, 380. *Carrel v. Collins,* 2 Bibb, 431. See also *Morford v. Ambrose,* 3 J. J. Marsh. 690. *Crump v. Mead,* 3 Mis. 233. *Miller v. Ward,* 2 Conn, 494. *Clendennen v. Paulsel,* 3 Mis. 230. *Webster v. Coffin,* 14 Mass, 196. 1 Pick. 287. *Seymour v. Bennet,* 14 Mass, 268. *Clark v. Moody,* 17 Mass, 149. *Cooper v. Mowry,* 16 Mass. 7.[178]

Lincoln won this appeal when the court reversed the judgment against his clients. The court relied solely on Lincoln's meager but well-chosen citation. It first quoted, without attribution, the black-letter statement from the *Digest:* "It is well settled, that *he who prevents, or dispenses with the performance of a condition, cannot take advantage of the non-performance.*" It then cited seven cases to support this statement of law. All seven were listed in the *Digest;* the first five cases were cited in the order they appear in the *Digest.*[179]

Lincoln used the *United States Digest* as both a case-finding tool and as a substitute for the reported cases. An 1851 letter shows how Lincoln relied on the *Digest.* Lincoln in this letter discussed "the competency of a stockholder to testify" in a stock subscription case and cited two cases. He first gave his client a citation to a Pennsylvania case but admitted "this book is not here & I find a reference to it in the Suplt. U. S. Dig: Vol. 2 page 976, Sec. 405."[180] Lincoln was referring to the 1847 *Supplement to the United States Digest.*[181] The case that Lincoln cited was summarized under the topic "Witnesses" and was under the heading "Members of Corporations, and unincorporated Societies." Lincoln next cited a Kentucky case, "7 Dana 99." Lincoln also had found this case using the 1847 *Supplement.* It was listed on the same page as the other case.[182] Lincoln, however, had read this case; he reported that "this case is full and plump; and is, perhaps, the only reported case, exactly in point."[183]

Lincoln also relied on the *Illinois Digest,* which collected decisions from the Illinois Supreme Court.[184] In one brief, Lincoln cited three Illinois cases to support his successful argument that the appeal should be dismissed because the judgment was against three defendants while the appellate bond named only two of the defendants.[185] Lincoln had not looked long for authority. All three cases he cited were in the section entitled "Appeals and Writs of Error" in the 1856 *Illinois Digest.* Two cases appeared under the heading "When Appeal is Prayed by Several, etc."[186] The synopsis of these cases explained that "the appeal was dismissed because all the defendants did not join the bond." The third case Lincoln cited appeared under the heading "When They Will be Dismissed."[187] Using the *Digest,* Lincoln would have found all three cases in less than five minutes. Digests, like treatises, allowed a lawyer like Lincoln to wait "till he had a case in which the question was involved" to study the law.

Table 3—LEGAL DIGESTS CITED BY LINCOLN

O. L. Barbour & E. B. Harrington, An Analytical Digest of the Equity Cases Decided in the Courts of the Several States, 3 vols. (Springfield, Mass.: G. & C. Merriam, 1837)	*Davis v. Harkness*, 6 Ill. (1 Gilm.) 173 (1844)
George Ticknor Curtis, A Digest of the Decisions of the Courts of Common Law and Admiralty (Boston: C. C. Little & James Brown, 1846–1847) (United States Digest, vols. 2 & 3)	*Anderson v. Ryan*, 8 Ill. (3 Gilm.) 583 (1846) *People ex rel. Harris v. Browne*, 8 Ill. (3 Gilm.) 87 (1846)
William Johnson, A Digest of the Cases Decided and Reported in the Superior Court of the City of New York, the Vice-Chancellor's Court, the Supreme Court of Judicature, Being a Supplement to Johnson's Digest (Philadelphia: E. F. Backus, 1838)	*Cannon v. Kinney*, 4 Ill. (3 Scam.) 9 (1841) *Schlencker v. Risley*, 4 Ill. (3 Scam.) 483 (1842)
Theron Metcalf & Jonathan C. Perkins, A Digest of the Decisions of the Courts of Common Law and Admiralty (Boston: Hilliard, Gray & Co., 1840) (United States Digest, vol. 1)	*McCall v. Lesher*, 7 Ill. (2 Gilm.) 46 (1845) *Risinger v. Cheney*, 7 Ill. (2 Gilm.) (1845) *Henderson v. Welch*, 8 Ill. (3 Gilm.) 502 (1846)
Richard Peters, A Full and Arranged Digest of Cases, Decided in the Supreme, Circuit, and District Courts of the United States, 3 vols. (Philadelphia: Thomas, Cowperthwait & Co., 1838–1839)	*Spear v. Campbell*, 5 Ill. (4 Scam.) 424 (1843)
John Phelps Putnam, Supplement to the United States Digest, 2 vols. (Boston: Charles C. Little & James Brown, 1847)	*Pearl v. Wellman*, 11 Ill. 352 (1849) AL to William Martin, March 6, 1851 [93970], *Alton & Sangamon R.R. v. Barret* [L02610] casefile, LPAL
John Phelps Putnam, United States Digest: Annual Digest for 1847 (Boston: Charles C. Little & James Brown, 1848) Motion for new trial, Aug. 23, 1851 [45853], *Perkins v. Hall* [L01244] casefile, LPAL	Motion for new trial, Aug. 23, 1851 [45853], *Perkins v. Hall* [L01244] casefile, LPAL
John Phelps Putnam, United States Digest: Annual Digest for 1848 (Boston: Charles C. Little & James Brown, 1849)	Motion for new trial, Aug. 23, 1851 [45853], *Perkins v. Hall* [L01244] casefile, LPAL

Lincoln and his contemporaries also would have kept up with legal developments by reading law journals such as the Cincinnati-based *Western Law Journal* or the Boston-based *Law Reporter.* The rise of antebellum law journals—48 journals had been published by 1860—was part of a larger trend toward what Edgar Allan Poe in 1845 called "our Magazine literature." Poe noted that this increase in magazines was "a sign of the times—and indication of an era in which men are forced upon the curt, the condensed, the well-digested—in a word upon journalism in lieu of dissertation."[188] Law journals typically included articles on legal topics, reviews of law books, and summaries of recent cases.[189] The *Western Law Journal,* in particular, would have drawn Lincoln's attention. It was founded by Ohio judge Timothy Walker, author of the popular treatise *An Introduction to American Law* (1837). For a brief time, one of its editors was Charles Gilman, the reporter for the Illinois Supreme Court, who resigned his position to launch the short-lived *Western Legal Observer.*[190] Lincoln's anonymous article on the Trailor murder case was reprinted in the *Western Law Journal* in October 1846 and the circuit court opinion from the Matson case was published in the journal in February 1848.[191]

Lincoln didn't have any intellectual curiosity about the law; he didn't study the law. He only read law when he had to. Fortunately, Lincoln was a very quick study, a trait he often would show in his political career.

Legal Education and the Self-Made Man

In 1844, Whig writer Calvin Colton depicted the United States as "a country, where men start from an humble origin, and from small beginnings rise gradually in the world, as the reward of merit and industry, and where they can attain to the most elevated positions, or acquire a large amount of wealth." "This," concluded Colton, "is a country of *self-made men.*"[192] Lincoln also believed that opportunity existed for all, "that every man can make himself."[193] Lincoln's own achievements were a powerful part of his free-labor message. He told audiences that "there is no such thing as a man who is a hired laborer, of a necessity, always remaining in his early condition." Lincoln said "the general rule is otherwise. I know it is so, and I will tell you why. When at an early age, I was myself a hired laborer, at twelve dollars per month; and therefore I do know that there is not always the necessity for actual labor because once there was propriety in being so."[194] Lincoln made his own story part of the message; his story proved there was "no fixed condition of labor."[195]

Despite changes in the practice of law, Lincoln continued to advise prospective lawyers to prepare for the bar as he had done twenty years before. His professional identity as a lawyer had come from reading law books; he had "read hard—day & night—terribly hard." He didn't become a lawyer by drafting documents or practicing oratory or attending lectures.

Although law schools were located nearby in Cincinnati and Lexington, Lincoln never suggested to prospective lawyers that they attend law school.[196] He never suggested first receiving some college education. Lincoln, in fact, never suggested that the would-be lawyer apprentice or study in a lawyer's office. He consistently stressed one path to becoming a lawyer—reading law books. Lincoln told William H. Grigsby in 1858 that he should "attach no consequence to the *place* you are in, or the *person* you are with."[197] To Isham Reavis, he said that "it is but a small matter whether you read *with* any body or not. I did not read with any one."[198] He advised James T. Thornton that "when a man has reached the age that Mr. Widner has, and has already been doing for himself, my judgment is, that he reads the books for himself without an instructer. That is precisely the way I came to the law."[199]

Lincoln also advised these would-be lawyers to read on their own because he believed what mattered in becoming a successful lawyer was the middle-class virtues of hard work and discipline. If someone was "resolutely determined," then "the thing is more than half done already. . . . Always bear in mind that your own resolution to succeed, is more important than any other one thing."[200] He told another aspiring lawyer: "Work, work, work is the main thing."[201] But Lincoln failed to inform his aspiring students that his friendship with John T. Stuart was critical to his success. Lincoln's early success at the bar was tied to Stuart's established practice. He did not venture out on his own but instead became a partner with an established lawyer and important Whig politician.[202] Lincoln took Henry Dummer's place as partner with Stuart, and Stuart and Dummer apparently had been the most successful partnership in Springfield.[203]

Nor did Lincoln tell his correspondents that the law had changed dramatically in the twenty years that had passed since he read Blackstone underneath a tree. Herndon later recalled that the courts in the 1850s "were becoming graver and more learned, and the lawyer was learning as a preliminary and indispensable condition to success that he must be a close reasoner, besides having at command a broad knowledge of the principles on which the statutory law is constructed."[204] A law catalogue that Lincoln received in the summer of 1859 shows how the law had become more complicated. The catalogue promoted John Livingston's book-ordering service for lawyers; it listed over 1,100 treatises available from New York booksellers.[205] The body of law that developed with the coming of the railroads also signaled this change.[206]

Lincoln certainly was aware that the profession was changing.[207] In 1858, the Illinois Supreme Court promulgated new rules for the "license of attorneys." The new rules allowed for all applicants residing in the "third grand division" (which included Chicago) to present a certificate "to the effect that the applicant for examination has studied two years continuously, one year of which must have been with an attorney in this state." Nineteen out of sixty Chicago lawyers who were admitted to the bar in the 1850s attended law school; forty-five received some college education.[208]

Lincoln's son, Robert Todd, also became a lawyer. Unlike his father, Robert did not study on his own. Robert first studied in the college preparatory department of Illinois State University. After failing his entrance examination to Harvard, Robert attended Phillips Exeter Academy. He then was accepted to Harvard and graduated in 1864. When he decided to become a lawyer, he told his father that he "was going back to Cambridge and enter Law School." Robert later wrote that his father said "he thought I was right." He attended the law school for the 1864–1865 school year. When Robert returned to Illinois, he studied in a law office in Chicago for over a year and attended law courses at the University of Chicago.[209]

Unlike most lawyer-politicians of his day, Lincoln was led to law by politics. His path to law was also unusual. Unlike most antebellum lawyers, who had read in lawyers' offices and copied documents, Lincoln "studied with nobody." His self-directed training for law, however, was similar in depth to most antebellum lawyers'. His training was even more unusual when compared to that of other prominent members of the Illinois bar. His colleagues who enjoyed equal success had attended college or law school. However deficient his preparation might have been, Lincoln was able to recognize the legal issues presented in a case and research those issues. By the 1850s, preparing for the bar through self-study was starting to look anachronistic. Lincoln, a self-made man, continued to advise would-be lawyers to prepare as he had in the 1830s. For Lincoln, work, work, work remained the main thing.

CHAPTER THREE

A Whig in the Courthouse

Legal historians tend to neglect the work of lawyers.[1] This neglect is apparent in antebellum legal historiography, where lawyers—when they appear at all—are portrayed as being allied with commercial interests and seeking to shape the law to accommodate capitalists.[2] This chapter uses Lincoln's law practice to present an alternative portrait of the antebellum bar.[3]

While the records of few antebellum lawyers are readily available to modern researchers, the Lincoln Legal Papers project has recovered thousands of records pertaining to Lincoln's practice. When the legal papers of Daniel Webster were published, several legal historians noted the problems in claiming that any one lawyer, especially one of Webster's prominence, was typical of the entire profession.[4] Webster, who argued an unsurpassed 171 cases before the United States Supreme Court, had a remarkable career.[5] Lincoln's practice certainly makes him a more representative figure of the antebellum bar than Webster. The attractiveness of studying the materials discovered by the Lincoln Legal Papers project may be their very ordinariness. While Lincoln had an extraordinary life, he also had a relatively ordinary law practice. If Lincoln hadn't become president, it's doubtful that his law practice would have been noticed by later historians. His reputation was such that a list of great antebellum lawyers would not have included him but for his political prominence.[6]

Lincoln's law practice does not provide any support for a theory about a lawyer-capitalist alliance bent on changing legal rules to accommodate capitalism or to exploit the working class. Lincoln's legal career instead exhibited a Whig concern for order and orderly law instead of an instrumentalist concern for the promotion of industry and the development of the economy. The primary value Whig lawyers like Lincoln found in the justice system was not the imposition of an economic agenda but the maintenance of order. Whig politicians favored a developmental economic agenda, but Whig lawyers did not necessarily carry this agenda into the courtroom. For example, Lincoln never adopted an instrumentalist agenda in railroad litigation, despite railroads' playing an integral part in Lincoln's economic vision. Whig lawyers like Lincoln were not unaffected by economic considerations; however, the scramble for business meant that these lawyers were ready to represent any client.

Lincoln, Law, and Whig Ideology

Lincoln was a Whig before he was a lawyer, and his law practice paralleled his affiliation with the Whig party from the time he was first licensed to practice until 1855. Lincoln shared the Whig enthusiasm for market capitalism and endorsed Whig programs of internal improvements and tariffs that would encourage economic development.[7] In an autobiographical "little sketch" written in 1859, Lincoln declared that he had been "always a whig in politics, and generally on the whig electoral tickets, making active canvasses."[8] Lincoln had a long association with the Whig party; in 1860 he wrote that he "belonged to the Whig party from it's origin to it's close."[9] While he served as an Illinois state legislator, he was the Whig minority leader in the lower house. He campaigned for William Henry Harrison in 1840 and was the head of the Illinois campaigns for Henry Clay in 1844 and Zachary Taylor in 1848. In 1843, he was one of the three drafters of the Whig party's Address to the People of Illinois. He was elected to congress as a Whig in 1846. In 1852 he campaigned for Whig presidential candidate Winfield Scott.[10] Lincoln was not fully committed to the Republican party until 1856.[11] David Donald once wrote an essay that depicted Lincoln as a "Whig in the White House," describing how Whiggish notions of the executive influenced Lincoln's presidency.[12] It's not surprising that we also would find a Whig in the courthouse.

The Whig Party attracted lawyers because of the congruence between the Whig commitment to order and tradition and the lawyers' attachment to order and precedent.[13] A preoccupation with legalism and order was one of two responses to the violence and rioting that marked Jacksonian America.[14] According to historian George Fredrickson, Americans who were worried about what they perceived as anarchy or mobocracy had two distinct conceptions of how the Republic could be saved. One was evangelical and idealized a moral community; the other was legalistic and idealized a procedural community. The evangelists and the legalists were predominantly Whig in their political loyalties in the 1830s and 1840s. For legalists, the main restraints to mobocracy were common-law tradition and American constitutionalism. Legalists had abiding faith in procedure—the ever-present threat of anarchy and lawlessness was forestalled by maintaining a rational means for peaceful and orderly adjudication of disputes. For legalists, communities were nothing more than individuals who were able to live together peaceably because they had agreed to resolve disputes through the rule of law.[15] For legalists, the use of courts to resolve disputes was not a sign of disharmony but a means to maintain social cohesion. Ideology for lawyers in Jacksonian America meant no more than a dedication to the judicial process.[16] This devotion to the rule of law had deep resonances in American culture.[17]

Lincoln's early speeches reflected the conservative response to Jacksonian "mobocracy."[18] William Henry Herndon, Lincoln's law partner, described Lincoln as "a conscientious conservative: he believed in Law & Order."[19] In a speech in the Illinois legislature on January 11, 1837, Lincoln declared that he opposed "encouraging that lawless and mobocratic spirit . . . which is already abroad in the land; and is spreading with rapid and fearful impetuosity, to the ultimate overthrow of every institution, or even moral principle, in which persons and property have hitherto found security."[20] One institution in which persons and property found security was the court system.

Lincoln again turned to the theme of lawlessness and mobocracy in his most famous early speech, the address before the Young Men's Lyceum of Springfield on "The Perpetuation of Our Political Institutions."[21] This 1838 address consisted of standard Whig rhetoric.[22] Unlike the strained interpretations by modern psychohistorians, Herndon's view was that "the essence of that speech was obedience to & respect for law."[23] Lincoln discussed "something of ill-omen, amongst us," the "increasing disregard for law which pervades the country; the growing disposition to substitute the wild and furious passions, in lieu of the sober judgment of Courts; and the worse than savage mobs, for the executive ministers of justice." Lincoln described "accounts of outrages committed by mobs" that constituted "the every-day news of the times." Lincoln was horrified by the potential consequences of unpunished mob action. First, the "mob of to-morrow" might target the innocent as well as the guilty and "thus it goes, step by step, till all the walls erected for the defense of the person and property of individuals, are trodden down." Second, the "lawless in spirit" would be "encouraged to become lawless in practice" and, without the threat of punishments, would be "absolutely unrestrained." Third, and most importantly, "good men, men who love tranquility, who desire to abide by the laws" would become disgusted with a "Government that offers them no protection." The "strongest bulwark of any Government," "the attachment of the People," would be lost.[24]

After describing the breakdown of the rule of law, Lincoln next turned to its solution. Like other Whigs, he did not advocate coercion.[25] Instead, Lincoln preached self-restraint and self-control. Like other Whigs, he encouraged "reverence for the laws."

> Let every American, every lover of liberty, every well wisher to his posterity, swear by the blood of the Revolution, never to violate in the least particular, the laws of the country; and never to tolerate their violation by others. . . . Let

> reverence for the laws, be breathed by every American mother, to the lisping babe, that prattles on her lap—let it be taught in schools, in seminaries, and in colleges;—let it be written in Primers, spelling books, and in Almanacs;—let it be preached from the pulpit, proclaimed in legislative halls, and enforced in courts of justice.

Lincoln, in short, wanted reverence for the laws to become "the political religion of the nation."[26] One year later Whig lawyer Timothy Walker gave an address with a similar message. Walker said that "however objectionable a law may be" it was "still to be revered, because it is the law." Reverence for the law, according to Walker, "is the first and deepest lesson of patriotism."[27]

Antebellum lawyers did not resolve all disputes with a formal adjudication; lawyers also served as informal mediators.[28] By advising potential clients to either settle disputes or forgo litigation, Lincoln, like many of his antebellum colleagues, served as a gatekeeper to the formal legal system. Herndon once described Lincoln's method of interviewing clients.

> After the man was done telling his story fully and after Lincoln was done asking questions, he would generally think awhile before answering. When he answered, it was—"You are in the right," or "You are in the wrong." If Mr. Lincoln was not satisfied of the law as applicable to the man's case, he would say—"I am not exactly satisfied about some point; come into the office in an hour or so, and I will give you my opinion, a positive one." The man would call again and then Lincoln would say—"You are in the right," or: "You are in the wrong of the case and I would advise you to compromise, or if you cannot do that do not bring a suit on the facts of your case because you are in the wrong and surely get defeated and have to pay a big bill of costs." This was Lincoln's general way of doing business.[29]

A former law clerk, John Littlefield, would recall, "I have heard him tell would-be clients again and again—You have no case; better settle."[30]

Lincoln, as a Whig lawyer, had a near-religious reverence for law and order. The court system allowed disputes to be peaceably resolved through adjudication or settlement. Through the courts lawlessness and mobocracy would be avoided.

Judges and Juries

Lincoln's legal career does not provide much support for the notion that the antebellum bench and bar allied with commercial interests to curtail the power of juries. Lincoln himself was a successful trial lawyer, who often told his law partner Herndon that "If I can free this case from technicalities and get it properly swung to the jury, I'll win it."[31] In Illinois, the concern seemed to be with curtailing the power of judges, not juries.

Some historians have interpreted the rise of written jury instructions as part of the antebellum subjugation of the power of juries.[32] Although Illinois accepted the separation of law and fact in civil cases, its law on jury instructions does not show a shift toward increasing the power of trial courts at the expense of juries. The Illinois legislature intended its law on jury instructions to restrict what judges could tell jurors. The 1827 Practice Act stated that "the circuit courts in charging the jury, shall only instruct as to the law of the case."[33] The law, according to Illinois politician John Reynolds, was enacted "to restrain the judges of the circuit courts from charging the petit juries on facts, and commenting on the evidence submitted to them." Before the 1827 law was enacted, judges were giving verdict-influencing speeches to the jurors instead of instructions. The 1827 act was intended to keep judges from interfering with the province of the jury.[34] In 1847, the legislature amended the provision on jury instructions, strengthening "its terms against the judges of the circuit courts addressing the juries." The 1847 law provided no judge could instruct the jury unless the instructions were reduced to writing. The instructions were prepared by the parties who wanted them, and the court could either refuse or give the requested instructions. The court verbally could not qualify, modify, or explain the written instructions.[35] The Illinois Supreme Court in 1857 reversed a civil case when the appellant's bill of exceptions complained that the trial judge had modified and explained the written instructions; the court noted that the statute "plainly inhibits the Circuit Courts from changing or in any measure affecting orally the law as stated in written instructions given; and in a case of so clear intention of the law-making power, there is no room by construction to avoid consequences, however inconvenient in practice, or detrimental to the administration of justice." It didn't even matter that the oral explanation or qualification was immaterial; any change from the written instructions was forbidden.[36] The Illinois Supreme Court consistently held that judges could not invade the province of the jury by giving instructions that either drew inferences from the evidence or determined what the evidence did or did not prove.[37] Other state legislatures also stripped the power to comment on evidence from trial judges, which also affected the ability of the trial judge to dominate the jury.[38]

While the juries were "the judges of the facts only" in civil cases, Illinois juries were "the judges of both law and fact" in criminal cases.[39] Throughout Lincoln's legal career, criminal juries remained the judges of both law and fact.[40] The power of the Illinois jury was such that Lincoln in an 1859 murder case argued that a question over the admissibility of a dying declaration must be decided in the jury's presence.[41] Modern lawyers accept without question the notion that issues of admissibility should be decided outside the jury's presence, but the timing of this procedural change is quite murky.[42] When the court suggested that the arguments over admissibility be conducted outside the presence of the jury, Lincoln objected, saying that he "had never heard of such a law." The next morning when the trial resumed the court decided "whether the evidence on the dying declarations should be heard & discussed in the presence or absence of the jury." When the court ruled that "the jury must be excluded while the Court first heard & decided upon the competency of the testimony," Lincoln excepted to the ruling.[43]

Illinois was one of the nineteen states where constitutional conventions held between 1846 and 1860 approved constitutions that allowed for the popular election of judges. Whigs had differing views on the popular election of judges. Conservative Whigs tended to oppose an elected judiciary while moderate Whigs favored it. Conservative Whigs argued that appointed judges with lifetime tenure assured judicial independence from the passions and prejudices of the day. Moderates, however, saw popular election as increasing the power and legitimacy of judges.[44] In Illinois, Whigs agreed with Democrats that judges should be elected. At the 1847 constitutional convention delegates from the two parties generally agreed on elections and differed only on whether supreme court judges would be elected by districts or statewide.[45] Lincoln also did not oppose the popular election of judges. In a letter to Orville Browning, written while the Illinois constitutional convention was meeting, Lincoln confessed that he was "satisfied with them as they are; but shall not care *much* if the judges are made elective by the People, and their terms limited."[46]

Whig Lawyers and Instrumentalism

Whig politicians wanted to develop a commercial republic, but Whig lawyers were not the shock troops of capitalism.[47] Lincoln, like many other Whig lawyers, was not an instrumentalist—he didn't see law as an instrument to implement pro-development or pro-capitalist legal rules. Lincoln as a lawyer was not allied solely with corporations.

The legal ideology of the Whigs forestalled the adoption of a litigation strategy dedicated to commercial interests. Lincoln's practice is often portrayed as becoming increasingly one-sided as he aligned with business corporations and railroads; but he also was regularly fighting *against* corporations and railroads throughout his career.[48] Lincoln took business as it came.[49]

Whig lawyers like Lincoln did not appear in court solely on behalf of corporations. The career of Rufus Choate, a prominent Whig lawyer in Massachusetts, demonstrates the Whiggish dedication to legal process in his willingness to work both for and against corporations. Choate didn't display any overarching commitment to commercial interests; he could advance either a narrow or a broad reading of precedent, depending on his client's interests.[50] Choate in 1839 represented an injured railroad worker in one of the first employee injury lawsuits brought against a railroad; he argued for an "extensive legal duty of care owed by the corporation." He also represented the plaintiff in an 1857 personal injury lawsuit against the Boston and Worcester Railroad and secured a $22,500 award, the highest jury verdict of its time.[51]

The legal career of South Carolina Whig James Louis Petigru also fails to demonstrate an alliance between the bar and commercial interests. Petigru, for example, was involved in a series of appellate cases from 1838 to 1847 that changed the common-law rule for fire damage to cargo. The South Carolina courts adopted a new rule that allowed steamboats and railroads to contractually limit liability, a shift from the earlier rule that protected shippers from such losses. At one time or another, Petigru represented all parties involved in shipping cargo—planters, insurance companies, railroads, and steamboats. Because his clients' positions differed, Petigru could hardly advance a consistent position from case to case.[52]

The primary value Whig lawyers found in the justice system was not the imposition of a developmental economic agenda but the maintenance of order. For Whig lawyers, law remained primarily an agency for resolving disputes. How the dispute was resolved was less important than the fact that it was resolved through peaceful, orderly means. This was particularly true for new settlements in the West where "the privilege of litigation" was not seen as "an expensive luxury" but as "one of the prime necessaries of life."[53]

Lincoln explained that the judicial system was one of those "desirable things which the individuals of a people can not do, or can not well do, for themselves." According to Lincoln, the legitimate objects of government fell into two classes: those relating to wrongs and those things unrelated to wrongs that required "combined action." Lincoln gave such examples of "combined action" as schools and roads. Those things relating to wrongs embraced "all crimes, misdemeanors, and non-performance of contracts." Lincoln noted that "the injustice of men" was responsible for civil and criminal courts: "If some men will kill, or beat, or constrain others, or despoil them of property, by force, fraud, or noncompliance of contracts, it is a common object with peaceful and just men to prevent it."[54]

Before the Illinois Supreme Court

Lincoln's most impressive legal work was before the state supreme court. Lincoln first began to flourish as an appellate lawyer under Logan's tutelage; Lincoln & Herndon later handled an average of fifteen appellate cases per year during their partnership.[55] Here, his appellate work fails to reveal any instrumentalist pattern. Lincoln wasn't using his appeals to advance any agenda beyond getting his client some relief. Indeed, this lack of a pattern meant that an earlier legal victory often would later ensure defeat when Lincoln argued the other side. His most formidable opponent in many cases was himself; Lincoln would be hoist with his own precedent.

For example, Lincoln argued both sides of an evidentiary matter: whether the relative wealth of the plaintiff and the defendant could be considered by the jury when it assessed compensatory and punitive damages. In *Grable v. Margrave,* Thomas Margrave sued William G. Grable to recover damages for the seduction of his daughter. The trial judge allowed Margrave to introduce evidence showing that he was a poor man and that Grable was a rich man. The jury awarded damages for "loss of services" and "compensation for the dishonor and disgrace cast upon him and his family, and for the being deprived of the society and comfort of his daughter." Margrave also recovered "smart money" or "vindictive" damages designed to punish Grable.[56] Grable appealed, arguing that the evidence of the parties' wealth was improper. Lincoln represented Margrave, the poor, aggrieved father, on appeal. The court sustained Lincoln's position. The court first held that evidence of Grable's wealth was proper because of the punitive nature of the award—a rich defendant would scarcely feel an award that would bankrupt a poorer one. The court also held that evidence showing that Margrave was a poor man was proper because this allowed the jury to understand the impact of the injury upon him.[57]

Three years later, Lincoln again was involved with this question. He now found himself on the other side of the issue, arguing on appeal that it was improper for the trial judge to admit evidence on the relative wealth of the parties. George A. King had sued Charles McNamara for assault and battery after McNamara had attacked him. The trial court allowed King to prove that he was a poor man with a large family and that the defendant was a wealthy man with no children. The court also instructed the jury that they had a right to consider the circumstances of the parties. After the jury awarded King $650 in damages, McNamara appealed. The Illinois Supreme Court rejected Lincoln's argument that the evidence on wealth was improper. The court adhered to its holding in *Grable,* which it cited in the opinion. In rejecting Lincoln's argument that evidence on wealth was improper, it closely followed the reasoning advanced by Lincoln in the earlier case. Lincoln's earlier victory secured his defeat. Evidence concerning "the condition of life, and circumstances of the parties are peculiarly the proper subjects for the consideration of the jury in estimating the damages." Evidence about the plaintiff's wealth was proper because "the consequences of a severe personal injury would be more disastrous to a person destitute of pecuniary resources." Evidence about the defendant's wealth was proper because "the more affluent, the more able he is to remunerate the party he has wantonly injured." Vindictive damages in such cases were designed to punish the defendant.[58]

This lack of pattern in Lincoln's representation of clients also appears in other cases, such as medical malpractice cases. Once he represented the plaintiff-patient; once he represented the defendant-doctors. In *Fleming v. Crothers,* Lincoln was one of six lawyers hired by the defendants. Fleming was an elderly man who had broken his leg and complained that the doctors had negligently reset the leg, resulting in a limp. Lincoln successfully argued that the plaintiff "should get down on his knees and thank your Heavenly Father, and also these two Doctors that you have any legs to stand on at all."[59] In the second case, Lincoln represented the patient on appeal and was unable to overturn the trial verdict. The supreme court held that, although the evidence showed that the doctor did not properly treat his patient's wrist injury, the patient failed to show up for a second visit, which rendered the patient "liable for all injury."[60]

As president, Lincoln often claimed that his policy was to have no policy.[61] This statement applies equally to his law practice. Lincoln was willing to represent any side in a dispute, regardless of the argument that he would have to present. He never adopted an instrumentalist agenda.

Lincoln's Railroad Litigation and Instrumentalism

Although railroads were an integral part of his economic vision, Lincoln, as a typical Whig lawyer, refrained from adopting an instrumentalist agenda in railroad litigation. His personal and political commitment to railroads did not prevent him from regularly suing them.[62] He never was just a "railroad lawyer."

Railroads were an important part of Lincoln's developmental program.[63] He had hailed the future of railroads as early as 1832 during his first campaign for the state legislature. He told the voters of Sangamon County that "no other improvement" could "equal in utility the rail road." Lincoln added that "it is a never failing source of communication, between places of business remotely situated from each other."[64] Fifteen years later, he signed an open letter on behalf of the proposed Springfield and Alton railroad. The letter predicted that "at no distant day, a railroad, connecting the Eastern cities with some point on the Mississippi, will surely be built." If the Springfield and Alton road was not built, then this national road "may pass us in such a way as to do us harm rather than good." But an existing road "will attract the other, and so become, not merely a local improvement, but a link in one of a great national character."[65] A month later, an open letter on the proposed railroad appeared in the *Sangamo Journal*. This letter stated that "constructing a railroad from Alton to Springfield, is viewed but as a link in a great chain of railroad communication which shall unite Boston and New York with the Mississippi."[66] Despite this deep commitment to railroads, Lincoln represented clients who were averse to railroads. In fact, in his first known case involving a railroad, Lincoln sued the Sangamon & Morgan Railroad Company on behalf of John B. Watson.[67] Watson had delivered one hundred and twenty thousand cross ties to the railroad but had not been paid. Watson was represented by Lincoln & Herndon and Stuart & Edwards. All four lawyers were Whigs.[68]

Lincoln or his partners participated in lawsuits that involved at least thirteen different railroads. He was aligned with six railroads: Alton & Sangamon (7 cases); Chicago, Alton, & St. Louis (7); Chicago & Mississippi (6); Illinois Central (52); Ohio & Mississippi (2); and Wabash Valley (1).[69] Lincoln appeared against seven other railroads: Chicago, Burlington & Quincy (1); Great Western (25); Illinois River (3); Peoria & Hannibal (1); Sangamon & Morgan (2); St. Louis, Alton & Chicago (3); and Terre Haute & Alton (23).[70] Lincoln & Herndon represented the Tonica & Petersburg Railroad four times and represented defendants who had been sued by the railroad three times.[71]

Lincoln the lawyer in cases against railroads took positions inimical to those of Lincoln the politician. In *Chicago, Burlington & Quincy Railroad Co. v. Wilson,* the railroad had petitioned the circuit court to appoint commissioners to assess damages of condemned land the railroad wanted to use to build repair shops. The court denied the petition, finding that the railroad's charter didn't grant it the power to condemn land for shops. The railroad then asked the supreme court to order the circuit judge to appoint commissioners. Lincoln forcefully argued against the railroad's position, asserting that the power granted for eminent domain must be narrowly construed and that the power to condemn land ended when the railroad began its operation. He later wrote his client, "I do not think I could have argued the case any better than I did." The court rejected his arguments, stating that Lincoln's view would yield a "disastrous rule" that a railroad must acquire all the land it would ever need "in the first instance." Justice Caton, writing for the court, sounded like a pro-development Whig politician; indeed, he sounded very much like Lincoln the pro-railroad politician. Although the land where the railroads were being built was "at present almost entirely unimproved," soon the land would be "peopled with an industrious and prosperous population, affording an immense business to the roads which pass through them." Illinois was destined "to be brought into as high a state of productiveness as any of the older States." This growth, fueled by the introduction of railroads, meant that railroads necessarily would create a greater need for machine shops, depots, and other accommodations.[72]

Lincoln understood that economic development in the West depended on capital formation. In 1832, he lamented how Sangamon County's infant resources temporarily prevented the construction of a railroad.[73] In the 1850s, Lincoln was involved in several lawsuits over capital stock subscribers defaulting on their obligations. A railroad's ability to enforce subscription agreements was critical to its future success. Yet in the cases that reached the Illinois Supreme Court, Lincoln twice represented the railroad and twice represented the defaulting subscriber.[74]

In his first subscription cases, Lincoln represented the Alton & Sangamon Railroad.[75] Lincoln sued four subscribers of the railroad's capital stock who had defaulted on their payments. In a letter to Isaac Gibson, the secretary of the corporation, Lincoln wrote that "I suppose it is a matter of interest to the Company that we should not fail in these suits, as such failures might encourage others to stop payments."[76] Soon after he was hired, Lincoln reported that "one of my men 'caved in' & paid his instalments yesterday." In fact, Thomas Kirkpatrick paid up the day he was sued by Lincoln.[77] Three weeks later, Lincoln reported that "another of my victims, J. M. Burkhardt, has 'caved in' and paid his instalments." Burkhardt had been sued the same day as Kirkpatrick; he probably settled after Lincoln filed a notice of a commission to take the deposition of Gibson.[78]

Lincoln was unable to settle with the two other subscribers. One of the subscribers, James A. Barret, had subscribed for thirty shares of capital stock at one hundred dollars per share. He owned 4,215 acres that bordered along the railroad's originally proposed route, and his complaint, according to Lincoln, was the railroad's "changing the road away from New Berlin, near which the principle part of his real estate lies."[79] Barret claimed that the alteration in the charter was so extensive that it dissolved the subscription agreement. The railroad's New York lawyer believed that (in Lincoln's words) "the change of the location of road makes a serious question as to the release of stockholders." Lincoln disagreed, arguing that "the change will not work a release."[80]

Lincoln proceeded to trial against Barret, winning a judgment for the amount of the overdue installments. Barret appealed. The supreme court held that, when examining whether the "alteration in the charter" relieved Barret from payment, "the special reasons which may have influenced him to become a subscriber to the stock of the company can not be taken into consideration." What mattered was the contract, which showed that Barret agreed to subscribe to thirty shares of stock. The court found that it "was wholly immaterial whether he became a subscriber because he believed that the stock would of itself be a profitable investment, or because of the incidental benefit which he might receive from the construction of the road in the immediate vicinity of his lands." It did not matter that Barret was "deprived of any incidental benefit" but whether "the amendment of the charter worked such a change in the company as releases the subscribers from their engagements." An amendment that changes the nature or objects of a corporation would not be binding on the stockholders; however, the court found that "the straightening of the line of the road, the location of a bridge at a different place on a stream, or a deviation in the route from an intermediate point" did not "destroy or impair" the contract between the corporation and the stockholders. The supreme court affirmed the judgment.[81] Lincoln also succeeded in the lawsuit against another subscriber, Joseph Klein. The supreme court affirmed the judgment against Klein, holding that he "entered into a binding obligation, when he made the payment, which he can not now repudiate."[82]

Lincoln's success with the Alton & Sangamon cases led to other subscription cases.[83] After Herndon was hired by the Tonica & Petersburg Railroad, he informed the railroad's president in October 1857 that he had been asked by the railroad's subscribers "to defend in those Cases." Herndon then suggested that it would be prudent "in your Co. to make a permanent Engagement with some one—say pay them $500., a little more or less, Commencing from this date?"[84] Within a week, Herndon filed suit for the railroad in a subscription case, and later he secured a default judgment.[85] When the railroad did not immediately retain Lincoln & Herndon on Herndon's terms, he wrote again. Subscribers in Athens, Illinois, had offered him five hundred dollars "*to tear up the County subscription to your Road.*" He was giving the railroad an opportunity to retain him: "I have always studied your side of the case, and would rather take your view; because I am so Educated—have always studied your side but am put up on the other side well enough to defeat you." Herndon's meaning was not lost on the railroad. The letter has the notation "W H Herndon Wants retainer or will take other side and defeat you."[86] Herndon neither received a retainer nor defeated the railroad.

The following year, the railroad hired Jacksonville lawyers Lynn McNulty Greene and David A. Smith to represent it in a subscriber suit against William McNeeley. After McNeeley lost in the circuit court, he contacted Lincoln, who agreed to represent him on appeal.[87] Lincoln & Herndon did not get to represent the subscriber because the railroad already had hired Herndon to assist Smith on the appeal, which the railroad won.[88] In *Tonica & Petersburg Railroad v. Stein,* Lincoln & Herndon represented the railroad and failed on appeal to overturn a judgment in favor of the defaulting subscriber.[89] During the January 1860 term, Herndon again represented the losing side in the supreme court. A judgment in favor of the railroad against the defaulting subscriber was reversed and remanded because of a pleading error.[90] That spring the railroad—this time represented not by Lincoln & Herndon but by Lynn McNulty Greene and Thomas P. Cowan—filed three lawsuits against subscribers.[91] Herndon represented all three subscribers. Despite his earlier boast that he could beat the railroad because he was "so Educated" in subscription cases, Herndon lost two trials and apparently settled the third lawsuit.[92]

The precedents Lincoln established in the Illinois Supreme Court in favor of railroads later stood in his way when he represented subscribers. In *Sprague v. Illinois River Railroad,* Lincoln and Henry E. Dummer represented Charles Sprague. Sprague was a citizen of Cass County, and Cass County had voted to subscribe fifty thousand dollars to the railroad in 1853. At that time the proposed road would have run from Jacksonville through Cass County to LaSalle. In 1854, the legislature amended the railroad's charter, providing that the railroad could consolidate or connect with any railroad at any point on the route and not be required "to build that portion of the road north of such connection." By 1857 the railroad apparently had decided to end the line at the juncture of the Peoria and Hanni-bal Railroad at Pekin. Sprague believed these changes were "an absurd proposition"; he sued to enjoin the county from issuing bonds to the rail-road.[93] The trial court ultimately dismissed Sprague's bill.[94]

The supreme court affirmed the dismissal, holding that the amendment to the charter did not authorize "an essential and material departure from the purposes and objects specified, in the original charter of that company, so as to make it a separate and distinct enterprise." A corporation couldn't be prevented by the "various collateral considerations" of different share-holders from making changes to its charter. The rule implicitly espoused by Lincoln and Dummer—a subscriber only consents to what is expressly au-thorized by the charter at the time he subscribes and opposes all subse-quent changes—would mean that "one stupid or obstinate holder of one share" would "tie up the hands of all the rest, to their utter ruin." The au-thor of the opinion, Chief Justice John D. Caton, stated that "we have no where met with a more satisfactory exposition of the general principles of law, governing the respective rights of corporations and individual stock-holders therein" than in *Barret v. Alton & Sangamon Railroad*.[95] Lincoln's ear-lier victory secured his defeat. After the court had announced its decision Lincoln wrote his co-counsel that he had "presented your brief, but pointed a[r]gument to the court; to which I subjoined as good a one of my own as I could; but, as it has resulted, all to no purpose."[96]

Lincoln again was stymied by his earlier successes when he represented subscribers in seventeen separate Shelby County lawsuits brought by the Terre Haute & Alton Railroad in 1856.[97] The railroad sued its subscribers be-cause they had defaulted when "installments and assessments became due and payable." Two cases were dismissed in October 1856 after Lincoln de-murred to the railroad's pleadings; the basis of his successful argument is not clear from the extant documents.[98]

The remaining fifteen cases weren't resolved until four years later. In those cases, Lincoln prepared the defensive pleas of the defendants. He ar-gued that, while each defendant had subscribed to build a railroad from Terre Haute to Alton, the railroad had changed the "real terminus of the road" from Alton to Illinoistown, which was twenty-five miles from Alton. When the railroad demurred to this plea, the court overruled the demurrer. One case, *Terre Haute & Alton Railroad v. Earp,* was appealed by the railroad while the other fourteen cases remained on the circuit court's docket. In 1859, the Illinois Supreme Court reversed the circuit court's judgment in fa-vor of Earp and held for the railroad. Justice Caton lamented that "if what we have said" in the earlier subscription cases "has not shown satisfactory reasons for the rule of law which we hold on this subject, we despair of do-ing so now." Caton cited four earlier cases to make his point; Lincoln was involved in two of them.[99] After the supreme court ruled in *Earp*, the re-maining cases, which had been put on hold while the appeal was pending, were settled.[100] Seven cases, including the remanded *Earp* case, were dismissed by consent of the parties during the 1860 April Term; eight cases were dismissed during the following October term.[101] Lincoln's unsuccessful representation of the seventeen subscribers was largely the result of precedent that he himself had established in earlier cases.

In the early railroad subscription cases, Lincoln won a significant victory for railroads in Illinois. A few years later, Lincoln & Herndon broadened the liability of railroads, ensuring that railroads would be responsible for injuries to their passengers.[102] In this case, Lincoln & Herndon represented Joseph Dalby after Dalby was assaulted by a train conductor and brakeman; the conductor apparently believed Dalby owed twenty cents for his ticket. The railroad argued that it was not responsible for its employees' "willful and intentional assault and battery." Justice Caton framed the issue as one "of paramount importance, as settling a principle which must affect all railroad companies, and that is, whether a private corporation can, in any case, become liable for an assault and battery." Caton reviewed the history of American corporations, noting that while "they have become among the greatest means of state and national prosperity…, their multiplication is astonishing, if not alarming." The issue of a railroad's liability for "wrongs done by their servants," wrote Caton, "is well settled by the adjudication of both the English and American courts." The court rejected the defense that a corporation can not be liable for the intentional act of one of its agents, holding that "a corporation may as well be liable for an assault and battery, as for any other tort which may be committed by its servants."[103] This decision was part of a larger trend in nineteenth-century English and American courts expanding liability for railroads when passengers—not workers—were injured.[104]

Nor was *Dalby* the only case where Lincoln & Herndon sued for personal injuries against a railroad. In March 1854, Lincoln filed suit for Jasper Harris against the Great Western Railroad in Sangamon County Circuit Court, alleging that Harris, a railroad worker, was injured when he was "thrown down and his right foot, ankle, leg and thigh, greatly torn, crushed, and broken." Harris was "sick, lame, and disordered" for four months and eventually his right leg was amputated above the knee. Lincoln sued for ten thousand dollars. The case apparently was settled as Harris later dismissed his lawsuit.[105] In February 1857, Lincoln & Herndon filed another personal injury lawsuit against the Great Western Railroad. Lewis Freidlander, who was a railroad passenger, alleged that the train "carelessly and negligently" collided with cars on a sidetrack, which resulted in his breaking his leg. Like Harris three years earlier, he asked for $10,000 in damages. Freidlander later settled for $500.[106]

Lincoln appeared in personal injury cases involving business or governmental entities in only three instances.[107] For example, Lincoln represented Samuel Grubb in a lawsuit against John Frink and Martin O. Walker, the proprietors of the Midwest's largest stagecoach business.[108] Because of the defendants' "want of due care and attention to their duty," Grubb had been injured in a pre-dawn accident in a stagecoach not fitted with lamps.[109] After a default was entered against John Frink & Co., the parties apparently settled.[110] Lincoln's involvement in few personal injury cases was typical of antebellum law practice.[111]

Lincoln also took different sides on whether railroads could build bridges across rivers without facing lawsuits from vessel interests that claimed the bridges obstructed navigation. In the more well-known case, Lincoln represented the owners of the bridge.[112] The bridge was at Rock Island, Illinois, and was the first to span the Mississippi. The owners of the bridge were the Rock Island Bridge Company and its parent company, the Chicago and Rock Island Railroad. The owner of the vessel *Effie Afton,* John S. Hurd, sued the owners of the bridge after the vessel was damaged when it collided with the bridge.[113]

Lincoln's closing argument stressed the importance of the railroad in the development of the West. He told the jury that he "had no prejudice against steamboats or steamboatmen, nor any against St. Louis" but "there is a travel from East to West, whose demands are not less important than that of the river." That travel was "growing larger and larger, building up new countries with a rapidity never before seen in the history of the world." Lincoln alluded "to the astonishing growth of Illinois, having grown within his memory to a population of a million and a half, to Iowa and the other young and rising communities of the Northwest." Lincoln also pointed out the utility of the railroad bridge: "from September 8, 1856, to August 8, 1857, 12,586 freightcars and 74,179 passengers passed over this bridge." In the winter, the bridge was "as useful as ever" while the river was "useless." Lincoln concluded that "this shows that this bridge must be treated with respect in this court and is not to be kicked about with contempt."[114] Although Lincoln and his co-counsel were able to convince nine of the twelve jurors, the jury was unable to reach a verdict. Because the case was not retried, as a practical matter, Lincoln's side won. Even with the jury deadlock, the pro-bridge *Chicago Daily Tribune* noted, "The bridge is still standing, despite the Chamber of Commerce at St. Louis and all the prejudiced, sore head pilots on the river."[115]

Again we cannot read too much into Lincoln's representation. Several years earlier, he had represented the insurers of a canal boat that had struck a pier in a railroad bridge in the Illinois River.[116] In *Columbus Insurance Co. v. Curtenius,* Lincoln sued the railroad bridge for damages. The defendants, stockholders of the Peoria Bridge Company, pleaded "an act of the legislature of Illinois authorizing the construction of the bridge." Lincoln demurred to the plea, arguing that a state did not have the power to "authorize a total obstruction of a navigable stream running within its territorial limits." The federal judge sustained the demurrer.[117] The case was later settled.[118] In these similar, but not identical situations, Lincoln was willing both to represent and to sue the railroads. In these cases, as in other cases, Lincoln refrained from adopting an instrumentalist agenda.

In 1855–1856, Lincoln represented landowners in at least nineteen Vermilion County lawsuits that involved disputes with the Great Western Railroad over the assessment of damages for right of way.[119] Fifteen of these cases settled after the commissioners' awards were appealed from the county court to the circuit court.[120] In six cases, the terms of the settlement weren't disclosed on the court's dockets.[121] In the remaining nine cases, the settlement terms were memorialized with an agreed judgment that appeared in the court's docket book.[122] For example, in *Price v. Great Western Railroad*, the court's docket reflected that the railroad agreed to pay $125.33 for the right of way, which was described, agreed to build fences on both sides of the right of way, and agreed to allow Price to put up and maintain gates and crossings and to let him remove the timber from the right of way.[123]

Four of the landowners' disputes with the railroad were tried to juries. In these cases, Andrew Makemson recovered a total of $560 in damages; James Makemson, $372; Ezekiel McDonald, $350.[124] In the three cases with Andrew Makemson and James Makemson, before the juries assessed damages, the railroad stipulated that it would "maintain a good and sufficient fence," maintain crossings over the road, and allow the landowners the timber on the right of way.[125]

The Economics of the Law Office

The failure of Whig lawyers to carry a developmental agenda into the courtroom was not necessarily the result of selfless devotion to the legal process. Economics played an important role; Whig lawyers, particularly ones on the frontier, simply could not afford to take only one side in important legal issues. Although lawyers were willing to sell their services to the highest bidder, the winning bids usually were very low and the winning bidders included more than corporations.

Illinois lawyers like Lincoln charged relatively modest fees and depended upon handling a large volume of cases to generate income. Lawyers in antebellum Chicago were mainly concerned with finding clients, not evaluating the merits of their cases.[126] Circuit-riding lawyers, Illinois Supreme Court justice John Dean Caton later observed, "had to practice law on the wing," receiving "their retainers about the time court opened."[127] Fees charged by lawyers in Lincoln's Eighth Circuit did not increase much from 1839 when the circuit was formed until when Lincoln was elected President. Lawyers generally charged between ten and twenty dollars for services rendered.[128]

Lincoln was in three successive two-lawyer partnerships; Lincoln and his partners handled over 5,600 cases or legal matters during that time.[129] The fee book of Lincoln and his first law partner, John T. Stuart, reveals small fees for legal work, with fees ranging from $2.50 to $50.[130] By way of comparison, the account book of Illinois lawyer-politician Adam W. Snyder for this same period reveals very similar fees, ranging from $5 to $20.[131] Logan & Lincoln's average fee for an appeal to the Illinois Supreme Court was $20.[132] Although Lincoln was an accomplished lawyer and a prominent politician, the fees charged by Lincoln & Herndon were not much different from those charged by Stuart & Lincoln.[133] In 1855, Lincoln represented the Illinois Central in fifteen cases in McLean and De Witt counties. He charged $150 for his services, explaining to the railroad's general counsel that he "concluded to lump them off at ten dollars a case." Despite Lincoln's modest charges, he had the circuit judge, David Davis, add a notation to the letter that he thought "the charges very reasonable."[134]

Lincoln and his partners also used contingent fees—they wouldn't be paid at all unless they were successful. The antebellum rise of contingent fee arrangements meant that ordinary Americans could afford the services of skilled lawyers.[135] Lincoln, Logan, and Stuart sued James Adams, alleging that Adams had defrauded Joseph Anderson out of ten acres of land.[136] The lawyers had a contingent fee contract with Anderson's widow and children: the heirs would pay them "one half of the said piece of ground for their services, provided they recover the same; but are not bound to pay any thing unless the said piece of ground be recovered."[137] In an 1855 slander case, Isaac Cossens agreed to pay Lincoln and Ward Hill Lamon one-half of "whatever judgment may be recovered" against the defendant.[138]

Lincoln once remarked that "the matter of fees is important, far beyond the mere question of bread and butter involved."[139] Lincoln's letters to his clients often reflect some anxiety about whether he would be paid for his work. Lincoln addressed the issue of fees in a letter he wrote to James S. Irwin, a Jacksonville lawyer who had enquired about Logan & Lincoln handling appellate cases. Lincoln said that the fees charged wouldn't be unreasonable and the two lawyers "would always be easily satisfied, provided we could see the money—but whatever fees we earn at a distance, if not paid *before*, we have noticed we never hear of after the work is done." Lincoln confessed to "growing a little sensitive on that point."[140] After another client, Thomas A. Howland, wrote Lincoln in 1859 to warn him that Howland's draft for a $100 retainer might be returned, Lincoln curtly responded, "Do not let it come upon again; or we might be provoked to dismiss your suit."[141] After reporting an appellate victory in another case, Lincoln gently prodded his client about getting paid: "As the dutch Justice said, when he married folks 'Now, vere ish my hundred tollars.'"[142]

In a practice built on volume, every fee counted, which may explain why Lincoln and his partners sued to recover their fees at least seventeen times.[143] Lincoln advised lawyers to take fee notes from clients, and it appears that Lincoln did sue on delinquent notes.[144] Lincoln's suit to recover a $5,000 fee against the Illinois Central is the best known of these suits over unpaid fees.[145] But Lincoln also sued five times for less than $10 in fees.[146] In 1855, he recovered a $6.22 judgment in the Christian County Justice of the Peace Court against his former client, Samuel Brown; three years earlier, Lincoln had obtained for his client a dismissal in an assault with a deadly weapon prosecution.[147]

Lincoln tended to take any case with at least an arguable basis. He worked for fees instead of the triumph of personal convictions.[148] Lawyers could not afford to do otherwise. Corporate business was relatively scarce and, before the advent of the widespread use of retainers, unpredictable. Herndon later observed that when Lincoln practiced law "there were no great corporations . . . retaining for counsel the brains of the bar in every county seat." Herndon remembered that "the greatest as well as the least had to join the general scramble for practice."[149] Herndon's statement that there were no great corporations retaining the "brains" of every county suggests that Herndon believed that things had changed by the time he published his biography of Lincoln in 1889. By the late nineteenth century, corporations (particularly railroads) tried to use retainers to monopolize legal talent. Other corporations would co-opt lawyers who had sued them by conditioning settlements upon those lawyers' agreeing not to sue them again. While these attempts to monopolize legal talent were not entirely successful, they did result in trial lawyers being divided into a plaintiffs bar and a defense bar.[150] This stratification of the bar wasn't yet present in Lincoln's Illinois.

David Davis suggested to Lincoln that, instead of returning to law practice from Congress in 1849, he take a position as Commissioner of the General Land Office. Davis believed that "the practice of law in Illinois at present promises you but poor remuneration for the labor."[151] Stephen A. Douglas in 1835 complained that of "the long list of Lawyers" that came to Illinois only one out of one hundred made "one half business enough to pay his expenses the first year nor enough to pay his expenses for three of the first years."[152]

These statements by Lincoln's Illinois contemporaries mirror other accounts of the antebellum legal profession. One Ohio lawyer believed that few lawyers were economically successful. In 1849, he explained in the *Western Law Journal* that "in this country, great fortunes are not acquired at the bar, and few become rich." The legal profession was "overstocked by a body of men, ingenious, ambitious, needy, and sometimes unscrupulous." With the same amount of effort, any lawyer could make more money doing something else.[153] Joseph Baldwin in *The Flush Times of Alabama and Mississippi* (1853) recalled law practice in the old Southwest as full of young lawyers "cultivating the cardinal virtues of Faith and Hope in themselves, and the greater virtue of Charity in their friends—the only briefs as yet known to them being brief of money and brief of credit."[154] In the September 1844 issue of the *Knickerbocker* magazine, John G. Saxe offered "A Legal Ballad" on the economics of the legal profession.

> Most unfortunate man that I am,
>   My only client is Grief;
> The case is, I've no 'case' at all,
>   And in brief, I have ne'er had a 'brief.'
>
> The profession's already so full
>   Of lawyers so full of profession,
> That a modest young man like myself
>   Can't make the smallest impression.
>
> They grant I'm acquainted with 'grants,'
>   Can devise a 'devise,' or a plea,
> Can make a good deal in 'fee simple,'
>   But I can't get the simplest 'fee.'

Saxe's young lawyer commits suicide at the end of the poem. The coroner's jury decides the cause of death "was no doubt for the want of 'a cause.'"[155] Antebellum lawyers often blamed this "general scramble" for business on overcrowding.[156] Stephen A. Douglas described economic opportunity in Illinois in 1834 as good for "every kind of business" except "professional business; for we have Lawyers, Doctors, and Ministers here in abundance."[157] Blaming overcrowding wasn't unreasonable. In 1830, Illinois had 73 lawyers among its population of 157,445 (1:2,156); by 1840, lawyers numbered 429 and the population 476,183 (1:1,110).[158] The population had grown 300 percent; the number of lawyers, nearly 600 percent. In 1850, Illinois had one lawyer for every 1,042 people while Indiana had one for every 1,069 people and Wisconsin one for every 733.[159] According to *Livingston's Law Register,* Illinois had 710 lawyers in 1851, and 862 in 1852.[160] One-third of the lawyers who opened a practice in Chicago between 1833 and 1847 left within two years.[161] An 1849 article in the *Western Law Journal* observed that "the profession of the bar has a large number of members in proportion to the business, and that they are constantly increasing." The profession grew as "the farmer abandons his plough, the tailor his thimble, the clerk his desk, and without study or education, they rush into a profession which is, in their view, the avenue to fame and fortune."[162] A Virginia lawyer in 1853 echoed this complaint. Richard Hawes believed "there is a super abundance of Lawyers, but a dearth of clients." Hawes wrote, "Blessed are they who expect nothing for they shall not be disappointed."[163]

Whig lawyers refrained from carrying a developmental agenda into the courtroom. Not only ideology but the economics of the law office helped dictate this decision. Part of the willingness of Whig lawyers to represent any side in a dispute was because they could not afford to turn away clients. A foolish consistency would have resulted in fewer clients.

Conclusion

The evidence from Lincoln's law practice does not provide support for the notion that antebellum lawyers worked assiduously for the triumph of market capitalism. Lincoln as a Whig politician favored a developmental economic agenda, but Lincoln as a Whig lawyer did not advance this agenda every time he entered a courtroom. The primary value Whig lawyers like Lincoln found in the justice system was the maintenance of order. The economics of the law office ensured that Whig lawyers were ready to represent any client because they could hardly afford to do otherwise. Lincoln, for example, believed that railroads were vitally important for economic development in the West, but he never adopted an instrumentalist agenda in railroad litigation. He was ready to sue railroads and to establish precedent that would have hindered his economic vision. Because of Lincoln's flexibility, early legal victories often would ensure later defeats.

None of this is all that surprising. The English legal historian S. F. C. Milsom may have accurately described the relationship between lawyers and legal change when he wrote:

> Lawyers have always been preoccupied with today's details, and have worked with their eyes down. The historian, if he is lucky, can see why a rule came into existence, what changes left it working injustice, how it came to be evaded, how the evasion produced a new rule, and sometimes how that new rule in its turn came to be overthrown by change. But he misunderstands it all if he endows the lawyers who took part with vision on any comparable scale, or attributes to them any intention beyond getting today's client out of his difficulty.[164]

Lincoln, like most antebellum lawyers, worked with his eyes down, doing his best to get his clients out of their difficulties. At some point, perhaps after the Civil War, things changed, and a sizeable number of lawyers, unlike their antebellum counterparts, consistently sided with commercial interests.[165]

CHAPTER FOUR

Law on the Prairie

Lincoln always seemed comfortable with the lawyering style demanded by purely local lawsuits. Like most lawyers in small communities, he was keenly aware that the community orientation of those disputes favored mediation and compromise, and he thus tried to serve as a mediator or peacemaker.

Lincoln's first case as a lawyer reflected the community orientation of his early practice. Lincoln and John T. Stuart represented David Wooldridge, the defendant in a series of cases brought by James P. Hawthorn. Wooldridge and Hawthorn were both farmers in Sangamon County. By the summer of 1836, their relationship had become so severely strained that Hawthorn filed two lawsuits against Wooldridge. On July 1, 1836, Hawthorn sued Wooldridge for "trespass on the case of promises," claiming that Wooldridge had asked him to break up prairie sod during "breaking season" in exchange for payment and the use of some of the land for farming. Wooldridge, however, broke his promise. Hawthorn asked for one hundred dollars in damages. That same day, he also sued Wooldridge for personal injuries, filing a trespass *vi et armis* (force and arms) action. Wooldridge, he claimed, had assaulted him, tearing "divers large quantities of hair" from his head, striking him with a stick, beating him with his fists, kicking him while he was on the ground, and, for good measure, gouging his eyes with his "thumbs and fingers." As a result, he was "sick sore wounded and partially blind." He asked for $500 in damages.[1] That fall Hawthorn also filed a replevin action against Wooldridge, asking for the return of one yoke of steers and a "prairie plough" that he claimed Wooldridge and another man had wrongfully detained. He estimated the value of the property at eighty dollars and asked for an additional twenty dollars in damages.[2]

That fall, Wooldridge retained Lincoln's mentor Stuart; Lincoln, who was not yet licensed as a lawyer, prepared several documents for the case. One response drafted by Lincoln asked that Hawthorn post security for costs in the lawsuits filed during the summer. Wooldridge asserted that Hawthorn would be "unable to pay the costs of this suit" because he was a "young man without family" and had no property. If the request for security was a strategic maneuver, then Stuart and Lincoln and their client may have been surprised when Hawthorn promptly posted security. Lincoln also itemized various charges that Wooldridge claimed offset what he might owe Hawthorn, including one for "boarding from the first day of April to the first day of November 1835" and another for the "use of waggon & team." Wooldridge turned the tables by filing his own trespass *vi et armis* lawsuit against Hawthorn on the same day that Hawthorn's trespass case against him was tried.[3]

A jury heard Hawthorn's personal injury lawsuit against Wooldridge on October 8, 1838. Wooldridge was held liable but damages were limited to thirty-six dollars and costs.[4] The following March the remaining lawsuits were settled. Hawthorn and Wooldridge agreed to dismiss all three remaining lawsuits with Wooldridge paying court costs in Hawthorn's assumpsit suit, Hawthorn paying the court costs in his replevin suit, and each party splitting the costs in Wooldridge's trespass *vi et armis* suit against Hawthorn.[5] The settlement and division of costs as well as the subject matter show the community base of Lincoln's early practice.

Land and Litigation

Land was the cornerstone of the predominantly agricultural frontier communities, and it is not surprising that many of Lincoln's cases involved disputes over land.[6] A recent study of the circuit court in Knox County, Illinois, in the 1840s found that one-fifth of all cases filed involved disputes over land.[7] Lincoln's practice also reflects a heavy proportion of such cases. For example, Lincoln was involved in over 140 suits to partition real estate.[8] These suits generally arose when a landowner died, leaving undivided interests in land to his heirs. The Illinois statute on partition required the circuit court, upon petition, to divide the property or to sell it if a partition could not "be made without great prejudice to the owners."[9] The petition was to be verified by affidavit; Lincoln noted that this was an "indispensable" requirement.[10] In any event, the court would appoint three "entirely disinterested" commissioners to go upon the land and "make partition" by "metes and bounds" or report that a division of the property could not be made "without manifest prejudice."[11]

Partition suits were, as Lincoln once noted, "not likely to be litigated."[12] The statute required notice to heirs and interested parties, who would be named as the defendants.[13] But the statute, by its language, also expressly recognized that defendants most likely would not contest the petition either by not answering (default) or by filing a "confession by plea."[14] Adult defendants appear not to have filed answers to the petition for partition in about half of the suits Lincoln and his partners were involved in.[15] Although the statute required a guardian *ad litem* to be appointed to represent the interests of minors, the appointed attorney would typically file an answer that stated that he knew no good reason why the petition shouldn't be granted, but he nonetheless would require "full proof."[16] The task was made even easier when the lawyer for the plaintiffs prepared an answer for the guardian ad litem's signature. Lincoln, for example, as *ad litem* signed an answer prepared by the plaintiff's attorney in both *Fields v. Fields* and *Rogers v. Rogers* and, as plaintiff's attorney, wrote the answer for the *ad litem* attorney's signature in *Bruner v. Bruner, Crow v. Crow, Prettyman v. Prettyman,* and *Smith v. Green.*[17]

Some partition suits did represent real disagreements among family members over how the land was to be divided. An example of a hotly contested partition is *Welsh v. Welsh,* a case from Clark County. In 1857, Lincoln & Herndon appealed a chancery court decision in a partition suit that had begun some fourteen years earlier. Henry Welsh had conveyed land to his brother, John Welsh, in 1823. The deed recited that the tract contained eighty-two acres. After John Welsh died, one of his children filed a petition in chancery to establish dower for his widow and to partition his land among his children.[18] The court appointed three commissioners to survey the land and to divide it.[19] When the commissioners surveyed the land according to the description of the physical boundaries contained in the deed, they discovered that the tract contained 134 acres and recommended that these 134 acres be divided. A controversy then arose over whether the children of John Welsh were entitled to more land than the eighty-two acres enumerated in the deed. Although Henry Welsh had died, a third brother, James Welsh, filed a cross-bill in the chancery court. James complained that Henry had never intended to convey more than eighty acres to John and that the additional fifty-four acres belonged to the legal heirs of Henry Welsh (Henry's brothers and sisters) and not the heirs of John Welsh (John's children).[20]

Uncles and aunts battled nephews and nieces for fourteen years. But the position of the aunts and uncles was not supported by law. Chancellor Kent, for example, in his *Commentaries* confidently stated that the rule was that "the mention of quantity of acres, after a certain description of the subject by metes and bounds or by other known specification, is but matter of description."[21] The circuit court dismissed James Welsh's cross-bill and affirmed the former order in favor of the children of John Welsh in 1852. Five years later, Lincoln & Herndon appealed the chancery court's order. Lincoln & Herndon claimed the court erred by partitioning the land without first determining the rights of the parties.[22] Three times, the parties asked that the appeal be continued, and the case languished on the court's docket until the supreme court granted Herndon's motion to dismiss the appeal in January 1861.[23] Thus, after eighteen years this dispute over land ended, and the children of John Welsh legally acquired the land owned by their father.

Other cases were less formulaic; Lincoln sometimes called upon courts to regulate the fairness of land sales. For example, in 1849 Lincoln & Herndon represented William Enyart in a chancery suit, seeking to rescind Enyart's sale of ninety acres to Smith McAtee. The bill of complaint written by Lincoln claimed that Enyart had conveyed the land to McAtee for the "expressed consideration of three hundred and fifty dollars." The price was "greatly below the real value of the interest in said land"; the land itself was worth "at least one thousand dollars."[24] McAtee actually had paid even less than that amount; he "really" had paid two hundred dollars and a horse saddle and bridle not worth one hundred dollars.

Lincoln's bill of complaint explained that Enyart had sold the land for so little because he "had been subject to a habit of intoxication by the immoderate use of spiritous liquors." When intoxicated, "his reason was dethroned" and he was "wholly incapable of any rational management of his affairs." Moreover, McAtee was well acquainted with Enyart and his "habit of intoxication and with the effect of intoxication upon his mind." When Enyart had conveyed the land he "was so much intoxicated as to be incapable of any rational actions." He did not even remember selling the land "when he afterwards became sober." McAtee had used "cunning and artifice" to get Enyart drunk and then took advantage of his condition by fraudulently inducing him to execute a deed for the inadequate consideration.[25]

McAtee denied that he used "cunning or artifice" or that he knew Enyart was drunk at the time of the sale. Enyart had accepted his offer because it was "the best he could get at the time" and it was a "fair and adequate price." According to McAtee, Enyart also had sold the land because he was under indictment for larceny and "he was in haste to avoid arrest and flee from Justice." Enyart was "prepared to do so upon almost any terms" and, with a "fleet horse," "leave for parts unknown." He also claimed that Enyart had agreed to submit the dispute to arbitration, which had been resolved in his favor.[26]

After McAtee filed his defensive plea, Lincoln received permission from the court to amend his original bill. In response to McAtee's mention of the alleged arbitration, Lincoln wrote that "said allegation in said answer is intended as a setting up of a submission and award between the parties as a bar" to Enyart's complaint and denied that there was any such "submission and award." Lincoln amended the bill to allege that Enyart "was in great distress of mind because of a charge pending against him of petty larceny." McAtee was aware of the "joint effects of his distress in consequence of the charge of larceny . . . and of intoxication as to be incapable of any rational action." McAtee had "used cunning and artifice to excite your orators shame and fear" and then induced him to drink. Lincoln, in support of the amendment, testified in court that he had not met Enyart before he drew the original bill and that he had framed the original bill from what he had learned from his associate counsel.[27]

Of the nineteen witnesses testifying at the hearing, many supported Lincoln's depiction of Enyart as a helpless alcoholic. One observed that "when in liquor he is the dummest fellow you ever saw." Another reported that "very little liquor made a fool of him." A third testified that Enyart was a "little high" and "pretty groggy" the day that he sold the land to McAtee.[28]

Enyart won; the court found the allegations in the bill of complaint to be true and vacated the deed. McAtee then appealed to the Illinois Supreme Court, where Enyart won again. The supreme court noted that "the difference between the value of the land and the price for which it was sold would not, of itself, justify the interposition of a court of equity." A seller may dispose of his property "on such terms and for such prices as he pleases. . . . He must abide the consequences of an injudicious bargain, if voluntarily and fairly made." Courts would not interfere with a sale "unless there has been some fraud, mistake or undue influence." An inadequate price generally was not a "sufficient ground for setting aside a conveyance of property." While the inadequacy of price in Enyart's case did not "necessarily indicate the least fraud or unfairness," the circumstances in the case showed that "the conveyance was obtained through improper influence, and ought therefore to be set aside." Enyart was "an ignorant and weak-minded man at best, and incapable of the rational management of his affairs when under the influence of spiritous liquor."[29] One wonders how Enyart celebrated his legal victory.

In 1838, Springfield lawyer Josephus Hewett filed a bill of complaint in chancery on behalf of three young girls, Nancy, Elizabeth, and Sally Ann Orendorf. The three girls, all under the age of thirteen, were the daughters of the deceased Charles Orendorf. According to the bill, their father had improved a tract of land but had "deferred entering said tract of land to a future day." A "long and distressing illness terminating in his death" prevented Orendorf from formally owning the land. When Orendorf was on his deathbed, he asked his father-in-law, James Stringfield, to use "any monies which might remain after the settlement of his estate" to purchase the tract of land. After Orendorf died, Stringfield used eighty dollars from the estate for the purchase of the tract of land. Stringfield often said that he intended to convey the land to the daughters, but he died before making the transaction. After Stringfield's death, his heirs decided to "defraud and defeat" the rights of Orendorf's daughters; they had "by fraud and cunning obtained and gotten possession" of the tract. Stringfield's heirs then had sold forty acres of the tract to one Booker Preston. The bill concluded that the daughters were "utterly remediless by the strict rules of the common law" and requested that the daughters be granted equitable relief.[30]

In their answer, William and Rowland Stringfield denied that their father James Stringfield had used money from Orendorf's estate to purchase the tract; on the contrary, he had purchased the land with his own money. They denied that he had said that the land belonged to his granddaughters or that the land was purchased with money belonging to the granddaughters. Although he may have said he intended to give the land to his granddaughters, he was not obligated to convey the land to them. The two Stringfield heirs also pleaded the statute of frauds: if James had made any contract or agreement to convey the land, it was not put in writing as required by law. The Stringfield heirs ignored how a resulting trust in favor of the Orendorf girls would have been exempt from the statute of frauds.[31]

Lincoln became involved in the case when the Orendorf girls' original attorney left for Mississippi. Informed that the case was ready to be submitted to the court, Lincoln filed a replication to the Stringfield's plea. (A replication is a pleading that avers the truth of the allegations in the bill and denies the truth of those in the answer; its purpose is to put the case at issue.[32]) But, in fact, Lincoln erred. The case, as pleaded, was not ready because the original bill contained a fatal defect: it ignored the third-party purchaser of the land.[33] If Booker Preston, who bought the land from the Stringfields, did not have notice of the girls' claim, it would have been extinguished.[34] If, on the other hand, Preston knew about the girls' claim, then his purchase would have been subject to it.[35] The original bill of complaint, however, did not say whether Preston had notice of the girls' claim.[36] Lincoln explained the rule on notice in an 1854 letter to a client:

> After you sold and deeded your property to Edmons, for a consideration which is worthless and fraudulent, any person who buys or takes a mortgage from Edmons, without Notice of the fraud, will hold the property against you; but whoever buys or takes a mortgage after your Bill is filed, is conclusively presumed to have had notice of the fraud, and therefore can have no better right against you than Edmonds himself had. This is the whole law of the case.[37]

As pleaded, the case was doomed. When it was submitted in July 1839, the daughters' bill of complaint was dismissed.[38]

Lincoln moved quickly to recover from his error. Two days later, he filed an affidavit by John Strode, the guardian of the three girls. Lincoln explained how he "had no acquaintance with the case until just as he was called on for that purpose" and wasn't aware of what was necessary to properly plead the case. But he was "now informed that the Bill was defective when issue was joined." The affidavit also claimed that the girls would be able to prove that Preston knew about their claim and that it had been a "matter of anxious deliberation" for him before he purchased the land. Moreover, the original bill of complaint had been amended to allege that the third-party purchaser, Booker Preston, knew that the land was being held in trust for the three girls. Strode hoped "that the rights of the innocent and the destitute will not be submitted to suffer from any of the untoward occurrences herein named." The day after the affidavit was filed, the court set aside its order dismissing the bill. In March 1840, the case was submitted to the court, which ordered that the land be conveyed to the Orendorf girls. Stephen T. Logan appealed the court's order to the supreme court for the Stringfield heirs, but there is no record of the supreme court ever reaching the appeal.[39]

Because land was the most valuable asset in these rural communities, it figured predominantly in disputes over wills. In *Barnes v. Marquiss*, a Macon County case, John M. Barnes sued Lincoln's client, Abraham Marquiss, to set aside the will of Abraham's sister. Permilla Marquiss had died in 1837, leaving an estate worth "five thousand dollars in money goods & chattels rights and credits" entirely to her brother. Barnes, Permilla's nephew, twelve years later charged that his aunt suffered from a "great imbecility of mind and was a person incapable from defects of understanding to make a will." He also claimed that Abraham had controlled Permilla's disposition of property through "fraud, compulsion, undue influence & possession."[40] Lincoln represented Abraham Marquiss. The judge's notes on the case show that Lincoln cited the Illinois "Statute of Wills."[41] Lincoln probably argued that Barnes was too late in contesting the will; the Illinois statute prescribed a five-year period from the probate of a will to contest the validity of a will.[42] In any event, the case was submitted to the court, and the court held that Barnes was not entitled to any relief.[43]

Mares and Marauding Hogs

In addition to routine debts and disputes over land, Lincoln also handled other matters typical of predominantly rural communities such as suits over the ownership of animals. For example, in 1842, Logan & Lincoln filed a replevin suit to recover possession "of a Sorrel Mare" for Thomas Watkins. Watkins claimed that John White had wrongfully detained his mare. White, however, claimed that Thomas Watkins's son, Joseph, had sold the mare to James Maxey; Maxey had sold the mare to John Constant, and Constant had sold the mare to him. He also asserted that Watkins "well knew" that Constant had the mare but had "suffered him so to refrain the possession . . . without hindrance or molestation." Watkins testified at trial that he had kept the mare in a fenced area, and that one night, shortly before his son sold it, someone took the mare. The son was under age and was not living with his father. He had not returned to his father's house until "he was hauled there helpless and sick about two or three days before his death." Watkins also testified that he had sent a hired hand to Springfield to search the livery stables and other places for the mare. The judge instructed the jury that if Watkins knew "for more than a reasonable time" that the mare was in Springfield in someone else's possession, then Watkins "had ratified the sale of the mare." The jury found for White. Lincoln won on appeal when the supreme court reversed, holding that the instruction was "entirely too general." Watkins, like any party, did not have to sue "immediately for any injury he may sustain."[44] Lincoln handled a similar case in *Cannon v. Kenney,* where he sued to recover a sorrel horse for Manly Cannon. After the circuit judge instructed a verdict against his client, Lincoln prevailed in an appeal to the supreme court.[45]

Other disputes involved the legal consequences of cattle and hogs running at large.[46] In Illinois, cattle and hogs were allowed to roam on unenclosed prairie. Before the 1850s few settlers enclosed their pastures to "fence in" their cattle or hogs; instead, other settlers enclosed their fields to "fence out" grazing stock.[47] This custom was ratified by the Illinois Supreme Court in 1848, when it refused to adopt the English common-law rule that required owners of cattle or hogs to "fence in" their animals.[48] In that case, William Peters had sued Samuel Seeley for damages to his wheat field caused by Seeley's marauding hogs. Seeley proved at trial that Peters's field "was so badly fenced that hogs which were not breachy could go in and out at pleasure, and that said fence was entirely insufficient to turn hogs."[49] The court instructed the jury that the condition of Peters's fence did not matter because "the owner of a field is not obliged to keep up a fence around his inclosure to keep out his neighbor's cattle or hogs." This instruction reflected the English common-law rule of "fencing in." The jury found for the plaintiff Peters, and Seeley appealed. Herndon represented Peters on appeal and argued "by the common law all persons were bound to keep up their own cattle." The supreme court, however, held that "no principle of the common law" was "so inapplicable to the condition of our country and people as the one which is sought to be enforced. It had been the custom in Illinois so long, that the memory of man runneth not to the contrary, for the owners of stock to suffer them to run at large." The English rule "on account of the inapplicability of the common law rule to the condition and circumstances of our people, that it does not and never has prevailed in Illinois." The court held the instruction to jury was erroneous and reversed the circuit court's judgment.[50]

In an 1850 Christian County lawsuit, Thomas Woods claimed that Christopher Ketcham, Josephus Ketcham, and William Brown "drove, chased, and hurried with their dogs and horses" his herd of cattle to "divers places to the Said Plaintiff unknown." Woods was "not only put to great trouble and expense" in finding his cattle but he also lost several steers. He asked for one thousand dollars in damages.[51] Lincoln answered for Christopher Ketcham. In his plea, he gave notice that he would prove at trial that Woods's cattle "were trespassing upon the said defendants grounds and crops" despite Ketcham's "good and sufficient fences." Ketcham drove the cattle away but "no more & no farther than was necessary for the protection of his said grounds and crops."[52] The case later was dismissed.[53]

Bite, Gouge, and Be Sued

Physical disputes led to legal ones. Historians have written about the acceptance of "rough-and-tumble fighting" in antebellum America.[54] These historians assert that these fights were ritualized violence that restored order and allowed the participants to display courage and masculinity. Lincoln and his partners handled civil lawsuits arising from physical violence that tell a different story. Some fights disrupted order, produced enemies, and led to lawsuits. When those lawsuits went to trial, Illinois juries showed little respect for the defendants' manliness or physical courage. Lincoln and his partners were involved in thirty-five civil lawsuits where plaintiffs complained about defendants' physically assaulting them. Plaintiffs dismissed six cases, which probably indicates some settlement was reached. Courts ruled for defendants five times either on a procedural point before any trial or after a trial to the bench. Two cases were abated because of the deaths of the plaintiffs. But juries did decide twenty-two cases and found for the plaintiffs twenty times.[55] Only one jury found a defendant not guilty.[56] In one case, the jury found one defendant liable and one not liable.[57] The pattern was somewhat different for the thirty-five criminal assault cases handled by Lincoln or his partners. Twenty cases were dismissed before trial and five trials resulted in at least one of the defendants on trial being found not guilty.[58]

Many of the civil cases may have made it to court because they weren't "fair fights." In fifteen cases, plaintiffs told stories of being shot; stabbed; beaten with axe handles, iron rods, clubs, and sticks; and, in one case, hung "between the heavens and earth" and then beaten.[59] In Lincoln's Illinois, one historian has suggested frontier fighting was almost without rules.[60] But there's a difference between fighting without rules and fighting almost without rules and that difference played out in Illinois courtrooms. The nearly unanimous jury verdicts against defendants suggest the existence of at least two norms that these defendants failed to observe. Many defendants violated a basic rule of fairness: they weren't supposed to use guns, knives, and clubs when their opponents were unarmed. The other rule, which can be inferred from the plaintiffs' pleadings, was that both parties had to be willing participants. Nor did it help defendants that they continued their assaults once their victims were on the ground.[61] Then as now, don't kick someone when he's down.

George L. King sued Charles McNamara for stabbing him with a knife, inflicting "deep and dangerous wounds." The attack was so severe that "his intestines & bowels gushed out through his wounds." The defendant McNamara was able to "disable him for life & rendered him weak & sickly so that he is wholly unable to labor & support a large family."[62] The jury awarded King $650.[63] Lincoln unsuccessfully argued on appeal that the damages were excessive and that the jury should not have been able to consider that the plaintiff was a poor man with a large family and the defendant was a rich man with no children.[64]

No jury found any defendant "not guilty" because of self-defense. In the six cases that went to juries where defendants pleaded self-defense, defendants were found guilty five times and the jury couldn't reach a verdict in the sixth case. The plea of self-defense, however, apparently affected the award of damages. The amount awarded in four of the five cases was much smaller than the awards given plaintiffs in cases where self-defense wasn't raised. Benjamin Burt received five cents; Benjamin Seaman, $3; Jacob Lahr against Blair, $12; Lahr versus Swarens, $20.[65] On the other hand, a jury awarded Samuel Johnson $130.[66]

Benjamin Burt sued James F. Jennings for "Trespass A & B" (assault and battery), claiming that Jennings attacked him with a pocket knife, which left him "sick, sore, lame, disabled and his eye sight injured." Jennings, who was represented by Lincoln, pleaded self-defense, claiming that Burt "would then and there have beat, bruised, and ill-treated" Jennings if he "had not immediately defended himself." Burt then filed a replication to the plea of self-defense, which complicated matters even more; he claimed that Jennings used "more force and violence than was necessary." Such a plea of excessive force seemingly conceded that Burt was the initial aggressor. The jury found for Burt, but only awarded five cents.[67] The jury wasn't convinced by Sigler Lester's plea of self-defense and awarded Samuel Johnson $130. Self-defense didn't explain Lester stabbing Johnson several times, beating him with a club, and then ripping his clothes.[68]

Other defendants pleaded the use of legitimate force based on their status, either as sheriffs or constables apprehending scofflaws or as a master disciplining an apprentice. Joseph Haines sued John Jones and William Gaither because they "beat and illtreated him" and then took him from his home to the Tazewell County courthouse where they imprisoned him "without any legal authority." Jones was the clerk of the circuit court and Gaither was the sheriff of Tazewell County. Lincoln, who represented Gaither, pled that Gaither was acting pursuant to a writ issued by the clerk and used "no more force than was necessary." The jury found the sheriff not guilty and the clerk guilty and assessed damages at $10.[69]

The Lawyer as Peacemaker

Abraham Lincoln, like most antebellum lawyers, believed that lawyers should serve as peacemakers. His slander cases show that he often took advantage of opportunities for mediation and compromise. He was able to resolve many cases by repairing the damage to the plaintiffs' reputation. In several cases, the defendant attested to the good reputation of the slandered plaintiff, which settled the case. In some cases, the defendant consented to a large judgment, which the plaintiff then agreed to reduce to a much smaller sum. In others, the plaintiff, after a jury had awarded damages, agreed to remit most or all of the award. Lincoln acted as a peacemaker and showed sensitivity to what was actually at stake in those cases.

Antebellum lawyers celebrated the "sober judgement of Courts" as a means to maintain social order.[70] At the same time, however, they also believed that they should serve as peacemakers who prevented disputes from going to court. Thus, they reflected a larger ambiguity in American culture about the use of courts to settle disputes. Americans acknowledged the importance of law in maintaining order but often saw the invocation of formal law as an antisocial act and disruptive force.[71] As Noah Webster explained in his *American Spelling Book* (1823), "Somebody is always the worse for lawsuits, and of course society is less happy."[72]

Law and Reputation

Antebellum lawyers in general, and Lincoln in particular, did not want to resolve all disputes with a formal adjudication. Lawyers were not simply courtroom advocates for their clients; they also served a mediating role. As Robert W. Gordon notes, antebellum lawyers "who seriously took their status as republican mediators were encouraged to run their office as little chancery courts."[73] That mediating role was particularly important in small communities where lawyers were keenly aware of the social context of purely local disputes.[74] One of Lincoln's former law clerks recalled that "the very character of this simple litigation drew the lawyer into the street and neighborhood, and into close and active intercourse with all classes of his fellow-men."[75]

Like many antebellum lawyers, Lincoln described the lawyer's role as that of a peacemaker. (Lawyers may have chosen "peacemaker" because it echoed one of the Beatitudes from the Sermon on the Mount: "Blessed are the peacemakers: for they shall be called the children of God."[76]) In his notes for a law lecture, he wrote: "Discourage litigation. Persuade your neighbors to compromise whenever you can. Point out to them how the nominal winner is often a real loser in fees, expenses, and waste of time. As a peace-maker, the lawyer has a superior opportunity of being a good man."[77] That was a common conception of the lawyer's role in the nineteenth century; it reflected the deep ambivalence about court use in American society.[78] After the 1880 death of Stephen Trigg Logan, who was Lincoln's second law partner, John T. Stuart (Lincoln's first law partner), observed, "Logan, in his office, was the just, ripe and safe counsellor, grasping with readiness the facts of the cases submitted to him, separating the truth from the coloring given it by the passion of the client, and readily seeing the point in the case, he was able to give sound advice, which his sense of justice directed to the right. He was not a promoter of litigation. He settled more controversies than he brought suits. He was a peacemaker." Springfield lawyer Benjamin S. Edwards also described Logan as a lawyer who "never encouraged litigation, but as a friend and neighbor strove for the peaceful adjustment of all controversies."[79]

Kentucky lawyer George W. Robertson similarly described the lawyer's role in his *Scrap Book on Law and Politics, Men and Times* (1855), a book Lincoln owned: "He should never advise a suit unless it is the interest of his client to 'go to law.' If the case be frivolous, or the right doubtful, he should advise forbearance or compromise. He should never encourage litigation."[80]

Following such advice, when faced with local disputes, Lincoln often tried to serve as a mediator or peacemaker. Lincoln represented Abram Bale in a suit over $1,000 worth of wheat. One of the defendants was Virgil Hickox, a prominent Springfield Democrat whom Lincoln had crossed paths with many times in central Illinois courtrooms. In 1850 he wrote his client Bale: "I sincerely hope you will settle it. I think you *can* if you *will*, for I have always found Mr. Hickox a fair man in his dealings. If you settle I will charge nothing for what I have done, and thank you to boot. By settling, you will most likely get your money sooner; and with much less trouble and expense." Six weeks later the case settled.[81]

Representing the Alton and Sangamon Railroad in a subscriber lawsuit, he advised the railroad to settle with the defendant because "it is better to get along peaceably if possible."[82] In 1859 he represented Haden Keeling in a $45 dispute over a cellar Keeling had built but not been paid for. Lincoln advised his client to drop his lawsuit: "I do not think there is the least use of doing any more with the law suit. I not only do not think you are sure to gain it, but I think you are sure to lose it. Therefore the sooner it ends the better." Keeling didn't drop the lawsuit when advised; instead, it took a long, fruitless journey from the Fulton County Justice Court to the circuit court to the Illinois Supreme Court and then back again to the circuit court.[83]

Lincoln helped to restore peace to the neighborhood through his efforts to mediate and settle slander lawsuits. He or one of his partners handled at least ninety-two slander lawsuits during the course of his career.[84] A self-educated lawyer, he became well versed in the law of slander as shown by an 1846 motion for rehearing filed in the Illinois Supreme Court where he offered to furnish the court a "new edition, in two volumes of Starkie on Slander."[85]

Those cases, however, involved much more than the sterile application of the formal law of slander to the facts of each lawsuit. Slander cases, by their very nature, were community-oriented, regulating acceptable forms of behavior in small communities.[86] Litigants in slander suits were involved in the "small politics" of everyday life: reputation, gossip, and insult.[87] Standing in a small community was based on reputation, and reputations were built or destroyed through gossip.[88] Lincoln recognized the importance of reputation; he confessed in 1832 that his "peculiar ambition" was "being truly esteemed of my fellow men."[89]

The Illinois law of slander had both statutory and common-law elements. As early as 1821, the Illinois General Assembly defined slander as criminal behavior that could be punished with a fine not exceeding $1,000.[90] In 1822, the legislature made certain words actionable in civil proceedings. The legislature declared that falsely stating that any person had been guilty of adultery or fornication or had sworn falsely were actionable.[91] That legislation thus rejected the narrower English common-law rule that required "an express imputation of some crime liable to punishment, some capital offence, or other infamous crime or misdemeanor."[92] Several other state courts did follow the English rule, which held that an imputation of adultery or fornication was not actionable.[93] In Illinois, it was.

Many of Lincoln's slander cases involved accusations of adultery or fornication; Lincoln thus was involved heavily in maintaining community reputations and relationships. In fact, he represented plaintiffs or defendants in at least thirteen such cases, all but one of which concerned a woman accused of adultery or fornication.[94] These slander suits confirm that female reputation was based primarily on sexual propriety.[95] False swearing (lying under oath) and adultery and fornication, the two seemingly neutral categories of actionable slander as defined by the legislature, were gendered: men sued over accusations of false swearing, women over adultery and fornication. The slander lawsuits filed in central Illinois counties reflected the unequal status and roles of men and women. The domestic work of women in the rural Midwest remained hidden, whereas the work and social life of men took place in a public world.[96] The aspect of a man's reputation that was considered important enough to sue over was honesty in that public realm.

Slander suits more narrowly protected women's sexual reputation. For example, Lincoln and Herndon represented Charles Cantrall and Emily Cantrall—under the doctrine of coverture, a married woman could not sue without her husband's joinder—in 1849 in a suit against one John Primm for publicly saying that "William King screwed Charles Cantrall's wife twice while he was gone; and before that he crawled in bed with her and her husband and screwed her." The Cantralls requested $1,000 in damages.[97] In an 1845 case, the plaintiffs, William Beaty and Martha Ann Beaty, sued Jonathan Miller and Susan Miller, claiming that Susan had said that "Mrs. Beaty and Dr. Sulivan were seen together in Beaty's stable one morning very early in the very act" and that "Mrs. Beaty and Dr. Sulivan were seen in the very act." The defendants were represented by Lincoln and Herndon. The jury found the defendants liable and assessed damages at $45.[98]

Eliza Cabot, represented by Lincoln, sued Francis Regnier in a slander case that was first tried in Menard County in 1843 and then retried in Morgan County in 1844; she complained Regnier had said that Elijah Taylor was "after skin and he has got it" with Eliza, that Taylor had "rogered" Eliza, and that "the captain has got some skin there as much as he wanted."[99] When the case went to trial in Menard County, Lincoln delivered a "denunciation" of Regnier that was "as bitter a Phillippic as ever uttered" but Eliza received a verdict for only twelve dollars.[100] Lincoln moved for a new trial based on jury misconduct, and the judge set aside the verdict.[101]

When the case was retried in Morgan County, Eliza received a $1,600 verdict, which was later sustained by the Illinois Supreme Court.[102] In an 1850 Shelby County lawsuit, Sarah Allsop sued John Sturgeon, who Allsop claimed had called her a "regular whore."[103] Lincoln represented Sturgeon.[104] The jury agreed that she had been slandered and assessed damages at $500.[105]

Other sexual-slander cases reflect racism and fears of miscegenation. Ambrose P. Edwards and his wife sued William Patterson and his wife over Mrs. Patterson's remark that "Mrs. Edwards has raised a family of children by a negro, and I can prove it." The Edwards claimed that these words, by innuendo, charged Mrs. Edwards with the crimes of adultery and fornication. The jury agreed and awarded $220 in damages. In a rare appeal of a slander lawsuit, the supreme court reversed the judgment and remanded the case to the trial court, holding that "the words spoken . . . do not in their plain and popular sense, or in common acceptation, necessarily amount to a charge of fornication and adultery."[106] In an 1851 case brought in Christian County, John M. Saunders and Katharine Saunders claimed that Aaron Dunham had slandered Katharine by saying she "had a Negro child," imputing that she "had been Guilty of fornication with a Negro man, and had borne a child—the issue of an illicit intercourse with a Negro man." The case was later dismissed by agreement of the parties with the plaintiffs "stipulating not to sue again for same cause of action."[107]

Only one slander suit filed by a woman did not involve rumors of adultery or fornication. In an 1843 Livingston County case, Moses Allen and his wife Eliza Allen sued Garret M. Blue for alleging that Eliza "swore a lie" in a court proceeding.[108] After the plaintiffs received a $250 default judgment, the defendant overturned that judgment on appeal.[109] Two of the ten appeals from slander cases with female plaintiffs heard by the Illinois Supreme Court from 1837 until 1860 involved accusations of larceny, and the other eight appeals involved accusations of adultery or fornication (two of those eight were Lincoln cases).[110]

Women appeared as plaintiffs in only twenty-one of the ninety-two cases. Of these twenty-one lawsuits, seven were filed by single women and fourteen by married couples.[111] The relative lack of lawsuits involving women as the target of defamatory speech is somewhat surprising. Here, roughly twenty-three percent of the plaintiffs were single women or married couples when women comprised nearly half of the Illinois population.[112]

The lack of women plaintiffs may reflect the relative isolation of women in the rural Midwest. Rural women were denied entry to the public world outside the family. Because of the division of labor and settlement patterns, most wives were isolated in their homes. In contrast to the village life of antebellum New England, central Illinois had thinly spaced homesteads that resulted in a population density of eight people per square mile.[113]

Even fewer women were named as defendants. Under antebellum law, a husband and wife were jointly sued for the wife's slander. But only eight of the ninety-two slander cases had female defendants; seven had been sued with their husbands.[114] In six of the suits with female defendants, the slanderous remarks had been directed at a woman.[115] In the seventy lawsuits where men were the targets of defamatory speech, only twice did a man sue because of something a woman allegedly said about him.[116] John F. Skinner sued Dabner Overstreet and his wife Jane Overstreet in Menard County because they said he was the father of a "bastard child." A jury found the Overstreets not guilty.[117]

Cyrus B. Chase sued John Blakely and his wife Phebe Blakely, claiming that Phebe had said he stole their sheep skin, chickens, and eggs, and poisoned their colt. Lincoln, E. D. Baker, and John J. Hardin represented the defendants. The jury found for Chase but only awarded one cent for damages.[118] I have found only one instance where an unmarried woman was sued for something she said. America Toney (represented by Lincoln, Oliver L. Davis, and Ward H. Lamon) sued Emily Sconce in an 1853 Vermilion County case because Sconce had said that Toney was guilty of fornication.[119] The preponderance of male defendants in nineteenth-century slander cases may reflect the relative ability of men to pay judgments, but it is more likely that the preponderance of male defendants reflects the unimportance of female opinion in the social construction of reputation.[120]

Men rarely sued over their sexual reputation. Not counting cases involving charges of having sex with animals, I have found only one case where a male sued because of an accusation of fornication. This was the suit by John F. Skinner, represented by Herndon, against the Overstreets.[121] The Overstreets offered to retract this statement on the day of trial, but Skinner rejected their offer. The case was tried and the jury found the Overstreets not guilty.[122]

Skinner may have sued to forestall either a seduction suit, bastardy action, or breach of promise to marry suit from being filed against him. The mother of an illegitimate child could initiate a statutory action against the father for support. The father of the "unfortunate female" could sue for damages in a seduction suit. According to the Illinois Supreme Court, damages would be for the "loss of character and happiness of the unfortunate female, and the consequent injury inflicted on the heart of the parent" or for loss of services, "dishonor and disgrace cast upon him and his family," and the loss of society and comfort of his daughter. A woman also could sue for breach of promise to marry and recover damages for her "disgrace and ruin," including damages arising from seduction and the birth of an illegitimate child. In Champaign County, Lincoln separately filed all three causes of action against one Albert G. Carle. For Nancy Jane Dunn he initiated a bastardy action and a breach of promise of marriage suit, and for her father, Zephaniah Dunn, he filed a seduction suit. In the bastardy lawsuit, Carle was found to be the father of the child and was ordered to pay $50 a year in support. Despite what Judge David Davis noted as "desperate" attempts by Carle's lawyers to "blacken" Nancy Jane's character in the seduction suit, Zephaniah Dunn won a $180 jury verdict, which he remitted in exchange for Carle's agreeing not to interfere with Nancy Jane's custody of the child.[123]

That men sued but once over slander involving fornication or adultery and women sued twelve times over adultery or fornication suggests the existence of a double standard where a man's reputation was not damaged by gossip about adultery and fornication.[124] The existence of a double standard is best shown in the willingness of men to implicate themselves in the very sexual misconduct that they used to defame women.[125] In an 1858 Vermilion County lawsuit, Nancy M. Martin—represented by Lincoln, Oliver L. Davis, and Oscar F. Harmon—sued Achilles M. Underwood for his detailed, public accounts of his alleged sexual conquest of her. Underwood boasted that:

> One Sunday I was down here and in the evening some of the folks come by going to Georgetown to meeting so I went along and fell in company with Nance Rolly and I didn't think anything more than just a cousin so I devilled along and we got back to the gate we stopped and Nance said let's watch the rest and she stepped up to and hugged me up tight and said O. Morg you can't tell how well I love you and shoved her belly up against me and it was so light she was afraid they'd see us from the house but I slipped my hand down and pulled up her clothes a little and she said don't and I pulled them up and she said don't and set one foot in the crack of the fence and I slapt it into her and she exclaimed don't knock me up for God's sake don't knock me up.

He said that on another occasion he "followed Nance in the kitchen room and cornered her and popped it to her again." He also said that "Nance Rolly has been fucked more times than I have fingers and toes for damned if it ain't so big I can almost poke my fist in."[126] Underwood chose to defend the claim against him by pleading truth as a justification for the words spoken: Martin had been guilty of fornication, "had had sexual intercourse with various persons" and had been guilty of "licentious conduct, lewd and obscene language." The jury rejected this defense, found Underwood guilty, and ordered him to pay $237 in damages.[127] Similarly, Lewis Hatch was sued by Dorinda Potter and her husband John for saying Dorinda "slept with me one night before she was married and I screwed her." The jury awarded the Potters $425, and the supreme court affirmed the judgment.[128] Lincoln represented the Potters on appeal.

While a male sued only once over an accusation of fornication, on at least four occasions male plaintiffs sued because of accusations of bestiality.[129] In an 1847 Christian County lawsuit, Lincoln & Herndon represented William Torrance in a suit against Newton Galloway, claiming that Galloway had slandered Torrance by imputing an "infamous crime against nature with a beast." Galloway had said that Torrance had "caught my old sow and he fucked her as long as he could." He also said that Torrance had impregnated his sow; she was "bellying down and will soon have some young bills." Torrance requested one thousand dollars in damages. The case later was dismissed with Torrance paying the court costs.[130]

Roughly seventy-seven percent of the targets of the defamatory speech were males, whose local reputations were vital for their community relationships. While slander lawsuits with female plaintiffs had been most concerned about accusations about sexual promiscuity, male plaintiffs were attacked on their honesty.[131] Slander cases with male plaintiffs typically involved accusations of false swearing or larceny. Male plaintiffs sued at least twenty-six times over accusations of theft[132] and sixteen times over accusations of false swearing.[133] For upland southerners in the Midwest, male reputation, as historian Nicole Etcheson has shown, depended on manliness, and two requisite qualities of manliness were honesty and integrity.[134] In the emerging (and male-dominated) market economy, a reputation for honesty was critical for financial success.[135] Lincoln filed his first slander case in 1838 on behalf of George W. Thompson of Sangamon County, who sued Stephen Osborn because Osborn had said that he was guilty of swearing falsely.[136] The case later was dismissed by agreement.[137]

The modern literature on gossip and scandal suggests those in the striving middle class are most concerned about gossip.[138] In antebellum Illinois, it appears that all social classes were concerned with the consequences of slander. Reputation, for example, was vital for the success of professionals: doctors, lawyers, and successful merchants all filed slander actions. And antebellum slander law gave special protection to professional reputations. One commentator explained in 1850 that "the law is clear, that words not actionable in the case of a common person, may become so when spoken of another in relation to the office he fills, or the trade or profession which he carries on."[139]

Lincoln represented fellow lawyer David B. Campbell in a slander suit against Abraham Smith. Lincoln's declaration claimed that Smith had charged Campbell "in his capacity of States attorney, of *drunkenness,* of *neglect of duty,* and of *drawing indictments wrong purposely that the accused might escape.*" The case went to trial, and Lincoln prepared the court's instructions to the jury: if the jury believed that Smith said the words, then Smith had to prove that all the charges were true; "proof of *drunkenness* will not justify the charge of *neglect of duty,* nor proof of drunkenness and neglect *both* justify the charge of collusion with persons accused." The jury also was instructed that "a mere *preponderance* of evidence is sufficient to prove that the defendant spoke the words; but that *more* than a preponderance, that is proof inducing belief beyond a reasonable doubt is necessary to prove that the words spoken were true." The jury awarded Campbell $450 in damages.[140]

While in most cases, the parties managed the lawsuit outside of court and determined whether it would settle or proceed to trial, there were some procedural obstacles for plaintiffs. The technical requirements of common-law pleading did not present much of an obstacle: only one of Lincoln's slander suits was dismissed because a demurrer to a declaration was sustained. The dismissal probably resulted from the plaintiff suing the defendant for calling him a "damned rogue"; under the law of slander, *rogue* was considered too general a term of abuse to be actionable.[141] Plaintiffs also could be required to obtain security for court costs. Under Illinois law, a defendant or "any officer of the court" could suggest to the court that the plaintiff was unable to pay the costs of the lawsuit. If the court agreed, then it could require the plaintiff to file a bond for costs by "some responsible person."[142] If the plaintiff failed to file a bond, then the court would dismiss the lawsuit.[143] This requirement discouraged the filing of lawsuits that did not have some community support, or, at least, someone willing to post the bond. In at least twenty-one cases, plaintiffs had to file bonds for costs.[144] The court dismissed two cases because the plaintiff, after initiating the action by summons, failed to file a declaration before the second term of court.[145] The plaintiffs probably failed to file declarations to maintain their lawsuits because the emotions that led to initiating the lawsuit cooled or they realized the financial or social costs of the lawsuits outweighed any potential benefit.

One striking statistic is the relative lack of default judgments in slander cases. A default judgment is a type of forfeit by the defendant: the plaintiff wins because the defendant has failed to answer or appear in court. Plaintiffs only obtained two default judgments, and one of the two was reversed on appeal to the Illinois Supreme Court.[146] Thus, default judgments were obtained in roughly two percent of the cases. In contrast, roughly forty percent of the common-law actions filed in the Knox County, Illinois, circuit court ended with default judgments during the 1840s.[147] Roughly thirty percent of the civil cases filed in the St. Louis Circuit Court also ended in default judgments during the same time period.[148] Successful resolution of slander cases, however, apparently required some kind of formal appearance by the defendant. The goal of a plaintiff suing on a promissory note was to obtain a judgment that memorialized the debt; whether the defendant appeared in court was irrelevant. The goal of a plaintiff in a slander suit was to vindicate honor and repair reputation. That goal required the defendant to participate by appearing in court.

Defendants had relatively little success in obtaining "not guilty" verdicts. Plaintiffs won roughly thirty-five of the forty-five cases that were tried to juries.[149] The success rate for plaintiffs reflects the community disapproval of malicious gossip. An 1838 article in a Jacksonville newspaper described the pernicious effects of the slanderer: "amidst the innumerable number of actors, probably none have been more successful in causing human misery—in sowing the seeds of discord—and disturbing the happy scenes of the family circle, than that of the base slanderer." The article concluded that the slanderer was "an arch-fiend—a demon in human shape— the prime minister of his Satanic Majesty—and in whose breast virtue has no abiding place."[150]

If a case proceeded to trial, a defendant generally used one of two strategies: either claim he had not spoken the slanderous words or prove that the words spoken were true and, therefore, not slanderous.[151] If a defendant denied saying the slanderous words, then that defendant would plead the general issue of "not guilty." If a defendant claimed that the spoken words were true, then the defendant had to assert the special plea of justification.[152]

In at least twenty-one slander cases, the defendant pleaded truth as a justification to the plaintiff's charges.[153] In five cases, Lincoln pleaded that the plaintiffs who sued for being called hog thieves were, in fact, hog thieves.[154] In five other cases, Lincoln offered to prove that the plaintiff, in fact, had sworn falsely in a prior proceeding.[155] In two cases, Lincoln pleaded that the plaintiffs were guilty of larceny.[156] In one case, Lincoln gave notice that he would prove that the plaintiff was guilty of fornication, and in another he pleaded that the plaintiff really was guilty of forgery.[157]

Justification was a risky strategy. First, the defendant had to admit speaking the words alleged by the plaintiff.[158] Second, the defendant carried a strict burden in proving that the charged words were true.[159] Third, before 1854, a jury in Illinois could be instructed that a plea of justification aggravated the original slander if the defendant failed to sustain the plea. In 1854 the Illinois Supreme Court held that the jury could consider the plea a reiteration of the slander and increase its award accordingly only when the jury believed that the defendant had pleaded justification without any expectation of proving it.[160]

In only four of the twenty-one cases where justification was pleaded, the strategy was wholly successful: the defendant obtained "not guilty" jury verdicts.[161] The parties dismissed two other cases.[162] The defendants received adverse jury verdicts in the remaining cases that pleaded justification, with the amounts of verdicts varying widely. In four cases, the award was substantial: $1,000 in *Linder v. Fleenor;* $1,012 in *Richey v. Adams;* $1,600 in *Cabot v. Regnier;* $2,000 in *Nordyke v. Fleenor.*[163] In three of those cases, however, plaintiffs agreed to remit part of the jury's verdict.[164] In four other cases where the defendant lost after pleading justification, the jury awarded $215, $237, $250, and $500.[165] In the remaining cases, the plea of justification may have helped minimize damages. In six cases where justification was pleaded, the defendants were ordered to pay $5, $30, $50, $55, $78, and $80.[166] In one case, the plaintiff was awarded only five cents.[167]

Lincoln had particular success pleading justification when the defendant was sued for calling the plaintiff a hog thief. In those five cases, Lincoln secured two "not guilty" verdicts and two dismissals.[168] David Adkin filed two lawsuits in Macon County in 1839, claiming that Robert Hines and Levi Meisenhelter had called him a "damned pig thief" and a "damned infamous pig thief."[169] Considerable bad blood existed between Adkin and Meisenhelter, who had been charged with fighting (an "affray") in November 1838.[170] Lincoln represented both defendants and pleaded in both lawsuits that the plaintiff did "feloniously steal take and carry away" five pigs and five hogs. His clients "lawfully" had called the plaintiff a "hog thief."[171] The suit against Hines was tried in June 1839, with the jury apparently agreeing with Lincoln: they found his client not guilty of slander.[172] Adkin dismissed the second lawsuit in the following term of court after agreeing to pay court costs.[173] Adkin was charged with larceny in October 1839, and, ironically, Lincoln was appointed to defend him. The jury found Adkin not guilty.[174] Lincoln apparently convinced the jury in the slander suit that Adkin was guilty of larceny and later convinced the jury in the criminal case that he wasn't.

Other defenses were available. The statute of limitations for "actions on words" provided a procedural defense if the plaintiff failed to sue within one year of the alleged slander.[175] Lincoln or one of his partners pleaded limitations seven times but apparently was never successful in pressing that defense.[176] A defendant also could avoid liability or mitigate damages by showing that the slanderous words were spoken in "heat and passion." Malice was the "gist" of a slander case, and if the words were spoken in heat and passion, then there was no malice.[177] In at least two cases, Lincoln submitted jury instructions that said if the jury believed the words were spoken but also believed "they were spoken through mere heat of passion, they are to find for the defendant."[178] In one of those cases, Lincoln submitted an additional instruction that charged the jury that if they found that the words were spoken "so much in the heat of passion as to be free from all deliberate malice, this is to go in mitigation of damages."[179] A defendant also could avoid liability by showing that he or she merely had repeated what others had said about the plaintiff and had not been motivated by malice.[180] Lincoln pleaded that defense in *Beaty v. Miller*. Lincoln's answer disclaimed any intent of "affirming the truth of the supposed slanderous words" but instead claimed that since the defendant was repeating what her husband had heard from one Thomas Vandergriff, she "did speak the said words . . . as lawfully she might." The jury didn't believe that defense and awarded the plaintiffs $45.[181]

Community-oriented litigation involved not only vindicating the aggrieved party, but also ensuring that the damages awarded were fair. In addition to showing that the defendant had not spoken the slanderous words or that the words were not slanderous, a defendant's lawyer could adopt a strategy of minimizing damages. Under Illinois law, a defendant in a slander case could mitigate damages by "showing the general bad character of the plaintiff" and by "showing any circumstances which tend to disprove malice, but do not tend to prove the truth of the charge."[182] In a Shelby

County slander lawsuit, Lincoln's client was sued for saying that the plaintiff had sworn falsely. Although the jury found for the plaintiff, the award was only $5.[183] In an 1842 Vermilion County case, Lincoln's client, who also was sued for saying the plaintiff had sworn falsely, was found guilty but was ordered to pay only $10 in damages (the plaintiff had demanded $5,000).[184]

In three cases, the jury gave the smallest possible award: one cent.[185] Such an award occurred in an 1853 Sangamon County case. Lincoln and Herndon represented the plaintiff, while Lincoln's former partner, Stephen Logan, represented the defendant. Although the jury found Logan's client guilty of slander, they awarded only one cent for damages.[186] In other jurisdictions based on English common law, the practice of juries in slander cases awarding the "lowest coin of the realm" gave rise to a formal doctrine that rationalized this award.[187] In appeals from nineteenth-century slander lawsuits in Canada, Australia, New Zealand, and England, such an award became known as "contemptuous damages."[188] In the United States, no such formal doctrine developed, but juries in Illinois and elsewhere practically expressed their disapproval of some slander plaintiffs by awarding only one cent in damages. Although a plaintiff might be awarded only one cent in damages, that plaintiff still could recover the costs of the lawsuit. In one slander case, the jury award was one cent, but the plaintiff was allowed to recover the costs of the suit, which were $45.70.[189]

Even in slander cases, Lincoln valued mediation and compromise. He did not try every slander claim; he often was able to settle them. In several instances, the parties settled before trial when the defendant agreed to a large adverse judgment, which the plaintiff then agreed to remit in part or in total. The earliest example from Lincoln's practice came in 1838, when Stuart & Lincoln helped Edward D. Baker represent Patricius Moran in a slander lawsuit against John W. Baddeley. The case settled when Baddeley withdrew his defensive pleas and allowed a default judgment against him for $2,000, which was the amount pleaded for by Moran. After the court ordered recovery for that amount, Moran then remitted all $2,000 of damages.[190] Two years later, in an 1840 Livingston County lawsuit, Stuart & Lincoln represented William Popejoy, who sued Isaac Wilson because he had said Popejoy had stolen meat. The case settled when Wilson in open court said he could not "gainsay" Popejoy's claim and confessed judgment "for the sum of Two Thousand Dollars, the amount of Damages claimed in Plaintiff Declaration"; the judge then ordered that Popejoy recover the "Two Thousand dollars so confessed"; and "thereupon" Popejoy then agreed to remit the entire amount except court costs.[191] Note the careful timing: Popejoy's magnanimous gesture came only after Wilson in open court said he couldn't say anything against Popejoy's claim and had confessed judgment to the entire claimed amount. The parties didn't just announce a settlement where Wilson agreed to pay costs but instead acted out a set piece. The trial was used by the parties to enact what anthropologists call a ritual reconciliation.[192]

Four years earlier in a Springfield courtroom (and one year before Lincoln became a lawyer), Lincoln was present when a nearly identical performance resolved a slander lawsuit brought by William G. Green against John Purcapile. Lincoln, who had been summoned as a witness for the plaintiff, was present when the defendant Purcapile withdrew his pleas, saying that he couldn't "gainsay the plaintiffs action against him" and that the plaintiff had sustained damages of $5,000. The court then ordered the plaintiff to recover the $5,000, and then the plaintiff released all damages except costs.[193]

Other cases were settled before trial in the same fashion. Lincoln settled an 1853 Vermilion County case by having the defendant withdraw her plea and consent to a $5,000 judgment and having the plaintiff remit all but $50. The plaintiff, America Toney, had sued Emily Sconce for saying that after America had gone to her room with one Whitcomb late one evening the bed was "rattling and jiggling" and when America later came out of the room at three in the morning her clothes and hair were "rumpled," her face was "very red," and she "very much excited."[194] In an 1845 Coles County case, the defendant Jonathan Hart agreed to a $2,000 judgment and the plaintiff Thomas McKibben then remitted $1,700 and agreed not to execute on the remaining $300 for twelve months.[195] That same year, Lincoln and Herndon represented the plaintiff in a Sangamon County slander suit. The case was settled when the parties agreed to a $500 judgment, which the plaintiff agreed to remit except for costs.[196] Lincoln pursued an identical strategy when he helped represent Dr. Julius Lehman in an 1859 McLean County lawsuit. Lehman sued another doctor, Herman Schroeder, for slander. The case was settled when Schroeder agreed in open court to a $5,000 judgment against him and Lehman agreed to remit all but $50 and to stay execution for three months.[197]

Henry Clay Whitney, an Urbana lawyer who often was associated with Lincoln on the circuit, recalled one slander case in which Lincoln, one of the defendant's lawyers, "made most strenuous and earnest efforts to compromise the case, which was accomplished by reason, solely, of his exertions."[198] The case arose in Kankakee County and involved a French Catholic priest named Chiniquy (from the French community of St. Anne's) and Peter Spink, a French Catholic from the nearby community of L'Erable. In a sermon, Chiniquy apparently accused Spink of perjury and refused to recant. Whitney noted that, after the suit was filed, "preparations were made for a 'fight to the finish,' by, not only the two principals, but the two respective neighborhoods, as well: for all became involved as principals or partisans." When the case was transferred to Champaign County, "The principals, their lawyers and witnesses, and an immense retinue of followers, came to Urbana. The hotels were monopolized, and a large number camped out."[199] The case was tried twice and resulted in a mistrial twice. At the next term of court, "All come to our county, camp-outfits, musicians, parrots, pet dogs and all, and the outlook was, that their scandal would have to be aired over again." Lincoln then intervened; Whitney noted that Lincoln "abhorred that class of litigation, in which [there] was no utility, and he used his utmost influence with all parties, and finally effected a compromise."[200] After convincing the parties to settle, Lincoln prepared the agreement of dismissal, which read: "This day came the parties and the defendant denies that he has ever charged, or believed the plaintiff to be guilty of Perjury; that whatever he has said from which such a charge could be inferred, he said on the information of others, protesting his own disbelief in the charge; and that he now disclaims any belief in the truth of such charge against said plaintiff." The parties agreed to divide court costs and to dismiss the case.[201]

The number of cases that Lincoln settled either before or after trial suggests that slander suits were intended more to restore or repair reputation than to collect damages. Richard Yates, an antebellum Illinois lawyer, argued to the jury in one slander lawsuit that his client's case was properly brought for "vindication of character," not "for mere revenge, for private malice, for filthy lucre's sake."[202] Lincoln settled at least three slander cases by having his client affirm the good reputation of the plaintiff, thus repairing the plaintiff's reputation in the community. As Lincoln later noted, "*Truth* is generally the best vindication against slander."[203] In an 1851 case in Tazewell County, Mary Ann Jacobus sued Milden Kitchell and Elizabeth Kitchell for slander. Jacobus claimed that Elizabeth Kitchell had said "Mary Ann Jacobus is a whore" and "Mary Ann Jacobus gets her fine clothes by whoring."[204] Lincoln, who represented the defendants, settled the case by having his clients deny in open court that "they or either of them ever made any charge against the chastity of the plaintiff" and assert that "neither of them has ever had any knowledge, information, or reasonable belief, of any want of chastity on the part of the plaintiff." The parties then dismissed the case by consent.[205]

In another slander case, the plaintiff agreed to dismiss the lawsuit when Lincoln filed into the court record the following statement signed by his client: "In this case, the defendant states that he has never spoken the slanderous words in the declaration alleged; that he always has believed, and still does believe the plaintiff to be an honest man; that he never has believed, and does not now believe that the plaintiff ever stole, embezzled, or in any way appropriated to his own use, any of defendant's money; and that he makes this statement to be placed upon the record as the most public and enduring vindication that he can make of the plaintiff's reputation, against such a charge."[206]

In a third case, Lincoln wrote a proposed judgment in which the defendant said that he had not "at any time accused the plaintiff of false swearing and does not believe him guilty of such offence." Lincoln's client had "spoken of a certain statement" by the plaintiff "as being incorrect, but that he has not characterized said statement a falsehood, as distinguished from a mistake." Lincoln's client agreed to pay court costs, and the plaintiff agreed to dismiss the lawsuit.[207] Lincoln thus showed sensitivity to what was actually at stake in those cases; he settled each case by repairing the damage to the injured party's reputation.

Lincoln also tried to use a similar tactic to settle the libel suit brought by Norman Judd against John Wentworth in 1859.[208] When Wentworth asked Lincoln to represent him in the lawsuit, Lincoln instead acted as a mediator.[209] He proposed that Wentworth file a disclaimer in court that said he had "made no reflection upon Mr. Judd morally, sociably, pecuniarily, professionally, and in no other way save politically, and if I have used Language capable of a different construction I have not intended it & now retract it." When David Davis analyzed Lincoln's proposal, he warned that Judd could continue the suit after Wentworth filed his retraxit, which would be "degrading" to Wentworth. Davis believed "the basis of a settlement should be the immediate withdrawal of the suits & that when Wentworth has placed on the files the above retraxit that he has done enough & that Judd should be satisfied with it."[210]

At least thirty-one of these slander cases never went to trial, and informal mediation probably was behind the dismissal of most of them.[211] When Lincoln acted as a peacemaker in slander suits, he played a role typical of Illinois lawyers. Between 1836 and 1860, at least thirty-seven slander lawsuits were filed in Sangamon County, yet only five went to a jury.[212] (Lincoln was involved in fifteen of the cases and four of the trials.[213]) Apparently, the parties settled three-fourths of the cases without a jury: twenty-six cases were either dismissed by the parties or disappeared from the court docket, while two were settled by agreed judgment.[214] Of the four remaining cases, the court dismissed two (for want of prosecution and for failure to post security for costs), sustained a demurrer to a declaration to another, and granted a default judgment in the fourth.[215]

In addition to settlements before trial, Lincoln was involved in at least nine cases where plaintiffs settled after the juries had returned sizeable verdicts against the defendants.[216] Plaintiffs were not avoiding an inevitable (or even likely) reversal by the Illinois Supreme Court; the court rarely overturned jury verdicts on the basis of excessive damages.[217] Nonetheless, successful plaintiffs willingly remitted most or all of the jury's award, again suggesting that the purpose of slander suits was to restore or repair reputations in the community. In three cases, plaintiffs remitted all of the jury's award except for costs.[218] In an 1851 slander case in Shelby County, for example, Lincoln was able to settle the case after the jury returned a verdict against his client. Emily Fancher had sued Lincoln's client, Daniel Gollogher, for slander, claiming in two counts of the pleading that Gollogher had said that Fancher had sworn falsely and in two other counts claiming that Gollogher had said Fancher had run away with a married man and had lived in a brothel. The jury found Gollogher guilty on the first two counts and not guilty on the last two counts, assessing $1,000 in damages. The judgment, however, recited that Fancher "remits the whole of said damages" except costs.[219] In an 1843 Coles County case, Lincoln's client was accused of saying that the plaintiff had broken into a man's house with his penknife, plundered his neighbor's smokehouse, and stolen a banknote from a woman's purse while he was courting her. The jury awarded the plaintiff $2,000, but the plaintiff's attorney "came into open court" and released the whole judgment except for costs.[220]

In other cases the plaintiff remitted most of the jury's award.[221] In a Shelby County slander case Elijah Mitchell and wife Missouri Mitchell sued James Mitchell, claiming that James Mitchell had called Missouri Mitchell a "base whore" and had said "the Nances have rode her in the corner of the fence many a time." The plaintiffs sought $500 in damages. Lincoln and Anthony Thornton represented the defendant James Mitchell. Lincoln prepared the defensive pleading, which stated that his client was not only not guilty but would prove at trial that Missouri Mitchell "was guilty of fornication with said Elijah before they were married." When the case was tried in May 1852, the jury awarded $500 in damages, of which the plaintiffs remitted $400.[222]

In *Linder v. Fleenor,* Lincoln represented the defendant, who received an adverse judgment of $1,000. John Linder claimed that Abram Fleenor had said that he had lied before a grand jury. Lincoln in his defensive pleading claimed that Linder had lied; Linder had committed "wilful and corrupt perjury" before the grand jury when he testified that Levi Fleenor and Emilion Fleenor had lived together without being married. The jury found for Linder, but Lincoln successfully negotiated an advantageous conclusion of the case: Linder "remitted and released . . . the sum of nine hundred and fifty Dollars of said verdict."[223] Thus, Lincoln was able to mediate and settle some cases even after juries had returned verdicts in favor of plaintiffs.

In *Richey v. Adams,* Lincoln used the threat of an appeal to reduce an adverse jury verdict. In the 1854 De Witt County Circuit Court lawsuit, the plaintiff claimed that Lincoln's client had slandered him by an accusation of false swearing and perjury. The jury agreed and awarded $1,012. Lincoln then filed a motion for new trial, claiming that the jury had expressed a "despotic passion" in its verdict and that his client had not received a fair trial. When the plaintiff remitted $500 of the judgment, the motion for new trial was overruled.[224]

Lincoln also negotiated a settlement after the jury's verdict in *Dungey v. Spencer,* an 1855 slander case in De Witt County. In that case, Lincoln represented the plaintiff William Dungey, who complained that his brother-in-law Joseph Spencer had said that he was "a negro." Spencer introduced deposition testimony that in Giles County, Tennessee (where Dungey had lived previously), "it was the general understanding of the People that [Dungey] was mixed blooded" and "had negro blood in him." The jury, however, found that Spencer had slandered Dungey and awarded $600 in damages. Lawrence Weldon, one of Spencer's attorneys, later recalled that Lincoln "had said that his client did not want to make money out of the suit, so we told Spencer the best thing he could do would be to get Dungey to remit some of the damage and be thankful." Lincoln and his client agreed to "release" $400 of the verdict in exchange for the defendant releasing "all errors which may exist in the record."[225]

In many slander cases, Lincoln was able to "persuade his neighbors to compromise." He settled some by repairing the damage to the plaintiff's reputation in exchange for defendant's attesting to the good reputation of the plaintiff. In other cases, the defendant consented to a large judgment, which the plaintiff agreed to reduce to a much smaller sum. That maneuver also repaired the damage to reputation and settled the case. In others, the successful plaintiff agreed to remit most or all of the jury's award. Lincoln advised that "as a peacemaker the lawyer has a superior opportunity of being a good man." His slander cases show that he often took advantage of such opportunities.

Debt Litigation

Commercial indebtedness in antebellum America was pervasive; most business dealings were based on credit.[226] As a consequence, debt cases formed the bulk of an antebellum lawyer's practice—and Lincoln's was no exception.[227] During Lincoln's legal career, over half of the cases he handled involved debt collection. During his four-year (1837–1841) partnership with John T. Stuart, Stuart and Lincoln handled approximately 700 cases; two-thirds of these cases involved debt collection. Stephen Logan and Lincoln handled over 850 cases during their four-year (1841–1844) partnership; seventy percent of the cases were debt collection. In seventeen years (1844–1861), Lincoln and Herndon handled 3,400 cases; half involved debt collection.[228] During his entire career, Lincoln himself represented creditors 1,319 times and debtors 713 times.

The outcome in a debtor-creditor case was rarely in doubt: defendants lost. They may have lost by default; they may have lost at trial; they may have lost when they confessed judgment; but they lost. The editors of the documentary edition of the Lincoln Legal Papers characterized 3,145 of Lincoln's cases as pertaining to "debtor and creditor." Of these cases, 1,044 resulted in default judgments—the defendant debtor never bothered to appear in court to contest the creditor's claim.[229] Another 786 were dismissed, which probably indicates the cases were settled.[230] Defendants confessed judgment in 214 cases.[231] Defendants won fewer than 200 cases, which is less than eight percent.[232] An example of a rare win by the debtor is *Phares v. Dockum,* an 1858 De Witt County case. After Allen Phares sued Maskell Dockum on three promissory notes for the sale of sheep, Dockum pleaded a failure of consideration because the sheep were diseased. At trial, Dockum—represented by Lincoln and Clifton Moore—was found not liable.[233]

This pattern of debtor losses was established early on in Lincoln's practice. Four cases filed by Stuart & Lincoln in Sangamon County Circuit Court in 1837 are representative. In *Billon v. White,* the plaintiff, Charles Billon, sued on a $143.24 promissory note; the defendant, Lawrence White, failed to answer; the court entered a default judgment against the defendant.[234] In *VonPhul & McGill v. Porter,* the plaintiffs sued on a $100 promissory note. The defendant, William Porter, in open court confessed that he was indebted to VonPhul & McGill for $136, and the court entered judgment for that amount.[235] In *Coffman v. Smith,* the plaintiff, Aaron Coffman, removed a house for the defendant, Thomas P. Smith, and then sued Smith when he wasn't paid. Because Smith had left the state, Stuart & Lincoln first had a writ of attachment issued against his property to fund the inevitable judgment. The court entered a default against Smith and ordered a writ of inquiry to ascertain the amount of damages. After a jury assessed damages at $31.50, the court ordered the sale of the property to satisfy the judgment.[236] In *Buckmaster v. Garrett,* the plaintiff, Thomas H. Buckmaster sued the defendant, Alexander Garrett, on a $352.92 promissory note. The parties apparently settled; the court entered an order stating Garrett withdrew his defensive plea and "by mutual consent and agreement of parties" the case was dismissed, with Garrett paying the costs of Buckmaster bringing suit.[237]

Debtors lost for several reasons. In general, they actually owed the debts. Once in court, the formal law of debtor-creditor relationships and community expectations almost inevitably assured judgments in the creditors' favor. If a creditor was willing to spend the time and expense of a lawsuit, the formal law placed few obstacles in the way once the suit was filed. After a successful judgment was obtained, Illinois law did protect some of the debtor's property—beds, utensils, household furniture, a stove—from seizure. Community expectations also played a role in the creditors' successes at the courthouse. The repayment of commercial debt was a vital part of the region's expanding market economy, which juries apparently recognized.[238]

But even with debt cases, there were some opportunities for the lawyers involved to fashion some compromise. After James Powers lost in the Coles County Justice of the Peace Court in May 1842, he appealed to the circuit court. Once there, Lincoln—it's not clear which side he represented—prepared an agreement between the parties that was read in open court; it stipulated that the $63.71 lower court judgment be affirmed but the execution of the judgment be stayed for one year.[239] This gave the creditors an enforceable judgment and gave the debtor some breathing room. In 1859, Lincoln agreed to a similar proposal. He represented law partners Orville H. Browning and Nehemiah H. Bushnell, who had sued Kersey H. Fell and Franklin Price for assumpsit on a note that Lincoln described as "a sort of 'insolvent fix-up'" with their creditors. After a $370 judgment was entered against the defendants, Fell wrote Lincoln saying that he would gladly pay "that little Judgement" but couldn't and proposed a partial payment of $150 with the remainder to be paid within a year. Lincoln agreed to the partial payment with "execution staid a year from the date of judgement."[240]

As Lincoln's practice and Illinois's economy matured together, some aspects of his debt collection changed while other aspects of these cases had an unvarying sameness. Three related cases provide an example. In March 1856, Stuart & Edwards filed three lawsuits against the Chicago, Alton & St. Louis Railroad in federal district court. Lincoln represented the railroad. In two respects, these cases were different from the debt cases Lincoln had handled nearly two decades earlier. The amounts were larger; the amounts claimed in the declarations totaled over $700,000.[241] The cases were also filed in federal district court, not in a state circuit court where most of Lincoln's earlier debt cases were filed. Because the plaintiffs were from out of state, the suits could be filed in federal court under diversity jurisdiction. Despite these differences, these cases were similar to the earlier debt cases in one important aspect—the results were preordained; Lincoln, as the railroad's attorney, offered little or no resistance. The declarations were filed on March 3; all three cases were tried less than two weeks later. After the parties waived trials by jury, the judge heard the evidence and entered judgment for all three plaintiffs. Brown Brothers recovered $257,524.76; Henry Hotchkiss, $51,496.85; New Haven County Bank, $107,381.39.[242]

Lincoln or his partners were involved in at least eighty-eight petitions to sell real estate to pay debts.[243] In such cases, the administrator of an estate would petition the court for permission to sell the property to pay the deceased's debts.[244] Generally, he could expect the petition to be granted. A guardian ad litem was appointed in each case to represent the interests of the infant heirs to the estate. At least ten times, Lincoln served as guardian ad litem and he never objected to any petition.[245] The answers he prepared merely recite that the guardian ad litem "knows of no reason consistent with the interest" of the heirs that the petition should not be granted.[246] The court's order routinely would direct the administrator to sell certain real estate or "so much thereof as should be sufficient to pay the debts against the estate."[247] That the guardian ad litem never protested any sale indicates a local consensus about the importance of paying one's debts. In fact, all eighty-eight petitions to sell real estate to pay debts were granted by the circuit court.[248] A widow's dower rights to a life interest to one-third of her husband's lands was not affected by these claims from creditors, which undoubtedly made things easier.[249] Unopposed by heirs, Lincoln and the other lawyers involved in these cases enforced the community's expectations and values.

In his early career Lincoln almost exclusively handled cases that were oriented around community-based disputes; in his later practice, he also handled cases that were based on the rise of a national market economy. When faced with local disputes, Lincoln often tried to serve as a mediator or peacemaker. Lincoln was in his element when handling lawsuits based on local disputes; the community orientation of these disputes favored mediation and compromise.

CHAPTER FIVE

In the Matter of Jane, A Woman of Color

In early October 1847, Abraham Lincoln traveled the ninety miles from his hometown of Springfield to Charleston, the county seat of Coles County. In previous years, Lincoln had practiced law often in Coles County, although it was not part of the circuit that he regularly rode.[1] Lincoln handled five circuit court cases that fall. Four of the cases were typical of Lincoln's practice: two slander suits, an assumpsit case alleging a $1,000 debt, and a chancery suit involving a conveyance of land. Lincoln didn't do particularly well with these four cases. He lost both slander suits and his client in the assumpsit case received a $828.57 judgment against him. He had won the chancery case in the previous term when the other side didn't show up; in October a commissioner appointed to divide the lands filed his report and was paid for his services.[2]

Lincoln lost the fifth case too. His participation in this particular case has baffled Lincoln scholars: Lincoln, the president who issued the Emancipation Proclamation, represented Robert Matson, a Kentucky slaveholder, in an unsuccessful attempt to establish property rights to an African-American woman named Jane Bryant and four of her children.[3]

The Matson case has been discussed by Lincoln biographers. J. G. Holland in his 1866 biography was the first to do so; he used Lincoln's representation of Matson to help prove that Lincoln regarded slaves as property under the Constitution. Lincoln recognized the Constitution's protection of slavery "not only in Congress, but on the stump and even in his business." Holland believed that "such a man as Mr. Lincoln would never have consented to act on this case if he had not believed that slaves were recognized as property by the Constitution." Yet Holland also insisted that Lincoln represented Matson poorly because his sympathies were for Jane and her children. Holland was wrong about lawyers in the case necessarily agreeing with the positions they took. Charleston lawyers Orlando Ficklin and Charles Constable, who helped win Jane and her children's freedom, were both originally from southern states and have been labeled by writers as pro-slavery (although it's more likely that they would have been more anti-black and antiabolitionist than pro-slavery). Both lawyers would have thought slaves were property under the Constitution.[4]

For many Lincoln admirers the case is unsettling. They believe that Lincoln was a lifelong opponent of slavery and that Lincoln, as a lawyer, did not represent unjust causes. For them, the case either challenges Lincoln's claim that he "always hated slavery" or raises the possibility that Lincoln fit the worst cultural stereotype of the "hired gun" who did not care whether he represented morally repugnant causes.[5] Many of those who have written about the case have reconciled Lincoln's antislavery convictions and his representation of a slaveholder by claiming that Lincoln was unable to commit himself fully to his client's cause. Some, in fact, suggest that he was "pitiably weak" and threw the case.[6] Still others have dismissed the notion that Lincoln didn't zealously represent Matson. These writers have suggested that Lincoln's spirited representation fulfilled his professional obligations as a lawyer. The modern notion of an adversary ethic for lawyers underlies this defense of Lincoln.[7]

Lincoln has not escaped criticism for his representation of Matson. Lincoln, in Edgar Lee Masters's eyes, was doubly damned: he first chose to represent Matson and then failed to represent him zealously. Masters in his debunking biography believed Lincoln showed he didn't have any moral scruples about whom he represented. Masters thus wrote that "one of the authors of the Stone-Lincoln resolutions which denounced slavery as founded in injustice and bad policy—this Lincoln came to Charleston, and there allied himself with Matson the slave owner to help him with legal ability and eloquence to win back his slaves." Masters, though, also believed that Lincoln later "in feebleness, without wit, stories, humor, invective or logic, got through a miserable performance." Conservative scholar M. E. Bradford used the case as evidence that Lincoln was a hypocrite when he spoke of his "hatred" for slavery.[8]

While Lincoln's representation of Kentucky slaveholder Robert Matson has not gone unnoticed, the accounts of the case are riddled with factual errors and ignorance of key sources, both of which have led to mistakes of interpretation. If we are to make sense of this apparent paradox, many questions must be answered. We need first of all to understand the factual background of the case. Who was Robert Matson and what was he doing with his slaves in a free state? Lincoln's role in the case has been misunderstood because the law that applied to the case hasn't been understood. Did Lincoln even provide competent representation or did he, as suggested by some writers, throw the case away? Lincoln's law practice is often examined in isolation, and the Matson case has been no different. But other northern lawyers faced similar choices. How does Lincoln's experience with the Matson case compare with those of other antebellum lawyers who were involved in similar cases? Lincoln has been criticized for representing Matson. What were the different models of professional responsibility that were prevalent during this period?

Robert Matson in Kentucky

Lincoln's client was Robert Matson from Bourbon County, Kentucky, who, according to one contemporary, was "one of the Kentucky aristocracy."[9] This appears to be an exaggeration. Matson does not appear to have been someone of great wealth or power. Born in Bourbon County in 1796, Matson as a teenager fought during the War of 1812. He was later commissioned as a general in the Kentucky state militia.[10] Running as a Clay Whig, Matson was elected to the Kentucky House of Representatives in 1832 and 1834.[11] For a southern "aristocrat," he owned very few slaves.

Slaveholding was different in Kentucky from elsewhere in the South: slaveownership was less concentrated than in most other slave states, with only Missouri having a smaller number of slaves per owner than Kentucky.[12] Slaveholding in Bourbon County was different from in the rest of Kentucky—it was more like the Deep South.[13] But Matson appears to have been merely an average slaveowner, at least in terms of the number of slaves he owned. In 1840, he owned seven slaves; by comparison, the average Kentucky slaveowner (in 1850) owned five.[14]

Matson was a frequent litigant in the Bourbon County Circuit Court. The portrait of Matson that emerges from those court records is that of someone who constantly had money problems, who did not get along with his brother, and whose slaves had tried to escape. Matson was sued thirty-three times in Bourbon County.[15] Most of the lawsuits against him were for debt. I was able to identify fourteen lawsuits filed against him from 1823 to 1846: thirteen were over unpaid notes[16] ranging from $1,221.29 to $81.20.

Matson was a plaintiff at least eight times from 1823 to 1842.[17] He fought with his brother Thomas and sued him three times. The earliest suit against his brother was for slander; he accused his brother of saying that "Nancy Mallory had had another child and Bob Matson killed it & buried it secretly & privately." The case settled when Thomas Matson stated for the record that he had never said Robert was a murderer: "he believes that Robert had no knowledge of Nancy Mallory having had a child or having murdered it."[18]

His brother also accused Robert of improperly influencing their father while he was dying. In 1826, Robert Matson and Nicholas Talbott, as executors of the estate of James Matson, sued Thomas Matson in chancery to get him to convey land.[19] Thomas in a deposition in that case asked a witness whether Thomas had complained that his father James was a "very old and infirm man" who had made several wills and that "all he did was under the influence of Robt Matson & Nancy Mallory."[20] Thomas, in turn, sued the executors of his father's estate, his brother Robert and Nicholas Talbot, for $12,000, pleading a "covenant broken."[21] In another 1827 suit, Matson sued his brother Thomas in trespass for $500, claiming Thomas tore down the fence that divided their property and "trampled on, consumed & spoiled the grass & wheat therein growing."[22]

At least four of Matson's cases involved slaves. The background of these cases foreshadows the events in Illinois; it shows that Matson's slaves had tried to escape before and that he had sold slaves before. Although such escape attempts apparently were quite rare in antebellum Kentucky, Matson inspired flight. Three of Matson's slaves tried to run to freedom in 1827.[23] In a later chancery suit, the pugnacious and tightfisted misanthrope sought to overturn a $20 award that Jesse Todd had received for apprehending some of Matson's slaves "who had Runaway & were endeavoring to make escape to the Ohio." Matson smugly claimed that Todd didn't deserve the reward; Matson, in fact, had anticipated "the flight of his Negroes" and had "directed his Overseer to keep a look out & pursue." Three of Matson's slaves (two women and a child) subsequently escaped with two male slaves belonging to other masters. In Augusta, Todd had helped recapture one of Matson's slaves; but the other two "had crossed the river" and were caught by others. Matson claimed that he had already paid his "portion of the reward & expenses which accrued at Augusta."[24]

Another series of lawsuits raised questions about whether Matson had the right to sell a slave. In an 1835 replevin suit, Peter Clarkson claimed Matson had taken "a negro man slave named Neptune" with a value of $800 and had unjustly detained him.[25] Matson apparently had obtained Neptune after executing on a judgment he had received against Clarkson; Matson then sold Neptune for $990 to Matthew Hughes.[26] Clarkson next sued Matthew Hughes and Otto Hughes in detinue "for the detention of a negro man slave named Neptune." Matson then hired attorney James S. Matson for the "preparation & prosecution of the Defence" of the suit because he "was concerned & interested as vendor & the warrantor of the title" to Neptune.[27] Matson stiffed his attorney on his bill; James Matson later sued him for $500 in legal fees. There was yet another suit over unpaid legal fees arising from Clarkson's lawsuits when, in 1846, John S. Williams, executor of the estate of attorney Thomas Elliott, sued Matson.[28]

Robert Matson and Jane Bryant in Illinois

In 1836, Matson bought some farmland in Coles County in central Illinois, which he named Black Grove.[29] Owning farms in both slaveholding Kentucky and free Illinois, Matson divided his time between the two. Records show that Matson lived and voted in both states. According to the

1840 census for Bourbon County, Matson owned five slaves under the age of ten, one aged between ten and twenty-five, and one aged between twenty-six and thirty-six. An 1846 Bourbon County lawsuit against Matson stated that he was "absent from the State of Kentucky" but owned "about sixty acres of land in Bourbon County."[30] Matson's mistress, one Mary Corbin, also stayed at Black Grove, and in Matson's absence ran the farm. Matson and Corbin had four illegitimate children; the oldest was born around the time that Matson bought Black Grove, which suggests that Matson may have purchased the land in Illinois to hide his mistress and illegitimate children from respectable society back in Bourbon County. The 1850 census lists four children for Robert and Mary Matson: Mary, age 14; Robert, age 12; Mildred, age 4; and, Henrietta, age 3 months. In 1850, Matson was 54 years old and Mary was 32.[31]

According to several accounts, each spring Matson brought a few of his slaves from Kentucky to Illinois to harvest crops, and each fall he returned these slaves to Kentucky.[32] Matson purportedly used different slaves each year to ensure that his slaves "would not lose their legal status as slaves or acquire any of the rights of freemen by having been in the State of Illinois."[33] These accounts seem doubtful because Matson, at least in the 1840 census, only had two slaves over the age of ten.[34] Matson may have brought his slaves to Illinois to evade creditors in Kentucky; the newspaper for Bourbon County often contained notices of judicial sales of slaves.[35]

Matson, in any event, allowed one Anthony Bryant to stay at Black Grove. One of the abolitionists who later assisted the Bryants referred to Anthony as a "freeman" in an October 1847 letter.[36] In August 1845, Bryant was joined by his wife, Jane, and four of her children.[37] Matson believed that Jane and her children remained his slaves in Illinois. Jane worked on the farm as a housekeeper. Jane, who was described as a "mulatto," may have been Matson's niece, as it was rumored that her father was Matson's brother.[38]

In the summer of 1847, Corbin, while Matson was away in Kentucky, told one of Matson's slaves that Matson now planned "to remove the children to his residence in Kentucky, and leave the old people childless in Illinois."[39] In other accounts, Corbin allegedly said that Matson planned to take all the slaves, including Jane and her children, back to Kentucky and sell them.[40] The sale of slaves was the most common method of disrupting slave families in Kentucky.[41]

Jane Bryant as "Runaway Slave": The Proceedings in the Coles County Justice Court

In any event, Jane's family, like so many other slave families, would be broken up. It was time for Jane and Anthony to act. Although Jane and her family had arrived in Illinois two years earlier, it would have been foolish to run away earlier—the laws of Illinois were exceedingly harsh for free blacks and Jane risked being kidnaped and subsequently being sold in a slave state.[42] While few slaves tried to escape to freedom from Kentucky, slaves who traveled in a free state were given opportunities to learn about freedom or to escape.[43] Their stay in Illinois provided Anthony and Jane both opportunities. Both Anthony and Jane believed that "by being brought from Kentucky, a slave state, to Illinois, a free state, she and her children became free."[44] Anthony, who was a Methodist lay preacher, first sought help from local white Methodists, who turned him away. He next approached Matt Ashmore, an abolitionist hotelkeeper in nearby Oakland. Ashmore was sympathetic and offered his assistance. He recruited fellow abolitionist Hiram Rutherford, a doctor originally from Pennsylvania, and together they hired Charleston lawyer Orlando B. Ficklin. The Kentucky-born Ficklin had served with Lincoln in the Illinois legislature in the 1830s and, at the time of the Matson case, was a Democratic representative to Congress.[45] Ficklin later remembered his clients as "the most thorough-faced abolitionists of that day."[46] Ashmore and Rutherford told Anthony to return to Black Grove. At some point, Anthony brought Jane and her children to Ashmore.[47]

Anthony and Jane somehow overcame what Lincoln later identified as the two stumbling blocks for slaves seeking freedom in a "free" jurisdiction: ignorance of their legal rights and lack of legal assistance. When discussing the introduction of slaves into the Nebraska Territory, Lincoln in 1854 noted that it "is good book-law" that slaves became free when they entered a jurisdiction that didn't have positive law that supported slavery, but it "is not the rule of actual practice." Lincoln described what would happen in "actual practice": "A white man takes his slave to Nebraska now; who will inform the negro that he is free? Who will take him before court to test the question of his freedom? In ignorance of his legal emancipation, he is kept chopping, splitting and plowing."[48]

Jane and Anthony at some point became aware they were possibly free under Illinois law, and they were able to obtain legal assistance. Whether Jane and Anthony sought out Ashmore and Rutherford because they believed they might be free under Illinois law or whether Ashmore and Rutherford had told them this when they met the two abolitionists isn't clear. But by the time the legal proceedings had begun, Jane surely wasn't ignorant of her possible "legal emancipation"; she believed she was free. Matson didn't meekly give up his claim to Jane and her children. When he discovered that they were missing, he began legal proceedings to have them returned to him. On August 17, 1847, he applied for a warrant under the federal fugitive slave law before William Gilman, the justice of the peace in Coles County. The 1793 federal act permitted a slaveowner to prove title to a runaway slave by presenting an affidavit or oral testimony to a county magistrate who would issue a certificate entitling the slave-owner to return the "fugitive from labour, to the state or territory from which he or she fled."[49] Matson swore in his affidavit that "by the request of said negroes," he brought Jane and her children to Illinois "on a temporary sojourn with the intention of returning" to Kentucky. They were "by the laws of Kentucky . . . his slaves" and owed him "labor and service in the state of Kentucky for and during their natural lives."[50] His slaves, however, had refused to return to their lawful service in Kentucky. Gilman commanded the sheriff to bring Jane and her children to appear before him to answer Matson's charges.[51]

Matson hired Usher F. Linder, a Kentucky-born Charleston lawyer, to represent him. Six years earlier in Alton, Illinois, Linder's fiery oratory had helped incite antiabolitionist sentiment, leading to the murder of newspaper editor Elijah Lovejoy.[52] After Lovejoy's death, Linder first helped prosecute those who had tried to protect Lovejoy's warehouse against the mob and then he helped defend those indicted for Lovejoy's murder. At the first trial, Linder spoke of the danger presented by "the African" with "his passions excited by [abolitionist] doctrine," a danger he compared to being "in the fangs of a wild beast."[53] Jane and her children were brought before Gilman on the "charge of being runaway slaves and the property of Robt Matson." The hearing lasted two days with Linder representing Matson and Ficklin representing Jane and her children. At its conclusion, Gilman did not issue a certificate but committed Jane and her children to the custody of the sheriff.[54]

No record of that hearing exists. Duncan T. McIntyre, a lawyer from Charleston, wrote an account of the hearing nearly sixty years later that was apparently based upon Rutherford's recollections.[55] According to McIntyre, Linder argued that Matson had never intended to free Jane and her children by bringing them to Illinois, but only had intended to "keep them here temporarily and return them to Kentucky at his convenience." The legal domicile of Jane and her children was Kentucky and the law of that domicile governed the case. Ficklin, in turn, argued that, although Jane and her children may have been Matson's slaves in Kentucky, they became free when Matson voluntarily brought them to Illinois. McIntyre also claimed that Gilman, who was "a pro-slavery man," held that he did not have jurisdiction over the case only because a large crowd had gathered outside and "it was plainly evident that in case the court should order Jane and her children back into slavery, desperate measures of resistance would surely be resorted to."[56] Ficklin did not mention any such crowd in his account of the case.[57]

It is possible, rather, that Gilman held he did not have jurisdiction because he, in fact, had none.[58] Although Matson had proceeded under the 1793 fugitive slave law, that law was inapplicable.[59] By swearing in his affidavit that he voluntarily had brought Jane and her children to Illinois and by presenting evidence at the hearing to that effect, Matson took the case outside the ambit of the fugitive slave law. The fugitive slave clause of the federal constitution applied to any "person held to Service or Labour in one State, under the Laws there of, *escaping into* another."[60] The 1793 congressional statute also was limited to a "person held to labor" who had *escaped into* another state.[61] State and federal courts repeatedly had held that the fugitive slave clause did not apply where slaveowners voluntarily brought slaves into a free state.[62] Jane and her children had not escaped into Illinois from Kentucky but, as Matson freely admitted, had been brought there voluntarily by him.

Gilman, in any event, did not rule whether Jane and her children were slave or free. He only found that they were "Runaway Slaves Ackording to the Law in Relation to the Runaway Law of the State of Illinois." Gilman then committed Jane and her children to the custody of L. R. Hutchason, the sheriff of Coles County, to "safly keep them untill discharged."[63] Sheriff Hutchason, in turn, posted a notice that "there was five Negroes taken up and committed to the Coles County Jail . . . to be dealt with as Runaway Negroes." The sheriff also described the "five Negroes":

> one Woman a Bright Mulatto 40 years old and calls her name Jane Briant[,] one about 14 years old a bright Mulatto named Mary Catherine[,] one about 12 years old a bright Mulatto named Sally Ann[,] and about 5 years old a bright Mulatto named Mary Jane[,] one about 3 years old named Robert Noah.[64]

In October, the sheriff posted another notice, this time proclaiming that he was ready to hire out for one month to the highest bidder "one Negro Woman[,] three Negro Girls and one Negro Boy."[65] The sheriff did not say what kind of work the three-year-old was ready to do.

Gilman and Sheriff Hutchason were dutifully following the provisions of the Illinois "Black Code."[66] This code was how Illinois had long regulated the presence of blacks within its borders. When Illinois was part of the Indiana Territory, territorial laws accommodated a system of slavery thinly disguised as indentured servitude.[67] These territorial laws later were adopted by the Illinois legislature.[68] While the Illinois Constitution of 1818 stated that "neither slavery nor involuntary servitude shall hereafter be introduced into this state," it also allowed for indentured servitude if the person entering the indenture was "in a state of perfect freedom" and the indenture was for "*bona fide* consideration." Section 2 of Article XI permitted slaves to be hired out in the "salt-works near Shawneetown" for up to a year at a time, but only until 1825.[69] Section 3 said that any person "bound to service by contract or indenture in virtue of the laws of Illinois Territory" was to be "held to specific performance of their contracts or indentures" and serve out the time remaining on the indenture. This status was inheritable: the children "born of such persons, negroes, or mulattoes" would become free at 21 years, if male, and at 18 years, if female.

In 1819, the Illinois legislature also took steps to discourage the immigration of free blacks into the state by requiring blacks to produce certificates of freedom.[70] In 1829, the Illinois legislature added more restrictive measures, including requiring free blacks to post bonds.[71] Illinois borrowed the idea of certificates and bonds from Ohio and Indiana, which required any "black or mulatto" person settling within state boundaries to produce a $500 bond in Indiana and both a certificate of freedom and $500 bond in Ohio.[72] White Illinoisans, prompted by hatred and fear of African-Americans, intended their version of these restrictive laws to discourage the immigration of free blacks into Illinois.[73]

The Black Code in effect when Jane was deemed a "runaway" provided that "no black or mulatto" could reside in Illinois without a "certificate of freedom" and without having provided a one-thousand-dollar bond to ensure that the free black would not become "a charge" to a county.[74] Any black or mulatto who did not possess a certificate of freedom was "a runaway slave or servant." Any Illinois resident could take "such black or mulatto person" before a justice of the peace, who would then commit the "runaway" to the custody of the sheriff of the county. Because Jane and her children did not have certificates of freedom, they were runaways under the statute. Once a supposed runaway was committed to the sheriff's custody, the sheriff was required to place a notice in a newspaper "stating a description of the most remarkable features of the supposed runaway." The sheriff then was required to hire out the supposed runaway "for the best price he could get" for one year. If no owner appeared to substantiate a claim within that year, then the supposed runaway would be considered a free person.[75]

The initial fallout from the fugitive slave hearing was a criminal charge brought against Matson. The day after Gilman had committed Jane and her children to the sheriff's custody, Matson was charged for "living in an open state of fornication" with Mary Corbin.[76] The timing of this charge was not coincidental: the justice of the peace who issued the warrant was Samuel C. Ashmore, Matt Ashmore's brother.[77] Samuel does not appear to have been acting as a neutral magistrate in this matter. In October Samuel, along with his brother and Rutherford, put up the bond to secure the Bryants' certificate of freedom.[78] The Ashmores intended the fornication charge to encourage Matson's return to Kentucky and to highlight the relationship between slavery and immorality.[79] In May 1848, Matson apparently was found guilty and fined $30.[80]

Legal Proceedings in Coles County Circuit Court

In the fall of 1847, the controversy over Jane and her children next moved to the circuit court where the parties filed three related actions. In September, Matson sued Ashmore and Rutherford under a provision of the

Black Code that prescribed fines for anyone "harboring" a negro or mulatto who did not have a certificate of freedom or who had not given the required bond.[81] Matson thus sued both abolitionists for $2,500 (a statutory penalty of five hundred dollars each for Jane and her children).[82] Ashmore and Rutherford were not dissuaded; they were "determined to test the right of the negroes to their freedom by writ of Habeas Corpus."[83] In October, Ashmore applied for a writ on behalf of Jane and her children, claiming that Jane and her children had been "restrained from the exercise of their liberty." They were "by virtue of the laws of the State of Illinois, free persons owing services to no person or persons."[84] In another pleading filed the same day, Ashmore explained the predicament of the five "runaways" in the county jail. The petition stated that Matson had brought Jane and her children to Illinois in 1845. Two years later, "believing that they were free under the laws and constitution of the state of Illinois," they left Matson's farm "to take steps to secure their freedom and to comply with the laws to free negroes." Matson, "desiring to recapture them," then "proceeded under the laws of Congress by affidavitt to reclaim them as fugitives." But they were "free and as freeman not liable to recaption and surrender into the custody of their former master."[85]

The petition for a writ of habeas corpus was to be heard by William Wilson, the chief justice of the state supreme court. Each member of the supreme court also rode the circuit; Wilson was the judge who sat on the trial bench in Coles County. He asked Samuel E. Treat, a fellow justice on the supreme court who was trying cases in nearby Edgar County, to hear the case with him. Wilson wanted Treat to join him, Ficklin believed, because the case was of "vital importance . . . involving as it did the question of African slavery."[86]

Enter Lincoln. Before the hearing on the habeas corpus petition, Lincoln joined Usher Linder in representing Matson. The circumstances surrounding Lincoln's retainer by Matson are not clear. Accounts differ about whether Matson had hired Lincoln before Lincoln arrived in the county seat of Charleston. In McIntyre's account, Matson rode to Springfield and retained Lincoln before any legal proceedings had begun.[87] This is unlikely because Linder, not Lincoln, represented Matson at the August hearing. It is more likely that Lincoln first became involved in the case in October. It is possible, some scholars have maintained, that Lincoln went to Charleston in October 1847 because he anticipated being retained in the Matson case. These scholars note that Lincoln, who had been elected to his only term in Congress, was preparing for his trip to Washington that fall and had failed to attend court in his regular circuit in either Vermilion or Edgar County the two previous weeks.[88] But he appears not to have had any cases pending that fall in Vermilion or Edgar County; he may have decided that he didn't want to take on any new business in those counties before leaving for Washington. In contrast, he had three pending cases in Coles County.[89]

Lincoln was capable of soliciting business if he thought the case would be significant, as he would show six years later in the McLean County tax case.[90] In that case, Lincoln was offered employment by the would-be plaintiff, the Illinois Central Railroad. After receiving the offer, Lincoln wrote the county clerk of McLean County because he believed the county had a prior right to his services, provided it chose "to secure me a fee something near such as I can get from the other side." He confessed that he did not want to miss "the largest law question that can now be got up in the State."[91] The case of Jane and her children also would have attracted considerable attention. Indeed, it was important enough for the Cincinnati-based *Western Law Journal* to publish Justice Wilson's opinion.[92]

But if Lincoln went to Charleston because he wanted to participate in this important case, he did not have to represent Matson. There was another side—the side of freedom—in this controversy. Lincoln, in fact, may have been approached by Rutherford, who asked him to defend the lawsuit that Matson had brought against him. Years later Rutherford insisted they had such a conversation in Charleston. After Rutherford told Lincoln the "story of my troubles" and asked Lincoln to represent him, Lincoln initially declined because he was already representing Matson.

> At length, and with apparent reluctance, he answered that he could not defend me, because he had already counseled with, in Matson's interest, and was therefore under professional obligations to represent the latter unless released. This was a grievous disappointment, and irritated me into expressions more or less bitter in tone. He seemed to feel this, and even though he endeavored in his plausible way to reconcile me to the proposition that, as a lawyer, he must represent and be faithful to those who counsel with and employ him, I appeared not to be convinced.

A few hours later, according to Rutherford, Lincoln sent word that "he had sent for the man who had approached him in Matson's behalf, and if they came to no more decisive terms than at first he would probably be able to represent me." Lincoln soon sent a second message: that "he could now easily and consistently free himself from Matson" and represent Rutherford. Rutherford rebuffed Lincoln because "his pride was up," and instead hired Charles H. Constable.

Rutherford's purported recollection may indicate the parameters of client loyalty in this period. Lincoln told Rutherford that he had to continue to represent Matson because of "professional obligations" yet he also was willing to represent Rutherford if Matson released him. If Lincoln did try to be released from his obligation, then he may have felt some uneasiness in representing Matson after talking with Rutherford. Whatever uneasiness he may have felt, it wasn't enough to cause him to withdraw from the case.[93]

The Law of Slavery in a Free State

For a "free" state, Illinois had a complicated law of slavery. If, on the eve of trial, Lincoln had reviewed this law, he would have discovered that the supreme court and legislature had crafted a variety of rules that addressed many different situations: the status of slaves introduced into the "Illinois country" by French settlers; the status of African-Americans under long-term contracts of indentured servitude; the status the children of those who had served under indentured servitude; and the status of slaves brought voluntarily into the state by their masters.[94]

Slavery had existed in Illinois long before it became a state; the Illinois Constitution of 1818 permitted slavery to persist after statehood merely by declaiming that "neither slavery nor involuntary servitude shall *hereafter* be introduced into this State."[95] This "hereafter" language didn't affect slaves who were already in the state; consequently, slavery in Illinois could persist for years.[96] The wording at least prevented the status of a slave from being inherited; the child of a slave born after 1818 could not be a slave because that would "hereafter" introduce slavery into the state.

The inheritability of slavery nevertheless became an issue with the "French slaves." French settlers, by 1752, had brought as many as 1,000 slaves to the Illinois Country. The descendants of the French settlers believed their rights to slaves were protected when Virginia ceded the territory to the United States.[97] This relatively narrow claim was defeated in 1845 in *Jarrot v. Jarrot* when the Illinois Supreme Court rejected the notion that the "descendants of the slaves of the old French settlers of the Illinois country" born since the adoption of the Northwest Ordinance could be slaves. The court found that the cession by Virginia didn't render void the prohibition of slavery in the Northwest Ordinance: "all persons of color, who were in this country before and since the passage of the ordinance of 1787, and their descendants, usually known by the appellation of 'French negroes,' are free."[98]

The Illinois Supreme Court in *Jarrot v. Jarrot* didn't address the status of "colored persons" under territorial contracts and indentures. The Illinois Constitution and the Black Code specifically addressed indentures.[99] The courts initially tolerated the quasi-slavery of lengthy indentures because those indentures were supported by these enactments. In the first case that addressed the status of an indentured servant, the court in 1826 approved an indenture from 1814 that had a forty-year term. The court in *Phoebe, a Woman of Color v. Jay* was faced with the conflict between the Northwest Ordinance, which flatly prohibited slavery and indentured servitude, and the territorial laws of Indiana and Illinois, which accommodated both. The court found that the indenture would be void because it violated the Northwest Ordinance except the Northwest Ordinance was itself abrogated when Congress permitted Illinois to become a state with a constitution that "requires that registered and indentured servants are bound to serve." Congress thus consented "to the abrogation of so much of the ordinance as was in opposition to our constitution."[100] In an 1828 case, the supreme court held that "indentured and registered servants" were "goods and chattels" that could be sold by court order to satisfy judgments. In 1843, the court held that an indenture was assignable. Lincoln may have been well aware of the use of such indentures—his partner, John T. Stuart, wrote an indenture in January 1839 for "Judah, a girl of color."[101]

In other cases involving indentured servants, the Illinois Supreme Court would carefully scrutinize the indenture to ensure that it complied with the requirements of the statute. In one case, it invalidated one indenture for not being registered in a timely manner; in another, it held that "the children of registered negroes and mulattoes" were unquestionably free.[102]

The case of Jane and her children involved the status of slaves brought voluntarily by their master into a free state. Here, for all involved, the two most important precedents were a British case, *Somerset v. Stewart* (1772), and a Massachusetts case, *Commonwealth v. Aves* (1836). Somerset was a "slave to Mr. Stewart, in Virginia" who was brought by Stewart to England. When Stewart was ready to leave England, he forcibly put Somerset on a vessel. A writ of habeas corpus was filed that challenged Stewart's right to detain Somerset. William Murray, Lord Mansfield, the chief justice of King's Bench, held that Stewart had no rights to Somerset that the laws of England recognized. In a passage that had a profound effect on antislavery jurisprudence in America, Lord Mansfield wrote:

> The state of slavery is of such a nature, that it is incapable of being introduced on any reasons, moral or political; but only positive law, which preserves its force long after the reasons, occasion, and time itself from whence it was created, is erased from memory: It's so odious, that nothing can be suffered to support it but positive law.

Mansfield concluded that "whatever inconveniences, therefore, may follow from a decision, I cannot say this case is allowed or approved by the law of England; and therefore the black must be discharged."[103] Sixty years later, Chief Justice Lemuel Shaw in *Commonwealth v. Aves* applied the *Somerset* holding in a Massachusetts case.[104] In *Aves*, Shaw held that a six-year-old slave named Med from Louisiana was freed when brought voluntarily by her mistress to Massachusetts for a visit with the slaveowner's relatives. Shaw stated the issue in the case as follows:

> [W]hether a citizen of any one of the United States, where negro slavery is established by law, coming into this State, for any temporary purpose of business or pleasure, staying some time, but not acquiring a domicile here, who brings a slave with him as a personal attendant, may restrain such slave of his liberty during his continuance here, and convey him out of this state on his return, against his consent.

Shaw noted that slavery was illegal under the constitution and laws of Massachusetts; the state Massachusetts had no positive law to support slavery. He held that the right to property in a slave, based on the law of Louisiana, could not be extended to Massachusetts. This extraterritorial application of the law would be "wholly repugnant to our laws, entirely inconsistent with our policy and our fundamental principles."[105]

Shaw also noted the inapplicability of the fugitive slave clause of the federal constitution under the facts of the case and discussed the historical context of the fugitive slave clause. When the federal constitution was formed, some states permitted slavery and considered it economically essential while other states had abolished slavery. One "party to this compact" wanted to enlarge and secure the rights of slaveowners while the other wanted to "limit and restrain them." The purpose of the fugitive slave clause "was intended to secure future peace and harmony, and to fix as precisely as language could do it, the limit to which the rights of one party should be exercised within the territory of the other." The "rights and powers of slave owners" could not be exercised in Massachusetts as a general rule, but the federal constitution limited the "operation of this general rule." The fugitive slave clause and the 1793 statute, however, "manifestly refer to the case of a slave escaping from a State where he owes service or labor, into another State or Territory." The fugitive slave clause could not be applied "to the case of a slave who has not fled from the State, but has been brought into the State by his master."[106]

Unlike the Massachusetts court, other antebellum courts adjusted the *Somerset* doctrine to accommodate the existence of slavery within a federal system. Both northern and southern appellate courts had little difficulty in ruling that slaves became free when brought into a free state by a slaveowner who had changed their domicile to the free state.[107] Southern courts generally were willing to accept the doctrine as it applied to slaves domiciled by their masters on free soil; northern courts generally agreed not to apply the doctrine to instances of slaveowners traveling through their states with their slaves. This distinction, recognized by northern courts and legislatures, represented a sectional compromise over the radical antislavery implications of *Somerset* and *Aves*.[108]

The courts in Illinois soon faced one issue that Shaw had avoided in *Aves*: whether transit through a free state would serve to emancipate a slave. Shaw had reserved the question "where an owner of a slave in one state is *bonâ fide* removing to another state where slavery is allowed, and in so doing necessarily passes through a free state," noting that Massachusetts's "geographical position exempts us from the probable necessity of considering such a case, and we give no opinion respecting it."[109] Geography forced Illinois courts to face this exact issue. An 1843 prosecution of abolitionist Owen Lovejoy for harboring fugitive slaves ended in an acquittal in the circuit court when Judge John Dean Caton, following the reasoning of *Somersett* and *Aves,* described how "slavery can only exist by the authority of positive law." Caton also concluded:

> By the Constitution of this State, slavery cannot exist here. If, therefore, a
> master voluntarily bring his slave within this State, he comes from that mo-
> ment free, and if he escape from his master while in this State, it is not an es-
> cape from slavery, but is going where a free man has a right to go; and the har-
> boring of such a person is no offense against our law; but the tie which binds
> the slave to his master can only be severed by the voluntary act of the latter.[110]

Although the master had been in transit through Illinois, Caton did not recognize any exception for transit through a free state.

Caton's unequivocal acceptance of *Aves* was not joined by his colleagues on the supreme court. Shortly after Lovejoy's acquittal, the Illinois Supreme Court recognized a distinction between a slave's brief transit through the state and a change in domicile.[111] It was at this point that the supreme court decided the law relevant to Jane. In *Willard v. People* (1843) the court held that a "slave does not become free by the Constitution of Illinois by coming into the State for the mere purpose of passage through it."[112] Jacksonville abolitionist Julius A. Willard had appealed his conviction under an Illinois statute that prohibited harboring or secreting a slave. On appeal, he argued that he didn't harbor a slave because when the African-American woman became free, she entered Illinois while traveling from Louisiana to Kentucky with her master. The court admitted that if the slave "upon entering our territory, although for a mere transit to another state, becomes free under the constitution," then Willard could not be guilty of harboring a slave.[113]

Willard's attorneys argued that "slavery is an artificial condition, created against natural right and justice; and cannot exist except by positive law." They cited both *Aves* and *Somerset.* They asserted that "slavery is local and cannot exist beyond the jurisdiction creating it." If a slave "is taken from a slave state to a free state, he resumes all his natural rights, and becomes a freeman." The state constitution declared that "all men are born equally free and independent"; slavery, therefore, was "repugnant to the constitution of the state, and contrary to public policy." This prohibition of slavery also "restrains the operation of slave laws of other states." The rule of comity, according to Willard's lawyers, did not apply to the case of slave property because comity only protects property that was "universally treated and recognized as property." Property rights derived from natural rights were worthy of protection, but "property in slaves owes its origin and existence solely to local law, and has no foundation in nature."[114]

The attorney general of Illinois, J. A. McDougall, responded to the arguments of Willard's lawyers. He asserted that the Illinois constitutional provision was intended to prevent the legislature from establishing the institution of slavery, not to prevent slaves from accompanying their masters in trips across the state. As for *Commonwealth v. Aves,* if Massachusetts had a similar law, the Massachusetts court would have held differently. McDougall also argued that someone's status—whether slave or free—was governed by the law of that person's domicile. The relationship between a master and a slave could not change "until they acquire a new domicile, and are operated upon by different and averse laws."[115] McDougall contrasted the facts in *Willard* with the facts in two cases that upheld the emancipation of slaves brought into free states. In *Rankin v. Lydia* (1820), the Kentucky Supreme Court rejected the argument that there is no difference between a slaveowner passing or sojourning in Indiana and one establishing a residence there. Thus, when Lydia's master brought his slave Lydia with him to Indiana and remained there for seven years, she became free. The court noted that while Lydia would be entitled to her freedom, a slave with a master traveling through the state would be unaffected.[116] In *Lunsford v. Coquillon* (1824), the Louisiana Supreme Court held that a slave became free when her owner moved from Kentucky to Ohio intending to reside there. The Ohio Constitution "emancipates, ipso facto, such slaves whose owners remove them into that state."[117] Because of this case law, McDougall narrowly tailored his argument to address only slaves in transit. He knew better than to argue against cases that held that slaves became free when they were brought into a free jurisdiction by their master who had intended to remain there.

The Illinois Supreme Court rejected Willard's appeal and affirmed his conviction. The court recognized a distinction between a slave's brief transit through the state and a change in domicile, holding that a "slave does not become free by the Constitution of Illinois by coming into the State for the mere purpose of passage through it." In his majority opinion, Justice Walter B. Scates concluded that not respecting "the right of transit with a slave" would produce "great and irremediable evils, and alienation of kind and fraternal feeling, which should characterize the American brotherhood, and tend greatly to weaken, if not to destroy the common bond of union amongst us, and our nationality of character, interest, and feeling." Thousands of southern slaveowners had depended upon "free and safe passage with their slaves across our territory, to and from Missouri." Scates believed that recognizing this right of free and safe passage did not violate the Illinois Constitution's prohibition against slavery because it did not introduce slavery in Illinois.[118]

Justice Samuel D. Lockwood, who had ruled against Willard in the circuit court, filed a concurring opinion. Lockwood noted that Julia, the slave whom Willard had harbored, was not a fugitive; consequently, she was not affected by the federal constitution's provisions on fugitives from labor. He also noted that under Illinois law "every person in this state, without any regard to the color of his skin, is presumed to be free." How then, Lockwood asked, did the court find that Julia remained a slave while in Illinois?

Lockwood believed that "the answer is that her case is taken out of the operation of the general rule by the law of comity." The courts of Illinois, under the laws of comity, had the discretion to determine "what laws of other states shall be recognised and enforced." Illinois courts should enforce the slave laws of these states because of "the geographic position of Illinois, as well as to the relations we sustain to our sister states." The courts of Illinois should protect the owner of slaves while passing through the state.[119]

Lincoln Argues for Slavery

Thus, under the *Willard* decision announced only four years earlier, Jane and her children would have remained Matson's slaves only if their stay in Illinois was temporary enough to be classified as a "sojourn" or a "transit," instead of a stay long enough to be considered a permanent change in "domicile."[120] Orlando B. Ficklin later explained that this distinction "was the hinge on which the case turned." Ficklin wrote: "If only crossing the state that act did not free them, but if located by the consent of the owner, even temporarily, that would emancipate them." Matson had understood the importance of this distinction between a brief stay and a change in domicile. Ficklin remembered that Matson "relied upon the fact that it was not Matson's intention to have the negroes remain permanently in Illinois." Each year that Matson brought his slaves to Illinois to work at his farm he would publicly declare in the presence of his white overseer that the slaves "were not to remain permanently in Illinois, but to be taken back to Kentucky."[121] Matson's formal ceremony of announcing his intent indicates that he may have sought legal advice before bringing slaves into a free state. Matson intended his legalistic maneuver to ensure some safety, but it would fail him in Jane's case. Jane and her children were not like the other slaves that Matson brought to Illinois each year to harvest crops; they had remained in Illinois for over two years.[122]

At the hearing on the petition for a writ of habeas corpus, Constable and Ficklin argued that Jane and her children had been "manumitted by the voluntary act of their master." They dismissed Matson's declaration of his intent as a self-serving statement that had no more significance than "any other declaration or verbal statements made in his own interests." The two lawyers asserted that the Northwest Ordinance and the Illinois Constitution prohibited slavery in Illinois and also supplied the court with English and American precedents.[123] Constable also quoted from Irish lawyer John Philpot Curran's then famous (and unsuccessful) 1794 defense of Hamilton Rowan, who had been charged with seditious libel. Curran had proclaimed that the "spirit of the British law" makes "liberty commensurate with, and inseparable from, British soil; which proclaims even to the stranger and the sojourner, the moment he sets his foot upon British earth, that the ground on which he treads is holy, and consecrated by the genius of UNIVERSAL

EMANCIPATION." When this stranger or sojourner "touched the sacred soil of Britain, the altar and the God sink together in the dust; his soul walks abroad in her own majesty; his body swells beyond the measure of his chains, that burst from around him; and he stands redeemed, regenerated, and disenthralled, by the irresistible genius of UNIVERSAL EMANCIPATION."[124] Lincoln, according to Ficklin, winced when Constable quoted Curran.[125] Ficklin didn't speculate about whether Lincoln winced because the argument landed a solid blow or because Lincoln felt personally convicted by Constable quoting Curran's speech.

Linder and Lincoln argued that Matson's declaration controlled the question of intent. Linder, according to Ficklin, also asserted that slavery enjoyed constitutional protection in every state a master ventured into with his slaves. Eleven years later, Lincoln would bitterly criticize the "logical conclusion" of the *Dred Scott* decision: "what Dred Scott's master might lawfully do with Dred Scott, in the free state of Illinois, every other master may lawfully do with any other *one,* or one *thousand* slaves, in Illinois, or in any other free state."[126] But in Charleston in 1847 Lincoln was allied with a lawyer whose argument, if successful, could have made Illinois a slave state. Lincoln, however, "did not endorse the extreme propositions of General Linder, but frankly admitted that if his client . . . had brought his slaves to Illinois and placed them on his farm as a permanent settlement, there to remain independently, that it worked out and effected their emancipation." Lincoln was not "giving his case away," as contended by Lincoln biographer Jesse Weik, but was characteristically stating his opponent's arguments with "seeming fairness" and a "liberality of concession." After reprising Ficklin and Constable's argument, Lincoln turned to presenting his case for Matson. Ficklin recalled how Lincoln's "trenchant blows and cold logic and subtle knitting together and presentation of facts favorable to his side of the case, soon dissipated all hope that any advantage was likely to be gained by Lincoln's liberal concession, but rather that he gained from the court a more patient and favorable hearing and consideration of the facts on which he relied for success." Focusing on Matson's public declarations that he had not brought any of his slaves to Illinois for "permanent settlement," he relied upon Matson never saying anything to the contrary. Ficklin recalled that Lincoln plausibly, ingeniously, and forcibly presented this argument to the court. Lincoln also argued that the English cases cited by Constable and Ficklin did not apply because the federal constitution "had established a rule different and much more liberal to the owners of slaves, than that laid down and declared by the English courts."[127]

Justices Wilson and Treat dismissed both Linder's extreme argument and Lincoln's more moderate one. Justice Wilson noted that "considerable importance is attached by counsel to the fact that Mateson [sic] retained his citizenship in Kentucky, and professed the intention of leaving his servants in Illinois but temporarily." These circumstances, however, were not "entitled to the consideration in this case claimed for them." Wilson stated:

> Neither the place of residence, nor the declared intentions of Mateson, countervail the fact that he voluntarily domiciled his servants here for two years or upwards. Even if, from some contingency, they had remained but a day, the circumstance of his having transferred their domicil from Kentucky, and fixed it in Illinois, would have produced the same result.

Wilson thus held that Matson, "by bringing Jane and her children into the State of Illinois, and domiciling them here, had forfeited all claim to their services, and entitled them to be discharged therefrom."[128]

Justice Wilson cited two cases "directly in point" to support his holding. Both were opinions by United States Supreme Court justices written while on circuit.[129] Justice John McLean in 1845 had considered very similar facts in *Vaughan v. Williams*. There, one Tipton, a Kentucky slaveowner, had moved to Illinois in October 1835 and built a house and told his neighbors he intended to reside in Illinois. He also brought his three slaves with him. After six months, he left for Missouri after realizing "there was much conversation in the neighborhood as to the right of the colored persons to their freedom." Tipton then sold his three slaves to someone who sold them to Vaughan. After the three slaves had escaped to Indiana, Vaughan sued Williams for rescuing his slaves. McLean concluded that Williams was not liable because the "colored persons [were] entitled to their liberty." He instructed the jury:

> Having been brought to the state of Illinois, which prohibits slavery, by their master, from the state of Kentucky, and kept at labor for six months, under a declaration of the master that he intended to become a citizen of that state, and who actually exercised the rights of a citizen by voting, there can be no doubt that the slaves were, thereby, entitled to their freedom.[130]

Jane had been "kept at labor" in Illinois for two years, not six months; the only arguable difference between the two cases was Matson's self-serving declaration of his intent.

Justice Wilson also adopted the reasoning used in both cited cases that explained the inapplicability of the fugitive slave clause where slaves had not "escaped" into the free state but had entered the free state with their masters. McLean in *Vaughan v. Williams* noted that the rights to a slave under the common law ceased when the slave reached a free jurisdiction.[131] Similarly, Justice Story noted in 1840 that "[i]t is well known, that, at the common law, a slave escaping into a state, where slavery is not allowed, would immediately become free, and could not be reclaimed." The fugitive slave clause created an exception to this common-law principle.[132] But in

Ex parte Simmons (1823), the other case cited by Wilson, Justice Bushrod Washington had ruled that the fugitive slave clause applied only to a slave escaping from one state to another and didn't apply to slaves "voluntarily carried by his master into another state."[133] Justice Wilson noted that the master would be entitled to the return of his slave only where the slave had escaped from one state into another. But Matson didn't claim Jane fell under the fugitive slave clause. Matson voluntarily brought Jane to Illinois in 1845.[134] The fugitive slave clause offered Matson no more protection before the circuit court than it had before the justice of the peace. Jane and her children were now free under the law.

The legal issue of Jane and her children's freedom was not a difficult one. At the time their freedom was decided, every antebellum court that had faced similar facts had ruled in favor of freedom.[135] Even courts in slave states consistently had held that slaves became free when they accompanied their masters who moved to a free state. The Supreme Court of Louisiana, for example, in 1840 recognized that an African-American woman became "ipso facto free" during a five-year residence with her master in Illinois; once free, she could not again be made a slave.[136] Missouri courts also had held that if slaveowners took slaves to Illinois with the intent to reside there, the slaves became free.[137]

Few southern slaveowners moving to Illinois acted as brazenly as Matson. When he went to court in 1847, no court—North or South—had refused to apply *Somerset* to cases where a slaveowner changed his residence to a free state. In Illinois, the writing already was on the wall by the 1830s. In 1831, a Kentucky slaveowner asked Illinois lawyer Henry Eddy if he could bring his "favorite servants" with him when he moved to Illinois. Eddy had advised that this "could not be done with safety."[138] Other southern slaveowners compromised their property rights to African-Americans once they arrived in Illinois. In 1838, after Daniel Cutright brought his slaves, Julia Ann and Major, into Illinois he went before the Sangamon County Commissioner's Court to record two indentures to the effect that Cutright had brought his two slaves to Illinois but that his slaves now claimed their right to freedom. The indentures "settle[d] the controversy" by announcing the agreement of the parties: Julia Ann and Major agreed to serve Cutright for two years; during those two years Julia Ann and Major initially would live with Cutright until December 25, 1838, and then Cutright would hire them out "at some good place" in Sangamon County; after the end of the term Cutright agreed to free Julia Ann and Major.[139] Cutright's willingness to compromise indicates he understood the weakness of insisting on his rights to property.

The law that governed the status of Jane and her children was clear, and there was no real dispute over the facts. The *Western Citizen*, an abolitionist paper published in Chicago, noted that Wilson's decision "may be considered an important decision in Illinois' jurisprudence, but it is only reaffirming decisions made in all parts of the country, even in the slave states. It is so plain a case that we wonder [sic] it was brought into court."[140] The abolitionist paper later noted that "we have it now laid down as the law, so plain that those who run may read, that if an owner brings his slave into this state, and 'domiciles' him here, that he becomes a free man, and those who take him in slavery are kidnappers of course."[141] While Illinois recognized the right of slaveowners to travel through the state with their slaves, Matson had left Jane and her children at this Illinois farm for two years. No honest judge would consider that an instance of transit, sojourn, or brief residence in the state. Jane and her children had changed their domicile, and with this change, Illinois courts would use Illinois law to determine their legal status.

Some writers, unfamiliar with Justice Wilson's opinion, have overestimated Lincoln's chances of success.[142] But Wilson's opinion is consistent with *Willard,* which merely protected the slaveowner's right of transit through Illinois. Jane's case did not present the issue of transit. Nor was Jane a seasonal worker: Jane and her children were not brought to Matson's farm along with other seasonal workers in the spring of 1847. Justice Wilson in his opinion stated that Matson brought Jane and her children to Illinois in 1845 and that "since then she has lived upon his farm in the capacity of housekeeper."[143]

The Aftermath

Lincoln's involvement with the case ended with the court's decision on the habeas corpus petition that freed Jane and her children. On October 25, Lincoln left Springfield to visit his wife's relatives in Kentucky, and in November he was on his way to Washington to serve his only term in Congress.[144] There, he announced that he intended to introduce legislation that would provide for gradual emancipation in the District of Columbia. All children born of slave mothers after January 1, 1850, would be free; those children had to be "reasonably supported and educated" by the owners of their mothers and would serve as apprentices; officers of the federal government who were "citizens of the slave holding states" could bring their servants into the district while on "public business"; all persons who were lawfully held as slaves in the district when the legislation went into effect would remain as slaves unless their owners wanted to receive "full value" for their emancipation; and the municipal authorities in Washington and Georgetown would be required to provide an "active and efficient means to arrest and deliver up to their owners all fugitive slaves escaping into the district."[145] The fugitive slave provision would later lead the abolitionist Wendell Phillips to refer to Lincoln as "that slave hound from Illinois." But the *New York Tribune* in 1849 referred to Lincoln as "a strong but judicious enemy to Slavery."[146]

Lincoln was following the moderate antislavery position that he had outlined more than ten years before in the Illinois legislature. He had held then that Congress had the power to abolish slavery in the District of Columbia "but that power ought not to be exercised unless at the request of the people" in the district.[147] Lincoln failed to introduce formally his bill to abolish slavery and his comments that he made when he introduced his resolution were the only ones that he made about slavery while he was in Congress.[148] He later explained that upon "finding that I was abandoned by my former backers and having little personal influence, I dropped the matter knowing that it was useless to prosecute the business at that time."[149]

Although Lincoln was no longer involved in the case, loose ends remained in the Coles County Circuit Court. After the court granted the writ of habeas corpus, Ashmore and Rutherford's attorneys moved to dismiss Matson's lawsuits against their clients. The motions to dismiss were held over to the next term of court.[150] The outcome of the habeas corpus hearing did not necessarily moot Matson's lawsuits against Ashmore and Rutherford. It did not matter under Illinois law that Jane and her children were "free" when Ashmore and Rutherford helped them: the Illinois statute prohibited anyone from harboring or employing or even feeding a "negro or mulatto" who did not have either the required certificate of freedom or the one-thousand-dollar bond; Jane and her children had neither when the two abolitionists had aided their quest for freedom. One week after the habeas corpus hearing, Rutherford wrote that whether Matson "will return to attend to the suits against Mr. Ashmore and myself is uncertain."[151] Matson, however, did not return the following spring when the cases were heard on the docket.[152] The docket book for the Coles County Circuit Court noted in the May 1848 term that Matson "by his attorney" moved to dismiss, at his costs, both lawsuits; the court ordered both cases dismissed and that Matson be assessed costs.[153] The court later noted that the costs were unpaid because no property was found in the county to pay them.[154]

Matson, according to some accounts, returned to Kentucky without paying either Lincoln's fee or the court costs. The court costs amounted to two hundred dollars, including the sheriff's expenses for "keeping & dieting" Jane and her children for forty-eight days.[155] Not paying Lincoln would have been consistent with Matson's behavior in Kentucky, where he had problems paying a number of people, including his lawyers. But Lincoln may have received a fee note from Matson; Lincoln's father, who lived in Coles County, wrote his son in 1848 that he had tried to sell a note from "Robert Mattison."[156]

Matson married Mary Ann Corbin on November 23, 1848, in Gallatin County, Illinois.[157] By 1850, Matson was living in Fulton County, Kentucky, with Mary and four children. He owned $3,500 worth of land, which placed him among the ten wealthiest landowners in the county.[158] He died in Fulton County on January 26, 1859. His headstone reads: "An affectionate husband, an indulgent parent, and a good citizen, he died contented and by all respected as an honest man."[159]

The Bryants did not stay in Illinois. Ashmore, who must have supported colonization (as did many whites in central Illinois), helped them leave for Liberia. The Sangamon Colonization Society had 150 members in the 1840s, and a statewide colonization society was formed in 1848. Supporting colonization was the path chosen by white northerners caught between their antislavery convictions and either their own racism or the racism of other white Americans. At the time Lincoln represented Matson, he supported colonization; but he later concluded it was impractical.[160]

Northern blacks generally rejected colonization because of its racist underpinnings. While blacks in Illinois rejected colonization schemes, the Colored Baptist Association of Illinois sent one of its members, Elder S. S. Ball, to Liberia in 1848 to investigate the viability of emigrating to that country. There, by chance, he encountered Anthony, Jane, and Jane's children, whom he found in a "deplorable condition." Ball later reported that Anthony told him he had left Coles County with a promise that money would be raised for him and his family. But little money was raised and the Bryants arrived in Liberia without money. They were sick and depressed. Anthony asked Ball if he could take them back to the United States. When Ball said he couldn't, Anthony asked him if he could at least take Anthony and his son back.[161]

Lincoln, Whig Lawyers, and Slavery

The representation of southern slaveowners by northern lawyers necessarily had a political dimension. When Lincoln represented Matson, he held moderate antislavery views—he believed slavery was morally wrong but constitutionally protected. Lincoln told Robert H. Browne in 1858 that the "slavery question often bothered me as far back as 1836–1840. I was troubled and grieved over it."[162]

Lincoln made his first public pronouncement on slavery in 1837 when he was a member of the Illinois legislature.[163] In December 1836, the governor of Illinois sent to the legislature some of the resolutions passed by other state legislatures that criticized abolitionists.[164] The Alabama legislature, for example, had condemned abolitionists who distributed to slaves "millions of essays, pamphlets, and pictures" that were calculated "to deluge our country in blood." In January, the Illinois legislature passed a resolution that also condemned "the misguided and incendiary movements of the abolitionists." Abolitionists had "forged new irons for the black man and added an hundred fold to the rigors of slavery."[165] Six weeks after the resolution had passed, Lincoln and Dan Stone, another Whig representative from Sangamon County, entered a "protest" against a resolution passed by both houses of the General Assembly. The two Whigs agreed with the resolution's criticism of abolitionists, stating that "the promulgation of abolition doctrines tends rather to increase than to abate [slavery's] evils." Lincoln and Stone also wrote that Congress did not have the "power, under the constitution, to interfere with the institution of slavery in the different states," but it did have the power to abolish slavery in the District of Columbia. The point of the protest was to declare that "the institution of slavery is founded on both injustice and bad policy."[166] Lincoln in 1860 said that this protest "briefly defined his position on the slavery question; and so far as it goes, it was then the same that it is now."[167]

Whigs were constitutional unionists and favored enforcement of the fugitive slave law. Whig judges like Joseph Story and Lemuel Shaw stressed the importance of the fugitive slave clause in the making of the federal constitution.[168] Story in *Prigg v. Pennsylvania* (1842) claimed that the fugitive slave clause "was so vital to the preservation of [the slaveholding states'] domestic interests and institutions, that it cannot be doubted that it constituted a fundamental article, without the adoption of which the Union could not have been formed."[169] Shaw in *Commonwealth v. Aves* (1836) wrote that the fugitive slave clause "was intended to secure future peace and harmony."[170] In *In Re Sims* (1851), Shaw claimed that the fugitive slave clause was essential to the constitution's ratification.[171] Whig lawyers believed that enforcement of the fugitive slave clause rested upon the "obligation of citizenship."[172] The Whig enthusiasm for enforcing the fugitive slave clause also may have rested on their devotion to property rights.[173]

Throughout northern courtrooms, lawyers had to decide whether to represent slaveowners in proceedings that, if successful, would result in blacks being enslaved. Some northern Whig lawyers represented slaveowners because they believed that effective enforcement of the fugitive slave clause was essential for the Union. Boston lawyer Benjamin R. Curtis, for example, represented slaveholders in two well-known cases. In 1836, he represented the Louisiana owner of the six-year-old slave Med, where he forcefully argued that Med remained a slave when she accompanied her mistress on a trip to Massachusetts. Curtis distinguished Somerset because the federal union presented "the question of national comity" that was not present in the English case: "None of the considerations which grow out of our close and peculiar relation with the State of Louisiana, there existed."[174] Fifteen years later, Curtis and his father-in-law Charles P. Curtis were rumored to have been "the secret legal advisers and chamber counsel of the southern slave-hunters" in *In re Sims*, another famous Massachusetts case. In that case, Curtis did appear in court as counsel for the United States marshal.[175]

Curtis's participation in these cases was politically driven. As early as 1835 he was convinced that "unless something is done here to check the Abolitionists, and convince the South that the opinions of the great body of the people of the Northern States are unfavorable to the [Antislavery]

Society, the Union will not continue for a single year."[176] Curtis believed "the moral duty we owe our country and its laws" was paramount. In a speech delivered at Faneuil Hall in Boston after the passage of the 1850 Fugitive Slave Law, Curtis stressed the primacy of the Whig commitment to law and order:

> For I understand we have come here, not to consider particular measures of government, but to assert that we have a government; not to determine whether this or that law be wise or just, but to declare that there is law, and its duties and power; not to consult whether this or that course of policy is beneficial to our country, but to say that we yet have a country, and intend to keep it safe.[177]

Curtis also believed that "without an obligation to restore fugitives from service," the North "could not expect to live in peace with the slave-holding states."[178] Curtis's concerns were typically Whiggish.

Lincoln, like Curtis, Daniel Webster, Rufus Choate, Timothy Walker, and other Whig lawyers, also accepted the fugitive slave clause and its enforcement as part of the price of union.[179] But Lincoln on at least one occasion in the 1840s represented an abolitionist who had been charged with aiding fugitive slaves.[180] Other Illinois lawyer-politicians, including Lincoln's fellow Whigs, refused to handle such cases because of possible political repercussions. Jacksonville lawyer E. D. Baker, for example, in 1843 declined, for political reasons, to represent two abolitionists charged with harboring an escaped slave.[181] Lincoln successfully represented Marvin Pond in an 1845 criminal proceeding in Menard County where Pond was charged with harboring a fugitive slave. When the case was tried in November 1845, the jury returned a not-guilty verdict.[182] Six months before he represented Matson, Lincoln may have represented three abolitionists charged with harboring escaped slaves. Two residents of Woodford County were acquitted; the charges against the third were dismissed.[183]

After the passage of the 1850 fugitive slave law, which was part of the Compromise of 1850, Lincoln did not appear in another case that involved fugitive slaves or abolitionists. The 1850 act was intended to placate southerners who complained the 1793 act was ineffectual.[184] One Springfield resident later recalled that Lincoln "didn't want to be a party to a violation of the fugitive slave law."[185] Throughout the decade Lincoln consistently supported the enforcement of the 1850 act, the passage of which had been championed by his political heroes, Daniel Webster and Henry Clay.[186] During one of his debates with Douglas in 1858, Lincoln said that, while he had "no taste for running and catching niggers," he supported a fugitive slave law because he could not support the Constitution without supporting the rights guaranteed in it.[187] As Lincoln explained in an 1855 letter to his friend Joshua Speed of Kentucky:

You know I dislike slavery; and you fully admit the abstract wrong of it. So far there is no cause of difference. But you say that sooner than yield your legal right to the slave—especially at the bidding of those who are not themselves interested—, you would see the Union dissolved. I also acknowledge your rights and my obligations, under the constitution, in regard to your slaves. I confess I hate to see the poor creatures hunted down, and caught, and carried back to their stripes, and unrewarded toils; but I bite my lip and keep quiet. . . . You ought rather to appreciate how much the great body of the Northern people do crucify their feelings, in order to maintain their loyalty to the constitution and the Union.[188]

Lincoln in his first Inaugural Address again expressed his support for the enforcement of the fugitive slave clause: "It is scarcely questioned that this provision was intended by those who made it, for the reclaiming of what we call fugitive slaves; and the intention of the law-giver is the law."[189]

Lincoln's own reluctance to participate in fugitive slave cases after 1850 can be contrasted with the actions of his own law partner, William Henry Herndon, who represented escaped slaves on at least two occasions after the passage of the 1850 fugitive slave law.[190] In 1857, Herndon unsuccessfully represented Frederick Clements; part of his defense was based on the "presumption, when a negro is arrested in a free state, . . . that he is free."[191] The presumption of freedom had been established in *Kinney v. Cook* and reaffirmed in *Bailey v. Cromwell*.[192] In 1860, Herndon unsuccessfully represented Edward Canton.[193] George M. Dickinson, Canton's owner, apparently agreed not to sell him when they returned to Missouri "in consideration of a verbal pledge not to run away again."[194] Not much is known about slaveowner Dickinson, but he appears to have been very gullible: a month after Canton gave Dickinson his "verbal pledge" he had escaped again and was passing through Springfield, heading north to Canada and freedom.[195]

Lincoln's Whiggish support for the enforcement of the fugitive slave clause does not explain his representation of Matson in 1847. The case does not fit within such a political context because it did not involve the operation of the fugitive slave clause. No Whig principle implicating "loyalty to the constitution and the Union" was at stake when Jane and her children sought freedom. Although Lincoln was a loyal Whig, there was no need for him to "bite his lip" and represent Matson.

It is possible that Matson lied to Lincoln about the applicability of the fugitive slave clause and that Lincoln took the case believing that the case involved a constitutional provision that he was bound to support. Nothing in his Kentucky background suggests Matson was a pillar of integrity. If his client had deceived him, then one wonders why Lincoln did not withdraw when he discovered the truth.

While some Whig lawyers like Curtis defended their representation of slaveholders on the basis of their commitment to constitutional unionism, others turned to notions of professional responsibility. According to Rutherford's recollection, Lincoln tried to explain his representation of Matson under "the proposition that, as a lawyer, he must represent and be faithful to those who counsel and employ him."[196] Other northern lawyers who represented slaveowners against escaped slaves gave similar justifications for their role. For example, when Boston lawyer Elbridge Gerry Austin represented a slaveholder in a fugitive slave case and was assailed by abolitionists as a "legal whore selling himself and the honor of Massachusetts for a slave-catching fee," Austin defended his actions as proper for a lawyer.[197] Austin believed that he had acted in his "professional capacity." He noted that "the counselling and advising of a stranger in the exercise of his constitutional privileges" was not a "crime." He also combined the Whig commitment to constitutional unionism with the lawyer's commitment to role morality: "citizens of the South, whenever they seek to enforce their rights, are entitled to the service of those persons, who, by education, are qualified to advise them how to observe the provisions of the Constitution and laws of their country."[198]

Lincoln's representation of Matson can be contrasted with the activism of Ohio lawyer and politician Salmon P. Chase.[199] The contrast is intriguing because Chase's legal and philosophical critique of slavery influenced Lincoln. Chase had linked "the antislavery natural rights philosophy as expressed in the Declaration of Independence to the Constitution," an argument that Lincoln later adopted.[200] Lincoln and Chase, however, had very different views on the enforcement of the fugitive slave clause.[201] Chase also had very different experiences as a lawyer in cases involving the status of slaves in free states. Chase's extensive antislavery litigation in trial and appellate courts earned him the nickname "Attorney General for Fugitive Slaves."[202] Chase approached his first antislavery cases in terms of his professional responsibilities. When some Cincinnati abolitionists asked him to represent them in a lawsuit against mob leaders who had destroyed their property, Chase initially hesitated. He later recalled that "wealth, influence, position, were all on the side of the slave owners, and the worst reputation a struggling young man could get was that of an abolitionist." Chase wondered whether his retainer would affect his career ("I had just begun to acquire a pretty good practice for a young man and among the gentlemen to be sued were several of my personal friends") but agreed to represent the abolitionists because "no lawyer could be found to undertake the case."[203] Chase later recalled his willingness "to surrender every professional prospect when the condition of retaining them is a departure from principle." Chase represented a runaway slave the following year and eventually participated in at least seven fugitive slave cases. Again, he later viewed these cases in terms of his professional responsibilities: "I never refused my help to any poor man black or white; and I like the office more . . . because [there] were neither fees or . . . salary connected with it."[204] Chase's sense of professional obligation differed from the typical Whig lawyer's. He cared about which party he represented. Whig lawyers were unconcerned with such matters; they were committed to a process of orderly dispute resolution.

What was different between Lincoln and Chase was their fundamental understanding of the role of law and lawyers. Unlike Lincoln, Chase approached law instrumentally. He was what Stephen A. Douglas called an "Abolition lawyer."[205] Chase was one of the many antebellum lawyers who strategically used litigation to advance the antislavery movement.[206] Chase explained his legal activism in an 1847 letter:

> It is strange that the pro-slavery construction of the constitution, so utterly indefensible upon history or by reason, should be so tamely acquiesced in by the courts, and I agree with you, that at the bar, and elsewhere, we should be open, bold, indignant, and emphatic in our denunciation of it. It cannot stand exposure and rebuke. If it finds sanctuary in courts of justice it must be dragged out and denounced before the people. In the result it must fall.[207]

Chase, unlike Lincoln, was ready to pursue an ideological and moral agenda in the courts. Illinois lawyers like James H. Collins of Chicago also pursued an antislavery agenda in the courts. Collins, who occasionally crossed paths with Lincoln in Illinois courtrooms, unsuccessfully represented before the Illinois Supreme Court abolitionists convicted of harboring escaped slaves and twice successfully represented abolitionists in circuit court proceedings.[208] Lincoln's own law partner represented escaped slaves; but, unlike Lincoln, he never represented a slaveowner in court.[209]

Writers often juxtapose Lincoln's representation of Matson with an earlier case where he is credited with winning the freedom of Nance, an indentured black girl, in *Bailey v. Cromwell*. The cases are paired to show Lincoln's pragmatic approach as a lawyer—he took business as it came.[210] But Lincoln both suing and representing railroads may not be the same thing as "freeing" Nance and attempting to enslave Jane and her children.

In any event, Lincoln in *Bailey v. Cromwell* didn't secure Nance's freedom. The facts of the case were not that dramatic. Cromwell's estate sued Bailey in assumpsit on a promissory note for Bailey's failure to pay for an indentured servant named Nance.[211] Bailey pleaded failure of consideration: Cromwell had represented that Nance was a slave and servant but had failed to provide proof. Earlier that year, the supreme court had held in *Kinney v. Cook*, "With us the presumption is in favor of liberty." This holding was technically wrong: a black in Illinois under the Black Code was presumed to be a slave. But under *Kinney v. Cook*, the circuit court nonetheless could presume that Nance was free, and Cromwell's estate failed to rebut this presumption. The Illinois Supreme Court concluded that "the sale of a free person is illegal, and that being the consideration for the note, that is illegal also, and consequently no recovery can be had upon the note." The decision by the Illinois Supreme Court meant that Bailey did not have to pay Cromwell's estate on the note. But Lincoln did not "win" the freedom of Nance in the Illinois Supreme Court. Nance had won it months before. The court's opinion noted that Nance had stayed with Bailey for six months and then had left, "asserting and declaring all the time that she was free."[212]

Lawyers, "Unjust Causes," and Antebellum Legal Ethics

Abolitionists rejected the rationalization of role morality used by northern lawyers who represented slaveowners. They instead believed that lawyers were morally accountable for their decisions to represent particular clients. Massachusetts abolitionist Theodore Parker complained that lawyers were "skilful in making nice technical distinctions, and strongly disposed to adhere to historical precedents on the side of arbitrary power, rather than to obey the instinctive promptings of the moral sense in their own consciousness." Parker, for example, attacked members of the Curtis family in Boston who were involved in several slave cases. Parker said that "when Mr. Webster prostituted himself to the Slave Power this family went out and pimped for him in the streets." When Parker examined Benjamin R. Curtis's and Charles P. Curtis's role as "counsel for the slave-hunters," he dismissed the defense that "this was only a lawyer pleading for his client." These lawyers were asking "the court to do a wicked thing"—to establish slavery in Massachusetts. When Boston lawyer Seth J. Thomas was hired to represent James Potter, the slaveowner who claimed Thomas Sims, an abolitionist newspaper called Thomas "the legal pimp of the slave catchers."[213]

The abolitionist critique of northern lawyers who represented slaveowners reflected a popular criticism of the antebellum legal profession. Antebellum lawyers were vilified by many Americans for their willingness to represent morally repugnant clients.[214] For example, the narrator of Edward Bonney's 1850 novel about Illinois admits that he has "an honest and well-founded contempt" for lawyers "whose trade it is, by means of their technical knowledge, to turn loose upon society men guilty of the blackest crimes and, for a paltry fee, to aid in the escape from the just penalty of the law murderers and assassins."[215] In the same month that Lincoln represented Matson, an article appeared in the New York–based *United States Magazine and Democratic Review* that complained about "the abuses of law courts." The writer described lawyers as "actuated by the strongest motives of the human breast, to pervert the principles of justice, and defeat the intentions of honest complainants by some of the devices of their wonderful arts." Lawyers stood ready to sell "their services to the highest bidder, to advocate even the most unworthy cause, and plighted their honor and reputation to prosecute it successfully."[216]

Antebellum lawyers were well aware of the popular critique of lawyers and reacted defensively.[217] In fashioning responses to this pervasive criticism of the ethics of the profession, lawyers offered two different models of professionalism and professional ethics.[218] Some legal writers, admitting that there was a difference between a lawyer's private morality and his public role, elaborated a professional duty based on detachment and isolation. Other legal writers dismissed as "vulgar notions" the idea that "a different code of morals and honor is recognized in professional practice than that would be allowed in the private dealings of man with man."[219] Ohio judge Timothy Walker cautioned in *An Introduction to American Law* (1837) that "there is not perhaps a more difficult question in casuistry, than that which every lawyer has to decide, in determining the nature and extent of his professional obligations."[220]

Baltimore lawyer and educator David Hoffman often is identified as the founder of American legal ethics. Hoffman in the second edition of his *Course of Legal Study* (1836) included an extensive discussion of "professional deportment." Contending that "what is morally wrong, cannot be professionally right," Hoffman rejected role morality and accepted limitations on the obligations lawyers owed to their clients: "neither loyalty to client nor compliance with the technicalities of the legal process could absolve an attorney from obeying the dictates of conscience and striving to do substantial justice to all parties." He believed that an attorney was bound morally not to use all available legal defenses for his client if injustice would result. The priggish Hoffman, for example, asserted that a lawyer should "never plead the Statute of Limitations when based on the *mere efflux of time*"; if the client owed the debt and "has no other defence than the *legal bar,* he shall never make me a partner in his knavery." When a lawyer represented "those charged with crimes of the deepest dye" and became convinced of their guilt, he was not obliged to "impede the course of justice, by special resorts to ingenuity—to the artifices of eloquence—to appeals to the morbid and fleeting sympathies of weak juries, or of temporizing courts." Someone of "atrocious character" was not entitled to "special exertions from any member of our pure and honourable profession." Hoffman's ideal attorney who is unwilling to represent unjust causes is identical to the model attorney of antebellum fiction and to the early biographers' conception of lawyer Lincoln.[221]

Simon Greenleaf, author of an influential treatise on the law of evidence—a book Lincoln cited to courts and recommended to would-be lawyers—and professor of law at Harvard Law School, expressed similar themes in an 1834 address. Lawyers needed to aspire to a "higher standard of morals," remembering "that we are not only lawyers, but citizens and men."[222]

The moralistic approach toward professional responsibility taken by Hoffman and Greenleaf represents the last vestiges of republicanism in antebellum legal thought.[223] Hoffman and Greenleaf stressed lawyers' overarching commitment to the community; lawyers, as guardians of civic virtue, would subordinate their obligations to their clients to the greater good.

In contrast to Hoffman's conception of the lawyer as independent moral agent, Judge George Sharswood, in his influential *A Compend of Lectures on the Aims and Duties of the Profession of Law* (1854), enjoined lawyers not to pass moral judgments on potential clients.[224] Sharswood wrote that a lawyer "is not morally responsible for the act of the party in maintaining an unjust cause, nor for the error of the court, if they fall into error, in deciding it in his favor." "The lawyer," Sharswood argued, "who refuses his professional assistance because in his judgment the case is unjust and indefensible, usurps the function of both judge and jury."[225]

Many other antebellum legal writers advocated suspending moral judgment of potential clients and letting courts determine the justice of their claims. In this way, Georgia lawyer J. F. Jackson observed in 1846 that "it is not for advocates to say whether a cause is just or unjust; for him to decide upon the justice or injustice of a case would be to usurp the province of the judge."[226] Timothy Walker likewise advised would-be lawyers not to decide "beforehand" which side was wrong "because there must be counsel on both sides, in order to make the scales of justice even." Walker warned that "if it be the duty of one lawyer to decline a prosecution, it is the duty of all to decline; and thus a cause is decided before it goes into Court."[227] Kentucky lawyer George Robertson in 1855 explained that a lawyer couldn't abandon his client if he discovered he was on "the wrong side." The lawyer still owed his client "his duty, whether in a good or bad cause, on the wrong side or the right, to present, in as imposing a manner as fair argument can exhibit, the stronger or more plausible points in his client's behalf, without expressing an uncandid opinion."[228]

An 1843 article in the *Law Reporter* scoffed at Hoffman's suggestion that a lawyer should refuse to plead the statute of limitations to defeat an "honest debt"; it asked, "if legislators make laws which are intended for general application, what right has a lawyer to set up his own scruples of conscience by denying to a citizen the protection of one of these laws?"[229]

Lawyers espoused this notion of role morality in more than articles and books. The same year Lincoln represented Matson, William Pitt Ballinger, a young Texas lawyer, wrote his uncle (who was also a lawyer) to question his complicity in using a Texas statute to work "an injustice" against two claimants. He plaintively asked, "Is this what the practice of law is all about?" His uncle answered that the law was not his "to ponder its meaning or purposes, but to uphold & enforce at all times. We do not make the law, the People do, & if they wanted them changed then it is their responsibility to do so. Your job is to ensure the People's wishes—nothing else."[230]

An 1840 English murder trial profoundly influenced the development of an American legal ethic based on role morality. This case involved Charles Phillips's defense of François Benjamin Courvoisier, a servant who was charged with the murder of his employer, Lord William Russell.[231] In final argument Phillips attempted to persuade the jury that other servants may have committed the crime. The jury did not heed Phillips's plea for his client; they found Courvoisier guilty of murder. After he was convicted and sentenced to death, Courvoisier confessed to the crime. At the same time his confession was made public, English newspapers also reported that Courvoisier earlier had confessed his guilt to his lawyer before Phillips gave his final argument. The English public was shocked by Phillips's attempt to convince the jury that his client was innocent, which he knew wasn't true.[232]

Phillips's role in the defense of Courvoisier became the subject of a spirited public debate over legal ethics in both England and the United States, raising important and disturbing questions about what duties lawyers owed to their clients.[233] American lawyers who wrote about the case disagreed about whether Phillips should be praised or condemned for his zealous defense of Courvoisier. An editorialist in the *American Law Journal* regretted that lawyers could even disagree about "whether a Counsellor can, *consistently with sound morals,* attempt to procure the acquittal of one who has, in sane mind, voluntarily confessed his guilt to his advocate."[234]

Other American legal writers supported Phillips's role in the Courvoisier case. The discussion of the case by these American lawyers helped establish the now dominant principle of American legal ethics: a lawyer's overriding duty was to the client. George Sharswood, for example, in his 1854 work on legal ethics included an appendix on the Courvoisier case, which contained Phillips's "vindication of himself."[235] The *Monthly Law Reporter* published several articles about the case.[236] In an 1846 article, an anonymous commentator wished to be "delivered from self-styled conscientious lawyers, who will engage for no parties that are not morally right, and who throw the weight of their own character into every cause they have." These lawyers had tried "their causes in their own chambers," but "the place to try causes is before the properly constituted tribunals."[237]

Although Sharswood and other commentators warned against lawyers "usurping" the role of juries, American lawyers never adopted the English "cab-rank" rule, which would have eliminated a lawyer's ability to choose his clients. In England, a barrister generally must accept those clients who seek their services.[238] In 1844 David Dudley Field thought it was widely held in the United States that "a lawyer is not at liberty to refuse any one his services."[239] An American commentator in 1846 regarded the "English rule" as "safer than our own practice, by which a counsellor may select his own causes." When a lawyer took cases that he considered "(upon the slightest possible testimony, that of his own client) the most just," he was "in danger of becoming identified with his client" or becoming "the slave of every artful man."[240] Sharswood, however, rejected the cab-rank rule; he conceded that a lawyer "has an undoubted right to refuse a retainer, and decline to be concerned in any cause, at his discretion."[241]

While Lincoln's career reflected aspects of both notions of professional ethics, on balance, he favored Sharswood's approach. Lincoln, in his notes for a lecture to law students, made some comments that were somewhat similar to those of Hoffman or Greenleaf yet did not reflect any deep thinking about legal ethics. Acknowledging "a vague popular belief that lawyers are necessarily dishonest," Lincoln warned that "no young man choosing the law for a calling" should yield to that popular belief. Instead, the young man should "resolve to be honest at all events; and if, in your own judgement you cannot be an honest lawyer, resolve to be honest without being a lawyer." Lincoln believed that "a moral tone ought to be infused into the profession."[242]

Yet Lincoln's hope for infusing a moral tone in the profession falls well short of Hoffman's maxim that "what is morally wrong, cannot be professionally right." Lincoln in his lecture gave two examples of "immoral" behavior by lawyers. One was a lawyer's stirring up litigation by searching deeds for defects in title "to stir up strife, and put money in his pocket." The other example given by Lincoln was the "dishonest" practice of selling fee notes before providing the service the fee secured. Lincoln's law lecture did not address the more problematic issue of whether a lawyer should be morally accountable for his choice of clients.

Lincoln rejected other aspects of Hoffman's moralistic approach to the practice of law. Hoffman believed that a lawyer shouldn't plead the statute of limitations against an honest debt; however, Lincoln in his practice used the defenses that were available to his clients, including the statute of limitations. Two examples will suffice. He unsuccessfully pleaded the statute of limitations in *Rice v. Blackman,* an 1860 case in federal court. Alphonso Rice was an engineer who had worked for the Mississippi & Atlantic Railroad; he had sued his employer when he wasn't paid. When the railroad didn't pay the judgment, Rice sued Curtis Blackman, a railroad stockholder, on the judgment. The trial court rejected Lincoln's defense that Rice had waited too long to sue Blackman and entered a judgment for Rice.[243] Four years earlier, Lincoln successfully interposed the defense of limitations in a debt case in Vermilion County brought by John McFarland against Moses Layton. After Lincoln asserted limitations, McFarland eventually dismissed his lawsuit against Lincoln's client.[244]

Unlike Hoffman's ideal lawyer, Lincoln was not above positioning a case to be decided upon a technical point of procedure rather than upon its merits. Five years before he represented Robert Matson, Lincoln represented Amos H. Worthing, who was the appellee in a case before the Illinois Supreme Court. Lincoln moved to dismiss the appeal because the appeal bond was executed by an agent of the appellant who lacked a document under seal giving him power to execute the bond for the appellant. The court sustained the motion and dismissed the appeal for "want of a sealed power."[245] The court's action brought a stinging dissent by Justice Sidney

Breese, who believed the rule advanced by Lincoln and relied upon by the court was "destitute of any good reason on which to base it, and altogether too technical for this age." It was time to save "such proceedings from the dominion of a rule so arbitrary, so technical, so wholly inapplicable to our condition, and so little calculated to promote justice."[246] That same year, Lincoln secured yet another triumph of form over substance; he successfully moved to dismiss an appeal because the appellant had not filed his assigned errors "in obedience to the rule of the Court."[247]

Whig lawyers like Lincoln did not approach law instrumentally; they cared more whether a dispute was settled in an orderly manner through the courts than whether they represented a particular side in the dispute. Lincoln was like Abiel Leonard, a Missouri lawyer and Whig. Leonard was involved with several freedom suits brought by Missouri slaves. Leonard took cases as they came and represented both slaves and slaveholders.[248]

This Whiggish conception of a lawyer's proper role reinforced the parallel development of a legal ethic that suspended a lawyer's moral judgment. A lawyer could not turn away a client for moral reasons because he was not in a position to make a moral judgment. Under the Whiggish conception of orderly law and the new conception of professional responsibility, lawyers renounced making ultimate judgments and left those to judges and juries. David Dudley Field in 1844 asserted that this faith in the system was flawed because it assumed that judges were infallible and the law always was certain.[249]

Conclusion

Lincoln was able to represent a slaveholder because he was able to suspend his moral judgment. Lincoln followed a model of professional responsibility that refused to hold a lawyer morally accountable for his choice of clients. This was not a case where Lincoln was ethically bound to represent Matson because he was "the last lawyer in town"; Matson already had a lawyer when Lincoln chose to help him.[250] At best, Matson had a legal claim but an objective that Lincoln otherwise would have recognized as immoral. Lincoln, at other times in his law practice, declined representation of a client because "some things legally right are not morally right." When he represented Matson, Lincoln had a sincere hatred of slavery, but the "masks of the law" allowed him to subordinate his personal beliefs to represent Matson.[251] His involvement in the case shows the corrupting influence of a legal ethic that minimized moral responsibility.

Working for the Railroad

One of the best-known and least-understood aspects of Abraham Lincoln's legal career is his representation of the Illinois Central Railroad in the 1850s. Gore Vidal, for example, has the characters in his novel on Lincoln and the Civil War refer to Lincoln as a "railroad lawyer" or to his association with the Illinois Central at least six times.[1] The standard biographies all refer to Lincoln and the Illinois Central.[2] But the full extent of Lincoln's work for the railroad is often overlooked. Lincoln's relationship with the railroad was relatively continuous after 1852; he was a trial lawyer for the railroad in two counties that he regularly attended on circuit and also represented the railroad before the Illinois Supreme Court. The railroad used Lincoln because of his trial and negotiation skills and his familiarity with the supreme court and elected officials.

Railroads and Lawyers

Railroads had transformed Illinois in the 1850s.[3] Nowhere in the United States was the development of railroads more dramatic. Illinois had no rail lines in 1830; 26 miles of rail lines were built by 1840; 118 miles by 1850; and an astounding 2,799 miles by 1860. In 1860 Illinois had more miles of rail than any other state in the Union except Ohio.[4] Railroads had a particularly profound impact on Lincoln's central Illinois.[5] The railroads opened up markets, created new towns, attracted laborers, and raised important legal issues.[6]

With the growth of railroads came the growth of railroad law.[7] American lawyers seized upon this new opportunity. Their attitude was typified by a Texas lawyer's 1860 diary entry: "I must make myself more thorough in Railroad law. Our State will soon be covered with lines & there will arise a no. of legal matters which we must be able to answer. RR's are the wave of the future & I must be prepared for their business."[8] A law journal in 1851 noted that "in this day of rail-roads, any lawyer's escape from the investigation of rail-road law, would be miraculous."[9] The legal literature of the period reflects this development. In 1851 two Boston lawyers compiled a two-volume set of "railroad laws and charters of the United States."[10] In 1854 a set of annotated reprints of leading American cases on railroad law was published. The editors of this two-volume publication, which was commonly known as *American Railway Cases,* the title on the book's spine, noted that "the introduction of railways has given rise to much litigation upon questions, either peculiar to that species of property, or involving novel applications of the principles of the common law."[11] The first American treatises on railroad law were both published in 1857.[12] In 1861, Herndon wrote Edward L. Pierce that his railroad law treatise "was most excellent—well-arranged, & somewhat massively condensed. Have often quoted it, and learned much from it."[13]

Lincoln served the Illinois Central in the courtroom, not the boardroom. While antebellum railroads were the forerunners of corporate management, Lincoln had no role in the Illinois Central's management.[14] Instead Lincoln's work for the railroad was limited almost entirely to handling trials and appeals. Nor was Lincoln the railroad's only trial or appellate lawyer. The railroad hired other lawyers throughout Illinois to defend lawsuits and handle appeals. The railroad also had lawyers on salary throughout this period. These company lawyers handled many important matters without Lincoln's assistance. For example, in the spring of 1855, the president of the railroad, John Griswold, and its general counsel, James F. Joy, negotiated the lucrative mail contract with the Post Office Department.[15]

Lincoln represented the Illinois Central Railroad in about fifty cases, although he seldom appeared alone.[16] Lincoln's trial work for the railroad was in Champaign, Coles, De Witt, Macon and McLean counties. Because all five counties were part of the Eighth Circuit, which Lincoln regularly traveled, he already was spending considerable time in these counties. Lincoln, while on the circuit in 1853, spent twenty-four days in Bloomington (McLean County) and eleven days in Clinton (De Witt County). In 1854 Lincoln spent twenty-two days in Bloomington and fifteen days in Clinton.[17] For Illinois Central business, Lincoln typically was hired by the lawyer in each county who had been hired directly by the railroad. In De Witt and Macon counties, Lincoln was associated with Clifton H. Moore, who resided in Clinton, the county seat of De Witt County. In McLean County, Lincoln and Asahel Gridley represented the railroad. Gridley lived in Bloomington, the county seat of McLean County. In Champaign County, Lincoln and Henry Clay Whitney, who resided in Urbana, the county seat, represented the railroad. Whitney recalled that "we had a contract that Lincoln was to take no case against us & I could call on him to help me when he was there: & when my clients wanted help I always got Lincoln."[18]

Lawyers involved in railroad litigation faced a challenging array of issues in the 1850s. An 1864 Illinois formbook provided sample pleadings for seven different types of routine railroad lawsuits. Six were actions in case; they described a plaintiff on a horse and buggy who was injured in a collision; a deceased on horse and buggy killed in collision; a passenger injured alighting a train; a plaintiff's wheat stacks destroyed by fire "communicated" by the train; a plaintiff's stock killed because the railroad failed to build fences and cattle guards; and vessel interests damaged by the obstruction of a river by a railroad bridge. The seventh declaration was for debt *qui tam* based on a railroad's failure to ring a bell when it neared a public highway crossing.[19]

The most prevalent dispute in antebellum railroad litigation involved the landowners whose property the roads crossed.[20] The extent of a railroad's liability to its customers—both shippers and passengers—also was decided in this period.[21] So too was a railroad's liability to its own employees for personal injuries.[22] Disputes between railroads and governmental entities often were resolved in courtrooms. Finally, railroads in Illinois often were embroiled in lawsuits with their stock subscribers.[23]

Lincoln handled many, but not all, of these issues for the Illinois Central. Almost half of Lincoln's circuit court cases involved disputes with landowners over damage to their land or the railroad's failure to build or maintain fences.[24] Lincoln's work for the railroad also addressed such routine matters as the exercise of eminent domain and its liability for damaged shipments and animals struck by trains. Lincoln also participated in three highly important taxation cases for the railroad. But Lincoln didn't face every legal issue involving railroads in his work for the Illinois Central. He wasn't involved in any litigation with shareholders because the Illinois Central, unlike other Illinois railroads, did not rely on local capital.[25] Lincoln also didn't defend the railroad in any personal injury lawsuits.

Right-of-Way Cases

Before a railroad could begin construction, it needed land. State legislatures aided this process by allowing railroads to exercise eminent domain, which permitted the railroad to take the land and then compensate the landowners.[26] Although eminent domain lawsuits involving railroads were frequently filed in antebellum courts, the building of the Illinois Central led to relatively few court cases.[27] Several of Lincoln's early Illinois Central cases involved the railroad's exercise of eminent domain. In these right-of-way assessment cases, he represented the landowner twice and the railroad twice.[28]

The Illinois legislature established the formal procedure for railroad companies to obtain right of way in the 1849 railroad incorporation act; the procedure was typical of its era.[29] If the legislature determined that a proposed road was "of sufficient public utility to justify the taking of private property," then the railroad had the right to condemn property along the proposed route. If the railroad and the landowner could not agree on the amount to be paid for the condemned land, then the railroad had to petition in the county circuit court for the appointment of commissioners. The court would appoint "five competent and disinterested persons as commissioners." After viewing the property and hearing "the proofs and allegations of the parties," the commissioners would certify the proper compensation for the condemned land.[30]

In 1852 the Illinois legislature changed the procedure for corporations to exercise eminent domain, seemingly to expedite the eminent domain process at a time when railroads were expanding rapidly. The number of commissioners was changed from five to three. More importantly, the commissioners would assess not only "compensation" for the right of way but "damages which may result from the construction and use of the road."[31] The Illinois Central considered the process so routine that it provided its attorneys preprinted fill-in-the-blank forms; these forms included a petition for filing in county court, an order for the appointment of commissioners, a certificate of commissioners, and a commissioners' final report.[32] The legislature also provided for an appeal from the decision of the commissioners to the county circuit court.[33] The new process ensured more rapid initial decisions but retained the property owner's recourse to the courts.

The formal process was irrelevant if the railroad and the landowner either successfully negotiated the value of the property or accepted the assessment of the commissioners.[34] The Illinois Central must have been very successful in negotiating agreements with landowners over the value of their property or both sides must have been very satisfied with the assessments: Lincoln was only involved in four appeals to the county circuit court from the assessments by the commissioners.[35] In the first such case, Lincoln represented the Illinois Central.[36] In two other 1853 cases, Lincoln represented the landowner. In May 1853, Lincoln and Leonard Swett represented John S. Barger, a De Witt County landowner who had appealed the commissioners' assessment for damages for right of way. Clifton Moore and John T. Stuart represented the railroad. In October, a jury awarded Barger $637.33 in damages. The judgment included a condition that the railroad would maintain a "good and substantial fence on each side of said strip of land covered by said right of way."[37]

Although Lincoln was involved in four disputes over the assessment of damages for right of way in the circuit courts, only one of these appeals to the circuit court of the commissioners' assessment was by the railroad. Dissatisfied landowners filed the three other appeals to the circuit court. Lincoln didn't handle any appeals to the Illinois Supreme Court that involved the railroad's exercise of eminent domain. Like most antebellum railroads, the Illinois Central was generally content with the commissioners' assessment of damages.[38] Appeals only would have led to protracted conflicts that wasted time and money. This pattern of acquiescence continued throughout the nineteenth century: railroad lawyers after the Civil War also tried to resolve questions about right of way as quickly and as amicably as possible.[39]

Lincoln's earliest case for the railroad reflected the railroad's eagerness either to settle the landowner's appeal of the commissioners' assessment or to minimize the jury's award. Lincoln filed an amended pleading of the original right-of-way petition that did nothing more than outline additional terms that the railroad unilaterally accepted. In the amended pleading, Lincoln stipulated the railroad's willingness to "perpetually maintain, a good and substantial fence on each side of the strip of land covered by the Right of Way." The railroad also stipulated that it would allow the landowner to "join" this fencing and would allow "any number of crossings not exceeding three at such points" that the landowner designated. This pleading precluded the landowner from arguing that part of the damages that he sustained would be his cost of building a fence.[40] Lincoln knew that, without these stipulations, the jury would be instructed that the railroad was not "bound to make fences" and that the landowner did not "have a right without the consent of the company, to make cattle guards." Armed with that instruction, a landowner could credibly argue for increased damages. Lincoln had learned this lesson over this instruction several months before in an appeal that he lost while representing the Alton & Sangamon Railroad.[41]

Lincoln had gained valuable experience with the assessment of damages in right-of-way cases while handling two appeals in the December 1852 term for the Alton & Sangamon Railroad.[42] In one appeal Lincoln complained that the jury assessing damages had been instructed that the railroad had no duty either to build fences or to allow landowners to build cattle guards. The railroad originally had filed a petition to assess damages when an agreement with George Baugh on "the price to be paid for the right of way" could not be reached. The railroad asked the Sangamon County Justice of Peace Court to appoint three "householders" to assess the damages "which they believe the owner thereof will sustain over and above the additional value which said Land will derive from the construction of said Rail Road." The three householders then assessed sixty-four dollars in damages. Baugh appealed to the circuit court, where a jury awarded him $480. Lincoln & Herndon then appealed the jury's verdict to the supreme court, where they complained about the instructions that were given to the jurors. The supreme court, however, upheld the lower court's instructions.[43]

In the other appeal Lincoln successfully argued that a jury should be instructed "in estimating the damage done to the land by the construction of the railroad, they are to deduct the advantage which they believe the land will derive from its construction."[44] Lincoln first had convinced the commissioners appointed to assess the land to consider the "advantages" that the railroad brought to the rest of the landowner's property.[45] This was not a novel approach; several state supreme courts had held that the benefit to the landowner's property could be considered when assessing compensation for land condemned by eminent domain.[46] In other states, legislatures had passed laws mandating such an approach. The charters for railroad companies in Ohio required that appraisers consider the "offsetting benefits" to landowners in right-of-way cases.[47]

The landowner appealed the assessment to the county circuit court where the circuit judge refused to instruct the jury to consider "the advantages accruing to said land from the construction."[48] Lincoln then appealed to the Illinois Supreme Court. The supreme court agreed with Lincoln, citing an 1848 decision from the Pennsylvania Supreme Court.[49] Lincoln's victory had little practical consequence: three months after he had convinced the commissioners to consider the increased value to the landowner's property the Illinois legislature prohibited commissioners from estimating any "benefits or advantages which may accrue to lands affected in common with adjoining lands."[50] While the Illinois Supreme Court agreed with Lincoln, it also realized the amended "statute, enacted since this proceeding was instituted," would govern future disputes.[51]

Damage to Property

While the first wave of cases against the Illinois Central involved landowners in disputes over the value of their land that was taken by the railroad, the next wave consisted of cases with landowners upset with the damage done to their property during and after the building of the railroad. De Witt County landowners, for example, filed at least eighteen lawsuits for damages incurred to their property after the railroad line was built. One particularly litigious landowner was Wilson Allen, who sued the Illinois Central seven times.[52] Allen also was a witness against the railroad for other De Witt County landowners in three other lawsuits and was a surety for other landowners in two other lawsuits.[53] In a November 1854 lawsuit, Allen complained in trespass that the railroad had dug "mines pits shafts and holes of great depth and breadth" upon his property. Lincoln and Moore represented the railroad. In October 1855, the case was tried and the jury awarded Allen $762.55. After the jury verdict, the parties entered an agreed judgment that stipulated that the parties had agreed to submit to the jury all "past present and future damages" and had further agreed that if the railroad paid the judgment, then "no future action shall be for a continuance of the matters mentioned in the declaration."[54]

Allen initiated two more lawsuits in 1857. In one, Allen sought $300 in damages. Lincoln filed a demurrer, which the court granted.[55] In the other, Allen sought damages for the railroad obstructing drainage; he sought two thousand dollars in damages. Lincoln filed a demurrer and a plea and notice, which argued that the railroad obstructed the stream by Allen's "leave and license."[56] The jury in this trial awarded $286.[57]

Allen filed yet another lawsuit in September 1859, claiming that the railroad had obstructed an "ancient drain." This obstruction caused a pond to form, which "became offensive and stagnant" and resulted in his family becoming ill. Allen also claimed that a different part of his property "had been injured by the washing of mud and sediment" caused by the improper construction of the railroad. Lincoln and Moore pleaded that a prior lawsuit precluded another suit against the railroad. In 1861, the venue was changed to Macon County where Allen two years later obtained a $25 judgment. The railroad appealed the verdict, and this litigation with Allen was not resolved until 1866 when the supreme court agreed that Allen could not again recover from the railroad.[58]

Another type of landowner lawsuit against the railroad involved the railroad's failure to build or maintain fences. The Illinois Central, like other railroads in Illinois, initially did not have a common-law or statutory duty to build or maintain fences along its road.[59] In 1855 the Illinois legislature imposed a duty on railroads to "erect and thereafter maintain fences" to "prevent cattle, horses, sheep and hogs from getting on to such railroad."[60] Even before the legislature acted, the Illinois Central in De Witt and Champaign counties had agreed to build fences when it purchased property from landowners.[61] Such agreements by railroads were not uncommon. Edward L. Pierce in his 1857 railroad-law treatise noted "there may be a special agreement to build the fence, as a part of the damages for taking the land."[62] Bad fences made good lawsuits: Illinois landowners could recover consequential damages for a railroad's breach of its agreement. The Illinois Supreme Court allowed landowners to recover the damages for crops destroyed by animals that should have been fenced out by the railroad.[63]

Lincoln tried to mediate these disputes. In March 1854, Lincoln wrote Brayman, the secretary of the Illinois Central, about an "old man from De Witt" who had asked him to sue the Illinois Central. The old man complained that the railroad "does not keep its covenants in regard to making fences." Because of his retainer, Lincoln had referred the farmer to John T. Stuart. Lincoln advised Brayman to mend fences, literally and figuratively. He reminded Brayman that "a stitch in time may save nine in this matter."[64]

The railroad was not always able to save nine. Instead, Lincoln and his colleagues ended up representing the railroad over its failure to build or maintain fences.[65] After Brayman reviewed the merits of fence cases filed in De Witt County, he concluded most of them were "vexatious" and he expected to dispose of them "without trouble."[66] Brayman may have been partially right about the outcomes of these cases: six of the nine of these types of cases were dismissed or settled. But the railroad certainly wasn't able to dispose of all of them without trouble. Two chancery suits—

brought by the irrepressible Wilson Allen—lingered for nearly nine years before they were dismissed by the court, with Allen amassing a staggering $550 in court costs.[67]

Lincoln did not go to trial on every lawsuit against the railroad. Nine of twenty-four lawsuits initiated by landowners in the circuit courts were dismissed. Brayman wrote that these disputes about fences would be "disposed of as soon as I can find the time to look at them personally, by arrangement; or if brought to trial, we shall prevail."[68] An example of a dispute over fences that was resolved "by arrangement" is *Spencer v. Illinois Central*. William and Catharine Spencer had sold right of way "over and through" their property in De Witt County in 1852. As part of the agreement, the railroad also consented to build crossings for "the accommodation of persons whose lands are divided" and to "erect and maintain such lawful fences." Three years later William Spencer sued the railroad for not maintaining crossings and for not building "lawful" fences. Spencer complained that he "was to put to great expense and labor and loss of time in watching and procuring others to watch and protect the crops" from damage from marauding hogs and cattle. Spencer also complained that he was put to great expense of time, labor, and money in putting up and keeping up the fences. Finally, Spencer complained that he had sustained "great damage to his crops" and his meadow. Spencer asked for five hundred dollars in damages. Lincoln and Moore represented the railroad. The case apparently was settled; it was dismissed in May 1856.[69]

In *Dye v. Illinois Central*, Lincoln negotiated a settlement for the railroad. Alexander Dye had sued the railroad for trespass and had claimed damages amounting to five hundred dollars. Dye charged that the railroad's crews had "crushed bruised damaged and spoiled" his grass and corn with their "carts wagons and other carriages." The railroad also had allowed cattle to devour his crops. The case was settled, with Lincoln writing the agreed judgment. Dye agreed to "waive all damages for the want of making and maintaining fence" and to "accept as sufficient" the "already made" fence and the railroad agreed to pay Dye one hundred dollars and costs.[70] In *Emery v. Illinois Central*, the case was settled before the jury reached its verdict and was dismissed by the court.[71] A case brought by George L. Hill of De Witt County in May 1854 was dismissed by agreement two years later.[72]

Of the fourteen cases brought by landowners that were heard by juries, Lincoln won outright courtroom victories for the railroad only twice.[73] The ubiquitous Wilson Allen was involved in both lawsuits; he appeared for one landowner as a surety and for another as a witness.[74] In one of the cases, Jacob Weaver had sued the railroad for trespass, claiming that the railroad's "servants and beasts" had "trod down destroyed and consumed" his crops and were responsible for "throwing down and laying open" his fence. He sued for $300. Lincoln and Moore defended the railroad. Moore first filed a suggestion that Weaver was "so unsettled as to endanger the officers of this court with respect to their legal demands" and would be unable to pay court costs. After Allen filed a bond for costs, Lincoln filed defensive pleas that asserted the railroad had not violated its right of way. The jury found for the railroad.[75]

The railroad and its lawyers believed that the railroad faced considerable hostility from juries. In the same 1854 report in which Brayman brashly predicted victory if the railroad went to trial, he also conceded, "A slight deviation from the letter of the Law will almost, with a willing jury (and juries are always with citizens against a corporation) carry a verdict against it."[76] Lincoln's fellow Illinois Central attorney, Henry Clay Whitney, wrote him during the senate campaign of 1858 that "if we can only turn the hatred of the people to the I.C.R.R. against Douglas no argument could be better." This hatred of the Illinois Central became more pronounced in 1857 when the railroad went into receivership and foreclosed upon thousands of mortgages.[77]

This unpopularity undoubtedly influenced how lawyers like Lincoln defended the railroad in court. Lincoln and his colleagues must have expected to lose on the issue of liability; their trial strategy was to minimize the amount of damages awarded by the jury. In light of the animosity that many held against the railroad, this strategy made sense and appears to have been successful. The railroad was satisfied with these tactics; Lincoln did not appeal any of the lawsuits involving disputes with landowners to the Illinois Supreme Court.

Lincoln and his co-counsel must have convinced juries that the landowners were overreaching. William Spencer filed another lawsuit against the railroad, charging that the railroad had "dug up turned and subvented the earth and soil" and asked for one thousand dollars in damages. Spencer technically won this lawsuit, but Lincoln and Moore successfully had held the damages to $6.50.[78] John Spencer filed a similar lawsuit; he recovered only $5.33 1/3 after asking for eight hundred dollars in damages.[79] In another 1854 lawsuit, Adam Lear of De Witt County asked for one thousand dollars in damages, claiming that the railroad had allowed "horses mares geldings cows oxen sheep & hogs eat up and depastured the grass corn wheat oats & potatoes." Lear was awarded only $225 at trial.[80] Of the three fence cases in De Witt County that went to trial, the railroad lost all three.[81] Although the landowners recovered verdicts in all three cases, none of the awards was close to the damages claimed by the plaintiff. Lewis Carey claimed $500 in damages and recovered $168.53; Abiel Cushman asked for $500 and received $89.50; and George Hill pleaded $5,000 in damages but only received $100.[82]

In *Cushman v. Illinois Central,* Lincoln exploited the evidentiary weakness of his opponent's case to exact an agreement that limited damages at trial. There, the plaintiff, Abiel P. Cushman, sued the railroad for breaking down the fence that surrounded his land and for trampling upon his grass and corn. He asked for five hundred dollars in damages. Lincoln wrote an agreement that stipulated that the railroad would consent to the admission of "evidence of questionable admissibility" if Cushman waived "now and forever all claims for damages which he might legally make for injuries accruing previous to the bringing to the suit because of the failure of said defendant to make and maintain a fence on one boundary of the close . . . according to the contract by which they acquired their Right of Way." After Lincoln negotiated this stipulation, which limited the damages that Cushman could recover, the jury awarded $89.50.[83]

While representing the Illinois Central in suits with landowners, Lincoln continued to represent landowners in suits against other railroads. For example, Lincoln in 1855 represented three co-owners of a parcel next to the Great Western Railroad's depot in Macon County, who complained that the depot's "privies, [and] water closets" were located on their land.[84]

Personal Injury Lawsuits

Curiously, Lincoln did not defend any personal injury lawsuits during the seven years he represented the Illinois Central. However, he did represent an injured worker in a lawsuit against the Great Western Railroad.[85] Lincoln's lack of personal injury cases for the Illinois Central was not a result of railroads' being injury-free. Accidents were common in nineteenth-century railroad work. In fact, the *Chicago Tribune* added the category "Killed on Railroad" when it published mortality statistics in the 1850s.[86] Three factors explain Lincoln's lack of personal injury cases for the Illinois Central. Railroad paternalism, unfavorable formal law, and social attitudes inhibited tort lawsuits against the Illinois Central by its employees. First, the railroad's own informal accident compensation procedures discouraged lawsuits by injured employees. During the nineteenth century, employer-employee relationships generally shifted from paternalistic ones where employers took care of injured workers, which made lawsuits by injured workers rare, to more impersonal relationships, which made lawsuits much more likely.[87] The Illinois Central took a somewhat different path: paternalism combined with releases from liability. The railroad took care of injured workers. For example, in 1857 an injured worker wrote a company official asking that the railroad compensate him for the loss of his foot, which had been severed by the driving wheel of a locomotive. The official replied that the railroad was "not bound for damages to employees on the Road," but offered to pay his medical bills and give him half-pay during his convalescence. Other injured workers also received financial assistance when they were deemed worthy by the railroad. The railroad also tried to find new jobs for workers who would be unable to return to their old ones.[88] Workers understood that filing a lawsuit jeopardized these voluntary payments and their future employment with the railroad. When the railroad paid financial assistance to injured workers or to the families of deceased workers it received signed releases from liability.[89] This release would bar any lawsuit for personal injury. There is no record of Lincoln's involvement with such releases.

The formal law governing injuries to railroad workers also discouraged lawsuits by injured employees.[90] In contrast to the great solicitude with which they approached suits by passengers, English and American courts took a much narrower view of railroad liability for injuries to employees.[91] In nineteenth-century English courts, passengers generally won their lawsuits and employees generally lost.[92] This same pattern applied to American courts generally and Illinois courts specifically.[93]

One legal obstacle to recovery for employees was the widespread adoption of the fellow-servant rule, which precluded recovery for an employee injured by the negligence of a co-worker.[94] The leading case was *Farwell v. Boston & Worcester Railroad,* a 1842 opinion by Chief Justice Lemuel Shaw of the Massachusetts Supreme Judicial Court.[95] In 1854 the Illinois Supreme Court adopted the fellow-servant rule, holding that an employer was not "liable to one servant for the carelessness of another servant." The court in a short opinion wrote that it was only "necessary to refer to *Farwell v. Boston & Worcester Railroad Corporation,* 4 Met. 49, where the whole argument upon the question is embodied in the opinion of Chief Justice Shaw." The court also noted, as had Shaw, that railroad workers were aware of "certain perils incident" to their employment and that railroad companies paid "a premium in enhanced wages to the servant in view of those very risks." With such a distribution of risk, "the misfortune must rest upon whom it has fallen."[96] By 1858 a railroad-law treatise could note that it was "mostly" well settled that "a servant, who is injured by the negligence, or misconduct of his fellow-servant, can maintain no action against the master for such injury."[97] A plaintiff, according to the Illinois Supreme Court, also had to show that "his own negligence or misconduct has not concurred with that of the other party in producing the injury."[98]

Finally, in small communities, the availability of formal remedies and courts is rendered meaningless when a lawsuit is considered an inappropriate response to injury. The social disapproval an individual faced for filing such a lawsuit for personal injuries may have prevented claims from being pressed in court.[99]

An Opinion on Preemption

On a handful of occasions, Lincoln was asked by a client to give a formal legal opinion on an issue to guide that client's actions.[100] He gave such an opinion for the Illinois Central at least once. On March 6, 1856, Lincoln wrote an opinion on whether there could "be any valid pre-emption on sections of land, alternate to the Sections granted to the Illinois Central

Railroad."[101] Preemptive rights were privileges accorded by federal and state governments to persons who had settled on public land before the land was to be sold. In 1841 Congress passed a general preemption law that allowed the head of a family who had settled, inhabited, and improved public lands the first choice or claim to buy the land at the minimum government price.[102] The 1841 law, however, exempted from preemption "sections of land reserved to the United States alternate to other sections granted to any canal, railroad, or other public improvement."[103] In 1852 Congress passed a law that was "to protect actual settlers upon the Land on the Line of the Central Railroad and Branches, by granting Preemption rights thereto." This law allowed someone to qualify for preemption if he was "now an actual settler and occupant" and had made "such an actual settlement and improvement" on public lands that were "alternate" to the lands granted to the Illinois Central.[104] In 1853 Congress extended preemptive rights "over the alternate reserved sections of public lands along the lines of all the railroads of the United States." The availability of preemptive rights was limited to persons who "settled or improved" lands before "the final allotment of the alternate sections to such railroads by the General Land Office."[105]

Lincoln carefully reviewed the applicable federal and state statutes before giving his opinion on preemptive rights. He concluded that "persons who settled on those reserved sections prior to the date of said 'final allotment' might have valid pre-emptions; and that those who settled theron after the date of said allotment, can not."[106] Lincoln's opinion on the availability of preemption may have influenced the railroad's decision to sell thousands of acres to over 1,000 settlers.[107] The validity of Lincoln's legal opinion was confirmed the following year. The Illinois Supreme Court held that the right of preemption did not extend to land on sections "alternate" to sections granted to the Illinois Central Railroad when "the facts of settlement and improvement" occurred after the day of final allotment.[108]

Supreme Court Appeals

Although Lincoln argued eleven cases before the Illinois Supreme Court that involved the Illinois Central Railroad, Lincoln was not the railroad's only appellate attorney. Lincoln's appellate caseload was limited to appeals that arose from the Second Grand Division of the state supreme court, and he did not even handle all of the appeals in that division. A. J. Gallagher and W. H. Underwood, for example, argued an appeal from Fayette County for the railroad in the December 1856 term.[109] The constitution of 1848 had divided the state into three judicial divisions. The Second Grand Division included thirty counties in the central part of the state. Once a year the court sat in Springfield to hear appeals from these counties. For appeals from the other two divisions, the court sat in Mount Vernon and Ottawa.[110]

Other attorneys handled appeals from the other two divisions. Chicago lawyer B. C. Cook, for example, argued at least six appeals for the railroad from 1856 to 1860.[111]

In one appeal, Lincoln successfully argued that the Illinois Central could contractually limit its liability to shippers.[112] This was one of six Illinois Central cases that involved the railroad's liability to its customers for shipments.[113] One of the two cases that reached the supreme court, *Illinois Central Railroad Company v. Morrison & Crabtree,* addressed a legal issue of "vast importance," according to a contemporary railroad law treatise.[114] The issue was important because a railroad's ability to limit liability contractually conflicted with its "insurer" status as a common carrier.[115] The case specifically involved injury to livestock, a common damage suit against railroads.[116]

In Illinois, as in most American jurisdictions, free-market ideology triumphed over the prior strict liability rule.[117] Morrison and his partner Crabtree had received a lower freight rate to ship cattle and had agreed to release the railroad from "all liability for escape or injury, except such as happened through the gross negligence or default" of the railroad. After their cattle suffered undue loss of weight in transit, they sued the railroad in Coles County Circuit Court, claiming that the railroad could not disclaim its liability as a common carrier. The railroad was represented by Orlando B. Ficklin. The plaintiffs' argument succeeded in the circuit court, where the trial judge refused to instruct the jury that the railroad was not a common carrier if there was a special contract for the shipment of the cattle; they received a $1,200 verdict.

The railroad appealed, with Lincoln and Whitney joining Ficklin on appeal. There, Lincoln and his colleagues successfully argued that the railroad had a right to restrict liability contractually. Justice Sidney Breese noted the appeal involved a question of "importance to the business public, and to the railroad interests." Breese began by noting that railroad companies were common carriers that were bound by common-law rules that made them insurers. Until the advent of railroads, courts had not permitted common carriers to limit their liability by "special contract." Railroads, however, meant that "new rules were found necessary, or modifications of old ones, as applicable to this new system." These new rules needed to protect the "magnificent and costly enterprizes" and guard the public from injury. It would be a "great injustice to require the company to pay for escaping risks, and then burden them with the losses against which, by fair contract, they have purchased exemption." The rule adopted in other jurisdictions was a "good one"; under that rule, railroads "have a right to restrict their liability as common carriers by such contracts as may be agreed upon specially, they still remaining liable for gross negligence or willful misfeasance, against which good morals and public policy forbid that they should be permitted to stipulate."[118] The case was remanded and Ficklin again represented the railroad. Somehow Ficklin had defeat snatched from the jaws of victory; he lost again despite the favorable ruling on the validity of the release from the supreme court. Instead of appealing again, the railroad paid the $1,069 judgment.[119]

Lincoln's appellate work for the railroad was not limited to matters of great importance. Seven of Lincoln's appeals were inconsequential. Six minor cases involving mechanics' liens were consolidated in one appeal. The Illinois statute was intended to protect artisans and suppliers by securing payment for labor or materials through a lien upon property.[120] The reporter for the *Illinois Reports* noted that "in the foregoing cases the petitions omitted to show that the work was to be completed within two years. This decision has been so often reported, that a further statement is deemed unnecessary." In a two-sentence opinion the circuit courts' judgments were reversed because the contracts did not say that the work was to be completed within two years, as required by the statute.[121] Lincoln also contended that a jury awarded excessive damages in a case that involved a shipment of hogs. The supreme court, in a one-paragraph opinion, rejected Lincoln's argument. The court noted that "the evidence clearly justified such verdict, and we do not regard it important, as it is a mere question of fact, to attempt, in this opinion, an analysis of the evidence before the jury."[122]

The Railroad and County Taxation

Lincoln handled three important tax cases for the Illinois Central in the supreme court. The Illinois Central specifically had engaged Lincoln to handle the appeal in the McLean County tax lawsuit. The issue presented in the case was whether counties had the right to tax the railroad. The railroad insisted that its charter precluded such taxes. State legislatures generously granted such tax exemptions to encourage the building of rail lines.[123]

McLean County asserted that the legislative charter was unconstitutional. Lincoln recognized that "the point to be made against us, [was] that the Constitution secures to the counties the right to tax all property, beyond the power of the Legislature to take it away."[124] The 1848 constitution provided that counties were "vested with power to assess and collect taxes" and that such taxes were "to be uniform in respect to persons and property within the jurisdiction of the body" that imposed the tax.[125]

The case began in September 1853 when Mason Brayman and Asahel Gridley filed a bill in chancery to enjoin McLean County's collection of taxes from the railroad. According to the railroad's attorneys, the county was attempting to tax property that was not "subject or liable to assessment and taxation for any purpose." They requested a perpetual injunction against the county. Both sides soon agreed that the matter had to be resolved by the Illinois Supreme Court as a matter of law. To this end, the circuit court, by agreement of the parties, entered a pro forma order that granted and then dissolved the injunction. The order dismissed the bill and allowed an appeal by the railroad. It also stipulated that the parties' agreement to limit the issue on appeal to "whether the property and franchises, attempted to be taxed by the Defendants . . . is in Law, liable to County Taxation."[126]

The case was on its way to the supreme court. Lincoln wrote the assignment of errors that was filed in the court.[127] The reporter's abstract of the case later summarized the railroad's two winning arguments. The railroad first argued that it was "within the constitutional power of the legislature to exempt property from taxation or to commute the general rate for a fixed sum." It asserted next that "the provisions, in the charter of the Illinois Central Railroad Company, exempting its property from taxation, upon the payment of a certain proportion of its earnings, are constitutional."[128]

Lincoln carefully prepared for the appeal. When Lincoln later sued for his fee, he claimed that he, "and not Joy, made the point & argument on which the case turned."[129] His notes for argument referred to twenty-six cases, including four decisions from the United States Supreme Court and twenty-two decisions from thirteen different state courts. The Illinois Supreme Court later cited thirteen of the twenty-six cases that Lincoln provided the court in his argument in its opinion.[130]

The legal issues were sufficiently complicated that Lincoln twice argued the case before the Illinois Supreme Court. The case was originally argued on February 28, 1854. Lincoln and James F. Joy argued the railroad's case and Lincoln's former partners, Stephen Logan and John Stuart, argued for the county. The court ordered the case "stood over" and reargued. Joy later recalled that "the case was long under advisement, and later the court complied with my request and gave us a rehearing."[131] The reargument took place in January 1856, nearly two years after the first argument. Chief Justice Scates later admitted in his opinion that the Illinois constitution's provisions on taxation had presented "apparently obvious difficulties" and that "a re-argument was ordered, that full discussion and deliberate examination might remove these apparent difficulties."[132]

Lincoln began his argument with the narrowest possible ground for the court to enjoin the county's collection of taxes. Lincoln argued for what was incontrovertible: that the railroad, under its 1851 charter, was exempt from any tax for six years. Lincoln asserted that the legislature exempted the property from taxation because it was held in trust to the state while the railroad was being constructed. As state property, it was "rightfully exempted from taxation." Lincoln also noted that Massachusetts and Pennsylvania courts had held that railroad property in those states was "in absence of statutory provisions, exempted from taxation" "on the ground that it is public property." Lincoln admitted that two other state courts had held otherwise.[133] Lincoln, however, asserted that, until the railroad was finished, its property was public property that could not be taxed by any county.[134] To support this point Lincoln cited *M'Culloch v. Maryland* (1819) and *Weston v. Charleston* (1829), two United States Supreme Court cases that involved the tax immunity of governmental entities.[135] In *M'Culloch,* the Court had held that the federal government was immune from state taxation; in *Weston*, the Court had held that stock issued for loans made to the federal government was also exempt from state taxation. By analogy, Lincoln argued the railroad's property was also immune from taxation so long as it could be considered state property.

In some ways this was a peculiar argument; after all, the railroad had requested a "perpetual" injunction. Lincoln's argument, if successful, would only delay the collection of taxes until the charter lines were finished. This meant that Lincoln would have won a six-month reprieve from county taxes for his client: the 705-mile charter line was completed later that year.[136] When the court issued its decision, Justice Skinner filed a concurring opinion that would have reversed the circuit court on this narrow basis.[137]

In the remainder of his argument, Lincoln squarely faced the county's constitutional argument that the constitution "secures to the counties the right to tax all property, beyond the power of the Legislature to take it away." To counter this argument that the railroad's exemption from county taxation was unconstitutional, Lincoln skillfully built a defense of the legislature's action. Lincoln first argued that, under the Illinois Central charter, the railroad was exempted from county taxes. After showing "by the Charter, the Co is not liable," Lincoln turned to "the question" presented by the case: "But was it constitutionally competent for the Legislature to grant the exemption?"[138] Lincoln made three points. First, he discussed the "general power of the Legislature." Second, he discussed similar "cases of exemption." Third, he compared the 1848 Illinois constitution with the 1818 constitution.

Lincoln first argued that the Illinois legislature was fully empowered to enact its will. Lincoln cited a particular page of Kent's *Commentaries* in a section on "statute law" to emphasize that "courts are to give the statute a reasonable construction." Kent wrote on that page that courts "will not readily presume, out of respect and duty to the lawgiver, that any very unjust or absurd consequences was within the contemplation of the law. . . . The will of the legislature is the supreme law of the land, and demands perfect obedience." Lincoln was selectively using Kent's *Commentaries* to make his point. If one of the judges had turned to the next page, he would have found that the cited comments were part of Kent's description of the English judiciary's approach to acts of Parliament, which Kent rejected. Kent explained that the "principle in the English government, that the parliament is omnipotent, does not prevail in the United States." Instead, American courts "have a right, and are duty bound, to bring every law to the test of the constitution."[139]

Lincoln also referred to an 1841 Illinois Supreme Court opinion that upheld a statute against an attack on its constitutionality.[140] There the court held that the legislature was "competent . . . to exercise all powers not forbidden by the constitution of the state, nor delegated to the general government, nor prohibited to the state by the constitution of the United States."[141] This argument about the power of the legislature resonates in the court's decision. Chief Justice Scates wrote that "courts will not seek by construction to deny or destroy the essential powers of the legislature, nor hold their acts void in mere cases of doubt."[142] Lincoln thus argued that the legislature should be allowed to exercise its proper powers without interference from courts.

In the second part of his argument, Lincoln discussed other cases of legislative exemptions from taxation. He discussed ten opinions from Illinois and other states where minor municipal corporations, such as counties, townships, and cities taxed corporations that previously had received legislative exemptions. In every case, declared Lincoln, the court decided in favor of the exemptions. (The supreme court later cited six of these ten opinions to support its ruling.[143]) Lincoln referred to an earlier Illinois Supreme Court decision. In *State Bank v. People,* the supreme court in 1843 had held that the circuit court erred in allowing lands owned by the State Bank of Illinois to be sold for taxes. The bank's charter exempted its property from taxation. The court reasoned that "its charter was in the nature of a contract, and the state would have no constitutional power thus to vary its terms or add to its burthens."[144]

The precise issue of the constitutional authority of the legislatures to grant exemptions from taxation was not discussed in these cases. Lincoln, however, then cited seven cases "where special taxes have been directly, or indirectly, imposed by legislative acts, and the constitutional competency questioned, and sustained."[145] Among the cases that Lincoln cited was an 1852 Pennsylvania decision that strongly asserted that "the taxing power must be left to that part of the government which is to exercise it."[146]

Lincoln then compared the 1848 state constitution with the 1818 state constitution. The 1835 charter for the State Bank of Illinois had "expressly exempted the bank from all taxes and impositions whatever." In 1843, the supreme court reviewed this charter under the 1818 constitution and held that the legislature had the power to make the contract with the bank.[147] To use this case as precedent, Lincoln had to compare the 1818 constitution with the 1848 constitution "in connection" with this case and show that they were substantially similar. The 1818 constitution had specified that "the mode of levying a tax shall be by valuation, so that every person shall pay a tax in proportion to the value of the property he or she has in her possession." The 1848 constitution, Lincoln noted, "has some provisions, supposed to bear on the case, which are not found in the other constitutions." Lincoln believed that this was "the exact and main question." He then analyzed specific provisions in the 1848 constitution.[148]

Lincoln concluded his argument by stating that "in no doubtful case will the court pronounce a legislative act to be contrary to the constitution." Lincoln cited two cases to support this argument. He referred to the 1844 Illinois Supreme Court decision in *People ex rel. Stickney v. Marshall* and the 1819 United States Supreme Court decision in *Dartmouth College v. Woodward*.[149] When faced with an attack on the constitutionality of legislation involving the state bank, the Illinois court had held that "it has been repeatedly decided, and is well settled by the highest tribunals in the nation, that it is seldom, if ever, in a doubtful case, or upon slight implication, that the court should declare the legislature to have transcended its authority."[150]

The court sustained Lincoln's position and held that the railroad was exempt from county taxation. Chief Justice Scates for the court held that the legislature had the power "to exempt, or rather to commute" the railroad's payment of county taxes by "the payment of a gross sum." The issue was not between the county and the railroad but between the county and the state. If the legislature had "the power exercised in this case," the court would not question the exercise of that power. Scates wrote that "there is no subject upon which the courts have sustained legislative power with greater liberality of construction" than taxation. A legislature needed to have a "power commensurate with the means required to furnish vitality to the body politic." After reviewing the case law provided by Lincoln, Scates held that the Illinois Central charter was constitutional.[151]

Lincoln had secured a significant victory. Decisions like the McLean County case were particularly important because they limited the local taxes that could be imposed on railroads, along with the associated financial burdens.[152] Lincoln believed he had saved the railroad $500,000.

The Railroad and State Taxation

The railroad soon faced another problem with taxes, which led to its settling its fee dispute with Lincoln in order to retain his expertise. Under its 1851 charter, the railroad was "exempt from taxation for the term of six years from the passage of this act." In 1857 the railroad faced its first assessment of state taxes. The charter provided that the railroad was to pay five percent of "the gross or total proceeds receipts, or income derived from said road and branches." The charter also provided for an "annual tax" upon the railroad's property and assets. If both assessments did not amount to "seven per cent. of the gross or total proceeds, receipts or income," then the railroad was to pay "the difference, so as to make the whole amount paid equal at least to seven per cent. of the gross receipts."[153] The railroad and Jesse Dubois, the state auditor, initially disagreed on how to interpret the charter: the railroad contended that the seven percent language set a ceiling on the tax (taxes couldn't exceed seven percent) and Dubois believed that the language set the minimum amount of tax owed (taxes could exceed seven percent).[154]

Dubois described the "serious question [that] has arisen between the state and the Illinois Central Railroad company" in his Biennial Report, which was filed in December 1858. The railroad's initial challenge to Dubois's assessment was that it exceeded what the railroad considered a cap on taxes in its charter. The railroad interpreted its charter to mean that the state could not impose any taxes that amounted to more than seven percent of the railroad's gross receipts. Dubois explained:

> The taxes upon the assessed value of the property of the company, when added to five per cent. provided to be paid into the state treasury, exceeded seven per cent of the gross earnings of the road for that year. The company insist, that under the law, its liability to the state for taxes, cannot in any event, exceed seven per cent of its gross earnings, whilst on the part of the state it is insisted that its liability to the state cannot be less than seven per cent of its gross earnings, but may be more, depending on the assessed valuation of the property.

Dubois noted that he had sued the railroad for the disputed taxes in an original suit filed in the Illinois Supreme Court and that "an authoritative construction of the law from that tribunal may be expected at its next term." Dubois concluded by noting, "nothing could be more dangerous and suicidal to the future interests of the people of the state" than to surrender to any corporation "the great constitutional privilege of taxing its property according to its value."[155] It's possible that Lincoln may have written this section of the auditor's report, but the evidence to support such a conclusion isn't particularly strong.[156]

With the lawsuit filed in supreme court, railroad officials knew that Lincoln's ability, reputation, and political connections would make his involvement with this issue crucial. These officials were aware that the state auditor had discussed retaining Lincoln. They knew that Lincoln, once again, was going to represent one side or the other. The railroad was able to employ Lincoln only after he—in the words of the railroad's general counsel—was "disarmed by our settlement of his claim & by our continued retainer."[157] In August, Ebenezer Lane wrote W. H. Osborn about the company's "narrow escape":

> While Lincoln was prosecuting his lawsuit for fees, it was natural for him to expect a dismissal from the Company's service & being a Politician aspiring to the Senate to entertain plans of making an attack upon the Company not only in a revengeful spirit, but as subservient to his future advancement.

The railroad, however, "settled with Lincoln & fortunately took him out of the field, or rather engaged him in our interests." The railroad did not just respect Lincoln's skill as a lawyer; it also realized that Lincoln was "not only the most prominent of his political party, but the acknowledged special adviser of the Bissell Administration."[158]

Some railroad officials believed that Lincoln himself was responsible for the charter tax problem. Ebenezer Lane thought Lincoln during the fee dispute had formed "plans of making an attack" on the railroad for the sake of revenge and political advantage. Lincoln had seen "the obscurity" of the provisions on tax in the charter and he briefly had discussed the issue with Dubois before the railroad settled the fee lawsuit with him. Lane, who saw Dubois as a "vain, self-sufficient but weak man," was under the impression that Lincoln gave Dubois "no detailed opinion, but expressed his sense of the great magnitude which the auditor was bound to protect. This had no other effect probably than to raise still higher the Auditor's opinion of himself."[159] Another railroad official was even more critical of Lincoln. David Stewart wrote Stephen Douglas in 1859 that "this thing has been put in motion by Lincoln & his special friend, not so much from a deceitful feeling connected with his [Senate] defeat as from his old quarrel with the Co. which you understand."[160]

Once engaged in the railroad's interests, Lincoln went to work. On December 21, 1857, he wrote a letter to Dubois, which John M. Douglass of the Illinois Central hand-delivered. Dubois and Lincoln had served as Whig representatives in the General Assembly. Dubois was a loyal supporter of Lincoln; in 1854 he wrote Lincoln that he was *"for you against the world."*[161] Lincoln explained that the railroad was prepared to pay $90,000 "into the Treasury now, if they have an assurance that they shall not be sued before Jany. 1859." Without such an assurance, the railroad would not pay any more of its disputed taxes. Lincoln hoped that Dubois would agree to his proposal. "Douglas says they *can not* pay more & I believe him." Lincoln was not writing the letter "as a lawyer seeking an advantage for a client; but only as a friend, only urging you to do, what I think I would do if I were in your situation." Lincoln admitted feeling "a good deal of anxiety" about the letter.[162] Dubois listened to Lincoln's plea; the state did not file suit against the railroad until November 1858.[163]

Lincoln and Douglass prudently shifted the railroad's strategy away from the construction of the charter. The lawyers apparently believed that it was unwise to rely upon a favorable construction of the charter; they hoped instead to argue for a lower valuation of the railroad's property. The auditor had used a figure of $19,000,000, which had been supplied by the railroad in its 1857 tax return. He then levied a tax on the entire valuation, which amounted to a tax liability of $132,067.44. If a cap of seven percent of gross receipts existed, then the assessment exceeded the supposed cap by over $94,000.[164] The problem with challenging the valuation figure was twofold. First, the railroad would be challenging a figure that it had provided. Second, it was unclear whether the supreme court could second-guess the auditor's figure.

The railroad and its lawyers adroitly executed a series of maneuvers to challenge the railroad's own valuation of its property. The railroad turned to the legislature, where it successfully lobbied in February 1859 for a law that prescribed a method to resolve disputes over its taxes. Cyrus W. Vanderen, a Republican state senator from Sangamon County, introduced a bill that supposedly was "intended to supply omissions" in the original charter.[165] At the same time, the railroad called upon Stephen Douglas to convince Democratic politicians from southern Illinois to support the bill.[166] The act said that it was the auditor's duty to list the railroad's "stock, property and assets," to "place a valuation thereon," and to "assess there on a tax for state purposes." If the company was dissatisfied with the auditor's "list and valuation," then it could appeal directly to the supreme court. The supreme court would handle the matter as an original suit; it would hear evidence and determine "the aggregate value of the stock, property and assets" of the railroad.[167]

In March, the company filed a drastically lower valuation of property for its 1858 and 1859 property. For its 1858 taxes, the railroad claimed that its property was worth $7,650,000; for its 1859 taxes, $4,942,000.[168] After the railroad filed its 1859 return, Dubois decided that he should see the railroad's entire property to assess its value. He arranged for a trip in July over the system, accompanied by Lincoln; Stephen T. Logan; the Secretary of State, O. M. Hatch; and the State Treasurer, William Butler. The trip began on July 14 and lasted nine days.[169] Dubois was not persuaded that the railroad's $4,942,000 figure was accurate; he formally "disapproved" the company's figure and determined that the value of the property was $13 million.[170]

Lincoln in October gave Dubois notice of an appeal of the 1859 valuation under the new act.[171] Lincoln succeeded in having the 1859 tax appeal heard before the 1857 case because the statute required the appeal to be heard "the next term succeeding the taking of such appeal." The 1859 case was heard in November 1859; the 1857 case in January 1860. At the November hearing Lincoln and Douglass presented ten witnesses, including the president of the Galena & Union Railroad, the Illinois Central's main engineer, the president of the Terre Haute & Alton Railroad, the president of the Great Western Railroad, the auditor of the Chicago & Burlington Railroad, and the auditor of the Chicago & Rock Island Railroad. These witnesses testified that the 1859 return was actually extravagant, "that railroad prospects in Illinois were not favorable, and that returns on railroad investments were poor."[172] The court later noted that "the most experienced and intelligent railroad men in the West, were fully examined on all the elements of value."[173] The state only called one witness, apparently because Dubois thought the case was set the following week.[174] The supreme court agreed that the company's valuation of this "stock, property and assets" was accurate and sustained its appeal. Its opinion in the appeal case has not survived.

The 1857 case was heard two months later. The outcome of the case was largely determined by the court's earlier decision and by the stipulations agreed upon by the parties. The parties originally stipulated that the court could hear evidence and could modify the 1857 assessment but could not reduce "the aggregate value of the stock, property and assets . . . below thirteen million of dollars." While the railroad's assessment bill was pending, the state's lawyers "agreed to remove the limit of thirteen million of dollars, and leave the valuation as entirely open to the court." The parties also stipulated that the evidence presented at the November hearing also could be considered by the court. The court held that the railroad's property valuation for 1857 was the same as it had found in the 1859 case.[175] Lincoln had helped secure another victory for the railroad. He was paid $500 for his efforts.[176]

Conclusion

Lincoln is often called a railroad lawyer or a corporation lawyer. In the modern sense, he was neither. While he practiced railroad law, he did not exclusively represent railroads; Lincoln frequently sued railroads. Nor was Lincoln a corporation lawyer. According to Robert L. Nelson, lawyers in modern corporate law practice generally fit one of two distinct roles. Corporate lawyers often have a long-term relationship with a corporation that is characterized by the lawyers knowing the intimate details of the workings of the corporation, a mutual dependence between the corporation and the lawyers, and the lawyers identifying with the interests of the corporation. The other role played by corporate lawyers is that of "hired gun" in a particular case or transaction. Corporations use these lawyers for their particular expertise in trial work or for their negotiating skills or for their "local knowledge" of courts and governmental bodies. These lawyers don't know everything about the company; they don't need to know everything to get their job done.[177]

Neither model fits Lincoln's relationship with the Illinois Central. Lincoln and other Western lawyers generally represented their clients on an ad hoc basis: they represented whoever asked them first. Lincoln frequently sued parties who had been clients and defended parties who had been adversaries. Lincoln, however, did develop some relatively long-term relationships with some clients in the 1850s. One such client was the Illinois Central. While Lincoln's relationship with the railroad was relatively continuous after 1852, it was also extremely narrow. Lincoln was a trial lawyer for the railroad in the circuits he regularly traveled and also represented the railroad in some appellate cases before the Illinois Supreme Court when it sat in Springfield. He did little "office work" for the railroad. The railroad hired Lincoln because of his trial and negotiation skills and his familiarity with the supreme court and elected officials, not because of any specialized knowledge about how the Illinois Central was structured. With the exception of the McLean County case, Lincoln's association with the railroad was not particularly lucrative. He received a $250 retainer and charged ten dollars a case for his assistance in trying cases. In contrast, some eastern lawyers received annual retainers from corporations of one or two thousand dollars.[178]

Lincoln's relationship with the Illinois Central shows the strains and tensions in Whig lawyering. The Whig ideal was based on the lawyer's independence to represent any client, and to serve a mediative role. Lincoln's acceptance of a retainer from the Illinois Central, however, meant that Lincoln was no longer free to accept any client. The Illinois Central hired Lincoln to represent it because he was well known to, and trusted by, rural juries. But this fame and trust were founded on the perception that Lincoln stood for something besides the self-interest of any particular client. The railroad wanted Lincoln to represent its own narrow interests, not to act as a mediator for the community's interests.

CHAPTER SEVEN

A Changing Legal Landscape

By the 1850s, Lincoln's clients included not only local litigants involved in land disputes or slander cases but also out-of-state business interests. The correspondence with these firms and their lawyers reveals his difficulty in adjusting to the different style of lawyering demanded by market-oriented litigation. Lincoln never fully adjusted to the quickened pace or the impersonal nature of these cases. He did not avoid these cases, but he remained ambivalent about representing corporations.

The rise of capitalism changed the rhythms of life, not only for society in general but also for lawyers. Socially, market capitalism was accompanied by a work- and time-discipline that was completely different from that associated with agriculture.[1] Lincoln, as Kenneth J. Winkle has shown, lived in two different worlds. He was born into a world that featured a subsistence economy based on family and self-sufficiency. The world Lincoln entered in New Salem and Springfield was the new market economy based on competition and enterprise.[2]

Some lawyers adjusted well to the demands of the emerging market economy, while others, like Lincoln, never fully adjusted to the new regimen. New York lawyer David Dudley Field observed in 1844 that "the bar is now crowded with bustling and restless men. . . . A feverish restlessness, and an overtasked mind, are the present concomitants of a leading position in the profession."[3] Lincoln, however, was neither feverish nor overtasked in the practice of law. Herndon relates how Lincoln would arrive at the office "about nine o'clock in the morning" and "the first thing he did was to pick up a newspaper, spread himself out on an old sofa, one leg on a chair, and read aloud." Lincoln did not read law books unless a case demanded legal research, and he depended on "the stimulus and inspiration of the final hour" for his effectiveness in handling cases. He generally ignored "the fees and money matters of the firm."[4] Lincoln was not temperamentally suited for the new style of lawyering associated with the rise of capitalism.

Lincoln's lack of organizational skills in his law practice is well documented. Herndon recalled how "Lincoln knew no such thing as order or method in his law practice. He made no preparation in advance, but trusted to the hour for its inspiration and to Providence for his supplies. . . . He was proverbially careless as to habits."[5] Lincoln's seeming lack of diligence can not be explained solely by his preoccupation with politics. In 1850, at a time when Lincoln said he "practiced law more assiduously than ever before," he wrote a client apologizing for "not sooner answering" the client's letter. Lincoln explained that he had put the letter "in my old hat, and buying a new one the next day, the old one was set aside, and so, the letter lost sight of for a time."[6] Lincoln had said he had hired Herndon "supposing that [Herndon] had system and would keep things in order, but . . . found that [he] had no more system" than Lincoln had.[7]

Lincoln's correspondence with the New York firm of Blatchford, Seward & Griswold illustrates the difficulty he sometimes had adjusting to this new style of lawyering. Blatchford, Seward & Griswold, the leading corporate law firm of its day, sent Lincoln a $120 collection case. The firm expected Lincoln immediately to sue the Springfield maker of the note. Lincoln, however, was not in a hurry.[8] When Lincoln received the case, he replied that he knew "the firm of T. J. V. Owen & Bro., and, although they are better pressed, I understand them to be good for all their debts."[9] Eight months later, the firm wrote it "have heard nothing from you on the note—Pray what has become of it."[10] Lincoln replied that it was his "impression" that "the note will ultimately be paid, but that its payment would not be accelerated by a suit." If the New York lawyers wanted Lincoln to file a lawsuit, however, he would "bring one at once."[11] Lincoln was out of step: the New York lawyers did not want him to evaluate the situation; they wanted him to file suit.

Lincoln's difficulties with out-of-state business clients are best illustrated by his relationships with S.C. Davis & Co. and Columbus Machine Manufacturing Co. S.C. Davis & Co. was a wholesale merchant in St. Louis, Missouri. In the late 1850s Lincoln & Herndon filed at least twenty-five lawsuits for the St. Louis firm in the federal district court for the Southern District of Illinois.[12] Twenty of the cases were filed in assumpsit to collect on promissory notes. The damages claimed in these twenty suits totaled $53,700. The highest amount of damages claimed in one suit was ten thousand dollars; the lowest amount claimed was five hundred dollars.[13] Three other suits were foreclosures; the firm had secured promissory notes with mortgages to land. The underlying notes in these three cases totaled $2,802.[14] These cases were very different from the collection cases that Lincoln had filed earlier in his career. The amounts sued for were much higher. The parties involved were business entities, not individuals. Instead of filing in state court, Lincoln & Herndon used diversity jurisdiction to file in federal court.

One case, *S.C. Davis & Co. v. Monical & Son,* seems fairly typical of the cases that Lincoln handled for this firm. There, Lincoln filed the declaration, which initiated the lawsuit, on May 26, 1858. The declaration itself was a preprinted form for suing on a note in federal court. Lincoln filled in the blanks in the forms for the names of the parties and the details of the promissory note. This was a slight advance from his earlier practice when he would copy declarations from Chitty's *Pleadings* and other formbooks. In this case, S.C. Davis & Co. had received a promissory note for $873 from George Monical and George W. Monical, who did business as "Monical & Son." The printed form told the rest of the story: "the said defendants (although often requested, &c) have not yet paid the said several sums of money above mentioned." Lincoln requested $1,200 in damages.[15] The court in January 1859 noted the defendants "being three times solemnly called came not but made default and entered a judgment for $939.07.[16]

Lincoln's task was to reduce these debt cases quickly to judgments. These cases typically ended with the defendant failing to answer and Lincoln & Herndon receiving a default judgment. Only one of the twenty-five cases filed for S.C. Davis went to trial; only two apparently settled. In the other twenty-two cases, Lincoln & Herndon obtained a default judgment for their client.[17] Of the nine cases Lincoln filed on December 7, 1857, he received eight default judgments a month later when the defendants failed to appear for trial. The judgments ranged from just under seven hundred dollars to more than five thousand dollars.[18] In all three of the foreclosure suits, Lincoln also received an order of foreclosure by default.[19]

A series of letters written by Lincoln document the problems he had with his client. After receiving judgments in the case filed in the January 1858 term, he wrote his client to express his "perplexity about the collection of these debts." He explained in a February 1858 letter that the federal marshal "now has the executions and will soon call on the defendants." If a defendant was able to "pay in money, or turn out sufficient of personal property," then that case would be "easy." Lincoln warned of another situation, where the defendant's only asset was real estate. A judgment creditor had to ensure that the chain of title was not defective and that the land was worth the amount of debt. In that instance, there was "no way to be safe, as to titles and value, but to visit the several localities, and examine carefully." Illinois was unlike Missouri, where the third parties who would buy property at execution sales would be responsible "to take care of themselves on titles and values." In Illinois, third parties "never bid & consequently plaintiffs have to buy in themselves & if not posted on titles and values, they get badly bit." This was also true in the three suits that Lincoln had filed to foreclose mortgages.[20]

On November 17, 1858, Lincoln angrily replied to a letter from S.C. Davis & Co. that had demanded an explanation of why its "interests have been so neglected." The firm had complained that "the lands of those against whom we obtained judgments last winter for you have not been sold on execution." Lincoln first stated that "you perhaps need not to be reminded how I have been personally engaged the last three or four months." (Lincoln had been campaigning for the Senate.) He then reminded the firm of his February letter that had warned how "the selling of land on execution is a delicate and dangerous matter; that it could not be done safely without a careful examination of titles." Such an examination would require "a canvass of half the State." Lincoln explained that he had sent the earlier letter because he was puzzled and needed instructions on how to proceed. S.C. Davis, however, had "sent no definite instructions." Lincoln had hired a young lawyer, William Fishback, to "visit all the localities, and make as accurate a report on titles and values as he could." After Fishback completed his report, Lincoln said he wrote the firm again, "asking if we should sell and bid in for you in accordance with this information." Lincoln faulted the firm: "this letter you never answered."

Lincoln informed the firm that he no longer wanted to handle "this class of business." He was willing to handle cases in court but he would not "follow executions all over the world." He suggested that S.C. Davis turn the cases over to Fishback. He further informed the firm that he had incurred legal fees of one hundred dollars. Lincoln, however, "would not go through the same labor and vexation again for five hundred."[21] The firm's apparent response to Lincoln's letter was to send the execution business to Fishback, as Lincoln suggested, and to send more cases for Lincoln to file in federal court.

The firm immediately replied to Lincoln's letter and within days he wrote again. He regretted that "there is still some misunderstanding." S.C. Davis in its latest letter had reminded Lincoln that he had "especially 'desired'" its business and had agreed to "attend to collection, Sales &c." Lincoln answered that "undoubtedly our taking the business, implied a promise that we would do what is usual for lawyers to do in such cases, and we have not blamed you for expecting this much of us." Lincoln's "determination to decline" the collection of judgment in future cases "implies no blame upon you." Lincoln admitted, however, "to a little impatience at your blaming us for not making sales, when, as we thought, the fault was your own, in not answering our letter requesting instructions." Lincoln was chagrined to discover that Fishback had moved to Arkansas, which "prevents the new arrangement." He asked for instructions from his clients on "what shall be done."[22]

The firm again turned to Lincoln to handle collecting the judgments. On November 30, Lincoln agreed to handle the executions of the judgments but again reminded S.C. Davis that he still had not received "your direction about making sales."[23] Lincoln wrote Fishback a couple of weeks later. He explained that S.C. Davis had complained that "lands had not been sold upon their executions" and that he had "answered them, saying it was their own fault, as they never answered after we informed them of the work you had done." When Lincoln discovered that Fishback had moved, he had "very reluctantly" agreed to "renew our effort to collect the money on their executions. And so we have pitched into it again." Lincoln asked Fishback to return to Illinois and "take charge of this business."[24]

Sometime in 1857 or 1858, the Columbus Machine Manufacturing Company of Columbus, Ohio, wrote Lincoln about one of their customers, James A. Barret of Springfield. The company had extended about five hundred dollars in credit to Barret and asked Lincoln for his opinion of Barret's "responsibility." Lincoln replied that he considered Barret "an honest and honorable man, having a great deal of property, owing a good many debts, and hard pressed for ready cash." After receiving Lincoln's balanced evaluation, the company extended Barret's credit "to near ten thousand dollars." The company then asked Lincoln "to take notes and a mortgage, and to hold on to the notes awhile to fix amounts." Lincoln, however, held on to both the notes and the mortgage, which allowed Barret to execute and record another mortgage on the property before the Ohio firm's mortgage was recorded. Barret later defaulted on the notes, and the company asked Lincoln to sue Barret.[25]

Lincoln filed suit against James A. Barret & Co. on December 9, 1858, during the January term of the federal court. The suit alleged $15,000 in damages, based on six promissory notes worth $11,324.60.[26] Lincoln also filed a separate chancery suit in federal court, which sought foreclosure on a mortgage deed that had secured four of the promissory notes. Lincoln admitted in this pleading that Barret had executed another mortgage in favor of Henry VonPhul after Barret executed the mortgage for Ambos. Lincoln also admitted that this "last mortgage was in fact first recorded." Lincoln asked the court that the property be sold to pay for the unpaid notes.[27]

After Lincoln filed suit, he received at least four letters from Ambos from January to April 1859. These letters reveal the company's anxiety about the lawsuit and about Lincoln's failure to answer its letters expeditiously.[28] Lincoln meanwhile had obtained a one-thousand-dollar partial payment on the debt.[29] The company continued to press Lincoln for news about the case because it was "very much embarrassed for want of funds to meet our present obligations and are in hopes this judgment has been settled or will be very soon."[30]

By June 1859, Lincoln was tired of the company's frequent correspondence and replied to "two or three letters" from the company. He informed Charles Ambos that Barret "has been telling me for three months past that there is some money at Christian Co. . . . which can be had when he and I can go there together to release a portion of the land involved." Lincoln and Barret planned to go to Christian County in a few days. This would again involve receiving only a partial payment of the debt, but Lincoln counseled that "it is so very much better to get the debt reduced by ac-

tual payments, than to push forward in the sole reliance upon the law."
Sensing that Ambos was dissatisfied by his efforts in the case, Lincoln offered to "very gladly surrender the charge of the case to anyone you
would designate, without charging anything for the much trouble I have
already had."[31]

Ambos apparently had Samuel Galloway, an Ohio lawyer and politician,
write Lincoln to express the company's continued desire for Lincoln to represent it but, at the same time, to express the company's concern about
how Lincoln was handling its case. Lincoln's response to the suggestion
that he had been lax in handling the claim was the same as when S.C.
Davis & Co. had criticized Lincoln: Lincoln blamed whatever problems that
existed on the client. Lincoln told Galloway that the case "has been a
somewhat disagreeable matter" to him. His chief annoyance was that the
company thought it was by his "neglect that they do not get their money."
Lincoln reminded Galloway that, when the company had inquired about
Barret's "responsibility" at a time when Barret had a "Credit of four or five
hundred dollars," Lincoln had pointed out that Barret had "a good many
debts" and was "hard pressed for ready cash." Lincoln was a "little surprised" to later learn that the Columbus Machine Manufacturing Co. "had
enlarged the credit to near ten thousand dollars." The company had asked
Lincoln "to take notes and a mortgage, and to hold on to the notes awhile
to fix amounts." Lincoln had "inferred" that both the notes and mortgage
were "to be held up for a time." Barret then "gave a second mortgage on
part of the premises, which was first recorded." Lincoln did not appreciate
that the company "blamed" him for not immediately recording the mortgage after Barret executed it.[32]

The company also apparently was concerned that Lincoln's personal relationship with Barret had affected the way he had handled the claim. Lincoln told Galloway that "there are no special relations between Barret and
myself. We are personal friends in a general way—no business transactions
between us—not akin, and opposed on politics."[33] Lincoln evidently did
not believe it was worth mentioning that he had sued Barret for the Alton
& Sangamon Railroad earlier in the decade and had won in both the trial
court and supreme court, and that he had sued Barret for nearly five thousand dollars for another client the previous year (the case was dismissed).[34]

Several months later, Lincoln again was barraged by letters from Peter
Ambos. Between January 14 and February 8, 1860, Ambos sent four letters
to Lincoln about the claim. On January 14, Ambos wrote after seeing a legal
notice in a Springfield newspaper about one of Barret's properties being
sold. Ambos was concerned because the company had a "claim either by
Lien or Mortgage" on the property. Ambos told Lincoln that the company
was "entirely in the dark as to the present situation of our case." While the
company had "full confidence" in Lincoln, it was concerned about how
this sale would affect its claim. While "it was our right to have had the first

mortgage on this property," it appeared that "we have failed in that." Ambos asked Lincoln to send a reply "as comprehensive as possible that it may be satisfactory to the Directors of this company who are as anxious about this matter."[35]

Lincoln sent a reply four days later, which Ambos answered on January 21. Lincoln apparently informed Ambos that not only was there a previously recorded mortgage on the property but also a mechanic's lien that superseded the mortgage. Ambos then complained that, while the company had instructed Lincoln to "make a settlement with Barret & Co. and take a mortgage," it also had instructed Lincoln "to make the settlement—as if it were your own case." The company now regretted that Lincoln did not take "a lien in place of a mortgage or both a lien and mortgage." Furthermore, the company had "certainly expected" Lincoln to record the mortgage he did receive and "not allow another to supersede ours." In fact, Ambos said that, if he was "rightly informed," Barret had told Lincoln that "he was very much disappointed when he learned that the subsequent mortgage he had given had superseded ours." Under the circumstances, the company was now willing to give Barret "further time" to pay. Ambos concluded by confessing his "disappointment" in Lincoln's management of the claim.[36]

On February 2, Ambos wrote again, asking Lincoln to take "prompt and energetic action to save our claims." Ambos had the "utmost confidence in your ability to save us from loss if you will only give the case the attention it requires." Ambos then complained about Lincoln giving Barret the "privilege to redeem the Christian County land," which would deprive the company of any security it held in the property.[37] Lincoln apparently again responded because, on February 8, Ambos sheepishly wrote "we are free to confess that we have misunderstood this matter entirely." As far as the mechanic's lien on the property, Ambos instructed Lincoln to "be governed by your own judgment as to the manner of preventing the sale." Lincoln apparently again had offered to retire from the case because Ambos said that "we feel satisfied you will do your best and we therefore prefer to leave the case entirely at your discretion."[38] When Ambos pointedly wrote that he would leave matters to Lincoln's judgment and discretion, he may have addressed the source of Lincoln's irritation.

On February 11, 1860, the claim against Barret neared a conclusion. Peter Ambos wrote Barret directly and advised that the company's board of directors had approved granting Barret "an extension of 1, 2, 3, 4, or even 5 years." Ambos regretted that the dispute with Barret had caused "so much trouble, ill feeling and embarrassment to our company" as well as to Barret. The company did not have "any particular complaint to make against you except as regards your inability to pay."[39]

Lincoln's stormy correspondence with S. C. Davis & Co. and Columbus Machine Manufacturing Co. shows his difficulties in representing cases for out-of-state business interests. While Lincoln was an eloquent defender of capitalism, he sometimes in his law practice failed to demonstrate qualities associated with the rise of capitalism such as diligence or organization. He also was irritated when these out-of-state clients second-guessed his assessment of how the lawsuits should proceed.

Lincoln's discomfort with aspects of a changing profession may help explain two significant career decisions. In 1849, Grant Goodrich, a lawyer in Chicago, asked Lincoln to go into partnership with him. According to David Davis, Lincoln refused the offer because "he would have to sit down and Study hard . . . it would kill him." Rather than being confined in an office studying the law, he "would rather go around the circuit."[40] In 1860, Lincoln reportedly was offered the position of general counsel for the New York Central Railroad at a salary of ten thousand dollars per year. After considering the offer for a few days, Lincoln turned it down.[41]

Lincoln found it difficult to adjust to the different style of lawyering demanded by market-oriented litigation. He was not temperamentally suited for this new style of lawyering. He disliked the hurried pace and the impersonal nature of these cases. While he did not avoid these cases, he remained ambivalent about representing corporations.

"I had sold myself out to you": Lincoln's Retainer with the Illinois Central

Lincoln's rocky relationship with the Illinois Central Railroad further illustrates his difficulties with corporate clients. Lincoln appreciated the fees he could garner from the railroad, yet he resented the loss of autonomy that resulted when he accepted its retainer. Although Lincoln was associated with the Illinois Central for at least seven years, the relationship between Lincoln and the railroad was tenuous and, at times, severely strained. Lincoln was willing to sue the railroad for his fee in the McLean County case although he believed that the lawsuit would end his relationship with the company. During his campaign for the Senate in 1858, Lincoln said he could not "comprehend" Stephen F. Douglas's charge that he was "on very cozy terms with the Railroad Company."[42]

Lincoln's association with the Illinois Central may have begun as early as 1851 when the railroad was struggling to obtain its charter from the Illinois Legislature. Douglas later charged that Lincoln was the "attorney of the Illinois Central Railroad, at the time the charter was granted" and had induced the legislature to change the state's tax on the railroad "from fifteen to seven per cent."[43] A member of the legislature later recalled that Lincoln was "engaged by the Illinois Central Railroad Company to obtain the charter for the company."[44] Others believe that Lincoln was employed by a competing group. W. K. Ackerman, who was president of the Illinois Central from 1877 to 1883, believed that Lincoln lobbied against the Illinois Central.[45] Robert Rantoul, the son of one of the incorporators of the Illinois Central, also claimed that Lincoln represented a competing group.[46]

Lincoln was busy doing some lobbying during the 1851 legislative session: Lincoln wrote one client in February 1851 that he "at last" had "time to attend to the business you left with me" with the "Legislature having got out of the way."[47] The strongest, although hardly compelling, evidence that Lincoln may have lobbied for the railroad is that he never explicitly denied Douglas's charge that he lobbied for the railroad. While it is possible that Lincoln lobbied for the Illinois Central, the evidence on this point is not conclusive.[48]

A pattern often seen in Lincoln's law practice emerges from his early involvement with Illinois Central litigation. In some cases, Lincoln sued the railroad; in others, he represented it. In March 1855, Stuart & Edwards, in association with Lincoln, wrote Martin L. Bishop of Bloomington about Bishop's claims against the Illinois Central. They asked for "particulars of damage you may have sustained by the failure of the C. RR Co. to comply with their agreements in the Deed by yrself & wife to the co."[49] A year earlier, they had filed two lawsuits for Bishop against the railroad—one in trespass on the case for damaging Bishop's property and one in assumpsit.[50] The trial court entered judgment for $470 based upon an arbitrator's award in the trespass on the case lawsuit in April 1854 and dismissed the assumpsit lawsuit with the railroad paying the costs of the suit in September 1856.[51]

Lincoln first represented the Illinois Central in court in April 1853. He and Asahel Gridley appeared for the railroad in a right-of-way case in McLean County.[52] The next month he again appeared for the railroad in a right-of-way case in Champaign County.[53] That same month Lincoln and Leonard Swett, however, represented a landowner in an appeal from the assessment of damages for right of way in the De Witt County Circuit Court.[54]

In the fall of 1853, the railroad put Lincoln on retainer and Lincoln agreed not to take any more cases against the railroad. In March 1854, Lincoln wrote Mason Brayman about an "old man from De Witt" who had asked Lincoln to sue the Illinois Central. Lincoln told Brayman that he did not take the farmer's case "as I had sold myself out to you."[55]

Lincoln's retainer with the railroad grew out of his involvement with the McLean County tax case. In the summer of 1853, the county assessor of McLean County announced plans to assess the property of the Illinois Central located in that county. Believing that its charter exempted the railroad from such taxes, the railroad filed suit to enjoin the collection of taxes by the county. In September, Lincoln wrote to Thompson R. Webber, the clerk of the Champaign County Circuit Court, about the McLean County lawsuit. Lincoln told Webber that "McLean County had assessed the land and other property of the Central Railroad, for the purpose of county taxation." Webber and Lincoln earlier had discussed Champaign County taxing the railroad. Lincoln revealed that the Illinois Central was "offering to engage me for them" but he felt "somewhat trammelled by what has passed between you and me." Champaign County had a "prior right to my services," provided that the county chose to pay Lincoln "something near such as I can get from the other side." Lincoln made it clear that he was going to represent one side or the other in this lawsuit. The issue involved, he said, "the largest law question that can now be got up in the state; and therefore, in justice to myself, I cannot afford, if I can help it, to miss a fee altogether."[56]

Three days later, John B. Thomas, the judge of Champaign County, wrote Webber about Lincoln's proposal. Thomas agreed with Webber that "no time is to be lost in securing the services of Mr. Lincoln." Thomas understood that the county had "no right to expect his services for a trifle." He suggested the county pay Lincoln a retainer of fifty dollars with an additional contingent fee of five hundred dollars.[57]

Lincoln, however, was not hired by Champaign County. In light of Lincoln's eventual five-thousand-dollar fee, he probably rejected the county's proposed five-hundred-dollar fee as not being "near" what he could "get from the other side." In any event, Lincoln wrote to Mason Brayman, the solicitor of the railroad, on October 3, 1853, and offered his services: "Neither the county of McLean nor any one on it's behalf has yet made any engagement with me in relation to it's suit. . . . I am now free to make an engagement for the Road; and if you think fit you may 'count me in.'"[58]

Brayman immediately wrote Lincoln back and enclosed a $250 check as a "general retainer." Brayman stated that "other charges to be adjusted between us as the character of the business in which you may be called upon to engage may render proper." Lincoln met with Brayman in Springfield shortly after receiving the retainer.[59] It was probably at this meeting that Brayman asked Lincoln not to take "any new cases against the company." Lincoln later explained to James F. Joy, a lawyer for the Illinois Central, that "it was at Mr. Brayman's request, made two years ago, I declined taking any new case against the company."[60] One week after being retained by the railroad, Lincoln was asked by Joy to serve as an arbitrator in a dispute between the Illinois Central and northern Indiana railroads. Apparently neither Lincoln nor Joy thought the retainer precluded Lincoln from serving as an impartial arbitrator.[61]

Lincoln was not reluctant to make sure that he did not lose money in accepting the retainer and its obligations. One year after the initial retainer, he wrote Brayman to explain that he had drawn one hundred dollars from the railroad's account at the McLean County Bank. Asking Brayman to "please see that it shall be honored," Lincoln explained:

> The reason I have taken this liberty is, that since last fall, by your request I have declined all new business against the road, and out of which I suppose I could have realized several hundred dollars; have attended, both at De Witt and here to a great variety of little business for the Co, most of which, however, remains unfinished, and have received nothing.[62]

Lincoln, when presenting his bill, reminded Brayman that he could have made "several hundred dollars" from clients who wanted to sue the railroad. This statement was intended, in a not very subtle manner, to encourage payment and also reflected Lincoln's resentment of his agreement not to take any more business against the railroad.

Lincoln had agreed not to take "any new cases against the company" but he continued to pursue at least one older case against the railroad. In November 1853, one month after Lincoln received the Illinois Central retainer, Stuart and Lincoln wrote Martin Bishop again. After consulting on the "propriety" of Bishop accepting an offer made by the railroad, Stuart and Lincoln advised him not to accept the railroad's proposed settlement. They believed the settlement proposed by Bishop was a better deal for him and asked him to refer the matter to them to "conclude this negotiation." Lincoln and Stuart apparently were unable to conclude the matter without litigation; they filed suit against the railroad on March 10, 1854 in the McLean County Circuit Court.[63]

The Bishop case went to trial the following month. Lincoln, Stuart, and Holmes represented Bishop and the jury returned a $583 judgment in Bishop's favor. One year later, a new trial was granted and the case was continued. The next year the court ordered that Bishop recover $470 from the railroad under the terms of an agreed arbitration award.[64]

Lincoln Sues the Illinois Central

After Lincoln won the McLean County tax case for the railroad, there remained the matter of his fee. Lincoln and the railroad had not agreed upon his fee in advance, and his appellate victory led to a dispute over the value of his services. In July 1856 Lincoln presented his bill to the railroad's lawyers in Chicago. One week later he wrote a railroad official that he was "very anxious for a decision in the premises." His anxiety probably resulted from his planning to use his fee (he requested either two thousand or five thousand dollars) to fund his 1858 race for the Senate. The railroad did not pay the requested fee, and he eventually sued the railroad.[65]

The circumstances surrounding the lawsuit over Lincoln's fee are not completely clear. Douglas charged in 1858 that Lincoln "was in the pay of the Illinois Central railroad, and had received $5000.00 from that company toward defraying his campaign expenses."[66] Lincoln himself explained his fee dispute in an 1858 speech.

> The Railroad Company employed me as one of their lawyers in the case, the county having declined to employ me. I was not upon a salary, and no agreement was made as to the amount of the fee. The Railroad Company finally gained the case. The decision, I thought, and still think, was worth half a million dollars to them. I wanted them to pay me $5,000, and they wanted to pay me about $500. I sued them and got the $5,000.[67]

Based on surviving documents, Lincoln's explanation generally appears to be accurate.

Herndon contributed two versions of the dispute between Lincoln and the railroad. In a lecture given in Springfield on December 26, 1865, Herndon said that Lincoln presented his bill to a "whiskered-ringed-mustachioed-curly headed-finely dressed pompous silly little clerk." According to Herndon, "this thing in boots" told Lincoln that "Daniel Webster would not have charged that much."[68] In Herndon's second account, the initial fee was two thousand dollars, and George B. McClellan gave the Daniel Webster retort. Lincoln then was convinced by six fellow lawyers that this amount was too low and that he should sue for five thousand dollars.[69] This account is marred by the fact that McClellan was not employed by the Illinois Central Railroad at that time.[70]

The Illinois Central has steadfastly maintained its own version of Lincoln's lawsuit against it. Lincoln's long relationship with the railroad presents a public relations coup of a major railroad "getting right with Lincoln."[71] Getting sued by Lincoln, of course, presents a slightly different story. The railroad thus has claimed that Lincoln pursued a "friendly" lawsuit that was a mere formality. The railroad's version of events recounts how "the then general counsel of the road advised Mr. Lincoln that while he recognized the value of his services, still, the payment of so large a fee to a western country lawyer without protest would embarrass the general counsel with the board of directors in New York, who would not understand, as would a lawyer, the importance of the case and the consequent value of Mr. Lincoln's services." The railroad suggested to Lincoln that "if he would bring suit for his bill in some court of competent jurisdiction, and judgment were rendered in his favor, the judgment would be paid without appeal."[72]

Some Lincoln scholars have advanced a third version of Lincoln's lawsuit against the railroad. This interpretation suggests that the lawsuit began in rancor, but Lincoln and the railroad settled their differences before the case was tried. The evidence for the settlement of the dispute is a letter written by Ebenezer Lane, resident director of the railroad, to W. H. Osborn, the president of the Illinois Central. In this letter, Lane wrote Osborn that the railroad had "settled with Lincoln and fortunately took him out of the field, or rather engaged him in our interests." In these accounts, the date given for the letter is May 14, 1857. Lincoln's lawsuit against the railroad was tried in June. The trial was nothing more than a formality to placate the railroad's board of directors in New York.[73]

The problem with these "friendly suit" interpretations is that they are all substantially based upon a typed copy of the letter from Lane to Osborn that states the railroad had "settled" with Lincoln. The typed copy, however, is incorrectly dated. The actual letter was not written the month before the trial; it was written two months after the trial.[74] While it reveals *why* the railroad settled with Lincoln, it does not establish *when* the railroad settled with Lincoln.

The available evidence suggests that Lincoln did not begin his lawsuit as a "mere formality." When the railroad rejected Lincoln's fee, Lincoln believed that his association with the railroad was over. When two lawyers from Paris, Illinois, asked Lincoln in February 1857 to handle a lawsuit against the railroad, Lincoln replied that he had "been in the regular retainer of the Co. for two or three years; but I expect they do not wish to retain me any longer." Lincoln said that he was going to Chicago to discuss his relationship with the railroad. He explained that he would "then ascertain whether they discharge me; & if they do, as I expect, I will attend to your business & write you."[75] Before he settled with the railroad, Lincoln also discussed the state's taxation of the railroad with the state auditor, Jesse K. DuBois. DuBois, according to an Illinois Central official, had "approached [Lincoln] with a view to retain him for the State for consultation. Lincoln answered he was not free from his engagement to us, but expected a discharge."[76]

Friction between Lincoln and James F. Joy had contributed to the fee dispute. Bloomington attorney Charles L. Capen later recalled that the "simple truth is that the whole trouble was with Mr. James F. Joy . . . whom Mr. Lincoln afterward despised."[77] Henry C. Whitney also believed that Joy had caused the dispute; Whitney said that Joy had disallowed Lincoln's fee and had dismissed Lincoln as a "common country lawyer."[78] Whitney wrote later that Joy "treated Lincoln rudely."[79] Lincoln sued for five thousand dollars, which was the same figure as Joy's railroad salary in 1854.[80]

Lincoln and Joy had clashed before over Lincoln's fees. In September 1855, Lincoln had his first dispute over fees with Joy. On September 14 Lincoln wrote Joy to explain that he had drawn $150 from the McLean County Bank. Lincoln explained that the money was "intended as a fee for all services done by me for the Illinois Central Railroad, since last September, within the counties of McLean and De Witt." Lincoln said that he had "assisted, for the Road, in at least fifteen cases" and had "concluded to lump them off at ten dollars a case." He asked Joy to honor the draft. Lincoln included an endorsement of his fees by David Davis, the circuit judge for De Witt and McLean counties. Davis wrote that the "above facts are true, and I think the charges very reasonable."[81]

The $150 draft reached Joy before Lincoln's letter. He sent Lincoln a "despach" demanding an explanation of Lincoln's actions. Lincoln first answered by telegraph and then answered by letter on September 19. He told Joy that he had written a letter that explained the draft and that "the draft and letter should have gone by the same mail, and I can not understand why they did not." He again described how for "two terms of court in each county" he had "attended to from fifteen to seventeen, cases for the I. C. Co., in the counties of McLean & De Witt for which I have not been paid." Lincoln thought the exact number of the cases and the names of the parties were unnecessary as Judge Davis had noted that Lincoln had performed the services and had charged reasonably. Lincoln concluded his letter with his understanding of his relationship with the railroad: "[I]t was at Mr. Brayman's request, made two years ago, I declined taking any new case against the company, and attended to these cases as they came up from time to time, and that he paid me for this class of business up to some time in September of 1854."[82] The friction between Lincoln and Joy resurfaced when Lincoln presented his fee for the McLean County case.

Lincoln's actual preparation for the trial contradicts the notion of a friendly lawsuit. Lincoln carefully prepared an outline of his "proof" for his claim. Lincoln first would document his retainer with "Brayman & Joy's letters, with proof of their signatures, and that they were the active agents of the Company." Then, Lincoln would prove that he "did the service, arguing the case twice." He next would describe the question involved in the case and how it was decided, pointing out that he, not his co-counsel from the railroad, "made the point & argument on which the case turned." The importance of the case to the railroad was obvious: the railroad owned "near two million acres" that could have been taxed by "twenty six counties." Lincoln estimated that $500,000 would "scarcely pay the tax." In summary, Lincoln posed the following question:

> Are, or not the amount of labor, the doubtfulness and difficulty of the question, the degree of success in the result; and the amount of pecuniary interest involved, not merely in the particular case, but covered by the principle decided, and thereby secured to the client, all proper elements, by the custom of the profession to consider in determining what is a reasonable fee in a given case.

Lincoln's answer to this question was "that $5000 is not an unreasonable fee in this case."[83] Lincoln also prepared to take the depositions of seven prominent Illinois lawyers—Norman Judd, Isaac N. Arnold, and Grant Goodrich of Chicago; Archibald Williams and Orville H. Browning of Quincy; Norman Purple of Peoria; and Stephen T. Logan of Springfield— who would testify on the reasonableness of his fee.[84]

The actions of David Davis also suggest that the lawsuit was not merely a formality. Davis, as the judge of the Eighth Circuit, should have tried Lincoln's lawsuit. Davis, however, swapped circuits with Judge Jesse O. Norton of Joliet when the suit was to be heard.[85] Davis's biographer, Willard L. King, suggested that Davis did not hear Lincoln's suit against the railroad because of Davis's close relationship with Lincoln and his prior assistance in helping Lincoln collect fees from the railroad.[86] If the trial was to be only a formality, then such considerations would be meaningless.

Lincoln's suit was called for trial on June 18, 1857. The docket entry reflects that "Defendant now came not"; no one appeared for the Illinois Central.[87] A jury was empaneled and, after hearing Lincoln present evidence, awarded Lincoln five thousand dollars. On June 23, Lincoln and the railroad's lawyer, John M. Douglass, agreed to set aside the judgment and try the case a second time. The docket entry reflects that the second jury heard "evidence of the parties and argument of counsel." Lincoln was awarded $4,800. Douglass, the attorney for the railroad, at the conclusion of the second trial, moved for a new trial, claiming that the verdict was "contrary to the law and the evidence." The court overruled the motion and Douglass excepted to the ruling. Douglass then announced his intention to appeal the court's judgment. He was given thirty days to file an appeal bond and a bill of exceptions.[88]

The second trial apparently lasted only a few minutes. The docket entry that the second jury heard evidence and argument of counsel hides more than it reveals. In April 1906 officials of the Illinois Central Railroad collected statements from three lawyers who claimed to have witnessed the trial between Lincoln and the railroad. The railroad was responding to an article by Frederick T. Hill that appeared in the April issue of *Century Magazine*. Hill briefly had discussed Lincoln's lawsuit against his "ungrateful client," the Illinois Central. Hill had noted that the railroad had "issued an elaborate pamphlet giving its side of this case" and that the railroad had tried to show that the trial "was merely a formality." Hill noted that "Lincoln's unusually careful brief on the law and the facts, however, does not bear out the contention that the litigation was friendly" and asserted the friendly suit notion was disputed by eyewitnesses who had spoken to Hill.[89] After this article appeared, John G. Drennan, a lawyer in the law department of the Illinois Central, collected statements from "the only living witnesses who heard this trial." Drennan wrote the president of the railroad that "we have 'got the goods' on Mr. Hill."[90]

All three lawyers had vivid memories of a nearly fifty-year-old case that had "lasted but a few minutes."[91] The three lawyers were James S. Ewing, Adlai E. Stevenson, and Ezra Prince. Ewing signed a one-page statement; Stevenson signed a two-paragraph statement that concurred in "the statement of facts made by Mr. Ewing."[92] Prince wrote a three-page letter to Drennan. Ewing recalled:

> Mr. Lincoln's statement of the case to the jury was very clear and impressive. After reciting the history of the case which he had tried, the question involved, the result of the case and the important benefits to the Railroad Company, he proceeded to comment on the elements which ought to enter into the determination of a reasonable fee for legal services; that is, the amount directly or indirectly involved in the suit, the amount of labor performed, the legal question decided and the result.[93]

Ewing also wrote that Lincoln announced that John Douglass "had kindly consented that a statement which he had written out and which had been signed by some of the prominent lawyers of the State, might be read in evidence with the same affect as if the depositions of these gentlemen had been taken." Lincoln concluded by saying "he had charged the Company, $5000 but Mr. Joy thought it was too much and they would have to leave the matter to a jury." Douglass, according to Ewing, then said Lincoln's "statement was substantially correct and fair and that he himself did not think the fee charged, was too much." The lawsuit "lasted but a few minutes and a verdict was promptly returned."[94]

Stevenson, a former vice-president of the United States, supported Ewing's account of the trial. Stevenson was a law student in Bloomington at the time of the trial and "was in court during the trial." Stevenson said that it "appeared" "to be in the nature of an amicable suit." He could not recall "that there was any display of ill feeling on the part of Mr. Lincoln or of Mr. Douglass during the trial."[95]

Ezra M. Prince provided the most detailed account of the trial. Some of the details are wrong. For example, Prince remembered that David Davis presided over the trial, but Davis had swapped benches for this trial. Although Prince wrote that he was providing his "recollection" of the trial, he also fit his recollection within the narrative framework supplied by the railroad. Prince wrote that he had been "informed that [Douglass] thought the bill reasonable, but in deference to others, it was agreed that an amicable suit should be brought; and the proceedings certainly bear out this view." Prince's description of the trial itself was substantially similar to Ewing's and Stevenson's, except that Prince said that Douglass stated, "he thought that the amount claimed was just and ought to be paid." Prince said that "the entire trial lasted but a few minutes, and in the ordinary meaning of the term was not a trial at all."[96]

Prince also wrote about the jury, "who promptly returned a verdict for Mr. Lincoln for $5000." Prince pointed out that Lincoln, "who had been attending the McLean County Court for years, knew every one of them and they knew him, and it would have taken a good deal of evidence on the part of the Railroad Company to convince them that Mr. Lincoln was asking an excessive fee."[97] The *Chicago Tribune* made a similar point about Lincoln in 1858. Lincoln had been visiting Vermilion County for fifteen years while on the circuit.

> Lincoln has been personally known to the citizens of Vermillion for the last fifteen years. Every man who has within that time been on the grand or petit jury, or whose business, or curiosity has called to the sitting of our courts, knows Abraham Lincoln. . . . Such has become the established integrity of Lincoln with us that let a jury be empaneled from any part of our populous county, to try a cause and they will take his exposition of the law and the facts of the case without a scruple, for they know, that as Lincoln has never misconstrued the law, nor perverted the evidence, they can follow him and do no wrong.[98]

Although the *Tribune* was a Republican paper that was supporting Lincoln when this article was published, the point about Lincoln's "established integrity" was undoubtedly correct.

The recollections of the three Bloomington lawyers, if accepted at face value, must be reconciled with the evidence that supports the notion that Lincoln had prepared for a contested trial the week before. There are two possible explanations. One is that Lincoln settled after he received the default judgment on June 18. Whitney, the railroad's lawyer in McLean County, recalled in 1887 that Douglass arrived in Bloomington "after the default" and asked Lincoln "to set it aside which L. did." Then Douglass "had a talk" with Whitney and David Davis and they "concluded that it was very poor policy to make an enemy of Lincoln so Douglass settled it for the full amt."[99] This explanation does not account for Lincoln's agreement to set aside the default judgment nor does it reveal why the second "trial" was necessary.

Another possible explanation does account for Lincoln's readiness to try a contested case on June 18 and for the uncontested case that was actually tried on June 25. The explanation lies in the default judgment that Lincoln received on June 18, which is often overlooked. This default judgment was an unexpected windfall for Lincoln; he received a five-thousand-dollar judgment when the railroad's lawyer, John M. Douglass, did not show up on time for trial. Douglass was mortified when he arrived late. He "did not want the record to show that the company had defaulted because of his absence."[100] Lincoln may have agreed to set aside the default judgment but would not let Douglass present a defense. Under Illinois law, Douglass would have been required to file a motion to set aside the default judgment with an affidavit that "clearly and specifically" gave the reasons for setting aside the default.[101]

While the default judgment was formally set aside, the effect of the default judgment was not. The trial then became a "mere formality." Douglass then convinced the railroad to settle the case; Douglass could truthfully state that the record contained nothing upon which an appeal could be based. This explanation would account for Lincoln's careful preparation, Davis's recusal, and the June 25 trial that appeared to witnesses to be an "amicable suit."

In any event, some time between June 18 (the day of the first "trial") and July 23 (the last day that the railroad could perfect its appeal from the second "trial"), Lincoln and the railroad settled the lawsuit. The Illinois Central had thirty days to perfect its appeal by filing a bond. No bond was filed. The railroad instead agreed to pay Lincoln the full amount of the judgment. On July 22, Lincoln left for New York, where he met with officials of the Illinois Central. On August 5, Lincoln returned to Springfield. On August 12, Lincoln deposited his $4,800 fee with the Springfield Marine and Fire Insurance Co. On August 31, Lincoln withdrew $4,800 from his account and took the money to his office, where he divided it with Herndon.[102] Herndon recalled that when Lincoln handed him his "share of the proceeds," Lincoln said, "Billy, it seems to me it will be bad taste on your part to keep saying the severe things I have heard from you about railroads and other corporations. The truth is, instead of criticizing them, you and I ought to thank God for letting this one fall into our hands."[103]

Conclusion

Lincoln early in his law practice had developed a Whiggish attitude toward law and the role of law in American society. Whig lawyers believed that the court system provided a neutral means to resolve disputes and maintain order. A lawyer's role in this system was to represent either side in a dispute—it didn't matter which side the lawyer took. Like most Whig lawyers, Lincoln stood ready to represent any party in court and give any argument. But these lawyers also believed they were guardians of community values.[104] Lincoln's slander cases show this keen awareness of the social stakes of lawsuits. These slander lawsuits helped restore reputations and to reestablish social equilibrium by defendants attesting to the good character of the injured plaintiffs and by successful plaintiffs magnanimously remitting judgments. Oddly enough, lawsuits could repair rifts in the community and not just create them.

As his practice changed during his nearly twenty-five-year career, Lincoln became less able to serve any client or to be in the position to help mediate disputes. Lincoln's early practice involved litigants who were primarily members of relatively small rural communities. These community-oriented cases allowed Lincoln to serve often as a mediator and not just as a courtroom advocate. While Lincoln continued to handle these types of disputes throughout his career, he also began handling cases that accompanied the rise of a market economy. Lincoln was irritated when his out-of-state clients didn't defer to his judgment. Lincoln also wasn't temperamentally suited for these cases. He resented the quickened pace and the impersonal style of lawyering that his corporate clients demanded, and he disliked the loss of autonomy that came with the increased supervision by his corporate clients of their claims.

During the "secession winter" of 1860, journalist Henry Villard observed that Lincoln was "indefatigable in his efforts to arrive at the fullest comprehension of the present situation of public affairs and the most proper conclusions as to its probable consequences." Villard noted that Lincoln "never contents himself with a superficial opinion based on newspaper accounts and arguments, but always fortifies his position by faithful researches for precedents, analogies, authorities, etc. He is at all times surrounded by piles of standard works to which constant reference is made."[105] Lincoln's "faithful researches" for precedents and authorities reflected his training as a lawyer.

A Note on Sources and Citations

Most of the citations to primary source materials are found in *The Law Practice of Abraham Lincoln: Complete Documentary Edition,* a three-DVD set published in 2000 by the University of Illinois Press. Thanks to the generosity of the Oliver Cromwell Nelson Foundation, every American Bar Association–accredited law school has a copy of this edition.

Every document in the Complete Documentary Edition database has a unique identifier. These documents are organized by case files, which also have unique identifiers. I have provided these identifiers when I have cited these materials, using this basic format:

Document name, date [document identifier], name of case file [case file identifier].

By using these identifiers, a researcher may directly access any document or case file that I have cited. I have tried to use the same terminology that editors of this edition have used for the names of the documents I have cited. I have substituted "judgment" for "order" when the court's action disposed of the case before it.

Court opinions published in reporters such as the *Illinois Reports* are also cited extensively. For these materials (and everything else I've cited) I have followed *The Bluebook: A Uniform System of Citation* (17th ed. 2000). These citations follow this basic format:

Style of case, volume of reporter • official reporter abbreviation (volume and nominative reporter abbreviation) • page case begins, specific page reference (year of decision).

A nominative reporter uses the name of the actual court reporter. For example, the volumes of *Illinois Reports* produced by Charles Gilman will have his name abbreviated as "Gilm." in the first parenthetical. The other two reporters for this period are Scammon ("Scam.") and Breese ("Breese").

Introduction

1. Fragment: Notes for a Law Lecture, 10 COLLECTED WORKS OF ABRAHAM LINCOLN 20 (Roy P. Basler ed., 1953–1990) (hereinafter "CW"). The notes are not dated. They first appeared in an 1894 edition of his complete works edited by his former presidential secretaries, John G. Nicolay and John Hay, who gave them a tentative date of July 1850. 1 ABRAHAM LINCOLN: COMPLETE WORKS 162 (John G. Nicolay & John Hay eds., New York: Century Co. 1894). Roy Basler, the editor of *Collected Works,* retained that date in the absence of any evidence to the contrary. Notes for a Law Lecture, CW 2:82. The editors of *The Law Practice of Abraham Lincoln: Complete Documentary Edition* suggest that the notes may have been related to a request to lecture at Ohio State and Union Law

College in Cleveland that Lincoln received in 1858. Description, *Lincoln prepared lecture on law* [N05375], THE LAW PRACTICE OF ABRAHAM LINCOLN: COMPLETE DOCUMENTARY EDITION (Martha L. Benner & Cullom Davis eds., 2000) (hereinafter "LPAL"); M.A. King to AL (Nov. 15, 1858), *available at* Abraham Lincoln Papers at the Library of Congress, <memory.loc.gov/ammem/alhtml/malhome.html>, Select: Search by Keyword, Enter: King 1858, Select: Item 1.

1—Lawyer Lincoln in American Memory

1. Randall Sanborn, *Who's Most Admired Lawyer?*, NAT'L LAW J., Aug. 9, 1993, at 24.

2. The entries on Lincoln's law practice in Mark E. Neely, Jr.'s, comprehensive The Abraham Lincoln Encyclopedia are instructive. *See* MARK E. NEELY, JR., THE ABRAHAM LINCOLN ENCYCLOPEDIA 179–80 (Law Practice), 8 (William "Duff" Armstrong), 96 (*Effie Afton* Case), 202 (*McCormick v. Manny & Company*), 204 (McLean County Tax Case), 207–08 (Matson Slave Case) (1982).

3. The Armstrong murder trial also forms the basis of the movie *Young Mr. Lincoln* (1939). *See* Norman Rosenberg, *Young Mr. Lincoln: The Lawyer as Super-Hero*, 15 LEGAL STUD. FORUM 215, 219–20 (1991).

4. *See, e.g.*, 2 ALBERT J. BEVERIDGE, ABRAHAM LINCOLN, 1809–1858, at 561–71 (1928).

5. *See generally* Anthony Chase, *Lawyers and Popular Culture: A Review of Mass Media Portrayals of American Attorneys*, 1986 AM. B. FOUND. RES. J. 281, 282–84.

6. *See, e.g.*, HAROLD M. HYMAN, *A Man out of Manuscripts: Edward M. Stanton at the McCormick Reaper Trial*, 12 MANUSCRIPTS 35 (1960); WILLIAM LEE MILLER, LINCOLN'S VIRTUES: AN ETHICAL BIOGRAPHY 410–18 (2002).

7. BENJAMIN P. THOMAS, ABRAHAM LINCOLN: A BIOGRAPHY 157 (1952).

8. *The Effie Afton Case*, ILLINOIS DAILY J. (Sept. 28, 1857) [126184], *Hurd v. Rock Island Bridge Co.* [L02289] case file, LPAL.

9. On the Lincoln image, *see generally* MERRILL D. PETERSON, LINCOLN IN AMERICAN MEMORY (1994).

10. STEPHEN B. OATES, WITH MALICE TOWARD NONE: THE LIFE OF ABRAHAM LINCOLN xv (1977).

11. ROY P. BASLER, THE LINCOLN LEGEND: A STUDY IN CHANGING CONCEPTIONS 130–31 (1935); DAVID HERBERT DONALD, LINCOLN RECONSIDERED: ESSAYS ON THE CIVIL WAR ERA 148 (2d ed. 1961); DAVID M. POTTER, THE SOUTH AND THE SECTIONAL CONFLICT 154–55 (1968).

12. DON E. FEHRENBACHER, LINCOLN IN TEXT AND CONTEXT: COLLECTED ESSAYS 181–83 (1987).

13. JAMES WILLARD HURST, THE GROWTH OF AMERICAN LAW: THE LAW MAKERS 252 (1950).

14. Robert C. Post, *On the Popular Image of the Lawyer: Reflections in a Dark Glass*, 75 CAL. L. REV. 379, 386 (1987).

15. Maxwell Bloomfield, *Law and Lawyers in American Popular Culture*, *in* LAW AND AMERICAN LITERATURE: A COLLECTION OF ESSAYS 138–39 (Carl S. Smith et al. eds., 1983); *see also* Donald G. Baker, *The Lawyer in Popular Fiction*, 3 J. POPULAR CULTURE 493 (1969).

16. Newspaper Reports [65588], *Hurd v. Rock Island Bridge Co.* [L02289], Trial Transcript, Aug. Term 1859 [123180], *People v. Harrison* [L04306] case file, LPAL; Robert Bray, *The P. Quinn Harrison Murder Trial*, 99 LINCOLN HERALD 59 (Summer 1997).

17. Charles B. Strozier, *The Lives of William Herndon*, 14 J. ABRAHAM LINCOLN ASS'N 1 (1993); DOUGLAS L. WILSON, LINCOLN BEFORE WASHINGTON: NEW PERSPECTIVES ON THE ILLINOIS YEARS 21–50 (1997).

18. POTTER, THE SOUTH AND THE SECTIONAL CONFLICT at 163; *see also* Louis A. Warren, *Herndon's Contribution to Lincoln Mythology*, 41 IND. MAG. HIST. 221 (1945).

19. JOHN P. FRANK, LINCOLN AS A LAWYER 15 (1961).

20. DONALD, LINCOLN RECONSIDERED at 154; DAVID HERBERT DONALD, LINCOLN'S HERNDON: A BIOGRAPHY 170–71 (1948); POTTER, THE SOUTH AND THE SECTIONAL CONFLICT at 162–64.

21. HERNDON'S LIFE OF LINCOLN: THE HISTORY AND PERSONAL RECOLLECTIONS OF ABRAHAM LINCOLN AS ORIGINALLY WRITTEN BY WILLIAM H. HERNDON AND JESSE W. WEIK 261–93 (Paul M. Angle ed., 1961) (1889) (hereinafter "HERNDON'S LINCOLN").

22. DAVID HERBERT DONALD, "WE ARE LINCOLN MEN": ABRAHAM LINCOLN AND HIS FRIENDS 71 (2003).

23. HERNDON'S LINCOLN at 276; Cullom Davis, *Law and Politics: The Two Careers of Abraham Lincoln*, 17 Q.J. IDEOLOGY 61 (June 1994); Abraham Lincoln (hereinafter "AL") to David Davis (Feb. 12, 1849), CW 10:12; Thomas F. Schwartz, *An Egregious Political Blunder: Justin Butterfield, Lincoln, and Illinois Whiggery*, 7 PAPERS OF THE ABRAHAM LINCOLN ASS'N 9 (1986).

24. THE HIDDEN LINCOLN: FROM THE LETTERS AND PAPERS OF WILLIAM H. HERNDON 427–28 (Emanuel Hertz ed., 1940); HERNDON'S LINCOLN at 270–71, 263.

25. *See, e.g.,* AL to Joshua F. Speed (Dec. 12, 1855), CW 2:328.

26. John A. Lupton, *Abraham Lincoln and His Informal Partners on the Eighth Judicial Circuit, in* PAPERS FROM THE THIRTEENTH AND FOURTEENTH ANNUAL LINCOLN COLLOQUIA 97 (n.d.).

27. PAUL M. ANGLE, A SHELF OF LINCOLN BOOKS 80 (1946).

28. HENRY CLAY WHITNEY, LIFE ON THE CIRCUIT WITH LINCOLN 53, 63–64 (1940) (1892); Lupton, *Abraham Lincoln and His Informal Partners on the Eighth Judicial Circuit, in* PAPERS FROM THE THIRTEENTH AND FOURTEENTH ANNUAL LINCOLN COLLOQUIA at 97; NEELY, ABRAHAM LINCOLN ENCYCLOPEDIA at 335.

29. NEELY, ABRAHAM LINCOLN ENCYCLOPEDIA at 96; Benjamin P. Thomas, *The Eighth Judicial Circuit*, BULL. ABRAHAM LINCOLN ASS'N (Sept. 1935); 2 BEVERIDGE, ABRAHAM LINCOLN at 219, 211, 215; WILLARD L. KING, LINCOLN'S MANAGER, DAVID DAVIS 71–98 (1960); WILLARD L. KING, *Riding the Circuit with Lincoln*, 6 AM. HERITAGE 48 (Feb. 1955).

30. WHITNEY, LIFE ON THE CIRCUIT WITH LINCOLN at 237–38, 233, 241, 123–24.

31. *See, e.g.,* 1 JOHN G. NICOLAY & JOHN HAY, ABRAHAM LINCOLN: A HISTORY 167–85, 298–309 (1909).

32. BLOOMFIELD, LAW AND LAWYERS IN AMERICAN POPULAR CULTURE at 135–38.

33. On Lincoln's campaign biographies, *see* Ernest James Wessen, *Campaign Lives of Abraham Lincoln, 1860*, PAPERS IN ILLINOIS HISTORY AND TRANSACTIONS FOR THE YEAR 1937, at 188–220 (1938).

34. G.S. Boritt, *Was Lincoln a Vulnerable Candidate in 1860?*, 27 CIVIL WAR HIST. 32, 33–34 (1981).

35. J.H. BARRETT, LIFE OF ABRAHAM LINCOLN 63–66 (Indianapolis, Asher & Co. 1860); D.W. BARTLETT, THE LIFE AND PUBLIC SERVICES OF HON. ABRAHAM LINCOLN 110–15 (Indianapolis, Asher & Co. 1860); J.Q. HOWARD, THE LIFE OF ABRAHAM LINCOLN 18–22 (Cincinnati, Anderson, Gates and Wright 1860); W.D. HOWELLS, LIFE OF ABRAHAM LINCOLN 35–36 (1938) (1860); HENRY J. RAYMOND, HISTORY OF THE ADMINISTRATION OF PRESIDENT LINCOLN 19–22 (New York, J.C. Derby & N.C. Miller 1864); WELLS' ILLUSTRATED NATIONAL CAMPAIGN HAND-BOOK FOR 1860, at 58–62 (New York, J.G. Wells 1860).

36. RICHARD HOFSTADTER, THE AMERICAN POLITICAL TRADITION 119 (1948).

37. LIFE OF ABE LINCOLN, OF ILLINOIS 7 (Printed for the Publishers, 1860).

38. THE ONLY AUTHENTIC LIFE OF ABRAHAM LINCOLN, ALIAS "OLD ABE" (American News Co. n.d.).

39. NEELY, ABRAHAM LINCOLN ENCYCLOPEDIA at 149; J.G. HOLLAND, LIFE OF ABRAHAM LINCOLN 77–78 (Springfield, Mass., G. Bill 1866).

40. HOLLAND, LIFE OF ABRAHAM LINCOLN at 80, 126.

41. BASLER, THE LINCOLN LEGEND at 13–14.

42. 1 NICOLAY & HAY, ABRAHAM LINCOLN at 304–05.

43. BENJAMIN J. SHIPMAN, HANDBOOK OF COMMON-LAW PLEADING 277 (1923).

44. *See, e.g.,* Demurrer, filed Mar. Term 1859 [6849], *Allen v. Illinois Central R.R.* [L00663] case file, LPAL.

45. EDMUND WILSON, PATRIOTIC GORE 115 (1962) (reprt. 1987); BASLER, THE LINCOLN LEGEND at 25.

46. CARL SANDBURG, *The Lawyers Know Too Much, in* COMPLETE WORKS 189 (1950).

47. 2 CARL SANDBURG, ABRAHAM LINCOLN: THE PRAIRIE YEARS 53–57, 47–48, 60, 42 (1926).

48. NEELY, ABRAHAM LINCOLN ENCYCLOPEDIA at 24; PETERSON, LINCOLN IN AMERICAN MEMORY at 278–82; Albert J. Beveridge, *quoted in* JOHN J. DUFF, A. LINCOLN: PRAIRIE LAWYER 141 (1960).

49. 2 BEVERIDGE, ABRAHAM LINCOLN at 275, 250–52.

50. *Id.* at 255–310.

51. *See* Mark E. Neely, Jr., *The Lincoln Theme Since Randall's Call: The Promises and Perils of Professionalism,* 1 ABRAHAM LINCOLN ASS'N PAPERS 10, 10 (1979); PETERSON, LINCOLN IN AMERICAN MEMORY at 298–310; JOHN HIGHAM, HISTORY: PROFESSIONAL SCHOLARSHIP IN AMERICA 68–76 (1989).

52. NEELY, ABRAHAM LINCOLN ENCYCLOPEDIA at 308; Benjamin P. Thomas, *Lincoln and the Courts, 1854–1861,* ABRAHAM LINCOLN ASS'N PAPERS (1933); Thomas, *The Eighth Judicial Circuit,* BULL. ABRAHAM LINCOLN ASS'N; Benjamin P. Thomas, *Lincoln's Earlier Practice in the Federal Courts 1839–1854,* BULL. ABRAHAM LINCOLN ASS'N (June 1935); Benjamin P. Thomas, *Abe Lincoln, Country Lawyer,* 193 ATLANTIC MONTHLY 57 (Feb. 1954).

53. THOMAS, ABRAHAM LINCOLN at 21, 66–67.

54. *Id.* at 94, 92, 155–56.

55. *Id.* at 410.

56. OATES, WITH MALICE TOWARD NONE at 112–13, 106, 109–10.

57. *Id.* at 113–14.

58. Cullom Davis, *Crucible of Statesmanship: The Law Practice of Abraham Lincoln,* 6 TAMKANG J. AM. STUD. at 5 (1988); Harold M. Hyman, *Neither Image Breaker Nor Broker Be,* 6 REV. AM. HIST. 73, 77 (Mar. 1978).

59. Robert W. Gordon, *The Devil and Daniel Webster,* 94 YALE L.J. 445, 445–46 (1984); Lyman Butterfield, *quoted in* R. Kent Newmeyer, *Daniel Webster and the Modernization of American Law,* 32 BUFFALO L. REV. 819, 819 (1983).

60. DONALD, LINCOLN'S HERNDON at 34–35; *see also* Benjamin Barondess, *The Adventure of the Missing Briefs,* 8 MANUSCRIPTS 20 (1955).

61. J.G. RANDALL, *Has the Lincoln Theme Been Exhausted?,* 41 AM. HIST. REV. 270, 272 (1936); *see also* Robert W. Johannsen, *In Search of the Real Lincoln, Or Lincoln at the Crossroads,* 61 J. ILL. ST. HIST. SOC'Y 229 (1968).

62. Neely, *The Lincoln Theme Since Randall's Call: The Promises and Perils of Professionalism,* 1 PAPERS OF THE ABRAHAM LINCOLN ASS'N 10, 29–30.

63. MARK E. NEELY, JR., THE LAST BEST HOPE: ABRAHAM LINCOLN AND THE PROMISE OF AMERICA 34 (1993); Ronald D. Rietveld, *Review Essay: Mark E. Neely, Jr., The Last Best Hope: Abraham Lincoln and the Promise of America,* 18 J. ABRAHAM LINCOLN ASS'N 17 (1997).

64. *See, e.g.,* William D. Beard, *Dalby Revisited: A New Look at Lincoln's "Most Far-reaching Case" in the Illinois Supreme Court,* 20 J. ABRAHAM LINCOLN ASS'N 1 (Summer 1999); William D. Beard, *"I have labored hard to find the law": Abraham Lincoln for the Alton and Sangamon Railroad,* 85 ILL. HIST. J. 209 (Winter 1992); Bray, *The P. Quinn Harrison Murder Trial,* 99 LINCOLN HERALD 57; Davis, *Law and Politics: The Two Careers of Abraham*

Lincoln, 17 Q.J. IDEOLOGY 61; Susan Krause, *Abraham Lincoln and Joshua Speed, Attorney and Client*, 89 ILL. HIST. J. 35 (Spring 1996); John A. Lupton, *A. Lincoln, Esq.: The Evolution of a Lawyer, in* ALLEN D. SPIEGEL, A. LINCOLN, ESQUIRE: A SHREWD, SOPHISTICATED LAWYER IN HIS TIME 18 (2002); Lupton, *Abraham Lincoln and His Informal Partners on the Eighth Judicial Circuit, in* PAPERS FROM THE THIRTEENTH AND FOURTEENTH ANNUAL LINCOLN COLLOQUIA 96–99; John A. Lupton, *Basement Barrister: Abraham Lincoln's Practice Before the Illinois Supreme Court*, 101 LINCOLN HERALD 47 (Summer 1999); John A. Lupton, *Selected Cases of A. Lincoln, Esq., Attorney and Counsellor-at-Law, in* AMERICA'S LAWYER-PRESIDENTS: FROM LAW OFFICE TO OVAL OFFICE 159–67 (Norman Gross ed., 2004); Christopher A. Schnell, *At the Bar and on the Stump: Douglas and Lincoln's Legal Relationship, in* PAPERS FROM THE THIRTEENTH AND FOURTEENTH ANNUAL LINCOLN COLLOQUIA 99–106 (n.d.); Paul H. Verduin, *A New Lincoln Discovery: Rebecca Thomas, His 'Revolutionary War Widow,'* 98 LINCOLN HERALD 3 (Spring 1996).

65. IN TENDER CONSIDERATION: WOMEN, FAMILIES, AND THE LAW IN ABRAHAM LINCOLN'S ILLINOIS (Daniel W. Stowell, ed.).

66. DAVID HERBERT DONALD, LINCOLN 16, 620, 148, 72 (1995).

67. WILLIAM E. GIENAPP, ABRAHAM LINCOLN AND CIVIL WAR AMERICA: A BIOGRAPHY 26, 44–45 (2002).

68. WILSON, LINCOLN BEFORE WASHINGTON at 21–50; DOUGLAS L. WILSON, HONOR'S VOICE: THE TRANSFORMATION OF ABRAHAM LINCOLN (1998).

69. WILSON, HONOR'S VOICE at 100–08, 316.

70. *See, e.g.,* Kelly Anderson, *Lincoln the Lawyer*, 58 OR. ST. BAR BULL. 13 (Feb./Mar. 1998); Marvin R. Halbert, *Lincoln Was a Lawyer First, Politician Second*, PA. L. J.-REP., Oct. 14, 1985, at 10; Steve Jordan, *Abe Lincoln Was Good for the Legal Profession*, 23 MONT. LAW. 16 (Oct. 1997); Martin Joseph Keenan, *Lincoln's Forgotten Profession*, 58 J. KAN. B. ASS'N 27 (Apr. 1989).

71. NIGHTLINE: WHY DO AMERICANS HATE LAWYERS SO MUCH? (ABC television broadcast, Aug. 4, 1993), *available in* LEXIS, Nexis Library.

72. DONALD, LINCOLN RECONSIDERED at 3–18.

73. *Sterling v. City of Philadelphia*, 378 Pa. 538, 106 A.2d 793, 804 n.5 (1954) (Musmanno, J., dissenting).

74. Frank J. Williams, *Lincolniana in 1992*, 14 J. ABRAHAM LINCOLN ASS'N 47, 66 (Summer 1993).

75. Jerome J. Shestack, *Abe Lincoln as a Lawyer*, 68 FLA. BAR J. 78 (Apr. 1994); Jerome J. Shestack, *Abe Lincoln, Lawyer*, 18 PA. L. 25 (Jan./Feb. 1996); Jerome J. Shestack, *Even today, Abraham Lincoln has a lesson for lawyers*, 140 CHICAGO DAILY LAW BULL. 6 (Feb. 11, 1994); Jerome J. Shestack, *The Lawyer as Peacemaker and Good Man*, 16 LEGAL TIMES 31 (Feb. 21, 1994); Jerome J. Shestack, *Abe Lincoln as a Circuit Lawyer*, 58 KY. BENCH & BAR 20 (Spring 1994).

76. Shestack, *Abe Lincoln as a Circuit Lawyer*, 58 KY. BENCH & BAR at 22.

77. Fragment: Notes for a Law Lecture, CW 10:19. A search in the JLR database on Westlaw found seventy-nine articles that quoted this portion of Lincoln's "law lecture."

78. David Luban, *The Lysistratian Prerogative: A Response to Stephen Pepper*, 1986 AM. B. FOUND. RES. J. 637 (*quoting* 2 WILLIAM H. HERNDON & JESSE WEIK, HERNDON'S LINCOLN 345n. [Chicago: Belford, Clarke & Co., 1899]), 638.

79. DON E. FEHRENBACHER & VIRGINIA FEHRENBACHER, RECOLLECTED WORDS OF ABRAHAM LINCOLN 305 (1996). Lord's original statement is reprinted in HERNDON'S INFORMANTS: LETTERS, INTERVIEWS, AND STATEMENTS ABOUT LINCOLN 469 (Douglas L. Wilson & Rodney O. Davis eds., 1998).

80. Edward J. Fox, *The Influence of the Law in the Life of Abraham Lincoln, in* REPORT OF THE THIRTY-FIRST ANNUAL MEETING OF THE PENNSYLVANIA BAR ASSOCIATION 350 (1925).

81. Julius E. Haycraft, *Lincoln as a Lawyer-Statesman*, 12 MINN. L. REV. (Supp.) 100 (1927).

82. Jesse K. Dunn, *Lincoln, the Lawyer*, 4 OKLA. L.J. 249, 260 (1906); *see also* George R. Peck, *Abraham Lincoln as a Lawyer*, REPORT OF THE ANNUAL MEETING OF THE WIS-CONSIN STATE BAR ASS'N HELD IN THE CITY OF MADISON, FEBRUARY 12 AND 13, 1900, at 112; Omar C. Spencer, *Abraham Lincoln, The Lawyer*, THIRTY SIXTH ANNUAL CONVENTION REPORT OF THE PROCEEDINGS OF THE WASHINGTON STATE BAR ASS'N 113, 140 (1924).

83. *See, e.g.,* Charles W. Moores, *The Career of a Country Lawyer—Abraham Lincoln, in* REPORT OF THE THIRTY-THIRD ANNUAL MEETING OF THE AMERICAN BAR ASSOCIATION 440–73 (1910).

84. JEROLD AUERBACH, UNEQUAL JUSTICE: LAWYERS AND SOCIAL CHANGE IN MODERN AMERICA 15–16 (1976). On the legal profession at the turn of the century, *see generally* THE NEW HIGH PRIESTS: LAWYERS IN POST–CIVIL WAR AMERICA (Gerald Gawalt ed., 1984).

85. AUERBACH, UNEQUAL JUSTICE at 15–16.

86. *See, e.g.,* Anderson, *Lincoln the Lawyer*, 58 OR. ST. BAR BULL. 13; Halbert, *Lincoln Was a Lawyer First, Politician Second*, PA. L. J.-REP. at 10; Jordan, *Abe Lincoln Was Good for the Legal Profession*, 23 MONT. LAW. 16; Keenan, *Lincoln's Forgotten Profession*, 58 J. KAN. B. ASS'N 27.

87. FREDERICK TREVOR HILL, LINCOLN THE LAWYER vx (1906); JOHN T. RICHARDS, ABRA-HAM LINCOLN: THE LAWYER-STATESMAN 43 (1916); ALBERT A. WOLDMAN, LAWYER LINCOLN v (1936); DUFF, A. LINCOLN: PRAIRIE LAWYER at v; FRANK, LINCOLN AS A LAWYER at 4–5.

88. WOLDMAN, LAWYER LINCOLN at v; RICHARDS, ABRAHAM LINCOLN at 91; HILL, LIN-COLN THE LAWYER at 300, 205.

89. 9 DICTIONARY OF AMERICAN BIOGRAPHY 30–31 (Dumas Malone ed., 1935).

90. HILL, LINCOLN THE LAWYER at 120–21, 240–41, 31–33.

91. *Id.* at 208, 109–10, 209–10.

92. RICHARDS, ABRAHAM LINCOLN at 90–91, v–vi, 92, 118–19, 145, 147–48.

93. WOLDMAN, LAWYER LINCOLN at v.

94. *Id.* at v, 142–43, 197, 186–87.

95. *Id.* at 184.

96. *Id.* at 4, 237, 136, 3, 2.

97. Arnold Gates, *John J. Duff, 1902–1961*, 54 J. ILL. ST. HIST. SOC'Y 419 (1961).

98. DUFF, A. LINCOLN: PRAIRIE LAWYER at 144–46, 109, 345.

99. *Id.* at 345, 368–69.

100. John J. Duff, *This Was a Lawyer*, 52 J. ILL. ST. HIST. SOC'Y 146 (1959).

101. William Eleroy Curtis, *Abraham Lincoln, in* 5 GREAT AMERICAN LAWYERS 498 (William Draper Lewis ed., 1908).

102. *Id.* at 125–26, 140–41; *see also* Alan T. Nolan, *Lawyer Lincoln—Myth and Fact*, 16 HARV. L. SCHOOL BULL. 9, 22 (Nov. 1964).

103. David Luban, *The Adversary System Excuse, in* THE GOOD LAWYER: LAWYERS' ROLES AND LAWYERS' ETHICS 84 (David Luban ed., 1983); *see also* Thomas L. Shaffer, *The Unique, Novel, and Unsound Adversary Ethic*, 41 VAND. L. REV. 697, 697 (1988).

104. John P. Frank, *Review*, 63 YALE L.J. 579, 579 (1954).

105. Willard King, *Review*, 55 J. ILL. ST. HIST. SOC'Y 96–99 (1962); *Review*, 6 AM. J. LEGAL HIST. 86 (1962).

106. FRANK, LINCOLN AS A LAWYER at v, 171, 52, 51, 191–92.

107. *Id.* at 143–44, 153, 172.

2—The Education of a Whig Lawyer

1. Remarks in United States House of Representatives Concerning Postal Contracts (Jan. 5, 1848), CW 1:426.
2. Allan G. Bogue et al., *Members of the House of Representatives and the Processes of Modernization, 1789–1960*, 63 J. AM. HIST. 275, 284 (1976); Donald R. Matthews, *United States Senators and the Class Structure*, 18 PUBLIC OPINION Q. 5, 13–18 (1954).
3. GLENN C. ALTSCHULER & STUART M. BLUMIN, RUDE REPUBLIC: AMERICANS AND THEIR POLITICS IN THE NINETEENTH CENTURY 97–105 (2000); 1 ALEXIS DE TOCQUEVILLE, DEMOCRACY IN AMERICA 280 (P. Bradley ed., H. Reeve trans., 1980) (1835); 2 ANTHONY TROLLOPE, NORTH AMERICA 265–66 (1968) (1862).
4. *See generally* Gordon, *The Devil and Daniel Webster*, 94 YALE L.J. 445; JAMES WICE GORDON, LAWYERS IN POLITICS: MID-NINETEENTH CENTURY KENTUCKY AS A CASE STUDY 112–13 (1981) (Ph.D. dissertation, University of Kentucky).
5. JAMES C. CONKLING, *Recollections of the Bench and Bar of Central Illinois, in* CHICAGO BAR ASSOCIATION LECTURES 38 (Chicago, Fergus Printing 1882).
6. Frank E. Stevens, ed., *Autobiography of Stephen A. Douglas*, 5 ILL. ST. HIST. SOC'Y J. 330, 336 (1912); *see also* Schnell, *At the Bar and on the Stump: Douglas and Lincoln's Legal Relationship, in* PAPERS FROM THE THIRTEENTH AND FOURTEENTH ANNUAL LINCOLN COLLOQUIA 100–01.
7. CONKLING, RECOLLECTIONS OF THE BENCH AND BAR at 38.
8. *The American Bar*, 28 U.S. MAG. & DEM. REV. 195, 199 (1851).
9. HERNDON'S LINCOLN at 276; *see also* HOFSTADTER, THE AMERICAN POLITICAL TRADITION at 121.
10. Jason Duncan to William H. Herndon (late 1866–early 1867), *in* HERNDON'S INFORMANTS: LETTERS, INTERVIEWS, AND STATEMENTS ABOUT LINCOLN at 540.
11. *Id.* at 170.
12. Bond for Title, dated Nov. 12, 1831 [N04996], Bill of Sale for Alexander Ferguson, dated Jan. 25, 1832 [N04998]; Summons, dated May 23, 1833, *Alley v. Duncan* [L05903] case file; Deed between Jesse Baker and wife Christina and James Eastep, dated July 26, 1833 [N05025]; Deed between James Cox and wife Nancy and Matthew Marsh and J.L. Clark, filed May 22, 1834 [N05270]; Deed between Isaac Colson and wife Jane and Matthew Young, dated Mar. 22, 1834 [N05230], LPAL.
13. Autobiography written for John L. Scripps, CW 4:65.
14. WILSON, HONOR'S VOICE 86–108; DEBORAH HAINES, CITY DOCTOR, CITY LAWYER: THE LEARNED PROFESSIONS IN FRONTIER CHICAGO, 1833–1860, at 109–10 (1986) (Ph.D. dissertation, University of Chicago). HERBERT ERSHKOWITZ, THE ORIGIN OF THE WHIG AND DEMOCRATIC PARTIES: NEW JERSEY POLITICS, 1820–1837, at 8 (1982).
15. MAXWELL BLOOMFIELD, AMERICAN LAWYERS IN A CHANGING SOCIETY, 1776–1876, at 142–44 (1976).
16. JOHN W. PITTS, ELEVEN NUMBERS AGAINST LAWYER LEGISLATION AND FEES AT THE BAR, WRITTEN AND PRINTED EXPRESSLY FOR THE BENEFIT OF THE PEOPLE 11–13, 42 (n.p. 1843).
17. Frederick Robinson, *A Program for Labor, reprinted in* SOCIAL THEORIES OF JACKSONIAN DEMOCRACY 330–32 (Joseph Blau ed., 1954).
18. Andrew Johnson, *quoted in* Thomas M. Green & William D. Pederson, *The Behavior of Lawyer-Presidents*, 15 PRES. STUD. Q. 343, 351 n.11 (1985).
19. Speech on the Appointment of Federal Clerks (May 31, 1848), *reprinted in* 1 PAPERS OF ANDREW JOHNSON 433 (Leroy P. Graf & Ralph W. Haskins eds., 1967).
20. Fragment: Notes for a Law Lecture, CW 10:20.

21. *The Election*, CHICAGO WEEKLY DEMOCRAT, Apr. 27, 1847 at 2; *see also* HAINES, CITY DOCTOR, CITY LAWYER: THE LEARNED PROFESSIONS IN FRONTIER CHICAGO at 218.

22. Maxwell Bloomfield, *Law vs. Politics: The Self-Image of the American Bar* (1830–1860), 12 AM. J. LEGAL HIST. 306 (1968).

23. GEORGE W. ROBERTSON, SCRAP BOOK ON LAW AND POLITICS, MEN AND TIMES 241 (Lexington, A.W. Elder 1855); AL to George Robertson (Aug. 15, 1855), CW 2:317–19.

24. Timothy Walker, *Ways and Means of Professional Success: Being the Substance of a Valedictory Address to the Graduates of the Law Class in the Cincinnati College*, 1 W. L.J. 543, 545–46 (1844). This was an 1839 address.

25. 1 TOCQUEVILLE, DEMOCRACY IN AMERICA at 280.

26. Cullom Davis, *Abraham Lincoln, Esq.: The Symbiosis of Law and Politics*, *in* ABRAHAM LINCOLN AND THE POLITICAL PROCESS: PAPERS FROM THE SEVENTH ANNUAL LINCOLN COLLOQUIUM (1992).

27. OLIVIER FRAYSSÉ, LINCOLN, LAND, AND LABOR, 1809–60, at 90 (Sylvia Neely trans., 1994).

28. Mark W. Granfors & Terence C. Halliday, *Professional Passages: Caste, Class and Education in the 19th Century Legal Profession*, Table 1 (Educational pattern by date of bar admission) (American Bar Foundation Working Paper 1987).

29. GORDON, LAWYERS IN POLITICS: MID-NINETEENTH CENTURY KENTUCKY AS A CASE STUDY at 155–56.

30. *But see* Harry E. Pratt, *The Genesis of Lincoln the Lawyer*, BULL. ABRAHAM LINCOLN ASS'N 3, 6 (Sept. 1939) (lawyers in Sangamon County in the 1830s lacked formal education).

31. PAUL M. ANGLE, ONE HUNDRED YEARS OF LAW: AN ACCOUNT OF THE LAW OFFICE WHICH JOHN T. STUART FOUNDED IN SPRINGFIELD, ILLINOIS, A CENTURY AGO 7–8 (1928); R. Gerald McMurtry, *Centre College, John Todd Stuart and Abraham Lincoln*, 33 FILSON CLUB HIST. Q. 117 (1959); MEMORIALS OF THE LIFE AND CHARACTER OF STEPHEN T. LOGAN 5 (Springfield, Ill., H.W. Rokker 1882); Thomas, *Lincoln and the Courts, 1854–1861*, ABRAHAM LINCOLN ASS'N. PAPERS at 68 (Logan); DONALD, LINCOLN'S HERNDON at 9–14, 17–18; KING, LINCOLN'S MANAGER, DAVID DAVIS at 11–18; MAURICE G. BAXTER, ORVILLE H. BROWNING: LINCOLN'S FRIEND AND CRITIC 2–4 (1957); GAILLARD HUNT, ISRAEL, ELIHU AND CADWALLADER WASHBURNE 164–67 (1925); HARRY C. BLAIR & REBECCA TARSHIS, COLONEL EDWARD D. BAKER: LINCOLN'S CONSTANT ALLY 5 (1960); NEELY, ABRAHAM LINCOLN ENCYCLOPEDIA at 139 (Hardin); Jack Nortrup, *The Education of a Western Lawyer*, 12 AM. J. LEGAL HIST. 294, 294–301 (1968) (Yates); Pratt, *The Genesis of Lincoln the Lawyer*, BULL. ABRAHAM LINCOLN ASS'N at 3, 6 (Dummer); Harry E. Pratt, *A Beginner On the Old Eighth Judicial Circuit*, 44 J. ILL. ST. HIST. SOC'Y 241, 241 (1951) (Swett).

32. KING, LINCOLN'S MANAGER, DAVID DAVIS at 17; *Cincinnati Law School*, 1 W. L.J. 522 (1844); *Law Schools: The Law Department of the Indiana University, at Bloomington*, 1 W. L.J. 92 (1843).

33. Craig Evan Klafter, *The Influence of Vocational Law Schools on the Origins of American Legal Thought, 1779–1829*, 37 AM. J. LEGAL HIST. 307, 323, 328–29 (1993).

34. W. Hamilton Bryson & E. Lee Shepard, Note, *The Winchester Law School, 1824–1831*, 21 LAW & HIST. REV. 393, 400–02 (2003); Andrew M. Siegel, Note, *"To Learn and Make Respectable Hereafter": The Litchfield Law School in Cultural Context*, 73 N.Y.U. L. REV. 1978 (1998).

35. ALFRED ZANTZINGER REED, TRAINING FOR THE PUBLIC PROFESSION OF THE LAW 152 (1921).

36. A Chicago lawyer offered a series of law lectures in 1847. This introductory series was intended to cover such subjects as pleading, evidence, and "outlines of the law of nature and nations." This endeavor was apparently short-lived. HAINES, CITY DOC-

TOR, CITY LAWYER: THE LEARNED PROFESSIONS IN FRONTIER CHICAGO at 347–48; ESTELLE FRANCIS WARD, THE STORY OF NORTHWESTERN UNIVERSITY 306 (1924). Another legal lecture series was offered in 1851–1852 by Judge D.V. Bell for his Commercial College, which had been founded to provide practical training for young men entering business. HAINES, CITY DOCTOR, CITY LAWYER: THE LEARNED PROFESSIONS IN FRONTIER CHICAGO at 348–49. The first law school in Illinois was formed in 1859 by the old University of Chicago. Robert A. Sprecher, *Admission to Practice Law in Illinois,* 46 ILL. L. REV. (NW. U.) 811, 839 (1952).

37. Josiah Quincy, *An Address Delivered at the Dedication of the Dane Law College in Harvard University, October 23, 1832, in* THE LEGAL MIND IN AMERICA FROM INDEPENDENCE TO THE CIVIL WAR 210–11 (Perry Miller ed., 1962); Joseph Story, *Law Studies,* 9 L. REP. 142, 142 (1846).

38. JOHN PENDLETON KENNEDY, SWALLOW BARN; OR, A SOJOURN IN THE OLD DOMINION 33 (Rev. ed. Philadelphia, J.B. Lippincott & Co. 1860).

39. Thomas W. Clerke, *An Introductory Discourse, on the Study of the Law, Delivered Before the New York Law School, in the City Hall, in the City of New York, on the 23d. Nov. 1840, in* RUDIMENTS OF AMERICAN LAW AND PRACTICE, ON THE PLAN OF BLACKSTONE; PREPARED FOR THE USE OF STUDENTS AT LAW, AND ADAPTED TO SCHOOLS AND COLLEGES XI (New York, Gould, Banks & Co. 1842).

40. Ann Fidler, *"Till You Understand Them in Their Principal Features": Observations on Form and Function in Nineteenth-Century American Law Books,* 92 PAPERS OF THE BIBLIOGRAPHICAL SOCIETY OF AMERICA 427, 435–37 (Dec. 1998).

41. HURST, THE GROWTH OF AMERICAN LAW at 256.

42. BELLAMY STORER, THE LEGAL PROFESSION: AN ADDRESS DELIVERED BEFORE THE LAW DEPARTMENT OF THE UNIVERSITY OF LOUISVILLE, KENTUCKY, FEBRUARY 20, 1856, at 10 (Cincinnati, C. Clark 1856).

43. Autobiography written for John L. Scripps, CW 4:65.

44. *Quoted in* HARRY E. PRATT, LINCOLN 1809–1839, at liv (1941).

45. JOSHUA FRY SPEED, REMINISCENCES OF ABRAHAM LINCOLN AND NOTES OF A VISIT TO CALIFORNIA: TWO LECTURES 20–21 (Louisville, John P. Morton 1884).

46. F.B. CARPENTER, SIX MONTHS AT THE WHITE HOUSE 313 (New York, Hurd & Houghton 1866). Carpenter reprints a supposed interview of Lincoln by J.P. Gulliver that appeared in 1864.

47. HERTZ, THE HIDDEN LINCOLN at 402–03. Don and Virginia Fehrenbacher concluded that Gulliver's article is "an excellent early example of pretended reminiscence at work constructing the Lincoln myth." FEHRENBACHER & FEHRENBACHER, RECOLLECTED WORDS OF ABRAHAM LINCOLN at 189–90.

48. Will of Joshua Short (dated Aug. 22, 1836), CW 1:51.

49. A. Christopher Bryant, *Reading the Law in the Office of Calvin Fletcher: The Apprenticeship System and the Practice of Law in Frontier Indiana,* 1 NEV. L.J. 19, 22 (2001); Bryson & Shepard, Note, *The Winchester Law School, 1824–1831,* 21 LAW & HIST. REV. at 398.

50. AL to James T. Thornton (Dec. 2, 1858), CW 3:344.

51. AL to John M. Brockman (Sept. 25, 1860), CW 4:121.

52. JOSEPH STORY, COMMENTARIES ON EQUITY JURISPRUDENCE AS ADMINISTERED IN ENGLAND AND AMERICA (Boston, Hilliard, Gray & Co. 1836).

53. The first American edition was JOSEPH CHITTY, A PRACTICAL TREATISE ON PLEADING; AND ON THE PARTIES TO ACTIONS, AND THE FORMS OF ACTIONS; WITH A SECOND VOLUME CONTAINING PRECEDENTS OF PLEADINGS (New York, Robert M'Dermut 1809). Six more American editions had appeared by 1837. Jenni Parrish, *Law Books and Legal Publishing in America, 1760–1840,* 72 LAW LIBR. J. 355, 386 (1979).

54. Joseph Story, Commentaries on Equity Pleadings, and the Incidents Thereto, According to the Practice of the Courts of Equity of England and America (Boston, C.C. Little & J. Brown 1838).

55. Simon Greenleaf, Treatise on the Law of Evidence (3 vols. Boston, Charles C. Little & James Brown 1842).

56. *See* Michael H. Harris, *The Frontier Lawyer's Library: Southern Indiana, 1800–1850, as a Test Case*, 26 Am. J. Legal Hist. 239, 249–51 (1972).

57. *See Ballentine v. Beall*, 4 Ill. (3 Scam.) 203 (1841); *Spear v. Campbell*, 5 Ill. (4 Scam.) 424 (1843); *Martin v. Dryden*, 6 Ill. (1 Gilm.) 187 (1844); *McCall v. Lesher*, 7 Ill. (2 Gilm.) 47 (1845); Brief, filed Dec. Term 1849 [5364], *Lewis v. Moffett & Johnson* [L03866] case file, LPAL.

58. *See Abrams v. Camp*, 4 Ill. (3 Scam.) 291 (1841); *Davis v. Harkness*, 6 Ill. (1 Gilm.) 173 (1844); *Broadwell v. Broadwell*, 6 Ill. (1 Gilm.) 599 (1844); *Hall v. Irwin*, 7 Ill. (2 Gilm.) 176 (1845); *Trumbull v. Campbell*, 8 Ill. (3 Gilm.) 502 (1846); and *Webster v. French*, 11 Ill. 254 (1849).

59. See *Martin v. Dryden*, 6 Ill. (1 Gilm.) 187 (1844); *Kincaid v. Turner*, 7 Ill. (2 Gilm.) 618 (1845); *Henderson v. Welch*, 8 Ill. (3 Gilm.) 340 (1845); *Pearl v. Wellman*, 11 Ill. 352 (1849); *Penny v. Graves*, 12 Ill. 287 (1850); *Whitecraft v. Vanderver*, 12 Ill. 235 (1850); *Smith v. Dunlap*, 12 Ill. 184 (1850); Brief, filed Dec. Term 1857 [5799], *King v. Wade* [L00856], Argument of Counsel, dated May 9, 1848 [5745], *Watson v. Gill* [L00733] case files, LPAL; Opinion on Wisconsin Land Titles (Mar. 24, 1846), CW 2:336. Herndon twice referred to Greenleaf's *Evidence* in his notes for the appeal in the *Dalby* case. Brief, dated Dec. Term 1857 [4793], *St. Louis, Alton & Chicago R.R. v. Dalby* [L01027] case file, LPAL.

60. *See Cannon v. Kinney*, 4 Ill. (3 Scam.) 9 (1841); *Averill v. Field*, 4 Ill. (3 Scam.) 390 (1842); *Field v. Rawlings*, 6 Ill. (1 Gilm.) 581 (1844); *Murphy v. Summerville*, 7 Ill. (2 Gilm.) 360 (1845); AL to William Martin (Feb. 19, 1851), CW 2:98–99.

61. AL to Isham Reavis (Nov. 5, 1855), CW 2:327; Andreas' History of the State of Nebraska (Chicago: Western Hist. Publishing Co. 1882).

62. Robert A. Ferguson, Law and Letters in American Culture at 305 (1986).

63. James M. Ogden, *Lincoln's Early Impressions of the Law in Indiana*, 7 Notre Dame L. 325, 328 (1932) (first quotation); David C. Mearns, *Mr. Lincoln and the Books He Read*, in Three Presidents and Their Books 61 (Arthur Bestor et al. eds., 1955) (second quotation).

64. Howells, Life of Abraham Lincoln at 31.

65. Howard, The Life of Abraham Lincoln 17.

66. Roy P. Basler, ed., *James Quay Howard's Notes on Lincoln*, 4 Abraham Lincoln Q. 387, 390 (1947).

67. Isaac Cogdal, *Interview (1865–1866)*, in Herndon's Informants: Letters, Interviews, and Statements About Lincoln at 440–41.

68. Wilson, Honor's Voice at 104.

69. AL to James T. Thornton (Dec. 2, 1858), CW 3:344; AL to John M. Brockman (Sept. 25, 1860), CW 4:121.

70. *Watkins v. White*, 4 Ill. (3 Scam.) 549 (1842); *Cook v. Hall*, 6 Ill. (1 Gilm.) 575 (1844); *Whitecraft v. Vanderver*, 12 Ill. (1 Scam.) 335 (1850).

71. Ferguson, Law and Letters in American Culture at 11, 15; *see also* Erwin C. Surrency, A History of American Law Publishing 132–33 (1990).

72. *Quoted in* J.G. Marvin, Legal Bibliography 124 (Philadelphia, T. & J.W. Johnson 1847).

73. William Blackstone, Commentaries on the Laws of England (1979) (4 vols. 1765–1769).

74. S.F.C. Milsom, *The Nature of Blackstone's Achievement*, 1 OXFORD J. LEGAL STUD. 1, 2–3, 10 (1981).

75. [Joseph Story], *Hoffman's Course of Legal Study*, 6 NO. AM. REV. 45, 52 (Nov. 1817).

76. Milsom, *The Nature of Blackstone's Achievement*, 1 OXFORD J. LEGAL STUD. at 11.

77. [Story], *Hoffman's Course of Legal Study*, 6 NO. AM. REV. at 52; *see also* Quincy, *An Address Delivered at the Dedication of the Dane Law College in Harvard University, October 23, 1832, in* THE LEGAL MIND IN AMERICA at 208.

78. TIMOTHY WALKER, AN INTRODUCTION TO AMERICAN LAW, DESIGNED AS A FIRST BOOK FOR STUDENTS at 12 (Philadelphia, P.H. Nicklin & T. Johnson 1837).

79. WILLIAM J. NOVAK, THE PEOPLE'S WELFARE: LAW AND REGULATION IN NINETEENTH-CENTURY AMERICA 32 (1996).

80. THOMAS JEFFERSON, WRITINGS 1806 (1984).

81. NOVAK, THE PEOPLE'S WELFARE at 34; *see also* Robert Cover, *Book Review*, 70 COLUM. L. REV. 1475 (1975).

82. Nathaniel Chipman, *Sketches of the Principles of Government* (1793), *reprinted in* THE LEGAL MIND IN AMERICA at 29–30.

83. WALKER, AN INTRODUCTION TO AMERICAN LAW 13.

84. *Walker's Introduction to American Law*, 45 NO. AM. REV. 485, 485 (1837).

85. *Walker's Introduction*, 1 W. LITERARY J. & MONTHLY REV. 107 (Dec. 1844).

86. CHARLES HUMPHREYS, COMPENDIUM OF THE COMMON LAW IN FORCE IN KENTUCKY x (Lexington, W.G. Hunt 1822).

87. FRANCIS HILLIARD, THE ELEMENTS OF LAW; BEING A COMPREHENSIVE SUMMARY OF AMERICAN JURISPRUDENCE iv (2d ed. New York, John S. Voorhies 1848).

88. CATHERINE SPICER ELLER, THE WILLIAM BLACKSTONE COLLECTION IN THE YALE LAW LIBRARY 37–51 (Yale Law Library Publications No. 6, June 1938); *see also* MARVIN, LEGAL BIBLIOGRAPHY 122–27.

89. Cover, *Book Review* 70 COLUM. L. REV. at 1477.

90. 1 ST. GEORGE TUCKER, BLACKSTONE'S COMMENTARIES: WITH NOTES OF REFERENCE TO THE CONSTITUTION AND LAWS, OF THE FEDERAL GOVERNMENT OF THE UNITED STATES AND OF THE COMMONWEALTH OF VIRGINIA iii–v (1969) (1803); Dennis R. Nolan, *Sir William Blackstone and the New American Republic: A Study of Intellectual Impact*, 51 N.Y.U. L. REV. 731, 737–38 (1976).

91. ELLER, THE WILLIAM BLACKSTONE COLLECTION at 60–61, 46, 49–50.

92. Brief Autobiography, June [15?] 1858, CW 2:459.

93. DAVID MELLINKOFF, THE LANGUAGE OF THE LAW 227 (1963).

94. CHARLES B. STROZIER, LINCOLN'S QUEST FOR UNION: PUBLIC AND PRIVATE MEANINGS 139 (1982); FERGUSON, LAW AND LETTERS IN AMERICAN CULTURE at 32.

95. Gary B. Nash, *The Philadelphia Bench and Bar, 1800–1861*, 7 COMP. STUD. SOC'Y & HIST. 203, 205–06 (1965).

96. Gerald W. Gawalt, *Sources of Anti-Lawyer Sentiment in Massachusetts, 1740–1840*, 14 AM. J. LEGAL HIST. 283 (1969); William R. Johnson, *Education and Professional Life Styles: Law and Medicine in the Nineteenth Century*, 14 HIST. EDUC. Q. 185, 187 (1974).

97. RICHARD ABEL, AMERICAN LAWYERS 40 (1989); Maxwell Bloomfield, *Law: The Development of a Profession, in* PROFESSIONS IN AMERICAN HISTORY 34–35 (Nathan O. Hatch ed., 1988); LAWRENCE M. FRIEDMAN, A HISTORY OF AMERICAN LAW 236–37 (3rd ed. 2005).

98. ROBERT H. WIEBE, THE OPENING OF AMERICAN SOCIETY 307–08 (1984); *see also* KENNETH ALLEN DE VILLE, MEDICAL MALPRACTICE IN NINETEENTH-CENTURY AMERICA 85–91 (1990).

99. An Act Concerning Attorneys and Counselors at Law, Mar. 1, 1833, STATUTE LAWS OF THE STATE OF ILLINOIS (Chicago, Stephen F. Gale 1839).

100. Pratt, Lincoln at liv.

101. Opinion Record Journal, Roll of Attorneys (Supreme Court Central Grand Division 1831–1843) (Illinois State Archives, Springfield, Illinois).

102. *In the Matter of Fellows*, 3 Ill. (2 Scam.) 369, 369 (1840).

103. John Dean Caton, Early Bench and Bar of Illinois 170 (Chicago, Chicago Legal News Co. 1893).

104. Plea, filed Oct. 5, 1836 [5174], Affidavit, filed Oct. 5, 1836 [5172], *Hawthorn v. Wooldridge* [L03504] (trespass vi et armis); Affidavit, filed Oct. 5, 1836 [5173], Account, filed Oct. 5, 1836 [5041], Judge's Docket, Mar. Term 1837, Sangamon County Circuit Court [100104], *Hawthorn v. Wooldridge* [L03505] (assumpsit) case files, LPAL.

105. Sangamo J. (Springfield), Apr. 15, 1837, at 3.

106. Caton, Early Bench and Bar of Illinois at 170–71; *see also* 1 Memoirs of Gustave Koerner 1809–1896, at 373–75 (Thomas J. McCormack ed., 1909).

107. "F.," *The Profession of the Law*, 7 W. L.J. 97, 112 (1849); *see also American Law*, 1 Sw. L.J. & Rep. 112, 116 (1844); *The Legal Profession, Ancient and Modern*, 4 Am. Rev. 242, 257 (1846); *Examination of Attorneys*, 5 W. L.J. 480 (1848).

108. 1 Diary of George Templeton Strong 164–65 (Allan Nevins & Milton Halsey Thomas eds., 1952).

109. 1 William T. Sherman, Memoirs of General William T. Sherman 140 (New York, D. Appleton & Co. 1875).

110. Angle, One Hundred Years of Law at 37–38 (examination of C.C. Brown); Jesse Weik, *A Law Student's Recollection of Abraham Lincoln*, 97 Outlook 311, 312–13 (1911) (examination of Jonathan Birch); Certificate of Examination for Hiram W. Beckwith and George W. Lawrence, dated May 27, 1854, CW 2:218; Recommendation for Henry S. Greene, dated Jan. 28, 1860, CW 3:515; Order, dated July 21, 1841 [130279], Admission of Benjamin F. James [N05306]; Recommendation, dated Feb. 12, 1845 [132971], Admission of Stanislaus P. Lalumiere [N05129]; Order, dated Dec. 21, 1841, Admission of Benjamin R. Hampton [N05307]; Order, dated July 8, 1841 [130278], Admission of Josiah McRoberts, John H. Murphy, and Joseph Peters [N05305]; Order (dated July Term 1842) [130286], Admission of Aguilla Parker and Isaac Stevens [N05308]; Motion (dated Nov. 27, 1844) [129836] case files, LPAL. Lincoln also twice moved for the admission in Illinois of two lawyers who were already licensed in Indiana. Order, dated Nov. 15, 1851 [129975], Admission of Robert M. Evans [N05215]; Motion [filed Oct. 23, 1851], Admission of Daniel M. Voorhees [N05255] case files, LPAL.

111. Weik, *A Law Student's Recollection of Abraham Lincoln*, 97 Outlook at 312–13.

112. *Quoted in* Angle, One Hundred Years of Law at 37–38.

113. The phrase is from Thomas Koenig & Michael Rustad, *The Challenge to Hierarchy in Legal Education: Suffolk and the Night Law School Movement*, 7 Res. In Law, Deviance & Soc. Control 189 (1984).

114. David Davis to AL (Jan. 10, 1860), Abraham Lincoln Papers at the Library of Congress, <memory.loc.gov/ammem/alhtml/malhome.html>, Select: Search by Keyword, Enter: David Davis legal, Select: Item 3.

115. C.H. Moore to AL (Jan.19, 1860), Abraham Lincoln Papers at the Library of Congress, <memory.loc.gov/ammem/alhtml/malhome.html>, Select: Search by Keyword, Enter: Clifton Moore, Select: Item 2.

116. Autobiographical Sketch (Sept. 1, 1838), *in* The Letters of Stephen A. Douglas 61 (Robert W. Johannsen ed., 1961).

117. AL to James T. Thornton (Dec. 2, 1858), CW 3:344.

118. Herndon's Lincoln at 274; William H. Herndon to Jesse Weik (Dec. 9, 1888), *in* Hertz, The Hidden Lincoln at 148.

119. HERNDON'S LINCOLN at 277, 274.

120. *Stephen T. Logan Talks About Lincoln*, BULL. LINCOLN CENTENNIAL ASS'N 3 (Sept. 1, 1928).

121. WHITNEY, LIFE ON THE CIRCUIT WITH LINCOLN at 242.

122. William H. Herndon to Jesse Weik (Feb. 18, 1887), *in* HERTZ, THE HIDDEN LINCOLN at 176; *see also* William H. Herndon to Jesse Weik (Oct. 22, 1885), Herndon-Weik Collection, Library of Congress.

123. M.H. Hoeflich, *The Lawyer as Pragmatic Reader: The History of Legal Common-Placing*, 55 ARK. L. REV. 87, 88–89 (2002).

124. John H. Littlefield, Brooklyn Eagle (Oct. 16, 1887), *quoted in* HERNDON'S LINCOLN at 265.

125. John Livingston to Abraham Lincoln (May 21, 1859), Abraham Lincoln Papers at the Library of Congress, <memory.loc.gov/ammem/alhtml/malhome.html>, Select: Search by Keyword, Enter: John Livingston, Select: Item 1.

126. WHITNEY, LIFE ON THE CIRCUIT WITH LINCOLN at 122.

127. Erwin C. Surrency, *Law Reports in the United States*, 25 AM. J. LEGAL HIST. 48, 50 (1981).

128. Thomas Jefferson to John Minor (Aug. 30, 1814), *in* 11 WORKS OF THOMAS JEFFERSON 423 (Paul Leicester Ford ed., 1905); Joseph Story, *Digests of the Common Law*, *in* MISCELLANEOUS WRITINGS OF JOSEPH STORY 380 (William W. Story ed., 1972) (1852).

129. DONALD, LINCOLN'S HERNDON at 37–38, 47–48; DONALD, "WE ARE LINCOLN MEN" at 71.

130. Law commonplace book [1849] [130384], Record of Legal Precedents [1861] [130383], Herndon Conducted Legal Research [N05453] file, LPAL.

131. 19 Ill. 353, 374 (1857); Legal Citations [Dec. Term 1857] [4793], *St. Louis, Alton, & Chicago R.R. v. Dalby* [L01027] case file, LPAL.

132. *William H. Herndon, Lincoln's "Ingratitude", reprinted in* HERTZ, THE HIDDEN LINCOLN at 419.

133. William H. Herndon to Wendell Phillips (May 12, 1857), *in* IRVING BARTLETT, WENDELL AND ANN PHILLIPS: THE COMMUNITY OF REFORM 1840–1880, at 157 (1979).

134. AL to Hezekiah M. Wead (Feb. 7, 1852), CW 2:118.

135. AL to Newton Deming & George P. Strong (May 25,1857), CW 11:13.

136. AL to Charles Hoyt (Jan. 16, 1856), CW 2:329.

137. 6 Ill. (1 Gilm.) 187, 197–206 (1844).

138. *Van Ness v. Pacard*, 27 U.S. (2 Pet.) 137, 144 (1829).

139. R. Ben Brown, *Judging in the Days of the Early Republic: A Critique of Judge Richard Arnold's Use of History in Anastasoff v. United States*, 3 J. APP. PRAC. & PROCESS 355 (2001).

140. 2 JOHN BOUVIER, A LAW DICTIONARY ADAPTED TO THE CONSTITUTIONS AND LAWS OF THE UNITED STATES OF AMERICA 9 (Philadelphia, T. & J.W. Johnson 1839).

141. *Law Intelligence*, CHICAGO TRIBUNE, Sept. 21, 1857 [132962], *reprinted in Hurd v. Rock Island Bridge Co.* [L02289] case file, LPAL.

142. PETER KARSTEN, HEART VERSUS HEAD: JUDGE-MADE LAW IN NINETEENTH-CENTURY AMERICA 26 (1997).

143. 1 JAMES KENT, COMMENTARIES ON AMERICAN LAW 442–43 (O. Halstead, New York 1826); Francis Lieber, *On Political Hermeneutics—Precedents*, 18 AM. JURIST 282–94 (1838); Frederick G. Kempin, Jr., *Precedent and Stare Decisis: The Critical Years, 1800 to 1850*, 3 AM. J. LEGAL HIST. 28 (1959); FERGUSON, LAW AND LETTERS IN AMERICAN CULTURE at 199–201.

144. *Law Reports*, 14 SOUTHERN LITERARY MESSENGER 255, 255 (Apr. 1848).

145. *Id.*; *see also* KARSTEN, HEART VERSUS HEAD at 35.

146. *See, e.g., Anderson v. Ryan*, 8 Ill. (3 Gilm.) 583, 584 (1846) (citing federal, Kentucky, and Massachusetts decisions); *Hawks v. Lands*, 8 Ill. 227, 227–28 (3 Gilm.) 227 (1846) (citing Indiana, Kentucky, Ohio, Massachusetts, New York, and English decisions); *Henderson v. Welch*, 8 Ill. 340, 341 (3 Gilm.) 340 (1846) (citing Maryland, Massachusetts, and New York decisions); *England v. Clark*, 5 Ill. (4 Scam.) 486, 487 (1843) (citing five English opinions); *Dorman v. Lane*, 6 Ill. (1 Gilm.) 143, 143–44 (1844) (citing Kentucky, Maine, Massachusetts, and English decisions).

147. *Law Reports*, 14 SOUTHERN LITERARY MESSENGER at 255.

148. *American Law Books. Story on Sales*, 5 W. L.J. 118, 118 (1847).

149. GRANT GILMORE, THE AGES OF AMERICAN LAW 29 (1977).

150. WARD HILL LAMON, THE LIFE OF ABRAHAM LINCOLN 316 (Boston, J.R. Osgood & Co. 1872).

151. *See* Louis A. Warren, *Lincoln's Law Library*, LINCOLN LORE, no. 619 (Feb. 17, 1941).

152. Many of these citations come from reported appellate opinions where the court reporter would list the authorities relied upon by the appellate lawyers. Because these lists don't appear in every opinion, this is an incomplete sample. The decisions that list the authorities that Lincoln cited on appeal represent roughly ten percent of Lincoln's appellate cases. As to the citations themselves, Lincoln would cite authority in an abbreviated format, such as "Babington on Auctions" or "Gould's Pl. Part IV, § 26." I used various reference materials to determine the treatise and the likely edition that Lincoln was citing. *See* MORRIS L. COHEN, BIBLIOGRAPHY OF EARLY AMERICAN LAW (1998) (6 vols.); MARVIN, LEGAL BIBLIOGRAPHY; Parrish, *Law Books and Legal Publishing in America* 72 LAW LIBR. J. 355; Mark E. Steiner, *General Catalogue of Law Books, Alphabetically Classified by Subjects (1859)*, 18 LEGAL REF. SERVS. Q. 47 (1999).

153. On Story's influence as a treatise writer, *see* ROSCOE POUND, THE FORMATIVE ERA OF AMERICAN LAW 154 (1938).

154. Robert Feikema Karachuk, *A Workman's Tools: The Law Library of Henry Adams Bullard*, 42 AM. J. LEGAL HIST. 160, 175 (1998).

155. The complete series is listed on pp. 300–01 of volume 319 of the NATIONAL UNION CATALOG (1974).

156. MARVIN, LEGAL BIBLIOGRAPHY at 449–50; *see also Critical Notice*, 5 AM. L. MAG. 246 (1845).

157. SURRENCY, A HISTORY OF AMERICAN LAW PUBLISHING at 167.

158. *Webster v. French*, 11 Ill. 254, 257 (1849); Brief, Dec. Term 1855 [3244], *Mayers & Mayers v. Turner* [L00960], LPAL. John M. Krum, Lincoln's co-counsel in *Martin v. Dryden*, cited specifically to the Law Library edition of Frederick Calvert's Treatise Upon the Law Respecting to Suits in Equity. 6 Ill. (1 Gilm.) at 198.

159. Legal Citations [dated Dec. Term 1857] [4793], *St. Louis, Alton, & Chicago R.R. v. Dalby* [L01027] case file, LPAL.

160. *See* [Louis A. Warren], *Lincoln's Law Library*, LINCOLN LORE, no. 619 (Feb. 17, 1941).

161. BROOKLYN DAILY EAGLE, Oct. 16, 1887 at 7.

162. List of Law Books Belonging to David Davis, Dec. 4, 1848, *in* Bound Volume Three, David Davis Papers, Abraham Lincoln Presidential Library & Museum, Springfield, Illinois.

163. *See* William H. Herndon to Jesse Weik (July 10, 1888), *in* HERTZ, THE HIDDEN LINCOLN at 215.

164. Petition for Rehearing, dated Jan. 12, 1847 [70483], *Gear v. Clark* [L02439] case file, LPAL. Lincoln wrote this motion for Jacksonville attorney David A. Smith, whose name Lincoln affixed to the document.

165. *Pearl v. Wellman*, 11 Ill. 352, 353 (1849); 2 J.I. CLARK HARE & H.B. WALLACE, SELECT DECISIONS OF AMERICAN COURTS (Philadelphia, T. & J.W. Johnson 1848).

166. AL to Newton Deming & George P. Strong (May 25, 1857), CW 11:13.

167. Petition for Rehearing, filed Jan. 23, 1846 [39617], *Patterson v. Edwards* [L00884] case file, LPAL.

168. *Patterson v. Edwards*, 7 Ill. (2 Gilm.) 720, 723–24 (1845).

169. *Id.* at 723.

170. Petition for Rehearing, filed Jan. 23, 1846 [39617], *Patterson v. Edwards* [L00884] case file, LPAL.

171. THOMAS STARKIE, A TREATISE ON THE LAW OF SLANDER AND LIBEL, AND INCIDENTALLY OF MALICIOUS PROSECUTIONS; FROM THE SECOND ENGLISH EDITION OF 1830, WITH NOTES AND REFERENCES TO AMERICAN CASES AND TO ENGLISH DECISIONS SINCE 1830 (2 vols. Albany, C. Van Benthuysen & Co. 1843). For a review of this edition, *see Critical Notice*, 2 AM. L. MAG. 247 (1843).

172. ARTHUR SYDNEY BEARDSLEY, LEGAL BIBLIOGRAPHY AND THE USE OF LAW BOOKS 270 (1937); Karachuk, *A Workman's Tools: The Law Library of Henry Adams Bullard*, 42 AM. J. LEGAL HIST. at 163; SURRENCY, A HISTORY OF AMERICAN LAW PUBLISHING at 111–13.

173. 1 NORMAN L. FREEMAN, THE "ILLINOIS DIGEST:" BEING A FULL AND COMPLETE DIGEST AND COMPILATION OF ALL THE DECISIONS OF THE SUPREME COURT iii (Cincinnati, Moore, Wilstach, Keys & Co. 1856).

174. *United States Digest*, 3 W. L.J. 239, 240 (1846).

175. *Critical Notices*, 6 AM. L. MAG. 471, 471–72 (1846).

176. MORRIS L. COHEN ET AL., HOW TO FIND THE LAW 83 (9th ed. 1989).

177. *Risinger v. Cheney*, 7 Ill. (2 Gilm.) 84, 84 (1845).

178. 1 THERON METCALF & JONATHAN C. PERKINS, DIGEST OF THE DECISIONS OF THE COURTS OF COMMON LAW AND ADMIRALTY IN THE UNITED STATES 540 (Boston, Hilliard, Gray, & Co. 1840).

179. *Risinger v. Cheney*, 7 Ill. (2 Gilm.) at 84, 90 (emphasis added).

180. AL to William Martin, dated Mar. 6, 1851 [93970], *Alton & Sangamon R.R. v. Barret* [L02610] case file, LPAL. Lincoln's abbreviation for "supplement" was rendered as "Septr." in CW 2:102.

181. 2 JOHN PHELPS PUTNAM, A SUPPLEMENT TO THE UNITED STATES DIGEST 976 (Boston, Charles C. Little & James Brown 1847).

182. 2 PUTNAM, A SUPPLEMENT TO THE UNITED STATES DIGEST at 976. Section 409 summarizes "*Turnpike Co. v. Burdett*, 7 Dana, 99."

183. AL to William Martin, dated Mar. 6, 1851 [93970], *Alton & Sangamon R.R. v. Barret* [L02610] case file, LPAL.

184. On the rise of state digests, *see* Joel Fishman, *The Digests of Pennsylvania*, 90 LAW LIBR. J. 481 (1998); Kurt X. Metzmeier, *Blazing Trails in a New Kentucky Wilderness: Early Kentucky Case Law Digests*, 93 LAW LIBR. J. 93 (2001); SURRENCY, A HISTORY OF AMERICAN LAW PUBLISHING at 114.

185. Motion to Dismiss, filed Jan. 5, 1860 [38906], Judgment, dated Jan. 19, 1860 [70184] *Headen v. True* [L00848] case file, LPAL.

186. 1 FREEMAN, THE "ILLINOIS DIGEST" at 193.

187. *Id.* at 201. Herndon also cited the *Illinois Digest* in the "argument of appellee" in *Smith v. Smith*. Argument of Appellee [dated Jan. Term 1858] [5612], *Smith v. Smith* [L00849] case file, LPAL.

188. Edgar Allan Poe, *Magazine Literature*, THE WEEKLY MIRROR 299 (Feb. 15, 1845).

189. Joel Fishman, *An Early Pennsylvania Legal Periodical: The Pennsylvania Law Journal, 1842–1848*, 45 AM. J. LEGAL HIST. 22 (2001); M.H. Hoeflich, *John Livingston and the Business of Law in Nineteenth-Century America*, 44 AM. J. LEGAL HIST. 347, 354–57 (2000).

190. WALTER THEODORE HITCHCOCK, TIMOTHY WALKER: ANTEBELLUM LAWYER 104–23 (1980) (Ph.D. dissertation, University of Mississippi).

191. *Remarkable Case of Arrest for Murder*, 4 W. L.J. 25 (Oct. 1846); *In the Matter of Jane, A Woman of Color*, 5 W. L.J. 202 (Feb. 1848).

192. CALVIN COLTON, THE JUNIUS TRACTS AND THE RIGHTS OF LABOR 15 (1974) (1844).

193. Speech at Kalamazoo, Michigan (Aug. 27, 1856), CW 2:364. For Lincoln's views on labor, *see* James A. Stevenson, *Abraham Lincoln on Labor and Capital*, 38 CIVIL WAR HIST. 197 (1992).

194. Speech at Cincinnati, Ohio (Sept. 17, 1859), CW 10:43–44.

195. Speech at New Haven, Connecticut (Mar. 6, 1860), CW 4:24–25.

196. Timothy Walker's Law Department of Cincinnati College advertised in the *Springfield Sangamo Journal. See, e.g.,* SANGAMO J., Sept. 24, 1841, at 3.

197. AL to William H. Grigsby (Aug. 3, 1858), CW 2:535.

198. AL to Isham Reavis (Nov. 5, 1855), CW 2:327.

199. AL to James T. Thornton (Dec. 2, 1858), CW 3:344.

200. AL to Isham Reavis (Nov. 5, 1855), CW 2:327.

201. AL to John M. Brockman (Sept. 25, 1860), CW 4:121.

202. 1 BEVERIDGE, ABRAHAM LINCOLN at 209.

203. THOMAS, ABRAHAM LINCOLN at 67.

204. HERNDON'S LINCOLN at 257.

205. Steiner, *General Catalogue of Law Books, Alphabetically Classified by Subjects (1859)*, 18 LEGAL REF. SERVS. Q. at 47.

206. FRIEDMAN, A HISTORY OF AMERICAN LAW at 223.

207. One memoirist wrote that Lincoln, after the Manny Reaper case, had said he was going back to Illinois to study law because college-trained lawyers were "coming west." MR. & MRS. RALPH EMERSON'S PERSONAL RECOLLECTIONS OF ABRAHAM LINCOLN 8–9 (1909). Don and Virginia Fehrenbacher concluded that this recollection had doubtful authenticity. FEHRENBACHER & FEHRENBACHER, RECOLLECTED WORDS OF ABRAHAM LINCOLN at 152.

208. Rules of Practice, *reprinted in* 19 Ill. xx (1858); Granfors & Halliday, *Professional Passages: Caste, Class and Education in the 19th Century Legal Profession*, Table 1.

209. JOHN S. GOFF, ROBERT TODD LINCOLN: A MAN IN HIS OWN RIGHT 23–30, 41–58, 62–63, 91 (1969).

3—A Whig in the Courthouse

1. John Henry Schlegel, *The Line Between History and Casenote*, 22 LAW & SOC'Y REV. 969, 974 (1988).

2. MORTON J. HORWITZ, THE TRANSFORMATION OF AMERICAN LAW 1780–1860 (1977); Robert W. Gordon, *The Elusive Transformation*, 6 YALE J.L. & HUMAN. 137, 137 (1994); Robert W. Gordon, *Critical Legal Histories*, 36 STAN. L. REV. 57, 96–97 (1984); CHARLES SELLERS, THE MARKET REVOLUTION: JACKSONIAN AMERICA 1815–1846, at 47–49 (1991); *but see* Mark Tushnet, *A Marxist Analysis of American Law*, 1 MARXIST PERSPECTIVES 96, 107 (1978); Alfred S. Konefsky, *Law and Culture in Antebellum Boston*, 40 STAN. L. REV. 1119, 1121 (1988); John Phillip Reid, *A Plot Too Doctrinaire*, 55 TEX. L. REV. 1307, 1310–11 (1977) (book review); William E. Gienapp, *The Myth of Class in Jacksonian America*, 6 J. POL'Y HIST. 232, 238–39 (1994).

3. The portrait of the antebellum bar that appears in chapter 5 of Horwitz's *The Transformation of American Law: 1780–1860* (1977) is but a small part of his overall argument about how antebellum legal changes enabled commercial groups to win a disproportionate amount of wealth and power. This chapter does not address the timing and

the extent of the changes described by Horwitz, which have been questioned by other scholars. *See, e.g.,* Comment, *The Creation of a Common Law Rule: The Fellow Servant Rule, 1837–1860*, 132 U. PA. L. REV. 579 (1984); Paula J. Dalley, *The Law of Deceit, 1790–1860: Continuity Amidst Change*, 39 AM. J. LEGAL HIST. 405 (1995); Peter Karsten, *"Bottomed on Justice": A Reappraisal of Critical Legal Studies Scholarship Concerning Breaches of Labor Contracts by Quitting or Firing in Britain and the U.S., 1630–1880*, 34 AM. J. LEGAL HIST. 213 (1990); Eben Moglen, Note, *Commercial Arbitration in the Eighteenth Century: Searching for the Transformation of American Law*, 93 YALE L.J. 135 (1983); A.W.B. Simpson, *The Horwitz Thesis and the History of Contracts*, 46 U. CHI. L. REV. 533 (1978); Jenny B. Wahl, *Twice-Told Tales: An Economist's Re-Telling of the Transformation of American Law, 1780–1860*, 37 TULSA L. REV. 879 (2002).

4. Stephen Botein, *Love of Gold and Other Ruling Passions: The Legal Papers of Daniel Webster* 1985 AM. B. FOUND. RES. J. 217, 223 (book review); Gordon, *The Devil and Daniel Webster*, 94 YALE L.J. 445 (book review); Hendrik Hartog, *The Significance of a Singular Career: Reflections on Daniel Webster's Legal Papers*, 1984 WIS. L. REV. 1105, 1110–11 (book review); R. Kent Newmyer, *Daniel Webster and the Modernization of American Law*, 32 BUFF. L. REV. 819 (1983) (book review).

5. William H. Rehnquist, *Daniel Webster and the Oratorical Tradition, in* YEARBOOK 1989, SUP. CT. HIST. SOC'Y 6 (1989).

6. BERNARD SCHWARTZ, MAIN CURRENTS IN AMERICAN LEGAL THOUGHT 257 (1993); FRANK, LINCOLN AS A LAWYER at 171.

7. On Lincoln and the Whig economic program, *see* GABOR S. BORITT, LINCOLN AND THE ECONOMICS OF THE AMERICAN DREAM 13–120 (1978).

8. AL to Jesse W. Fell (Dec. 20, 1859), CW 3:511–12.

9. AL to Samuel Haycraft (June 4, 1860), CW 4:70.

10. DANIEL WALKER HOWE, THE POLITICAL CULTURE OF AMERICAN WHIGS 264 (1979); Daniel Walker Howe, *Why Abraham Lincoln Was a Whig*, 16 J. ABRAHAM LINCOLN ASS'N 27 (1995); [Mark E. Neely, Jr.], *The Political Life of New Salem, Illinois*, LINCOLN LORE no. 1715 (Jan. 1981).

11. DON E. FEHRENBACHER, PRELUDE TO GREATNESS: LINCOLN IN THE 1850S, at 19–47 (1962).

12. David Donald, *Abraham Lincoln: Whig in the White House, in* LINCOLN RECONSIDERED at 187–208; Joel H. Silbey, *"Always a Whig in Politics": The Partisan Life of Abraham Lincoln*, 7 PAPERS OF THE ABRAHAM LINCOLN ASS'N 21, 22 (1986); *Kenneth Stampp, Abraham Lincoln: The Politics of a Practical Whig, in* THE ERA OF RECONSTRUCTION 24–49 (1965).

13. Robert W. Gordon, *Lawyers as the American Aristocracy*, 20 STAN. LAW. 2, 3 (Fall 1985); Anthony T. Kronman, *Precedent and Tradition*, 99 YALE L.J. 1029 (1990).

14. HOWE, THE POLITICAL CULTURE OF AMERICAN WHIGS at 127; David Grimsted, *Rioting in Its Jacksonian Setting*, 77 AM. HIST. REV. 361 (1972); Lorman Ratner, *Northern Concern for Social Order as Cause for Rejecting Anti-Slavery, 1831–1840*, 28 HISTORIAN 1 (1965); LEONARD L. RICHARDS, "GENTLEMEN OF PROPERTY AND STANDING": ANTI-ABOLITION MOBS IN JACKSONIAN AMERICA 3–19 (1970).

15. George Fredrickson, *The Search for Order and Community, in* THE PUBLIC AND PRIVATE LINCOLN 88 (G. Cullom Davis et al. eds., 1979). This paragraph heavily relies on Fredrickson.

16. GORDON, LAWYERS IN POLITICS: MID-NINETEENTH CENTURY KENTUCKY AS A CASE STUDY 24, 33–34 (1981) (Ph.D. dissertation, University of Kentucky).

17. *See generally* M.H. Hoeflich, *Law in the Republican Classroom*, 43 U. KAN. L. REV. 711 (1995); Peter R. Teachout, *Light in Ashes: The Problem of "Respect for the Rule of Law" in American History*, 53 N.Y.U. L. REV. 241 (1978).

18. Fredrickson, *The Search for Order and Community* at 91; *see also* Phillip S. Paludan, *Lincoln, the Rule of Law, and the American Revolution* 70 J. ILL. ST. HIST. SOC'Y 10, 12–14 (1977).

19. William Henry Herndon to Jesse Weik (Jan. 27, 1888), Herndon-Weik Collection, Library of Congress.

20. Speech in the Illinois Legislature Concerning the State Bank (Jan. 11, 1837), CW 1:68–69.

21. Address Before the Young Men's Lyceum of Springfield, Illinois (Jan. 27, 1838), CW 1:108–15. On the Lyceum speech, *see generally* Richard O. Curry, *Conscious or Subconscious Caesarism: A Critique of Recent Scholarly Attempts to Put Abraham Lincoln on the Analyst's Couch*, 77 J. ILL. ST. HIST. SOC'Y 67, 71 (1984); HARRY V. JAFFA, CRISIS OF THE HOUSE DIVIDED: AN INTERPRETATION OF THE ISSUES IN THE LINCOLN-DOUGLAS DEBATES 183–232 (1959); Thomas F. Schwartz, *The Springfield Lyceums and Lincoln's 1838 Speech*, 83 ILL. HIST. J. 45 (1990); GARRY WILLS, LINCOLN AT GETTYSBURG 81–85 (1992).

22. Silbey, *"Always a Whig in Politics"*, 7 PAPERS OF THE ABRAHAM LINCOLN ASS'N at 23 n.7.

23. WILLS, LINCOLN AT GETTYSBURG at 79–83; William Henry Herndon to Jesse Weik (Jan. 27, 1888), Herndon-Weik Collection, Library of Congress.

24. Address Before the Young Men's Lyceum of Springfield, Illinois (Jan. 27, 1838), CW 1:109; *see also* RICHARDS, "GENTLEMEN OF PROPERTY AND STANDING": ANTI-ABOLITION MOBS IN JACKSONIAN AMERICA at 8–14.

25. LAWRENCE KOHL, THE POLITICS OF INDIVIDUALISM: PARTIES AND THE AMERICAN CHARACTER IN THE JACKSONIAN ERA 154–55 (1989).

26. Address Before the Young Men's Lyceum of Springfield, Illinois (Jan. 27, 1838), CW 1:112. On reverence of law as a Whig virtue, *see* JEAN V. MATTHEWS, RUFUS CHOATE: THE LAW AND CIVIC VIRTUE 86–87, 180 (1980); KOHL, THE POLITICS OF INDIVIDUALISM at 162–63.

27. Walker, *Ways and Means of Professional Success*, 1 W. L.J. at 543, 549. This was an 1839 address.

28. WILLIAM F. ALLEN, AN ADDRESS DELIVERED BEFORE THE GRADUATING CLASS OF THE LAW DEPARTMENT OF HAMILTON COLLEGE, JULY 15, 1857, at 28 (Utica, Roberts 1857); SIMON GREENLEAF, A DISCOURSE PRONOUNCED AT THE INAUGURATION OF THE AUTHOR AS ROYALL PROFESSOR OF LAW IN HARVARD UNIVERSITY, AUGUST 26, 1834, at 16 (Cambridge, James Munroe & Co. 1837); ROBERTSON, SCRAP BOOK ON LAW AND POLITICS, MEN AND TIMES at 239.

29. William Henry Herndon, Lincoln as Lawyer, Politician & Statesman (manuscript), Herndon-Weik Collection, Library of Congress.

30. John Littlefield, *quoted in* Lupton, *A. Lincoln, Esq.: The Evolution of a Lawyer, in* SPIEGEL, A. LINCOLN, ESQUIRE: A SHREWD, SOPHISTICATED LAWYER IN HIS TIME at 41–42.

31. HERNDON'S LINCOLN at 278.

32. HORWITZ, THE TRANSFORMATION OF AMERICAN LAW at 28, 143.

33. An Act Concerning Practice in Courts of Law, approved Jan. 29, 1827, 5th G.A., sec. 37, ILL. REV. LAWS 310, 319 (1853).

34. JOHN REYNOLDS, MY OWN TIMES 175–76 (1968) (1855).

35. An Act to Amend the Practice Act, approved Feb. 25, 1847, 15th G.A., ILL. REV. LAWS 63 (1853).

36. *Ray v. Wooters*, 19 Ill. (9 Peck.) 82, 82 (1857).

37. *E.g.*, *Eames v. Blackheart*, 12 Ill. 195, 198 (1850).

38. Renee Lettow Lerner, *The Transformation of the American Civil Trial: The Silent Judge*, 42 WM. & MARY L. REV. 195 (2000).

39. *Wickersham v. People*, 2 Ill. (1 Scam.) 128, 130 (1834).

40. ILL. CRIM. CODE § 188 (1857); ILL. REV. STAT., Criminal Jurisprudence § 188 (1845); David J. Bodenhamer, *The Democratic Impulse and Legal Change in the Age of Jackson: The Example of Criminal Juries in Antebellum Indiana*, 45 HISTORIAN 206 (1983).

41. Trial Transcript [123180], *People v. Harrison* [L04306] case file, LPAL.

42. John H. Langbein, *Historical Foundations of the Law of Evidence: A View From the Ryder Sources*, 96 COLUM. L. REV. 1168, 1189 (1996).

43. Trial Transcript [123180], *People v. Harrison* [L04306] case file, LPAL.

44. Kermit L. Hall, *The Judiciary on Trial: State Constitutional Reform and the Rise of an Elected Judiciary, 1846–1860*, 45 HISTORIAN 337, 337, 341, 343 (1983).

45. THE CONSTITUTIONAL DEBATES OF 1847, at 458–68 (Arthur C. Cole ed., 1919) (Collections of the Illinois State Historical Library, vol. 14); *see also The Elective Principle as Applied to the Judiciary*, 5 W. L.J. 127, 128–29 (1847).

46. AL to Orville H. Browning (June 24, 1847), CW 1:394–95.

47. *But see* SELLERS, THE MARKET REVOLUTION: JACKSONIAN AMERICA 1815–1846, at 47–49.

48. For depictions of Lincoln as a corporate or railroad lawyer, *see* ROBERT KELLEY, THE CULTURAL PATTERN IN AMERICAN POLITICS 214 (1979); EDWARD PESSEN, THE LOG CABIN MYTH: THE SOCIAL BACKGROUNDS OF THE PRESIDENTS 92 (1984); GIENAPP, ABRAHAM LINCOLN AND CIVIL WAR AMERICA at 44–45.

49. THOMAS, ABRAHAM LINCOLN at 157–58 (1952); *see also* DONALD, LINCOLN at 157; WOLDMAN, LAWYER LINCOLN at 161.

50. HOWE, THE POLITICAL CULTURE OF THE AMERICAN WHIGS at 226. For examples of Choate "broadening or narrowing" the *Charles River Bridge* decision to suit the needs of his clients, *see* ABSTRACT OF THE ARGUMENTS OF THE HON. RUFUS CHOATE AND WILLIAM D. NORTHEND, ESQ. FOR THE PETITIONERS . . . FOR A RAILROAD FROM DANVERS TO MALDEN, BEFORE THE COMMITTEE ON RAILWAYS AND CANALS OF THE MASSACHUSETTS LEGISLATURE . . . SESSION 1847, at 20, 24, 25 (Boston, S.N. Dickinson & Co. 1847); SPEECH OF HON. RUFUS CHOATE BEFORE THE JOINT LEGISLATIVE RAIL ROAD COMMITTEE, BOSTON, FEB. 28, 1851, APPLICATION OF THE SALEM AND LOWELL RAIL ROAD COMPANY FOR A PARALLEL AND COMPETING RAIL ROAD FROM SALEM TO DANVERS 4–6 (Boston, J.M. Hewes & Co. 1851).

51. Christopher L. Tomlins, *A Mysterious Power: Industrial Accidents and the Legal Construction of Employment Relations in Massachusetts, 1800–1850*, 6 LAW & HIST. REV. 375, 394–402 (1988); *Shaw v. Boston & Worcester R.R.*, 74 Mass. (8 Gray) 45 (1857); MATTHEWS, RUFUS CHOATE at 166.

52. WILLIAM H. PEASE & JANE H. PEASE, JAMES LOUIS PETIGRU: SOUTHERN CONSERVATIVE, SOUTHERN DISSENTER 95–146 (1995).

53. Spirit of the Times (Jan. 9, 1841) at 543, *quoted in* Grimsted, *Rioting in Its Jacksonian Setting*, 77 AM. HIST. REV. at 370.

54. *Fragment on Government* [July 1, 1854] CW 2:220–22.

55. HERNDON'S LINCOLN at 278; Lupton, *A. Lincoln, Esq.: The Evolution of a Lawyer, in* SPIEGEL, A. LINCOLN, ESQUIRE: A SHREWD, SOPHISTICATED LAWYER IN HIS TIME at 27, 32.

56. *Grable v. Margrave*, 4 Ill. (3 Scam.) 372, 373 (1842). On "vindictive" damages or "smart money," *see* THEODORE SEDGWICK, A TREATISE ON THE MEASURE OF DAMAGES 39–46 (New York, John S. Voorhies 1847). Sedgwick cites the *Grable* case in the second edition of his treatise. THEODORE SEDGWICK, A TREATISE ON THE MEASURE OF DAMAGES 464 (2d ed. New York, John S. Voorhies 1852).

57. *Grable v. Margrave*, 4 Ill. (3 Scam.) at 373.

58. *McNamara v. King*, 7 Ill. (2 Gilm.) 432, 435–37 (1845).

59. Harry E. Pratt, *Lincolniana: The Famous "Chicken Bone" Case*, 45 J. ILL. ST. HIST. SOC'Y 164, 166 (1952); *see also* DE VILLE, MEDICAL MALPRACTICE IN NINETEENTH-CENTURY AMERICA 100–01.

60. *Ritchey v. West*, 23 Ill. 385 (1860); *see also* DE VILLE, MEDICAL MALPRACTICE IN NINETEENTH-CENTURY AMERICA at 49.

61. DONALD, LINCOLN RECONSIDERED at 131.

62. This point is often overlooked. *See, e.g.,* OATES, WITH MALICE TOWARD NONE at 113; Phil Patton, *Lincoln Fueled the Railroad Era's Engine*, N.Y. TIMES, Feb. 24, 1992 at A18.

63. Robert M. Sutton, *Lincoln and The Railroads of Illinois* in LINCOLN IMAGES: AUGUSTANA COLLEGE CENTENNIAL ESSAYS 41–60 (O. Fritiof Ander ed., 1960).

64. Communication to the People of Sangamo County (Mar. 9, 1832), CW 1:5.

65. Open Letter on Springfield and Alton Railroad (June 30, 1847), CW 1:397–98.

66. Report on Alton and Springfield Railroad (Aug. 5, 1847), CW 1:398–99.

67. Declaration, filed July 25, 1849 [126101], *Watson v. Sangamon & Morgan R.R.* [L04807] case file, LPAL; JOHN W. STARR, JR., LINCOLN AND THE RAILROADS 117–18 (1927).

68. ANGLE, ONE HUNDRED YEARS OF LAW 33–34.

69. *See, e.g., Alton & Sangamon R.R. v. Baugh* [L02615]; *Brown Bros. & Co. v. Chicago, Alton & St. Louis R.R.* [L02118]; *Allen v. Chicago & Mississippi R.R.* [L02541]; *Allen v. Illinois Central R.R.* [L00662]; *Eads & Nelson v. Ohio & Mississippi R.R* [L02137]; *McGrady & Allen v. Wabash Valley R.R.* [L02170] case files, LPAL. The Chicago, Alton & St. Louis Railroad was the successor to the Alton & Sangamon.

70. *See, e.g., Chicago, Burlington & Quincy R.R. v. Wilson* [L02355]; *Harris v. Great Western R.R.* [L03753]; *Allen & McGrady v. Illinois River R.R.* [L02099]; *Howland v. Peoria & Hannibal R.R.* [L02303]; *Sangamon & Morgan R.R. v. Hickox Bros.* [L04475]; *Scott v. St. Louis, Alton, & Chicago R.R.* [L01686]; *Terre Haute & Alton R.R. v. Armstrong* [L00680]; case files, LPAL. The Great Western Railroad was the successor to the Sangamon & Morgan Railroad.

71. *Tomlin v. Tonica & Petersburg R.R.* [L00885]; *Tonica & Petersburg R.R. v. Alkire* [L05843]; *Tonica & Petersburg R.R. v. Lukins* [L05870]; *Tonica & Petersburg R.R. v. McNeeley* [L02500]; *Tonica & Petersburg R.R. v. Miles* [L00134]; *Tonica & Petersburg R.R. v. Montgomery* [L05871]; *Tonica & Petersburg R.R. v. Stein* [L00160] case files, LPAL.

72. AL to Charles Hoyt (Jan. 16, 1856), CW 2:329; *Chicago, Burlington & Quincy R.R. v. Wilson*, 17 Ill. (7 Peck) 123 (1855).

73. Communication to the People of Sangamo County (Mar. 9, 1832), CW 1:5.

74. *Banet v. Alton & Sangamon R.R.*, 13 Ill. 504 (1851); *Klein v. Alton & Sangamon R.R.*, 13 Ill. 514 (1851); *Tomlin v. Tonica & Petersburg R.R.*, 23 Ill. 374 (1860); *Tonica & Petersburg R.R. v. Stein*, 21 Ill. 96 (1859).

75. *See generally* Beard, *"I have labored hard to find the law": Abraham Lincoln for the Alton and Sangamon Railroad*, 85 ILL. HIST. J. 209; GLEN V. GLENDINNING, THE CHICAGO & ALTON RAILROAD: THE ONLY WAY 18–19 (2002).

76. AL to Isaac Gibson (Feb. 26, 1851), CW 2:101.

77. CW 2:100; Declaration, filed Feb. 18, 1851 [4786], Order, dated Mar. 18, 1851 [5224], *Alton & Sangamon R.R. v. Kirkpatrick* [L02618]; Declaration, filed Feb. 18, 1851 [4789], Notice of Commission to Take Deposition [4788], Order, dated Mar. 18, 1851 [5225], *Alton & Sangamon R.R. v. Burkhardt* [L02616] case files, LPAL.

78. AL to William Martin (Mar. 6, 1851), CW 2:102.

79. AL to William Martin (Feb. 27, 1851), CW 11:6.

80. AL to William Martin (Mar. 6, 1851), CW 2:102.

81. *Banet v. Alton & Sangamon R.R.*, 13 Ill. 504 (1851). Barret's name was misspelled in the case reporter.

82. *Klein v. Alton & Sangamon R.R.*, 13 Ill. 514 (1851). The importance of the *Barret* and *Klein* decisions is reflected in the ten references to either *Banet* or *Klein* in the

1856 Illinois Digest. *See* FREEMAN, THE "ILLINOIS DIGEST" at 570–72. Edward L. Pierce in his 1857 treatise on railroad law cited *Banet* and *Klein* six times in his chapter on stock subscription. EDWARD L. PIERCE, TREATISE ON AMERICAN RAILROAD LAW 65, 73, 79, 91, 100, 108 (New York, John S. Voorhies 1857). Isaac Redfield in his 1858 railroad-law treatise cited *Banet* and *Klein* four times. ISAAC F. REDFIELD, A PRACTICAL TREATISE UPON THE LAW OF RAILWAYS 73, 78, 87, 95 (2d ed. Boston, Little, Brown & Co. 1858).

83. WOLDMAN, LAWYER LINCOLN at 162.

84. William Henry Herndon to Richard Yates (Oct. 6, 1857), *quoted in* DONALD, LINCOLN'S HERNDON 43. This account is drawn from Donald.

85. Narratio, filed Oct. 12, 1857 [7492]; Judgment, dated Nov. 10, 1857 [7497], *Tonica & Petersburg R.R. v. Miles* [L00134] case file, LPAL.

86. William Henry Herndon to Richard Yates (Oct. 20, 1857), *quoted in* DONALD, LINCOLN'S HERNDON at 43.

87. AL to William McNeeley (Nov. 30, 1858) [125502], *Tonica & Petersburg R.R. v. McNeeley* [L02500] case file, LPAL.

88. Assignment of Errors [filed Jan. Term 1859] [82203], *Tonica & Petersburg R.R. v. McNeeley* [L02500] case file, LPAL.

89. *Tonica & Petersburg R.R. v. Stein*, 21 Ill. 96 (1859).

90. *Tomlin v. Tonica & Petersburg R.R.*, 23 Ill. 374 (1860).

91. *See, e.g.,* Declaration, filed Mar. 23, 1860 [136099], *Tonica & Petersburg R.R. v. Alkire* [L05843] case files, LPAL.

92. Judgment, dated Apr. 11, 1860 [136114], *Tonica & Petersburg R.R. v. Alkire* [L05843]; Judgment, dated Apr. 11, 1860 [136137], *Tonica & Petersburg R.R. v. Lukins* [L05870]; Order of Dismissal, dated Apr. 13, 1860 [136148], *Tonica & Petersburg R.R. v. Montgomery* [L05871] case files, LPAL.

93. Bill of Injunction, filed Aug. 6, 1857 [20515], *Sprague v. Illinois River R.R.* [L02489] case file, LPAL.

94. Decree, dated Nov. 21, 1857 [20505], *Sprague v. Illinois River R.R.* [L02489] case file, LPAL.

95. *Sprague v. Illinois River R.R.*, 19 Ill. 174, 177–78 (1857).

96. AL to Henry E. Dummer (Feb. 7, 1858), CW 2:432–33.

97. *See, e.g., Terre Haute & Alton R.R. v. Armstrong* [L00680]; *Terre Haute & Alton R.R. v. Francisco* [L00684]; *Terre Haute & Alton R.R. v. Wright* [L00695] case files, LPAL.

98. Order, dated Oct. 10, 1856 [35989], *Terre Haute & Alton R.R. v. Auxer* [L00681]; Order, dated Oct. 10, 1856 [36040], *Terre Haute & Alton R.R. v. Moberly* [L00686] case files, LPAL.

99. *Terre Haute & Alton R.R. v. Earp*, 21 Ill. 290 (1859).

100. The supreme court ordered the *Earp* case remanded to the circuit court on Mar. 21, 1859. *See* Judgment, dated Mar. 21, 1859 [40901], *Terre Haute & Alton R.R. v. Earp* [L00980] case file, LPAL.

101. *See, e.g.,* Order, dated Apr. 16, 1860 [40905], *Terre Haute & Alton R.R. v. Earp* [L00980]; *Terre Haute & Alton R.R. v. Fleming* [L00682] case files, LPAL.

102. Bill Beard has persuasively argued that the *Dalby* case was handled by Herndon, not Lincoln. Beard, Dalby *Revisted: A New Look at Lincoln's "Most Far-reaching Case" in the Illinois Supreme Court*, 20 J. ABRAHAM LINCOLN ASS'N 1.

103. *St. Louis, Alton & Chicago R.R. v.* Dalby, 19 Ill. 352 (1857).

104. JAMES W. ELY, JR., RAILROADS AND AMERICAN LAW 219–20 (2001); R.W. KOSTAL, LAW AND ENGLISH RAILWAY CAPITALISM 1825–1875, at 254–56 (1994).

105. Declaration, filed Mar. 3, 1854 [5139], Judge's Docket (dated Mar. Term 1854) [103702], *Harris v. Great Western R.R.* [L03753] case file, LPAL.

106. Declaration, filed Feb. 21, 1857 [31361], Agreement, dated Oct. 9, 1857 [31377], *Freidlander v. Great Western R.R.* [L00869] case file, LPAL.

107. *See Browning v. City of Springfield*, 17 Ill. 143 (1855); Declaration, filed Aug. 13, 1852 [5109], *Grubb v. John Frink & Co.* [L03754]; Declaration, filed Apr. 17, 1858 [65824], *MacReady v. City of Alton* [L02171] case files, LPAL; *see also* SPRINGFIELD DAILY ST. J., July 2, 1858 at 3.

108. Declaration, filed Aug. 13, 1852 [5109], *Grubb v. John Frink & Co.* [L03754] case file, LPAL; Roger Martile, *John Frink and Martin Walker: Stagecoach Kings of the Old Northwest*, 95 J. ILL. ST. HIST. SOC'Y 119 (Summer 2002).

109. Declaration, filed Aug. 13, 1852 [5109]; Deposition, dated Dec. 22, 1853 [120952], *Grubb v. John Frink & Co.* [L03754] case file, LPAL.

110. Order, dated Mar. 23, 1853 [99227], *Grubb v. John Frink & Co.* [L03754] case file, LPAL.

111. *See* Thomas D. Russell, *Historical Study of Personal Injury Litigation: A Comment on Method*, 1 GA. J. S. LEGAL HIST. 109, 112, 117–18 (1991).

112. *See, e.g.*, DUFF, A. LINCOLN: PRAIRIE LAWYER at 345; Elwin L. Page, *The Effie Afton Case*, 58 LINCOLN HERALD 3 (1956).

113. *See* DUFF, A. LINCOLN: PRAIRIE LAWYER at 332–37.

114. Speech to the Jury in the Rock Island Bridge Case, Chicago, Illinois (Sept. 22, 1857), CW 2:415–16.

115. No Verdict, *Chicago Daily Tribune* (Sept. 26, 1857) [132966], *Hurd v. Rock Island Bridge Co.* [L02289] case file, LPAL.

116. *Illinois State Register* (Springfield), Dec. 20, 1851, at 2; *Illinois State Register*, Jan. 27, 1852, at 2; *see also* Thomas, *Lincoln's Earlier Practice in the Federal Courts 1839–1854*, BULL. ABRAHAM LINCOLN ASS'N at 8.

117. *Columbus Ins. Co. v. Curtenius*, 6 F. Cas. 186 (C.C.D. Ill. 1853) (No. 3, 045).

118. *Columbus Ins. Co. v. Peoria Bridge Ass'n*, 6 F. Cas. 191, 193 (C.C.D. Ill. 1853) (No. 3, 046).

119. *See, e.g., Campbell v. Great Western R.R.* [L01866], *Josephine Frazier v. Great Western R.R.* [L01899], *Samuel Frazier v. Great Western R.R.* [L01900] case files, LPAL.

120. *See, e.g.*, Order, dated May 30, 1855 [58665], *Campbell v. Great Western R.R.* [L01866]; Order, dated May 30, 1855 [59401], *Josephine Frazier v. Great Western R.R.* [L01899]; Order, dated May 30, 1855 [59405], *Samuel Frazier v. Great Western R.R.* [L01900] case files, LPAL.

121. *See, e.g.*, Order, dated May 30, 1855 [58665], *Campbell v. Great Western R.R.* [L01866] case file, LPAL.

122. *See, e.g., Hickman v. Great Western R.R.* [L01916]; case files, LPAL.

123. Order, dated May 30, 1855 [61332], *Price v. Great Western R.R.* [L02018] case file, LPAL.

124. Order, dated May 30, 1855 [59209], *Great Western R.R. v. Andrew Makemson* [L01909]; Order, dated May 30, 1855 [133424], *Andrew Makemson v. Great Western R.R.* [L01946]; Order, dated May 30, 1855 [60033], *James Makemson v. Great Western R.R.* [L01948]; Order, dated May 30, 1855 [60572], *McDonald v. Great Western R.R.* [L01970] case files, LPAL.

125. Order, dated May 30, 1855 [133424], *Andrew Makemson v. Great Western R.R.* [L01946]; Order, dated May 30, 1855 [60033], *James Makemson v. Great Western R.R.* [L01948] case files, LPAL.

126. DEBORAH HAINES, CITY DOCTOR, CITY LAWYER: THE LEARNED PROFESSIONS IN FRONTIER CHICAGO at 157.

127. CATON, EARLY BENCH AND BAR OF ILLINOIS 241–42.

128. HARRY E. PRATT, THE PERSONAL FINANCES OF ABRAHAM LINCOLN 36 (1943).

129. Complete Edition, Papers of Abraham Lincoln website, <http://www.papersof abrahamlincoln.org/complete_edition.htm>.

130. Stuart & Lincoln Fee Book [Apr. 1837] [127736], *Stuart & Lincoln collected and recorded fees* [N05068] file, LPAL.

131. Adam W. Snyder, Client Account Book, 1837-1841, Box 40, John Francis Snyder Papers, Abraham Lincoln Presidential Library & Museum, Springfield, Illinois.

132. PRATT, THE PERSONAL FINANCES OF ABRAHAM LINCOLN at 31.

133. *Id.* at 35; Lincoln & Herndon Day Book [1847] [124827], *Lincoln & Herndon collected and recorded fees* [N05178] file, LPAL.

134. Abraham Lincoln to James F. Joy (Sept. 15, 1855), CW 2:325. As Lincoln did not provide any details on the cases, Judge Davis's notation was probably directed more to substantiating the number of cases than the amount charged. Joy apparently balked at Lincoln's fee. *See* AL to James F. Joy (Sept. 19, 1855), CW 2:326.

135. KARSTEN, HEART VERSUS HEAD at 91–99.

136. Lincoln also rashly attacked Adams in a series of signed and unsigned letters in the *Sangamo Journal. See* WILSON, HONOR'S VOICE at 174–79; Second Reply to James Adams (Oct. 18, 1837), CW 1:101–06.

137. Contingent Fee Agreement, dated May 26, 1837 [5253], *Wright v. Adams* [L03870] case file, LPAL.

138. Contingent Fee Agreement, dated Apr. 14, 1855 [132040], *Cossens v. Parrish* [L01879] case file, LPAL.

139. Fragment: Notes for a Law Lecture, CW 10:19.

140. AL to James S. Irwin (Nov. 2, 1842), CW 1:304.

141. Thomas A. Howland to AL, dated July 16, 1859 [68739]; AL to Thomas A. Howland, July 23, 1859 [65761], *Howland v. Peoria & Hannibal R.R.* [L02303] case file, LPAL.

142. AL to Andrew McCallen (July 4, 1851), CW 2:106.

143. *Herndon v. Todd et ux.* [L03542], *Lincoln & Herndon v. Moffett* [L03869], *Lincoln v. Alexander* [L01656], *Lincoln v. Brown* [L01616], *Lincoln v. Gwinn* [L00711], *Lincoln v. Hall* [L01275], *Lincoln v. Hawley* [L01274], *Lincoln v. Huston* [L01709], *Lincoln v. Illinois Central R.R.* [L01660], *Lincoln v. McGraw* [L00574], *Lincoln v. Pollock* [L01661], *Lincoln v. Read* [L04947], *Logan & Lincoln ex rel. Tucker v. Smith* [L02510], *Logan & Lincoln v. Atchison* [L04001], *Logan & Lincoln v. Craig & Warner* [L02080], *Logan & Lincoln v. McClun & Harkness* [L01662], *Logan & Lincoln v. Smith* [L03897] case files, LPAL.

144. *See, e.g.,* Declaration, filed July 18, 1845 [5420], *Logan & Lincoln v. Atchison* [L04001] case file, LPAL.

145. *Lincoln v. Illinois Central R.R.* [L01660] case file, LPAL.

146. *Lincoln v. Brown* [L01616], *Lincoln v. Gwinn* [L00711], *Lincoln v. Huston* [L01709], *Lincoln v. McGraw* [L00574], *Lincoln v. Pollock* [L01661] case files, LPAL.

147. Judgment, dated Nov. 22, 1855 [1908], *Lincoln v. Brown* [L01616]; Judge's Docket, dated June Term 1852 [51498], Order of Dismissal, dated Nov. 15, 1852 [51500], *People v. Brown* [L01565] case files, LPAL.

148. BORITT, LINCOLN AND THE ECONOMICS OF THE AMERICAN DREAM at 151.

149. HERNDON'S LINCOLN at 171–72.

150. JOHN ANTHONY MORETTA, WILLIAM PITT BALLINGER: TEXAS LAWYER, SOUTHERN STATESMAN, 1825–1888, at 249–54 (2000); WILLIAM G. THOMAS, LAWYERING FOR THE RAILROAD: BUSINESS, LAW, AND POWER IN THE NEW SOUTH 43–44 (1999); KENNETH LIPARTITO & JOSEPH A. PRATT, BAKER & BOTTS IN THE DEVELOPMENT OF MODERN HOUSTON 28 (1991).

151. David Davis to AL (Feb. 21, 1849), Abraham Lincoln Papers at the Library of Congress, <memory.loc.gov/ammem/alhtml/malhome.html>, Select: Search by

Keyword, Enter: David Davis 1849, Select: Item 4.

152. S.A. Douglas to Julius N. Granger (May 9, 1835), *in* THE LETTERS OF STEPHEN A. DOUGLAS 15.

153. "F.," *The Profession of the Law,* 7 W. L.J. at 97, 110–11; *see also* Walker, *Ways and Means of Professional Success,* 1 W. L.J. at 543.

154. JOSEPH BALDWIN, THE FLUSH TIMES OF ALABAMA AND MISSISSIPPI 48 (1987) (1853).

155. John G. Saxe, *A Legal Ballad,* 24 KNICKERBOCKER 265–66 (Sept. 1844).

156. Willard Hurst warns that the persistence of these complaints by lawyers about overcrowding casts doubt upon their validity. HURST, THE GROWTH OF AMERICAN LAW at 313.

157. S.A. Douglas to Julius N. Granger (Nov. 14, 1834), *in* THE LETTERS OF STEPHEN A. DOUGLAS at 10–11.

158. Sprecher, *Admission to Practice Law in Illinois,* 46 ILL. L. REV. (NW. U.) 811, 813 n.17.

159. Howard Feigenbaum, *The Lawyer in Wisconsin, 1836–1860: A Profile,* 55 WIS. MAG. HIST. 100, 101 (1971–1972).

160. JOHN LIVINGSTON, LIVINGSTON'S LAW REGISTER v (New York, Monthly Law Mag. 1851); JOHN LIVINGSTON, LIVINGSTON'S LAW REGISTER FOR 1852, at 4 (New York, U.S. Law Mag. 1852).

161. HAINES, CITY DOCTOR, CITY LAWYER: THE LEARNED PROFESSIONS IN FRONTIER CHICAGO at 96–97.

162. "F.," *The Profession of the Law,* 7 W. L.J. at 98, 103.

163. *Quoted in* E. Lee Shepherd, *Breaking into the Profession: Establishing a Law Practice in Antebellum Virginia,* 48 J. S. HIST. 393, 404, 408–09 (1982).

164. S.F.C. MILSOM, HISTORICAL FOUNDATIONS OF THE COMMON LAW 7 (2d ed. 1981).

165. *See* Marc Galanter, *Why the "Haves" Come Out Ahead: Speculations on the Limits of Legal Change,* 9 LAW & SOC'Y REV. 95 (1974); JOHN P. HEINZ & EDWARD O. LAUMANN, CHICAGO LAWYERS: THE SOCIAL STRUCTURE OF THE BAR (1983); Kenneth Lipartito, *What Have Lawyers Done for American Business? The Case of Baker & Botts of Houston,* 64 BUS. HIST. REV. 489 (1990).

4—Law on the Prairie

1. Declaration, dated July 1, 1836 [5167], *Hawthorn v. Wooldridge* [L03504] case file, LPAL.

2. Jesse W. Weik, *Lincoln as a Lawyer: With an Account of His First Case,* 68 CENTURY MAG. 279, 282 (June 1904).

3. Affidavit of David Wooldridge, filed Oct. 5, 1836 [5172]; Plea, filed Oct. 5, 1836 [5174], Bond for costs, filed Oct. 6, 1836 [5043], *Hawthorn v. Wooldridge* [L03504]; Praecipe, filed Oct. 8, 1836 [98730], *Wooldridge v. Hawthorn* [L03506] case files, LPAL.

4. Judgment, dated Oct. 8, 1836 [88244], *Hawthorn v. Wooldridge* [L03504] case file, LPAL.

5. Order of Dismissal, dated Mar. 14, 1837 [88260], *Hawthorn v. Wooldridge* [L03505]; Order of Dismissal, dated Mar. 14, 1837 [88261], *Wooldridge v. Hawthorn* [L03506]

6. *See generally* FRAYSSÉ, LINCOLN, LAND, AND LABOR, 1809–60, at 159.

7. Terry Wilson, *The Business of a Midwestern Trial Court: Knox County, Illinois, 1841–1850,* 84 ILL. HIST. J. 249, 251, 255 (1991).

8. *See, e.g., Alexander v. Darneille* [L02528], *Braucher v. Sayles* [L02750], *Deardorff v. Mathews* [L03373], *Hazlett et ux. v. Drennan* [L03661], *McElmore v. Olcire* [L04030],

McLean v. Wiley [L01398], *Prickett v. Opdycke* [L01155], *Sheneman v. Goodpasture et ux.* [L00188], *Vanderen et ux. v. Baker* [L04786] case files, LPAL.

9. Partitions, approved Mar. 3, 1846, ILL. STAT. ch. 79, sec. I (Chicago: Keen & Lee 1856).

10. Partitions, approved Mar. 3, 1846, ILL. STAT. ch. 79, sec. II (Chicago: Keen & Lee 1856); AL to Wm McCullough, dated Jan. 16, 1856 [81869], *Bishop v. Bishop* [L01626] case file, LPAL.

11. Partitions, approved Mar. 3, 1846, ILL. STAT. ch. 79, sec. IX.

12. Fragment: Notes for a Law Lecture, CW 10:19.

13. Partitions, approved Mar. 3, 1846, ILL. STAT. ch. 79, sec. VI.

14. Partitions, approved Mar. 3, 1846, ILL. STAT. ch. 79, sec. VII. The statute stated that the court would "declare the rights, titles and interests" of the parties from "the evidence, in case of default, or from the confession by plea, of the parties if they appear, or from the verdict."

15. *See, e.g.,* the following partition suits from Sangamon County in LPAL: *Braucher v. Heirs at Law of Sayles* [L02750], *Broadwell v. Broadwell* [L02765], *Crow v. Heirs at Law of Crow* [L03098], *Merriman v. Merriman* [L03221], *Latham v. Latham* [L03826].

16. *See, e.g.,* Answer of Guardian Ad Litem [filed Apr. 15, 1852] [3870], *Rogers v. Rogers* [L01818], Decree, dated June 7, 1852 [51024], *Nichols v. Turpin* [L01558], Record, dated Nov. 3, 1837 [126319], *White v. Harris* [L04843] case files, LPAL. Lincoln was the guardian *ad litem* in these three cases.

17. Answer of Guardian Ad Litem [dated Apr. 25, 1853] [56098], *Fields v. Fields* [L01761], Answer of Guardian Ad Litem [dated Apr. 15, 1852] [3870], *Rogers v. Rogers* [L01818], Answer of Guardian Ad Litem [dated Apr. 9, 1842] [4617], *Crow v. Crow* [L03098], Answer of Guardian Ad Litem [dated May 5, 1840] [5320], *Bruner v. Bruner* [L01215], Answer of Guardian Ad Litem [dated June 3, 1853] [63515], *Martin v. Allen* [L01954], Answer of Guardian Ad Litem [dated June 14, 1854] [124473], *Smith v. Green* [L04597] case files, LPAL.

18. Bill of Complaint, dated Aug. 24, 1843 [38615], *Welsh v. Welsh* [L00842] case file, LPAL.

19. Decree, dated Oct. 3, 1843 [38617], *Welsh v. Welsh* [L00842] case file, LPAL.

20. Transcript, dated Feb. 28, 1857 [38680], *Welsh v. Welsh* [L00842] case file, LPAL.

21. 4 JAMES KENT, COMMENTARIES ON AMERICAN LAW 466 (New York, O. Halstead 1830).

22. Transcript, dated Feb. 28, 1857 [38680], *Welsh v. Welsh* [L00842] case file, LPAL.

23. Order, dated Feb. 6, 1858 [82337]; Order, dated Jan. 18, 1859 [82340]; Order, dated Jan. 20, 1860 [82343]; Order, dated Jan. 11, 1861 [82347], *Welsh v. Welsh* [L00842] case file, LPAL.

24. Transcript, filed Dec. 19, 1851 [97027], *McAtee v. Enyart* [L03188] case file, LPAL.

25. *Id.*

26. *Id.*

27. *Id.*

28. *Id.*

29. *McArtee v. Engart,* 13 Ill. (3 Peck) 242, 248–49 (1851).

30. Bill, filed Aug. 29, 1836 [76273], *Orendorf v. Stringfield* [L04168] case file, LPAL.

31. Answer, filed July 2, 1838 [76279], *Orendorf v. Stringfield* [L04168] case file, LPAL. 4 KENT, COMMENTARIES ON AMERICAN LAW at 300.

32. Replication, filed Sept. 26, 1838 [122600], *Orendorf v. Stringfield* [L04168] case file, LPAL; *Jameson v. Conway*, 10 Ill. (5 Gilm.) 227, 230 (1848).

33. Bill, filed Aug. 29, 1836 [76273], *Orendorf v. Stringfield* [L04168] case file, LPAL.

34. See 2 EDWARD SUGDEN, A PRACTICAL TREATISE OF THE LAW OF VENDORS AND PURCHASERS OF ESTATES 295–98 (Brookfield, Mass., E. & L. Merriam 1836); 4 KENT, COMMENTARIES ON AMERICAN LAW at 464; 1 JOHN TAYLOR LOMAX, DIGEST OF THE LAWS RESPECTING REAL PROPERTY, GENERALLY ADOPTED AND IN USE IN THE UNITED STATES 223 (Philadelphia, J.S. Littell 1839).

35. *Prevo v. Walters*, 5 Ill. (4 Scam.) 35, 37 (1842); *see also* 2 SUGDEN, A PRACTICAL TREATISE OF THE LAW OF VENDORS AND PURCHASERS OF ESTATES at 307; 1 STORY, COMMENTARIES ON EQUITY JURISPRUDENCE at 383–84; 1 LOMAX, DIGEST OF THE LAWS RESPECTING REAL PROPERTY, GENERALLY ADOPTED AND IN USE IN THE UNITED STATES at 215.

36. Bill, filed Aug. 29, 1836 [76273], *Orendorf v. Stringfield* [L04168] case file, LPAL.

37. AL to John D. Swallow (June 15, 1854), CW 2:219.

38. Decree, dated July 20, 1839 [91013], *Orendorf v. Stringfield* [L04168] case file, LPAL.

39. Affidavit, dated July 22, 1839 [122601], Decree, dated July 23, 1839 [91052], Decree, dated Mar. 17, 1840 [91177], Circuit Court Transcript, dated Apr. 28, 1840 [89942], *Stringfield v. Orendorf* [L04168] case file, LPAL.

40. Bill to Annul and Set Aside Will, dated Aug. 20, 1849 [31035], *Barnes v. Marquiss* [L00462] case file, LPAL.

41. Judge's Notes [Nov. 16, 1850] [3621], *Barnes v. Marquiss* [L00462] case file, LPAL.

42. 2 N.H. PURPLE, A COMPILATION OF THE STATUTES OF THE STATE OF ILLINOIS 1192 (Chicago, Keen & Lee 1856).

43. Order, dated Nov. 16, 1850 [31031], *Barnes v. Marquiss* [L00462] case file, LPAL.

44. Transcript, filed June 30, 1842 [126086], *Watkins v. White* [L04803] case file, LPAL; *Watkins v. White*, 4 Ill. (3 Scam.) 549 (1842).

45. Transcript, filed Aug. 19, 1839 [4665], *Cannon v. Kenney* [L02875] case file, LPAL; *Cannon v. Kenney*, 4 Ill. (3 Scam.) 9 (1841).

46. *See generally* Hendrik Hartog, *Pigs and Positivism*, 1985 WIS. L. REV. 899; Peter Karsten, *Cows in the Corn, Pigs in the Garden, and "the Problem of Social Costs": "High" and "Low" Legal Cultures of the British Diaspora Lands in the 17th, 18th, and 19th Centuries*, 32 LAW & SOC'Y REV. 63 (1998).

47. JOHN MACK FARAGHER, SUGAR CREEK: LIFE ON THE ILLINOIS PRAIRIE at 132 (1986).

48. For earlier departures from the English common-law rule on fencing, *see* DAVID THOMAS KONIG, LAW AND SOCIETY IN PURITAN MASSACHUSETTS: ESSEX COUNTY, 1629–1692, at 118–20 (1979); *see also* Note, *As to liability of owners for trespass of cattle*, 22 L.R.A. 55 (1894).

49. "Breachy" refers to animals that are "apt to break fences, and get out of inclosures." 1 COMPACT EDITION OF THE OXFORD ENGLISH DICTIONARY 267 (1971).

50. *Seeley v. Peters*, 10 Ill. (5 Gilm.) 130, 138, 142–43 (1848). Four years later Herndon represented another farmer on appeal who had sued the owner of cattle for damage to his cornfield. *Reed v. Johnson*, 14 Ill. 257 (1852).

51. Declaration, dated May 12, 1850 [52003], *Woods v. Ketcham* [L01604] case file, LPAL.

52. Plea & Notice, dated Aug. 23, 1850 [3430], *Woods v. Ketcham* [L01604] case file, LPAL.

53. Order, dated June 3, 1851 [52035], *Woods v. Ketcham* [L01604] case file, LPAL.

54. Elliot J. Gorn, *"Gouge and Bite, Pull Hair and Scratch": The Social Significance of Fighting in the Southern Backcountry*, 90 AM. HIST. REV. 18–43 (1985); NICOLE ETCHESON, THE EMERGING MIDWEST: UPLAND SOUTHERNERS AND THE POLITICAL CULTURE OF THE OLD NORTHWEST, 1787–1861, at 31 (1996); KENNETH J. WINKLE, THE YOUNG EAGLE: THE RISE OF ABRAHAM LINCOLN 67 (2001); JAMES E. DAVIS, FRONTIER ILLINOIS 287 (1998).

55. *See, e.g.,* Judgment [dated May 10, 1838] [133317], *Abrams v. Cordell* [L05546]; Judgment, dated May 30, 1854 [7619], *Foster v. Prather* [59381]; *Hornback b/n/f Hornback v. Dawson* [L05812]; Judgment, dated Oct. 5, 1855 [43872], *Seaman v. Duffey* [L01168]; Judgment, dated Mar. 22, 1854 [31219], *Selby v. Dunlap* [L01897] case files, LPAL.

56. Judgment, dated Nov. 27, 1854 [123296], *Perry v. Alexander* [L04322] case file, LPAL.

57. Judgment, dated Sept. 21, 1852 [46161], *Haines v. Jones* [L01258] case file, LPAL.

58. *See, e.g.,* Order of Dismissal, dated June 1, 1842 [51130], *People v. Babbitt* [L01564]; Judgment, dated Apr. 10, 1860 [135280], *People v. Baldwin* [L05851] (guilty verdict: four hours jail and $25 fine); Judgment, dated May 23, 1853 [12560], *People v. Barnettt* [L00318] (not guilty); Order of Dismissal, dated Mar. 31, 1859 [41392], *People v. Dudney* [L01018]; Judgment, dated Apr. 10, 1860 [12778] case files, LPAL.

59. ILL. ST. J., Dec. 9, 1856, *reprinted in Bryan v. Jones* [L02803] (defendant shot plaintiff); Amended Declaration, filed July 20, 1852 [46593], *Burt v. Jennings* [L10305] (defendant stabbed plaintiff with pocketknife); Declaration, filed Sept. 11, 1840 [131909], *Cannon v. Cormack* [L01615] (defendant beat plaintiff with axe handle); Declaration [filed Nov. Term 1846] [10485], *Elmore v. Moon* [L00238] (defendant shot plaintiff); Declaration, filed Feb. 18, 1841 [36686], *Ewing v. Goodman* [L00704] (defendant beat plaintiff with stick); Narratio, filed Oct. 9, 1847 [135608], *James Hornback b/n/f Andrew Hornback v. Dawson* [L05812] (defendant beat minor plaintiff with leather trace); Declaration, filed Nov. 19, 1845 [38718], *Johnson v. Lester* [L00844] (defendant stabbed plaintiff with knife); Narratio, filed Sept. 28, 1857 [48256], *Keeton v. Dunn* [L01379] (defendant beat plaintiff with stick); Declaration [filed Apr. Term 1845] [73677], *King v. McNamara* [L02466] (defendant stabbed plaintiff with knife); Declaration, filed Sept. 24, 1857 [56226], *Lahr v. Blair* [L01782] (defendant beat plaintiff with steel rasp or iron rod or wooden club); Declaration, filed Sept. 24, 1857 [56744], *Lahr v. Swarens* [L01783] (defendant beat plaintiff with steel rasp or iron rod or wooden club); Declaration, filed Apr. 9, 1853 [33768], *McCarrell v. Campbell* [L00554] (defendant beat plaintiff with stick); Declaration, filed Feb. 28, 1859 [53573], *Smith v. Crary* [L01702] (defendant hung, then beat plaintiff); Declaration, filed Nov. 4, 1839 [5569], *O'Neal v. Gatten* [L04163] (defendant beat plaintiff with "divers sticks, clubs, hoes, hoe-handles, malls, wedges, logs"); Declaration, filed Feb. 25, 1854 [62162], *Woods v. Henry* [L02063] (defendant beat plaintiff with a three-foot-long stick) case files, LPAL.

60. WILSON, HONOR'S VOICE at 25.

61. Declaration [filed Mar. Term 1852] [58607], *Brown v. Makemson* [L01864]; Declaration [filed May Term 1854] [59372], *Foster v. Prather* [L01897]; Declaration, filed Feb. 18, 1841 [36686], *Ewing v. Goodman* [L00704]; Declaration, filed Sept. 13, 1855 [43867], *Seaman v. Duffey* [L01168] case files, LPAL.

62. Declaration [filed Apr. Term 1845] [73677], *King v. McNamara* [L02466] case file, LPAL.

63. Judgment, dated Sept. 4, 1845 [73684], *King v. McNamara* [L02466] case file, LPAL.

64. *McNamara v. King*, 7 Ill. (2 Gilm.) 432, 435 (1845).

65. Judgment, dated Oct. 13, 1852 [46595], *Burt v. Jennings* [L01305]; Judgment, dated Oct. 5, 1855 [43872], *Seaman v. Duffey* [L01168]; Judgment, dated Oct. 8, 1857 [56233], *Lahr v. Blair* [L01782]; Judgment, dated Sept. 24, 1857 [56759], *Lahr v. Swarens* [L01783] case files, LPAL.

66. Judgment, dated May 7, 1847 [38754], *Johnson v. Lester* [L00844] case file, LPAL.

67. Amended Declaration, filed July 20, 1852 [46593], Plea, filed Oct. 15, 1852 [1866], Replication, Oct. 15, 1852 [1866], Judgment, dated Oct. 13, 1852 [46595], *Burt v. Jennings* [L01305] case file, LPAL.

68. Declaration, filed Nov. 19, 1845 [38718], *Johnson v. Lester* [L00844] case file, LPAL.

69. Declaration, filed Sept. 3, 1852 [46158], Plea, filed Sept. 18, 1852 [46157], Judgment, dated Sept. 21, 1852 [46161], *Haines v. Jones* [L01258] case file, LPAL.

70. Address Before the Young Men's Lyceum of Springfield, Illinois (Jan. 27, 1838), CW 1:108–15; Fredrickson, *The Search for Order and Community, in* THE PUBLIC AND PRIVATE LINCOLN at 86–98; HOWE, THE POLITICAL CULTURE OF THE AMERICAN WHIGS at 227–30, 269–71; MATTHEWS, RUFUS CHOATE 86-87, 180; KOHL, THE POLITICS OF INDIVIDUAL-ISM 162–63.

71. David M. Engel, *The Oven Bird's Song: Insiders, Outsiders, and Personal Injuries in an American Community*, 18 LAW & SOC'Y REV. 551–52 (1984).

72. NOAH WEBSTER, THE AMERICAN SPELLING BOOK; CONTAINING THE RUDIMENTS OF THE ENGLISH LANGUAGE 164 (Concord: H. Hill & Co. 1823).

73. Gordon, *Lawyers as the American Aristocracy*, 20 STAN. LAWYER 2, 7.

74. For a contemporary look at small-town law practice, *see* Donald M. Landon, *Clients, Colleagues, and Community: The Shaping of Zealous Advocacy in Country Law Practice*, 10 AM. B. FOUND. RES. J. 81 (1985); Donald M. Landon, *Lawyers and Localities: The Interaction of Community Context and Professionalism*, 7 AM. B. FOUND. RES. J. 1 (1982).

75. Milton Hay, *quoted in* 1 NICOLAY & HAY, ABRAHAM LINCOLN 168.

76. *Matthew* 5:9 (King James Version).

77. Fragment: Notes for a Law Lecture, CW 10:19.

78. GREENLEAF, A DISCOURSE PRONOUNCED AT THE INAUGURATION OF THE AUTHOR AS ROY-ALL PROFESSOR OF LAW IN HARVARD UNIVERSITY at 16; *Examination of Students*, 3 N.Y. LEGAL OBSERVER 395–96 (1845); SAMUEL WALKER, THE MORAL, SOCIAL, AND PROFESSIONAL DUTIES OF ATTORNEYS AND SOLICITORS 161 (New York: Harper and Brothers, 1849); Carol J. Green-house, *Courting Difference: Issues of Interpretation and Comparison in the Study of Legal Ide-ologies*, 22 LAW & SOC'Y REV. 687, 691 (1988).

79. MEMORIALS OF THE LIFE AND CHARACTER OF STEPHEN T. LOGAN 17, 22.

80. ROBERTSON, SCRAP BOOK ON LAW AND POLITICS, MEN AND TIMES at 239; AL to George Robertson (Aug. 15, 1855), CW 2:317–19; *see also* ALLEN, AN ADDRESS DELIVERED BEFORE THE GRADUATING CLASS OF THE LAW DEPARTMENT OF HAMILTON COLLEGE at 28 (avoid litigation if the cost of the lawsuit outweighs its anticipated success).

81. Declaration, dated Jan. 27, 1850 [9750], *Bale v. Wright & Hickox* [L00153] case file, LPAL; Lincoln to Abram Bale (Feb. 22, 1850), CW 2:76; Docket entry, dated Apr. 1, 1850 [9751], *Bale v. Wright & Hickox* [L00153] case file, LPAL.

82. AL to William Martin (Mar. 6, 1851), CW 2:102.

83. Lincoln to Hayden Keeling (Mar. 3, 1859), CW 3:371; Circuit Court Tran-script, dated Nov. 15, 1860 [39192], *Scott & Stipp v. Keeling* [L00875] case file, LPAL.

84. *See, e.g., Adkin v. Hines* [L00457], *Beaty et ux. v. Miller et ux.* [L02643], *Cockrell et ux. v. Tainter* [L03090], *Gaddie v. Ott* [L05856], *McDonough et ux. v. Donnelly* [L04010], *Popejoy v. Wilson* [L02070], *Scott et ux. v. Busher* [L00193], *Torrance v. Galloway* [L01595], case files, LPAL.

85. Lincoln was referring to a recent American edition of the English treatise. *See* STARKIE, A TREATISE ON THE LAW OF SLANDER AND LIBEL; Petition for Rehearing, filed Jan. 28, 1846 [39617], *Patterson et ux. v. Edwards et ux.* [L00884] case file, LPAL.

86. Andrew J. King, *The Law of Slander in Early Antebellum America*, 35 AM. J. LEGAL HIST. 1 (1991); Roger Thompson, *'Holy Watchfulness' and Communal Conformism: The Functions of Defamation in Early New England Communities*, 56 NEW ENGLAND Q. 504–07 (1983); HELENA M. WALL, FIERCE COMMUNION: FAMILY AND COMMUNITY IN EARLY AMERICA 30–48 (1990).

87. F.G. Bailey, *Gifts and Poison, in* GIFTS AND POISON: THE POLITICS OF REPUTATION 2–3 (F.G. Bailey ed., 1971); Peter Charles Hoffer, *Honor and the Roots of American Litigiousness*, 33 AM. J. LEGAL HIST. 295, 313 (1989).

88. Mary Beth Norton, *Gender and Defamation in Seventeenth-Century Maryland*, 44 WILLIAM & MARY Q. 1, 5 (1987).

89. Communication to the People of Sangamo County (Mar. 9, 1832), CW 1:8.

90. An Act Respecting Crimes and Punishments, ILL. LAWS 126, 128–29 (1821).

91. An Act Declaring Certain Words Actionable, approved Dec. 27, 1822, ILL. REV. LAWS 583 (1833).

92. *Onslow v. Horne*, 95 Eng. Rep. 999 (K.B. 1771), *quoted in* King, *The Law of Slander in Early Antebellum America*, 35 AM. J. LEGAL HIST. at 15.

93. King, *The Law of Slander in Early Antebellum America*, 35 AM. J. LEGAL HIST. at 15–17.

94. *Allsop v. Sturgeon* [L00667], *Beaty et ux. v. Miller et ux.* [L02643], *Cantrall et ux. v. Primm* [L03010], *Fancher v. Gollogher* [L00669], *Hatch v. Potter et ux.* [L02450], *Jacobus v. Kitchell et ux.* [L01063], *Martin v. Underwood* [L01953], *Mitchell et ux. v. Mitchell* [L00673], *Patterson et ux. v. Edwards et ux.* [L00884], *Patterson v. Moore* [L05591], *Regnier v. Cabot* [L00158], *Saunders et ux. v. Dunham* [L01583], *Skinner v. Overstreet et ux.* [L00144], *Toney v. Sconce* [L02050] case files, LPAL. On the gender dimensions of slander, *see* LAURA GOWING, DOMESTIC DANGERS: WOMEN, WORDS, AND SEX IN EARLY MODERN LONDON (1998); Andrew J. King, *Constructing Gender: Sexual Slander in Nineteenth-Century America*, 13 LAW & HIST. REV. 63 (1995); Norton, *Gender and Defamation*, 44 WM. & MARY Q. at 35–39.

95. King, *Constructing Gender: Sexual Slander in Nineteenth-Century America*, 13 LAW & HIST. REV. at 63, 68.

96. JOHN MACK FARAGHER, WOMEN AND MEN ON THE OVERLAND TRAIL 65 (1979); John Mack Faragher, *History from the Inside-Out: Writing the History of Women in Rural America*, 33 AM. Q. 537, 548 (1981).

97. Declaration, filed Aug. 11, 1849 [4664], *Cantrall et ux. v. Primm* [L03010] case file, LPAL.

98. Pleas, filed July 30, 1845 [94680], Judgment, dated Aug. 6, 1845 [94684], *Beaty et ux. v. Miller et ux.* [L02643] case file, LPAL.

99. Declaration, filed May 25, 1843 [4037], *Regnier v. Cabot* [L00158] case file, LPAL.

100. S.C. Parks to W.H. Herndon (Mar. 25, 1866), *in* HERNDON'S INFORMANTS: LETTERS, INTERVIEWS, AND STATEMENTS ABOUT LINCOLN at 239; Docket entry, dated Nov. 7, 1843 [8406], *Regnier v. Cabot* [L00158] case file, LPAL.

101. Motion for New Trial, dated Nov. 8, 1843 [4022], *Regnier v. Cabot* [L00158] case file, LPAL.

102. *Regnier v. Cabot*, 7 Ill. (2 Gilm.) 34 (1845).

103. Narratio, filed May 9, 1850 [35667], *Allsop v. Sturgeon* [L00667], LPAL.

104. The editors of The Law Practice of Abraham Lincoln note that the reference

work Lincoln Day by Day is the only source that associates Lincoln with this case. WILLIAM E. BARINGER, LINCOLN DAY BY DAY, VOL. II: 1849–1860, at 34 (1960). It is likely that the documents that supported concluding that Lincoln was involved have since been stolen or misplaced.

105. Jury Verdict [May 23, 1850] [35675], *Allsop v. Sturgeon* [L00667], LPAL.

106. *Patterson v. Edwards*, 7 Ill. (2 Gilm.) 720, 723 (1845). Illinois was one of several northern states to prohibit interracial marriages. DAVID W. FOWLER, NORTHERN ATTITUDES TOWARDS INTERRACIAL MARRIAGE: LEGISLATION AND PUBLIC OPINION IN THE MIDDLE ATLANTIC AND THE STATES OF THE OLD NORTHWEST, 1780–1930, at 134–40, 156–61 (1987). On racism and the fear of miscegenation, *see generally* John M. Rozett, *Racism and Republican Emergence in Illinois, 1848–1860: A Re-evaluation of Republican Negrophobia*, 22 CIVIL WAR HIST. 101 (1976).

107. Declaration, filed Nov. 7, 1851 [51134], *Order,* dated Nov. 17, 1851 [51135], *Saunders v. Dunham* [L01583] case file, LPAL.

108. Narratio, filed Sept. 14. 1843 [61131], *Blue v. Allen et ux.* [L01583] case file, LPAL.

109. Order, dated Sept. 14. 1843 [61142] (Livingston County Circuit Court); Order, dated Dec. 27, 1843 [67956] (Illinois Supreme Court), *Blue v. Allen et ux.* [L01583] case file, LPAL.

110. *See, e.g., Russell v. Martin*, 3 Ill. (2 Scam.) (2 Scam.) 492 (1840) (sexual slander); *Cummerford et ux. v. McAvoy*, 15 Ill. (5 Peck) 311 (1853) (larceny).

111. *See, e.g., Allsop v. Sturgeon* [L00667], *Fancher v. Gollogher* [L00669], *Hatch v. Potter et ux.* [L02450], *Jacobus v. Kitchell et ux.* [L01063], *Kipper et ux. v. Davis et ux.* [L01541], *Martin v. Underwood* [L01953], *Mitchell et ux. v. Mitchell* [L00673], *Patterson et ux. v. Edwards et ux.* [L00884], case files, LPAL.

112. For example, the white population of Shelby County in 1850 was fifty-two percent male (4,025) and forty-eight percent female (3,737). UNITED STATES CENSUS, 1850, SHELBY COUNTY, ILLINOIS (Judy Graven & Phyllis Hapner comps., 1983). *See also* Norton, *Gender and Defamation*, 44 WM. & MARY Q. at 5, 9.

113. Faragher, *History from the Inside-Out: Writing the History of Women in Rural America*, 33 AM. Q. at 548.

114. *Beaty et ux. v. Miller et ux.* [L02643], *Chase v. Blakely et ux.* [L00879], *Jacobus v. Kitchell et ux.* [L01063], *Kipper et ux. v. Davis et ux.* [L01541], *Patterson et ux. v. Edwards et ux.* [L00884], *Preston et ux. v. Townsend et ux.* [L04349], *Skinner v. Overstreet et ux.* [L00144], *Toney v. Sconce* [L02050] case files, LPAL; JOSEPH CHITTY, TREATISE ON PLEADING *92 (9th Am. ed., Springfield, Mass., G. & C. Merriam 1844).

115. *Beaty et ux. v. Miller et ux.* [L02643], *Jacobus v. Kitchell et ux.* [L01063], *Kipper et ux. v. Davis et ux.* [L01541], *Patterson et ux. v. Edwards et ux.* [L00884], *Preston et ux. v. Townsend et ux.* [L04349], *Toney v. Sconce* [L02050] case files, LPAL.

116. *Chase v. Blakely et ux.* [L00879], *Skinner v. Overstreet et ux.* [L00144] case files, LPAL.

117. Declaration, filed Oct. 23, 1849 [8708], Judgment, dated Apr. 5, 1850 [8660], *Skinner v. Overstreet et ux.* [L00144] case file, LPAL.

118. Deposition, filed Nov. 12, 1841 [39540], Judgment, dated Nov. 13, 1841 [39543], *Chase v. Blakely et ux.* [L00879] case file, LPAL.

119. Narratio in case, filed May 11, 1853 [61803], *Toney v. Sconce* [L02050] case file, LPAL.

120. King, *Constructing Gender: Sexual Slander in Nineteenth-Century America*, 13 LAW & HIST. REV. at 74 (preponderance of male defendants linked to ability of males to pay judgments).

121. Declaration, filed Oct. 23, 1849 [8708], *Skinner v. Overstreet et ux.* [L00144] case file, LPAL.

122. Plea, filed Apr. 5, 1850 [8707], Judgment, dated Apr. 5, 1850 [8660], *Skinner v. Overstreet et ux.* [L00144] case file, LPAL.

123. An Act to Provide for the Maintenance of Illegitimate Children, approved Jan. 23, 1827, ILL. STAT. 332 (1839); *Anderson v. Ryan,* 8 Ill. (3 Gilm.) 583, 588 (1846); *Grable v. Margrave,* 4 Ill. (3 Scam.) 372, 373 (1842); *Tubbs v. Van Kleek,* 12 Ill. (2 Peck) 446 (1851); Judgment, dated May 2, 1851 [48725], *People ex rel. Dunn v. Carle* [L01416], David Davis to Sarah W. Davis, dated May 3, 1851 [87215], Judgment, dated May 2, 1851 [47512], *Zephaniah Dunn v. Carle* [L01340], Judgment, dated May 3, 1850 [47509], *Nancy Jane Dunn v. Carle* [L01339] case files, LPAL.

124. *See generally* Keith Thomas, *The Double Standard,* 20 J. HIST. IDEAS 195 (1959).

125. *See* GOWING, DOMESTIC DANGERS: WOMEN, WORDS, AND SEX IN EARLY MODERN LONDON at 66; POLLY MORRIS, DEFAMATION AND SEXUAL REPUTATION IN SOMERSET, 1733–1850, at 291–92 (1985) (Ph.D. dissertation, University of Warwick).

126. Declaration, filed Oct. 16, 1857 [60127], *Martin v. Underwood* [L01953] case file, LPAL.

127. Declaration, filed Oct. 16, 1857 [60127], Pleas [dated Oct. Term 1857] [60152], Judgment, dated Apr. 27, 1858, *Martin v. Underwood* [L01953] case file, LPAL.

128. Narratio in case, filed Aug. 27, 1844 [129418], Judgment, dated Sept. 11, 1845 [129366], *Potter et ux. v. Hatch* [L02450] case file, LPAL; *Hatch v. Potter et ux.,* 7 Ill. (2 Gilm.) 725 (1845).

129. Declaration, filed Feb. 7, 1852 [55884], *Davidson v. McGhilton* [L01753]; Plea, filed Oct. 3, 1851 [5863], *Thompson v. Henline* [L01689]; Plea [5864], *Thompson v. Patton* [L01691]; Declaration, filed Nov. Term 1847 [58003], *Torrance v. Galloway* [L01595] case files, LPAL. In a fifth case, Gaddie sued Ott because Ott had said Gaddie lied under oath when he testified in a earlier court proceeding that Ott had sex with hogs and cattle. Plea, filed May 21, 1857 [136364], *Gaddie v. Ott* [L05856].

130. Declaration, filed Nov. Term 1847 [58003], Judgment, dated June 5, 1848 [51907], *Torrance v. Galloway* [L01595] case file, LPAL.

131. Norton, *Gender and Defamation,* 44 WM. & MARY Q. at 9, 35–39; *see also* Peter N. Moogk, *"Thieving Buggers" and "Stupid Sluts": Insults and Popular Culture in New France,* 36 WM. & MARY Q. 524, 541–43 (1979).

132. *See, e.g., Adkin v. Hines* [L00457], *Burson v. Newman* [L00700], *Henrichsen v. Laughery* [L01047], *Smith v. Poque* [L01823], *Watson v. Mullen* [L04804] case files, LPAL.

133. *See, e.g., Bagley v. Vanmeter* [L00699], *Noland v. Evans* [L00674], *Ray v. Cummins* [L00778]; *Spink v. Chiniquy* [L01448] case files, LPAL.

134. ETCHESON, THE EMERGING MIDWEST: UPLAND SOUTHERNERS AND THE POLITICAL CULTURE OF THE OLD NORTHWEST at 27–39.

135. WINKLE, THE YOUNG EAGLE: THE RISE OF ABRAHAM LINCOLN at 100–01.

136. Declaration, filed Sept. 29, 1838 [5865], *Thompson v. Osborn* [L04636] case file, LPAL.

137. Order, dated Mar. 7, 1839 [86981], *Thompson v. Osborn* [L04636] case file, LPAL.

138. Sally Engle Merry, *Rethinking Gossip and Scandal, in* 1 TOWARD A GENERAL THEORY OF SOCIAL CONTROL 272 (Donald Black ed., 1984).

139. 2 ASA KINNE, QUESTIONS AND ANSWERS ON LAW: ALPHABETICALLY ARRANGED, WITH REFERENCES TO THE MOST APPROVED AUTHORITIES 691 (New York: John F. Trow, 1850).

140. Jury Instructions [May Term 1853] [3745], Jury verdict, dated June 1, 1853 [61520], *Campbell v. Smith* [L02072] case file, LPAL.

141. Judgment, dated July 29, 1842 [96645], Declaration, filed Feb. 11, 1842 [4591], *Dormody v. Bradford* [L03146] case file, LPAL; Thomas Starkie, Law of Slander *24 (Am. ed. New York: Collins and Hannay 1832); *Caldwell v. Abbey*, 3 Ky. (1 Hard.) 539 (1808).

142. Ill. Rev. Stat. Ch. XXVI, sec. 2 (1845).

143. Ill. Rev. Stat. Ch. XXVI, sec. 2 (1856).

144. *See, e.g.*, Bond for Costs, dated June 30, 1839 [30956], *Adkin v. Hines* [L00457]; Bond for Costs, dated May 14, 1855 [33656], *Fairchild v. Madden* [L00548]; Bond for Costs, dated May 16, 1855 [38532], *Johnson v. Benson* [L00839]; Bond for Costs, filed Nov. 6, 1849 [8720], *Skinner v. Overstreet et ux.* [L00144] case files, LPAL.

145. Order, dated Oct. 26, 1856 [11320], *Keltner et ux. v. Keltner* [L00199]; Order, dated Sept. 28, 1859 [41433], *Shockey v. White* [L01028] case files, LPAL; An Act Regulating the Practice in the Supreme and Circuit Courts, approved Jan. 29, 1827, Ill. Rev. Laws, sec. 6 (1833); Ill. Rev. Stat. Ch. LXXXIII, sec. 8 (1845).

146. Judgment, dated Apr. 15, 1852 [55880], *Davidson v. McGhilton* [L01753] case file; Judgment, dated Sept. 25, 1843 [61142] (Livingston County Circuit Court), Judgment, dated Mar. 11, 1844 [61158] (Illinois Supreme Court), *Blue v. Allen et ux.* [L02069] case file, LPAL.

147. Wilson, *The Business of a Midwestern Trial Court: Knox County, Illinois* 84 Ill. Hist. J. at 255, 257.

148. Wayne V. McIntosh, The Appeal of Civil Law: A Political-Economic Analysis of Litigation 124 (1990).

149. *See, e.g.*, *Allsop v. Sturgeon* [L00667], *Blue v. Allen et ux.* [L02069], *Chase v. Blakely et ux.* [L00879], *Mitchell et ux. v. Mitchell* [L00673], *Skinner v. Overstreet et ux.* [L00144], *Watson v. Gill* [L00733], *Wright v. Busby* [L00726] case files, LPAL.

150. [Jacksonville] *Illinoian*, Apr. 14, 1838, at 1.

151. King, *The Law of Slander in Early Antebellum America*, 35 Am. J. Legal Hist. at 32.

152. 1 Joseph Chitty, A Treatise on Pleading and Parties to Actions 492–94 (J.C. Perkins ed., Springfield, Mass., G. & C. Merriam 1844).

153. *See, e.g.*, Plea, filed June 4, 1839 [3587], *Adkin v. Meisenhelter* [L00463]; Plea, filed May 18, 1855 [1964], *Fairchild v. Madden* [L00548]; Plea, dated Nov. 15, 1850 [30818], *Hill v. Whitley* [L00451]; Plea [dated Oct. 16, 1847] [5818], *Watson v. Gill* [L00733] case files, LPAL.

154. Plea, filed June 4, 1839 [3585], *Adkin v. Hines* [L00457]; Plea, filed June 4, 1839 [3587], *Adkin v. Meisenhelter* [L00463]; Plea [filed May 12, 1846] [1951], *Burson v. Newman* [L00700]; Plea, filed Oct. 2, 1846 [3194], *Slatten v. Branson* [L00641]; Plea, filed Oct. 19, 1842 [61555], *Smith v. Courtney* [L02037], LPAL.

155. Plea [filed Oct. Term 1847] [5383], *Linder v. Fleenor* [L00713]; Plea [filed Nov. Term 1851] [5523], *Mercer v. Evans* [L00672]; Plea [filed Nov. 3,1851] [3350], *Noland v. Evans* [L00674]; Plea, filed May 16, 1854 [3145], *Richey v. Adams* [L00590]; Plea, filed Oct. 2, 1846 [3194], *Slatten v. Branson* [L00641] case files, LPAL.

156. Plea, filed Apr. 11, 1844 [3876], *Boggs v. Overton* [L01742]; Plea [filed May 1852] [35773], *Johnson v. Hardy* [L00671] case files, LPAL.

157. Plea [filed May Term 1852] [35801], *Mitchell et ux. v. Mitchell* [L00673]; Plea [dated Oct. 16, 1847] [5818], *Watson v. Gill* [L00733] case file, LPAL.

158. 1 Chitty, A Treatise on Pleading at 496–97.

159. *Crandall v. Dawson*, 6 Ill. (1 Gilm.) 556, 558–59 (1844); *Darling v. Banks*, 14 Ill. 46, 48 (1852).

160. *Beasley v. Meigs*, 16 Ill. 139, 140 (1854); *Sloan v. Petrie*, 15 Ill. 426, 427 (1854); *see also* Sedgwick, A Treatise on the Measure of Damages 540–41 (2d ed.).

161. Judgment, dated June 6, 1839 [30938], *Adkin v. Hines* [L00457]; Judgment, dated April 12, 1844 [55476], *Boggs v. Overton* [L01742]; Judgment, dated May 11, 1847 [36546], *Burson v. Newman* [L00700] case files, LPAL.

162. Agreement to Dismiss, dated Oct. 18, 1839 [31080], *Adkin v. Meisenhelter* [L00463]; Agreement to Dismiss, dated Oct. 19, 1842 [61558], *Smith v. Courtney* [L02037] case files, LPAL.

163. Judgment, dated Oct. 14, 1847 [36836], *Linder v. Fleenor* [L00713]; Judgment, dated May 16, 1854 [34409], *Richey v. Adams* [L00590]; Judgment, dated Mar. 21, 1844 [31306], *Cabot v. Regnier* [L00158]; Judgment, dated May 25, 1843 [37404], *Nordyke v. Fleenor* [L00736] case files, LPAL.

164. In *Linder v. Fleenor*, the plaintiff remitted $950 of the $1,000 jury award; in *Richey v. Adams*, the plaintiff remitted $500 of the $1,012 jury award; in *Nordyke v. Fleenor*, the plaintiff released all $2,000 of the award. Judgment, dated Oct. 14, 1847 [36836], *Linder v. Fleenor* [L00713]; Order, dated May 18, 1854 [34412], *Richey v. Adams* [L00590]; Judgment, dated May 25, 1843 [37404], *Nordyke v. Fleenor* [L00736] case files, LPAL.

165. Judgment ($215), dated Oct. 16, 1847 [37343], *Watson v. Gill* [L00733]; Judgment ($237), dated Apr. 27, 1858 [60139], *Martin v. Underwood* [L01953]; Judgment ($250), dated Oct. 2, 1846 [35407], *Slatten v. Branson* [L00641]; Judgment ($500), dated May 24, 1852 [35811], *Mitchell et ux. v. Mitchell* [L00673] case files, LPAL. The $500 award was remitted to $100 in *Mitchell*.

166. Judgment ($5), dated Nov. 3, 1851 [35781], *Mercer v. Evans* [L00672]; Judgment ($30), dated May 21, 1857 [136396], *Gaddie v. Ott* [L05856]; Judgment ($50), dated May 24, 1852 [35768], *Johnson v. Hardy* [L00671]; Judgment ($55), dated May 19, 1855 [33662], *Fairchild v. Madden* [L00548]; Judgment ($78), dated Nov. 3, 1851 [35838], *Noland v. Evans* [L00674]; Judgment ($80), dated Oct. 25, 1843 [36179], *Bagley v. Vanmeter* [L00699] case files, LPAL.

167. Judgment, dated May 30, 1851 [30815], *Hill v. Whitley* [L00451] case file, LPAL.

168. Judgment (not guilty), dated June 6, 1839 [30938], *Adkin v. Hines* [L00457]; Judgment (not guilty), dated [May 11, 1847] [36546], *Burson v. Newman* [L00700]; Agreement to Dismiss, dated Oct. 18, 1839 [31080], *Adkin v. Meisenhelter* [L00463]; Agreement to Dismiss, dated Oct. 19, 1842 [61558], *Smith v. Courtney* [L02037]; Judgment ($250), dated Oct. 2, 1846 [35407], *Slatten v. Branson* [L00641] case file, LPAL.

169. Declaration, filed May 24, 1839 [30950], *Adkin v. Hines* [L00457]; Declaration, filed May 24, 1839 [31058], *Adkin v. Meisenhelter* [L00463] case file, LPAL.

170. Warrant, dated Nov. 19, 1838, Macon County Criminal case files, box 1, folder 17, Illinois Regional Archives Depository, University of Illinois–Springfield.

171. Plea, filed June 4, 1839 [3585], *Adkin v. Hines* [L00457]; Plea, filed June 4, 1839 [3587], *Adkin v. Meisenhelter* [L00463] case file, LPAL.

172. Judgment (not guilty), dated June 6, 1839 [30938], *Adkin v. Hines* [L00457] case file, LPAL.

173. Agreement to Dismiss, dated Oct. 18, 1839 [31080], *Adkin v. Meisenhelter* [L00463] case file, LPAL.

174. Order, Oct. 1839, Macon County Docket Book [132887], *People v. Adkin* [L00468] case file, LPAL.

175. An Act for the Limitations of Actions and for Avoiding Vexatious Law Suits, approved Feb. 10, 1827, ILL. REV. LAWS 441–42 (1833); ILL. REV. STAT. ch. 66, sec. 3 (1845).

176. Plea, filed May 21, 1850 [89888], *Allsop v. Sturgeon* [L00667]; Plea [dated Sept. Term 1838] [41977], *Bell v. Mitchell* [L01055]; Plea, filed Oct. 8, 1845 [5067], *Frost v. Gillinwaters* [L00705]; Plea [dated May Term 1852] [3354], *Johnson v. Hardy* [L00671]; Plea [dated May Term 1852] [935801], *Mitchell et ux. v. Mitchell* [L00673]; Plea, filed May

24, 1843 [1950], *Nordyke v. Fleenor* [L00736]; Plea, filed Oct. 19, 1842 [61555], *Smith v. Courtney* [L02037] case files, LPAL.

177. *McKee v. Ingalls*, 5 Ill. (4 Scam.) 30, 33 (1842).

178. Jury Instructions [dated May 23, 1850] [35679], *Allsop v. Sturgeon* [L00667]; Jury Instructions [dated Sept. 25, 1852] [37337], *Ramsey v. Marteny* [L01812] case files, LPAL.

179. Jury Instructions [dated Sept. 25, 1852] [57337], *Ramsey v. Marteny* [L01812] case file, LPAL.

180. *Cummerford v. McAvoy*, 15 Ill. 311, 313 (1853).

181. Plea, filed July 30, 1845 [94680], Judgment, dated Aug. 6, 1845 [94684], *Beaty et ux. v. Miller et ux.* [L02643] case file, LPAL.

182. *Regnier v. Cabot*, 7 Ill. (2 Gilm.) 34, 40 (1845).

183. Judgment ($5), dated Nov. 3, 1851 [35781], *Mercer v. Evans* [L00672] case file, LPAL.

184. Narratio, dated Sept. 24, 1842 [61391], Judgment [dated Oct. Term] [61403], *Scott v. Cox* [L02028] case file, LPAL.

185. Judgment, dated Mar. 25, 1853 [94546], *Archer v. Duff* [L02557]; Judgment, dated Nov. 13, 1841 [39543], *Chase v. Blakely et ux.* [L00879]; Judgment, dated Oct. 30, 1861 [41614], *Henrichson v. Laughery* [L01047] case files, LPAL.

186. Judgment, dated Mar. 25, 1853 [94546], *Archer v. Duff* [L02557] case file, LPAL.

187. CANADIAN ENCYCLOPEDIC DIGEST *Defamation* § 485, *available in* Westlaw database. *See also* JOHN G. FLEMING, THE LAW OF TORTS 595 (8th ed. 1992); MARGARET BRAZIER, STREET ON TORTS 507 (9th ed. 1993).

188. Plaintiffs in several slander cases in New South Wales in the 1820s and 1830s were awarded one farthing or one shilling in damages. *See, e.g., Threlkeld v. Lang* (1836); *Klensendorlffe v. Oakes* (1827); *Whitfield v. Caswell* (1837), Decisions of the Superior Courts of New South Wales 1788–1899, *available at* <www.law.mq.edu.au/scnsw>.

189. Writ of Fieri Facias, dated May 13, 1853 [74418], *Archer v. Duff* [L02557] case file, LPAL. Some jurisdictions required plaintiffs in slander suits to recover a minimal amount in damages before the plaintiff could be awarded costs that exceeded the damages. *See, e.g., Robinson v. Whitcher*, 2 Vt. 565 (1829) (under Vermont statute slander plaintiffs had to be awarded more than $7 to recover costs greater than the damage award).

190. Judgment [dated May 7, 1838] [133352], *Moran v. Baddeley* [L05557] case file, LPAL.

191. Declaration, filed Aug. 4, 1840 [3893], Judgment, dated Oct. 13, 1840 [61097], *Popejoy v. Wilson* [L02070] case file, LPAL.

192. *See generally* Andrew R. Arno, *Ritual Reconciliation and Conflict Management in Fiji*, 47 OCEANIA 49 (1976); Klaus-Friedrich Koch et al., *Social Structure, Ritual Reconciliation, and the Obviation of Grievances: A Comparative Essay in the Anthropology of Law*, 16 ETHNOLOGY 269 (1979).

193. Judgment, dated Mar. 26, 1836 [88203], *Green v. Purcapile* [L03394] case file, LPAL.

194. Agreement [filed Oct. Term 1853] [5890], Judgment, dated Oct. 29, 1853 [61811], Narratio, filed May 11, 1853, *Toney v. Sconce* [L02050] case file, LPAL.

195. Agreement, filed May 12, 1845 [5450], Judgment, dated May 12, 1845 [36910], *McKibben v. Hart* [L00716] case file, LPAL.

196. Judgment, dated Aug. 9, 1845 [126100], *Watson v. Mullen* [L04804] case file, LPAL.

197. Judgment, dated Jan. 8, 1859 [53253], *Lehman v. Schroeder* [L01659] case file, LPAL.

198. WHITNEY, LIFE ON THE CIRCUIT WITH LINCOLN 144–45.

199. *Id.* at 74.

200. *Id.* at 75.

201. Judgment [dated Oct. Term], *Spink v. Chiniquy* [L01448] case file, LPAL.

202. Speech to jury [n.d.], Richard Yates Papers, Abraham Lincoln Presidential Library & Museum, Springfield, Illinois.

203. Lincoln to Edwin M. Stanton (July 14, 1864), CW 7:440.

204. Declaration, filed Sept. 1, 1851 [42225], *Jacobus v. Kitchell et ux.* [L01063] case file, LPAL.

205. Proposed Judgment (Lincoln's draft) [filed Sept. 19, 1851] [42131], Judgment, dated Sept. 19, 1851 [42118], *Jacobus v. Kitchell et ux.* [L01063] case file, LPAL.

206. Defendant's Statement [dated Oct. 8, 1845] [1948], Judgment, dated Oct. 8, 1845 [36735], *Frost v. Gillinwaters* [L00705] case file, LPAL.

207. Proposed Judgment [filed Aug. 26, 1851] [4708]; Judgment, dated Aug. 26, 1851 [95234], *Brundage v. McCarty* [L02801] case file, LPAL.

208. *See generally* Don E. Fehrenbacher, *The Judd-Wentworth Feud*, 45 J. ILL. STATE HIST. SOC'Y 197 (1952).

209. John Wentworth to AL, Dec. 21, 1859, Abraham Lincoln Papers at the Library of Congress, <memory.loc.gov/ammem/alhtml/malhome.html>, Select: Search by Keyword, Enter: Wentworth, Select: Item 8.

210. David Davis to AL, Feb. 21, 1860, Abraham Lincoln Papers at the Library of Congress, <memory.loc.gov/ammem/alhtml/malhome.html>, Select: Search by Keyword, Enter: Wentworth, Select: Item 8.

211. For examples of cases dismissed by the plaintiff before trial, *see* Agreement to Dismiss, dated Oct. 18, 1839 [31080], *Adkin v. Meisenhelter* [L00463]; Agreement, filed Apr. 28, 1855 [58893], *Cossens v. Parrish* [L01879]; Proposed Judgment (Lincoln's draft) [dated Sept. 19, 1851] [42131], Judgment, dated Sept. 19, 1851 [42118], *Jacobus v. Kitchell* [L01063]; Judgment, dated Nov. 20, 1855 [123344], *Preston et ux. v. Townsend et ux.* [L04349]; Agreement to Dismiss, dated Oct. 19, 1842 [61558] case files, LPAL.

212. *Archer v. Duff*, judge's docket, 1849–53, 264; *Busher v. Strawn*, judge's docket, 1853–56, 290; *Cass v. Lawson*, court docket, 1845–49, 255; *Thurman v. Taylor*, court record, 1841–42, 346; *Yocum v. Newsom*, court docket, 1845–49, 80, Sangamon County Circuit Court Records, Illinois Regional Archives Depository, University of Illinois–Springfield, Springfield, Illinois.

213. *Archer v. Duff*, judge's docket, 1849–53, 264; *Bentley v. Cherry*, court docket, no. 2, 1858–59, 462; *Brundage v. McCarty*, judge's docket, 1849–53, 148; *Busher v. Strawn*, judge's docket, 1853–56, 208; *Cantrall v. Primm*, judge's docket, 1849–53, 9; *Cockrell v. Tainter*, judge's docket, 1856–57, 199; *Dormody v. Bradford*, court record, 1841–42, 456; *Jayne v. Benson*, judge's docket, 1856–57, 367; *McDonough v. Donnelly*, court docket, no. 2, 1858–59, 476; *Preston v. Townsend*, judge's docket, 1853–56, 472; *Rape v. Chambers*, judge's docket, 1853–56, 24; *Thompson v. Osborne*, court record, 1838–39, 321; *Thurman v. Taylor*, judge's docket, 1840–41, 116; *Watson v. Mullen*, judge's docket, 1845–49, 33; *Yocum v. Newsom*, court docket, 1845–49, 80, Sangamon County Circuit Court Records, Illinois Regional Archives Depository, University of Illinois–Springfield, Springfield, Illinois.

214. *See, e.g.*, *Bentley v. Cherry*, court docket, no. 2, 1858–59, 462; *Flynn v. Dempsey*, court docket, no. 1, 1857–58, 205; *Cockrell v. Tainter*, judge's docket, 1856–57, 199 Sangamon County Circuit Court Records, Illinois Regional Archives Depository, University of Illinois–Springfield, Springfield, Illinois.

215. *Bell v. Jones*, judge's docket, 1849–53, 90; *Dormody v. Bradford*, court record 1841–42, 456; *Huston v. Dunkin*, Docket Book B, 1836–40, 105; *Jayne v. Benson*, judge's

docket, 1856–57, 367, Sangamon County Circuit Court Records, Illinois Regional Archives Depository, University of Illinois–Springfield, Springfield, Illinois.

216. *Allsop v. Sturgeon* [L00667], *Dungey v. Spencer* [L00567], *Fancher v. Gollogher* [L00669], *Gay v. Short* [L03307], *Linder v. Fleenor* [L00713], *Mitchell et ux. v. Mitchell* [L00673], *Nordyke v. Fleenor* [L00736], *Richey v. Adams* [L00590], *Turney v. Craig* [L00731], *Wright v. Busby* [L00667] case files, LPAL.

217. For examples of jurists' reluctance to overturn jury verdicts for excessive damages, *see Blanchard v. Morris*, 15 Ill. 36 (1853), *McNamara v. King*, 7 Ill. (2 Gilm.) 436 (1845), and King, *The Law of Slander in Early Antebellum America*, 35 Am. J. Legal Hist. at 22–23.

218. *Fancher v. Gollogher* [L00669], *Nordyke v. Fleenor* [L00736], and *Turney v. Craig* [L00731] case files, LPAL.

219. Demurrer, filed May 21, 1850 [5045], Judgment, dated May 21, 1850 [35693], *Fancher v. Gollogher* [L00669] case file, LPAL.

220. Declaration, filed Apr. 25, 1850 [35686], *Fancher v. Gollogher* [L00669] case file, LPAL; Declaration filed Apr. 28, 1843 [37394]; Judgment, dated May 25, 1843 [37404], *Nordyke v. Fleenor* [L00736] case file, LPAL.

221. Judgment, dated May 23, 1850 [35671], *Allsop v. Sturgeon* [L00667] ($300 of $500 award remitted); Judgment, dated Oct. 14, 1847 [36836], *Linder v. Fleenor* [L00713] ($950 of $1,000); Judgment, dated May 24, 1852 [35811], *Mitchell et ux. v. Mitchell* [L00673] ($400 of $500); Judgment, dated May 13, 1847 [37211]; *Wright v. Busby* [L00726] ($950 of $1,000) case files, LPAL.

222. Declaration, filed May 13, 1852 [35807], Plea [May Term 1852] [35801], Judgment, dated May 24, 1852 [35811], *Mitchell et ux. v. Mitchell* [L00673] case file, LPAL.

223. Declaration, filed Aug. 24, 1847 [5382], Plea [Oct. Term 1847] [5383], Judgment, dated Oct. 14, 1847 [36836], *Linder v. Fleenor* [L00713] case file, LPAL.

224. Declaration, filed May 5, 1854 [34420], Judgment, dated May 16, 1854 [34409], Motion for New Trial, filed May 17, 1854 [4321], Judgment, dated May 18, 1854 [34412], *Richey v. Adams* [L00590] case file, LPAL. Under antebellum slander law, a new trial would not be granted on the basis of excessive damages unless the jury was influenced by "passion, prejudice or partiality." 2 Kinne, Questions and Answers at 273.

225. Declaration, filed Apr. 17, 1855 [4580], Deposition of Joseph Catrell, dated Oct. 8, 1855 [33945], Judgment, dated Oct. 18, 1855 [33951], *Dungey v. Spencer* [L00567] case file, LPAL; Judge Lawrence Weldon, *Reminiscences of Lincoln as a Lawyer*, The Independent, Apr. 4, 1895.

226. Edward J. Balleisen, Navigating Failure: Bankruptcy and Commercial Society in Antebellum America 26–32 (2001).

227. Gordon Morris Bakken, Practicing Law in Frontier California 51 (1991); Moretta, William Pitt Ballinger: Texas Lawyer, Southern Statesman at 81–82; Thomas D. Russell, *The Antebellum Courthouse as Creditors' Domain: Trial-Court Activity in South Carolina and the Concomitance of Lending and Litigation*, 40 Am. J. Legal Hist. 331 (1996); Wilson, *The Business of a Midwestern Trial Court: Knox County, Illinois* 84 Ill. Hist. J. 249.

228. Lupton, *A. Lincoln, Esq.: The Evolution of a Lawyer*, in Spiegel, A. Lincoln, Esquire: A Shrewd, Sophisticated Lawyer in His Time at 23, 26–27, 31. I am indebted to Lupton for the data presented in this paragraph.

229. *See, e.g.*, Judgment, dated July 12, 1838 [90323], *Ackley v. Hillman* [L02521]; Judgment, dated Nov. 16, 1847 [127006], *Betts v. Elkin* [L04927]; Judgment, dated Apr. 27, 1860 [93193], *Black v. Owens* [L02689] case files, LPAL.

230. *See, e.g.,* Agreed Order of Dismissal, dated May 30, 1838 [39164], *Atwood & Co. v. Shinn & Vittum* [L00886]; Order of Dismissal, dated Nov. 24, 1848 [93919], *Baker v. Camp* [L02579]; Order of Nonsuit, dated Oct. 5, 1858 [56295], *Forney v. L.C. Blakslee & Co.* [L01766] case files, LPAL.

231. *See, e.g.,* Judgment, dated Sept. 27, 1837 [133339], *A. & G.W. Kerr & Co. v. Covell* [L05551]; Judgment, dated May 18, 1855 [33672], *Fears v. Slatten* [L00549]; Judgment, dated Nov. 4, 1845 [10816], *Green v. Graham* [L00299] case files, LPAL.

232. *See, e.g.,* Judgment, dated Aug. 6, 1841 [95994], *Mallory v. Elkin* [L02960]; Judgment, dated Apr. 1, 1853 [98521], *McDonald v. Allen* [L04031] case files, LPAL.

233. Declaration [filed Oct. Term 1856] [34261], Affidavit for Continuance, filed Oct. 16, 1857 [34268], Plea [filed Mar. Term 1858] [34258], Judgment, dated Mar. 1858 [34273], *Phares v. Dockum* [L00582] case file, LPAL. *See also* Judgment, dated Mar. 17, 1838 [90252], Affidavit, filed Mar. 17, 1838 [5086], *Goodacre v. Simpson* [L03322] case file (consideration for note for sale of horse failed because horse older than represented).

234. Declaration, filed Sept. 22, 1837 [4725], Judgment, dated Oct. 18, 1837 [88441], *Billon v. White* [L02681] case file, LPAL.

235. Declaration, filed Sept. 22, 1837 [5798], Judgment, dated Oct. 16, 1837 [88418], *VonPhul & McGill v. Porter* [L04775] case file, LPAL.

236. Declaration, filed July 6, 1837 [4637], Order, dated July 3, 1837 [88311], Public Notice, *Sangamo J.,* July 22, 1837 [96412], Order, dated Oct. 16, 1837 [88418], Order, dated Oct. 20, 1837 [88465], Order, dated Oct. 21, 1837 [88478], *Coffman v. Smith* [L02895] case file, LPAL. This was one of ten lawsuits Stuart & Lincoln filed in 1837 against Smith, who had fled town in advance of his creditors. *See A.Y. Ellis & Co. v. Smith* [L03092], *Bryan v. Smith* [L02805], *Capps v. Smith* [L03011], *Ellis v. Smith* [L03177], *Herndon v. Smith* [L03544], *Klein v. Smith* [L03778], *Luckett v. Smith* [L03919], *Nation & Woods v. Smith* [L04133] case files, LPAL.

237. Declaration [filed Oct. Term 1837] [866], Order of Dismissal, dated Oct. 17, 1837 [88421], *Buckmaster v. Garrett* [L02848] case file, LPAL.

238. Russell, *The Antebellum Courthouse as Creditors' Domain,* 40 AM. J. LEGAL HIST. at 333–34; Act of Mar. 1845, ILL. STAT. ch. 57, § 33 (Chicago: Keen & Lee 1856); WINKLE, THE YOUNG EAGLE: THE RISE OF ABRAHAM LINCOLN at 96–100.

239. Proposed Judgment [Oct. 26, 1842] [1949], Agreed Judgment, dated Oct. 26, 1842 [37237], *Mount & Alexander v. Powers* [L00728] case file, LPAL.

240. AL to Orville H. Browning, dated June 29, 1857, CW 2:410; Judgment, dated Apr. 6, 1859 [133366], *Browning & Bushnell v. Price & Fell* [L05560] case file, LPAL; AL to Kersey H. Fell, dated July 8, 1859, CW 11:17.

241. Declaration, filed Mar. 3, 1856 [63253], *Brown Bros. & Co. v. Chicago, Alton & St. Louis R.R.* [L02118]; Declaration, filed Mar. 3, 1856 [65733], *Hotchkiss v. Chicago, Alton & St. Louis R.R.* [L02302]; Declaration, filed Mar. 3, 1856 [64325], *New Haven County Bank v. Chicago, Alton & St. Louis R.R.* [L02186] case files, LPAL.

242. Judgment, dated Mar. 17, 1856 [63254], *Brown Bros. & Co. v. Chicago, Alton & St. Louis R.R.* [L02118]; Judgment, dated Mar. 17, 1856 [65736], *Hotchkiss v. Chicago, Alton & St. Louis R.R.* [L02302]; Judgment, filed Mar. 17, 1856 [64330], *New Haven County Bank v. Chicago, Alton & St. Louis R.R.* [L02186] case files, LPAL.

243. *See, e.g., Baker v. Unknown heirs of Asahel Langworthy* [L02357], *Diamond v. Wiles's Heirs* [L03123], *Dorman et ux. v. Yost* [L01569], *Ex parte Kellogg* [L04424], *Kinkannon v. West* [L01929], *Pickrell v. Taft* [L03246], *Vredenburgh v. Harris* [L04777], *Warnick v. Warnick* [L00444] case files, LPAL.

244. A study of Knox County in the 1840s found that thirty-four of thirty-six

petitions to sell real estate to settle debt were granted. Wilson, *The Business of a Midwestern Trial Court: Knox County, Illinois* 84 ILL. HIST. J. at 265.

245. *See, e.g.,* Decree, dated Nov. 28, 1839 [91057], *Davenport v. Davenport* [L03121]; Decree, dated June 5, 1839 [132879], *Ex parte Butler* [L00472]; Answer [dated Nov. Term 1839] [1737], *Haines v. Haines* [L03408]; Decree, dated Aug. 11, 1845 [99324], *Lewis v. Matthews* [L03851] case files, LPAL.

246. Answer [May 26, 1840] [3588], *Ex parte Finley* [L00475]; Answer [dated Nov. Term 1839] [1737], *Haines v. Haines* [L03408] case files, LPAL.

247. This paragraph is based on the following case files in LPAL: *from Sangamon County, Ford v. Ford* [L03376], *Haines v. Haines* [L03408], *Henry v. Heirs of Whitwell* [L03426], *Keyes v. Heirs of Matheny* [L03758], and *West v. Stevens* [L04615]; and from Macon County, *Ex Parte Butler* [L00472], *Ex Parte Finley* [L00475], *Ex Parte Murphy* [L00476], and *Shepherd v. Shepherd* [L00433].

248. The supreme court reversed the granting of the petition to sell real estate three times and the circuit court reversed the county court once. *Dorman et ux. v. Yost,* 13 Ill. (2 Peck) 127 (1851); *Dorman et ux. v. Lane,* 6 Ill. (1 Gilm.) 143 (1844); *Fridley v. Murphy, Adm'r,* 25 Ill. (15 Peck) 146 (1861); Decree, dated Oct. 9, 1854 [44781], *Ex parte Doolittle* [L01207] case file, LPAL.

249. Daniel W. Stowell, *Femes UnCovert: Women's Encounters with the Law, in* STOWELL, ED., IN TENDER CONSIDERATION 32–33.

5—*In the Matter of Jane, A Woman of Color*

1. *See generally* CHARLES H. COLEMAN, ABRAHAM LINCOLN AND COLES COUNTY, ILLINOIS 80–111 (1955).

2. Judgment, dated Oct. 14, 1847 [36804], *Levick v. Eccles* [L00710] (assumpsit); Commissioner's Report, filed Oct. 15, 1847 [36768], Decree, dated Oct. 16, 1847 [36765], *Hodges v. Vanderen* [L00707] (conveyance); Judgment, dated Oct. 14, 1847 [36836], *Linder v. Fleenor* [L00713] (slander); Judgment, dated Oct. 16, 1847 [37343], *Watson v. Gill* [L00733] (slander) case files, LPAL.

3. *See generally* Anton-Hermann Chroust, *Abraham Lincoln Argues a Pro-Slavery Case,* 5 AM. J. LEGAL HIST. 299 (1961); DUFF, A. LINCOLN: PRAIRIE LAWYER at 130–49; Duncan T. McIntyre, *Lincoln and the Matson Slave Case,* 1 ILL. L. REV. (Nw. U.) 386 (1907); [Mark E. Neely, Jr.], *Some New Light on the Matson Slave Case,* LINCOLN LORE no. 1705 at 3 (Mar. 1980); ON THE ILLINOIS FRONTIER: DR. HIRAM RUTHERFORD 1840–1848, at 131–43 (Willene Hendrick & George Hendrick eds., 1981); Jesse W. Weik, *Lincoln and the Matson Negroes,* 17 ARENA MAG. 752 (Apr. 1897).

4. HOLLAND, LIFE OF ABRAHAM LINCOLN at 120–21; DUFF, A. LINCOLN: PRAIRIE LAWYER at 136; Weik, *Lincoln and the Matson Negroes,* 17 ARENA MAG. at 756; Chroust, *Abraham Lincoln Argues a Pro-Slavery Case,* 5 AM. J. LEGAL HIST. at 302.

5. WHITNEY, LIFE ON THE CIRCUIT WITH LINCOLN at 315 n.4; DUFF, A. LINCOLN: PRAIRIE LAWYER at 144; WEBB GARRISON, THE LINCOLN NO ONE KNOWS: THE MYSTERIOUS MAN WHO RAN THE CIVIL WAR 37 (1991); Speech at Chicago, Illinois (July 10, 1858), CW 2:492.

6. Weik, *Lincoln and the Matson Negroes,* 17 ARENA MAG. at 756; BEVERIDGE, ABRAHAM LINCOLN at 396; WOLDMAN, LAWYER LINCOLN at 64.

7. DUFF, A. LINCOLN: PRAIRIE LAWYER at 144–45; COLEMAN, ABRAHAM LINCOLN AND COLES COUNTY, ILLINOIS at 110–11; Nolan, *Lawyer Lincoln—Myth and Fact,* 16 HARV. L. SCHOOL BULL. 9, 22; Luban, *The Adversary System Excuse, in* THE GOOD LAWYER: LAWYERS' ROLES AND LAWYERS' ETHICS 84; Shaffer, *The Unique, Novel, and Unsound Adversary Ethic,* 41 VAND. L. REV. 697, 697.

8. Edgar Lee Masters, Lincoln the Man 120, 96 (1931); Fehrenbacher, Lincoln in Text and Context 207, 210–11; Basler, The Lincoln Legend 299; M.E. Bradford, *Against Lincoln: An Address at Gettysburg, in* The Historian's Lincoln: Pseudohistory, Psychohistory, and History 111 (Gabor S. Boritt ed., 1988).

9. O.B. Ficklin, *A Pioneer Lawyer*, Tuscola [Ill.] Rev., Sept. 7, 1922 (n.p.) (photocopy in Lincolniana Collection, Abraham Lincoln Presidential Library & Museum, Springfield, Illinois).

10. Matson Family Cemetery, Fulton County, Kentucky, USGenWeb Archives, <http://www.rootsweb.com/~kyfulton/Cemeteries/matson.html>.

11. 2 Lewis Collins, History of Kentucky 772 (Covington, Ky., Collins & Co. 1874).

12. Keith C. Barton, *"Good Cooks and Washers": Slave Hiring, Domestic Labor, and the Market in Bourbon County, Kentucky*, 84 J. Am. Hist. 436, 436 (Sept. 1997); Marion B. Lucas, A History of Blacks in Kentucky: From Slavery to Segregation, 1760–1891, at 2 (2d ed. 2003).

13. Barton, *"Good Cooks and Washers,"* 84 J. Am. Hist. at 437.

14. 1840 United States Census, Bourbon County, Kentucky 306; Lucas, A History of Blacks in Kentucky, at 62.

15. Defendant Index, Bourbon County Circuit Court, Bourbon County Courthouse, Paris, Kentucky.

16. Petition & Note, Oct. 1, 1823, *Joseph Hall v. Robert Matson* ($330 debt); Summons, filed Mar. 31, 1827, *Thomas Matson v. Robert Matson & Nicholas Talbot*, Executors of James Matson, Decedent ("plea of covenant broken," claiming $12,000); Petition & Note, filed Apr. 27, 1829, *Daniel Smith v. Robert Matson* ($115.50 debt); Petition, filed Oct. 27, 1831, *Benjamin Mills v. Robert Matson* ($185.75 note); Petition & Summons, filed May 22, 1835, *Jacob Miller v. Robert Matson & E.M. Mallory* ($156 debt); Petition, filed Dec. 25, 1835, *Peter Clarkson, Trustee v. Robert Matson* (replevin seeking $2,000 in damages); Notice, filed July 12, 1836, *Andrew Scott v. Robert Matson* (contribution sought for $1,221.29 on note that Matson was co-guarantor); Petition & Bond, filed Apr. 23, 1837, *John Berry v. Robert Matson* ($1,400 note); Petition & Note, filed Mar. 21,1839, *Andrew Scott, Administrator v. Robert Matson* ($102.50 debt); Petition & Note, filed Feb. 28, 1835, *Loyd Warfield v. Robert Matson* ($81.20 debt); Petition filed Mar. 6, 1839, *Thomas Eads v. Robert Matson* ($197.70 debt); Petition, filed Jan. 18, 1842, *James S. Matson v. Robert Matson* ($500 debt); Petition & Summons, filed Feb. 9, 1843, *James M. Cogswell v. Robert Matson* ($203.20 debt); Bill, filed Nov. 26, 1846, *John Williams, Executor v. Robert Matson & Samuel Muir* ($350.62 debt), Bourbon County Circuit Court Records, Public Records Division, Kentucky Dep't for Libraries and Archives, Frankfort, Kentucky (hereinafter "BCCCR").

17. Petition, filed July 12, 1823, *Robert Matson v. Thomas Matson* (slander); Bill, filed Apr. 3, 1826, *Robert Matson v. Joseph Hall*; Bill, filed May 29, 1826, *Robert Matson & Nicholas Talbott, Executors v. Thomas Matson*; Narratio, filed Mar. 17, 1827, *Robert Matson v. Thomas Matson*; Bill, filed Apr. 18, 1827, *Robert Matson v. Jesse Todd*; Petition, filed Oct. 19, 1835, *Robert Matson v. James McGuire* ($400 debt); Petition, filed Sept. 28, 1842, *Robert Matson for the use & benefit of Thomas Elliott v. John Curl* ($137.58 debt); Petition, filed Oct. 24, 1825, *Robert Matson for the use of Ann Mallory v. Phillip Shrader & Conrad Shrader* ($100 debt), BCCCR.

18. Terms of Compromise, filed Aug. 16, 1823, *Robert Matson v. Thomas Matson*; Order, dated Aug. 16, 1823, Order Book "T" 1823–1824, BCCCR.

19. Bill, filed May 29, 1826, *Robert Matson & Nicholas Talbott, Executors v. Thomas Matson*, BCCCR.

20. Deposition of Wm. A. Menzius, filed May 29, 1826, *Robert Matson & Nicholas Talbott, Executors v. Thomas Matson*, BCCCR.

21. Summons, filed Mar. 31, 1827, *Thomas Matson v. Robert Matson & Nicholas Talbot, Executors of James Matson, Decedent*, BCCCR.

22. Narratio, filed Mar. 17, 1827, *Robert Matson v. Thomas Matson*, BCCCR.

23. Lucas, A History of Blacks in Kentucky, at 62.

24. Bill, filed Apr. 18, 1827, *Robert Matson v. Jesse Todd*, BCCCR. Matson filed a chancery bill instead of a common-law suit because he had missed the deadline for appealing the judgment of the justice of the peace because of "the neglect of the Magistrate." *Id.*

25. Petition, filed Dec. 25, 1835, *Peter Clarkson, Trustee v. Robert Matson*, BCCCR.

26. Deposition, filed Mar. 15, 1847, *John S. Williams, Executor v. Robert Matson & Samuel Muir*, BCCCR.

27. Petition, filed Jan. 18, 1842, *James S. Matson v. Robert Matson*, BCCCR.

28. Bill, filed Nov. 26, 1846, *John S. Williams, Executor v. Robert Matson & Samuel Muir*, BCCCR.

29. The 1836 date is given in the published opinion in the case. Most accounts say that Matson bought the land in 1842, but apparently that was the date that Matson formally entered his deed to the land. *See* Coleman, Abraham Lincoln and Coles County, Illinois at 104 n.2.

30. 1840 United States Census, Bourbon County, Kentucky 306; *In the Matter of Jane, A Woman of Color*, 5 W. L.J. 202, 203; Bill, filed Nov. 26, 1846, *John Williams, Executor v. Robert Matson & Samuel Muir*, BCCCR.

31. 1850 United States Census, Fulton County, Kentucky 134.

32. Duff, A. Lincoln: Prairie Lawyer at 130; Weik, *Lincoln and the Matson Negroes*, 17 Arena Mag. at 753.

33. Weik, *Lincoln and the Matson Negroes*, 17 Arena Mag. at 753.

34. 1840 United States Census, Bourbon County, Kentucky 306.

35. McIntyre, *Lincoln and the Matson Slave Case*, 1 Ill. L. Rev. (Nw. U.) at 386; Whitney, Life on the Circuit with Lincoln at 315; *Valuable Negro Man at Commissioner's Sale* [Paris, Kentucky] Western Citizen, Sept. 3, 1847, p. 3, col. 6; *Take Notice Ten Valuable Slaves* [Paris, Kentucky] Western Citizen, Jan. 7, 1848, p. 3, col. 6. On slavery and debt litigation, *see generally* Thomas D. Russell, *Articles Sell Best Singly: The Disruption of Slave Families at Court Sales*, 1996 Utah L. Rev. 1161 (1996); Thomas D. Russell, *A New Image of the Slave Auction: An Empirical Look at the Role of Law in Slave Sales and a Conceptual Reevaluation of the Nature of Slave Property*, 18 Cardozo L. Rev. 473 (1996).

36. Dr. Hiram Rutherford to John J. Bowman (Oct. 25, 1847), *in* Coleman, Abraham Lincoln and Coles County, Illinois at 109.

37. Petition for Writ of Habeas Corpus, dated Oct. 16, 1847 [36858], *In re Bryant* [L00714] case file, LPAL.

38. Ficklin, *A Pioneer Lawyer*, Tuscola [Ill.] Rev. Jane was described as a "mulatto" in a legal notice posted by the sheriff of Coles County. Notice, dated Aug. 23, 1847, Matson case, Herndon-Weik Collection, Library of Congress.

39. Dr. Hiram Rutherford to John J. Bowman (Oct. 25, 1847), *in* Coleman, Abraham Lincoln and Coles County, Illinois at 109.

40. Ficklin, *A Pioneer Lawyer*, Tuscola [Ill.] Rev.; McIntyre, *Lincoln and the Matson Slave Case*, 1 Ill. L. Rev. (Nw. U.) at 386.

41. Lucas, A History of Blacks in Kentucky, at 24.

42. *See* Lea Vandervelde & Sandhya Subramanian, *Mrs. Dred Scott*, 106 Yale L.J. 1033, 1079–82 (1997).

43. LUCAS, A HISTORY OF BLACKS IN KENTUCKY, at 63.

44. McIntyre, *Lincoln and the Matson Slave Case*, 1 ILL. L. REV. at 386.

45. PORTRAIT AND BIOGRAPHICAL ALBUM OF COLES COUNTY, ILL. 187 (Chicago: Chapman Bros. 1887).

46. Ficklin, *A Pioneer Lawyer*, TUSCOLA [ILL.] REV.

47. Weik, *Lincoln and the Matson Negroes*, 17 ARENA MAG. at 753.

48. Speech at Peoria, Illinois (Oct. 16, 1854), CW 2:262.

49. 1 STAT. 302–5 (1793); DON E. FEHRENBACHER, THE SLAVEHOLDING REPUBLIC: AN ACCOUNT OF THE UNITED STATES GOVERNMENT'S RELATIONS TO SLAVERY 209–14 (1999); PAUL FINKELMAN, SLAVERY AND THE FOUNDERS: RACE AND LIBERTY IN THE AGE OF JEFFERSON 81–104 (2d ed. 2001).

50. Affidavit, dated Aug. 17, 1847 [5510], *Matson v. Bryant* [L00714] case file, LPAL.

51. Warrant, dated Aug. 20, 1847 [5512], *Matson v. Bryant* [L00714] case file, LPAL.

52. RICHARDS, "GENTLEMEN OF PROPERTY AND STANDING": ANTI-ABOLITION MOBS IN JACKSONIAN AMERICA at 100–11.

53. Bonnie E. Laughlin, *"Endangering the Peace of Society": Abolitionist Agitation and Mob Reform in St. Louis and Alton, 1836–1838*, 95 MO. HIST. REV. 1, 17–19 (2000).

54. Warrant, dated Aug. 20, 1847 [5512], *Matson v. Bryant* [L00714] case file, LPAL.

55. The editors of a book about Rutherford say that McIntyre "knew Dr. Rutherford well and had obviously heard Dr. Rutherford's narrative many times." ON THE ILLINOIS FRONTIER: DR. HIRAM RUTHERFORD 1840–1848, at 133.

56. McIntyre, *Lincoln and the Matson Slave Case*, 1 ILL. L. REV. at 387–88.

57. Ficklin, *A Pioneer Lawyer*, TUSCOLA [ILL.] REV.

58. On the formalism of antebellum judges who heard cases involving slavery, *see generally* ROBERT M. COVER, JUSTICE ACCUSED: ANTISLAVERY AND THE JUDICIAL PROCESS (1975); A.E. Keir Nash, *In Re Radical Interpretations of American Law: The Relation of Law and History*, 82 MICH. L. REV. 274 (1983).

59. Some writers have suggested that Matson was proceeding under state law when he filed the affidavit with Gilman. *See* 1 BEVERIDGE, ABRAHAM LINCOLN at 393; Chroust, *Abraham Lincoln Argues a Pro-Slavery Case*, 5 AM. J. LEGAL HIST. at 300. Matson's affidavit, however, tracked the language of the fugitive slave clause, not the state's "Black Laws."

60. U.S. CONST. art. IV, sec. 2 (emphasis added).

61. 1 STAT. 302–5 (1793) (emphasis added).

62. The earliest such decision was *Butler v. Hopper*, 4 F. Cas. 904 (1806), which was followed by *Ex Parte Simmons*, 22 Fed. Cas. 151 (C.C.E.D. Pa. 1823), and *Commonwealth v. Aves*, 35 Mass. (18 Pick.) 193 (1836). Justice Wilson noted in his opinion that "repeated decisions have given a uniform construction to these laws." *In the Matter of Jane, A Woman of Color*, 5 W. L.J. at 205; *see also Rights of the Slave-Holding States and the Owners of Slave Property Under the Constitution of the United States*, 23 AM. JURIST 23, 32 (1840).

63. Order, dated Aug. 20, 1847 [5512], *Matson v. Bryant* [L00714] case file, LPAL.

64. Notice, dated Aug. 23, 1847 [5509], *Matson v. Bryant* [L00714] case file, LPAL.

65. Notice, dated Oct. 8, 1847 [5507], *In re Bryant* [L00714] case file, LPAL.

66. ILL. REV. STAT. ch. 74 (1845); *see generally* Paul Finkelman, *Slavery, the "More Perfect Union," and the Prairie State*, 80 ILL. HIST. J. 248 (1987); Elmer Gertz, *The Black Laws of Illinois*, 56 ILL. ST. HIST. SOC'Y J. 454 (1963); 2 JOHN CODMAN HURD, THE LAW OF FREEDOM AND BONDAGE IN THE UNITED STATES 132–37 (Boston, Little, Brown & Co. 1862); Arvarh E. Strickland, *The Illinois Background of Lincoln's Attitude Toward Slavery and the Negro*, 56 ILL. ST. HIST. SOC'Y J. 474 (1963).

67. A Law Concerning Servants, Approved Sept. 22, 1803, Laws of the Indiana Territory, *reprinted in* STEPHEN MIDDLETON, THE BLACK LAWS IN THE OLD NORTHWEST: A DOCUMENTARY HISTORY 186–87 (1993); An Act Concerning Servants, Approved Sept. 17, 1807, Laws of the Indiana Territory, *reprinted in* MIDDLETON, THE BLACK LAWS IN THE OLD NORTHWEST: A DOCUMENTARY HISTORY at 190–91.

68. *Compare* An Act respecting Free Negroes, Mulattoes, Servants and Slaves, Approved Mar. 30, 1829, secs. 10–23, ILL. REV. STAT. (1845) *with* A Law Concerning Servants, Approved Sept. 22, 1803, secs. 1–11, Laws of the Indiana Territory, and An Act Concerning Servants, Approved Sept. 17, 1807, secs. 13–15, Laws of the Indiana Territory.

69. ILL. CONST. ART. VI, secs. 1–2 (1818).

70. An Act respecting Free Negroes, Mulattoes, Servants and Slaves, Approved Feb. 1, 1819, sec. 1.

71. An Act respecting Free Negroes, Mulattoes, Servants and Slaves, Approved Mar. 30, 1829, sec. 1.

72. An Act to Regulate Black and Mulatto Persons, Laws of Ohio, Jan. 5, 1804, *reprinted in* MIDDLETON, THE BLACK LAWS IN THE OLD NORTHWEST: A DOCUMENTARY HISTORY at 15; An Act to amend the last named act "An Act to Regulate Black and Mulatto Persons," Approved Jan. 25, 1807, Laws of Ohio, *reprinted in* MIDDLETON, THE BLACK LAWS IN THE OLD NORTHWEST: A DOCUMENTARY HISTORY at 17; An Act Concerning Free Negroes and Mullatoes, Servants and Slaves, Approved Feb. 10, 1810, Laws of Indiana, *reprinted in* MIDDLETON, THE BLACK LAWS IN THE OLD NORTHWEST: A DOCUMENTARY HISTORY at 202.

73. *See* EUGENE H. BERWANGER, THE FRONTIER AGAINST SLAVERY: WESTERN ANTI-NEGRO PREJUDICE AND THE SLAVERY EXTENSION CONTROVERSY 30–36 (1967).

74. ILL. REV. STAT. ch. 74, sec. 1 (1845). Illinois lawyer Mason Brayman derisively referred to a free black as "$1,000 nigger" in an 1860 letter. Letter (dated Nov. 5, 1860), Bailhache-Brayman Papers, Abraham Lincoln Presidential Library & Museum, Springfield, Illinois.

75. ILL. REV. STAT. ch. 74, sec. 4.

76. Docket Entry (transcription), dated Aug. 21, 1847, *People v. Robert Matson*, Matson case, Herndon-Weik Collection, Library of Congress.

77. The Ashmores are identified as brothers by Charles H. Coleman. *See* COLEMAN, ABRAHAM LINCOLN AND COLES COUNTY, ILLINOIS at 105 n.3.

78. Bond for freedom of Anthony Bryant, Jane Bryant and their children, dated Oct. 17, 1847 [5505], *In re Bryant* [L00714] case file, LPAL.

79. RONALD G. WALTERS, THE ANTISLAVERY APPEAL: AMERICAN ABOLITIONISM AFTER 1830, at 74 (1976).

80. Execution Docket, dated July 3, 1848 [36863], *State v. Matson*, Coles County Circuit Court, *In Re Bryant* [L00714] case file, LPAL.

81. ILL. REV. STAT. ch. 74, sec. 2. For a detailed account of two similar lawsuits for damages brought in Indiana and Iowa, *see* Paul Finkelman, *Fugitive Slaves, Midwestern Racial Tolerance, and the Value of "Justice Delayed,"* 78 IOWA L. REV. 89 (1992).

82. Declaration, dated Sept. 1, 1847 [36866], *Robert Matson individually and for the use of Coles County v. Rutherford, In re Bryant* [L00715] case file, LPAL.

83. Ficklin, *A Pioneer Lawyer*, TUSCOLA [ILL.] REV.

84. Petition for Writ of Habeas Corpus, dated Oct. 16, 1847 [5504], *In re Bryant* [L00714] case file, LPAL.

85. Petition of G.M. Ashmore, dated Oct. 16, 1847 [5506], *In re Bryant* [L00714] case file, LPAL.

86. Ficklin, *A Pioneer Lawyer*, TUSCOLA [ILL.] REV.

87. McIntyre, *Lincoln and the Matson Slave Case*, 1 ILL. L. REV. at 387.

88. Duff, A. Lincoln: Prairie Lawyer at 134.

89. *Levick v. Eccles* [L00710], *Hodges v. Vanderen* [L00707], *Linder v. Fleenor* [L00713] case files, LPAL.

90. Duff, A. Lincoln: Prairie Lawyer at 312–18.

91. AL to Thompson R. Webber (Sept. 12, 1853), CW 2:202.

92. *In the Matter of Jane, A Woman of Color*, 5 W. L.J. at 202. Because it was a circuit court case, the decision was not published in the *Illinois Reports*.

93. *Quoted in* Weik, *Lincoln and the Matson Negroes*, 17 Arena Mag. at 755.

94. *Joseph Jarrot, alias Pete, alias Joseph, a colored man v. Jarrot*, 7 Ill. (2 Gilm.) 1 (1845) (the "French slaves"); *Phoebe, a Woman of Color v. Jay*, 1 Ill. (Breese) 268 (1828) (indentured servitude); *Nance, a girl of color v. Howard*, 1 Ill. (Breese) 242 (1828) (indentured servitude); *Sarah, alias Sarah Borders, a woman of color v. Borders*, 5 Ill. (4 Scam.) 341 (1943) (indentured servitude); *Boon v. Juliet*, 2 Ill. (1 Scam.) 258 (1836) (children under indentured servitude); *Willard v. People*, 5 Ill. (4 Scam.) 461, 472–73 (1843) (slaves in transit).

95. Ill. Const. Art. VI, § 1 (1818).

96. Finkelman, Slavery and the Founders: Race and Liberty in the Age of Jefferson at 77.

97. James Simeone, Democracy and Slavery in Frontier Illinois: The Bottomland Republic 19 (2000).

98. *Joseph Jarrot, alias Pete, alias Joseph, a colored man v. Jarrot*, 7 Ill. (2 Gilm.) 1, 23–24 (1845).

99. *Id.* at 22.

100. *Phoebe, a Woman of Color v. Jay*, 1 Ill. (Breese) 268 (1828).

101. *Nance, a girl of color v. Howard*, 1 Ill. (Breese) 242 (1828); *Sarah, alias Sarah Borders, a woman of color v. Borders*, 5 Ill. (4 Scam.) 341 (1843); Decree, dated Jan. 24, 1839 [129550], *Stuart wrote indenture* [N05020] case file, LPAL.

102. *Choisser v. Hargrave*, 2 Ill. (1 Scam.) 317 (1836); *Boon v. Juliet*, 2 Ill. (1 Scam.) 258 (1836).

103. *Somerset v. Stewart*, 98 Eng. Rep. 499, 510 (K.B. 1772); *see generally* William M. Wiecek, The Sources of Antislavery Constitutionalism in America, 1760–1848, at 20–39 (1977).

104. Harold M. Hyman & William M. Wiecek, Equal Justice Under Law: Constitutional Development 1835–1875, at 99 (1982).

105. *Commonwealth v. Aves*, 35 Mass. (18 Pick.) 193, 207 (1836); Leonard W. Levy, The Law of the Commonwealth and Chief Justice Shaw 62–68 (1957).

106. *Commonwealth v. Aves*, 35 Mass. (18 Pick.) at 219.

107. Don E. Fehrenbacher, The Dred Scott Case: Its Significance in American Law and Politics 54 (1978); *Bush's Representatives v. White*, 19 Ky. (3 Mon.) 100, 104 (1825); *Rankin v. Lydia*, 9 Ky. (2 A.K. Marsh.) 467, 478–79 (1820); *Winny, A Free Woman Held in Slavery v. Whitesides*, 1 Mo. 472 (1824).

108. Fehrenbacher, The Dred Scott Case at 52–56.

109. *Commonwealth v. Aves*, 35 Mass. (18 Pick.) at 224–25.

110. [Chicago] Western Citizen, Oct. 26, 1843, at 2.

111. *Willard v. People*, 5 Ill. (4 Scam.) 461, 472–73 (1843); *see also* Merton L. Dillon, The Antislavery Movement in Illinois: 1809–1844, at 332–33 (1951) (Ph.D. dissertation, University of Michigan); Finkelman, *Slavery, the "More Perfect Union," and the Prairie State*, 80 Ill. Hist. J. at 254–55.

112. *Willard v. People*, 5 Ill. (4 Scam.) at 473; Mark E. Steiner, *Abolitionists and Escaped Slaves in Jacksonville: Samuel Willard's My First Adventure With a Fugitive Slave: The Story of It and How It Failed*, 89 Ill. Hist. J. 213 (1996).

113. *Willard v. People,* 5 Ill. (4 Scam.) at 471.

114. *Id.* at 463.

115. *Id.* at 463, 466, 468.

116. *Rankin v. Lydia,* 9 Ky. (2 A.K. Marsh.) 467, 478–79 (1820).

117. *Lunsford v. Coquillon,* 4 La. Rep. Ann. Ed. (2 Mart. N.S.) 401 (1824).

118. *Willard v. People,* 5 Ill. (4 Scam.) at 471–72.

119. *Id.* at 474, 476–77.

120. Fehrenbacher, The Dred Scott Case at 32.

121. Ficklin, *A Pioneer Lawyer,* Tuscola [Ill.] Rev.

122. *See In the Matter of Jane, A Woman of Color,* 5 W. L.J. at 205–06.

123. Ficklin, *A Pioneer Lawyer,* Tuscola [Ill.] Rev.

124. Weik, *Lincoln and the Matson Negroes,* 17 Arena Mag. at 757. Curran's speech in defense of Rowan was reprinted many times. *See, e.g.,* 1 William H. Curran, The Life of the Right Honorable John Philpot Curran 307–18 (London, Archibald Constable & Co. 1819); William O'Regan, Memoirs of the Legal, Literary, and Political Life of the Late the Right Honorable John Philpot Curran 62 (London, James Harper 1817); Speeches of the Right Honorable John Philpott Curran 169–70 (4th ed. London, Hurst, Rees, Orme, & Brown 1815); Report of the Trial of Archibald Hamilton Rowan 50 (New York, Tiebout & O'Brien 1794); *see also Eloquence of the Bar. Grattan—Curran,* 3 W. L.J. 241 (1846). Curran's speech was sufficiently well known for the abolitionist editor Benjamin Lundy to take the name of his antislavery newspaper, The Genius of Universal Emancipation, from it. 1 Beveridge, Abraham Lincoln at 397 n.2; Merton L. Dillon, The Abolitionists: The Growth of a Dissenting Minority 30 (1974).

125. Weik, *Lincoln and the Matson Negroes,* 17 Arena Mag. at 757.

126. Speech at Springfield, Illinois (June 16, 1858), CW 2:461, 464–65 ("House Divided" speech).

127. Ficklin, *A Pioneer Lawyer,* Tuscola [Ill.] Rev. *Id.*

128. *In the Matter of Jane, A Woman of Color,* 5 W. L.J. at 205–06.

129. *Id.* at 206.

130. *Vaughan v. Williams,* 28 F. Cas. 1115, 1116–17 (C.C.D. Ind. 1845) (No. 16, 903); *see also* Carl B. Swisher, The Taney Period 1836–64, at 555–56 (1974).

131. *Id.*

132. Joseph Story, A Familiar Exposition of the Constitution of the United States 291–92 (1986) (1840); *see also* 3 Records of the Federal Convention of 1787, at 325 (Max Farrand ed., 1937); Arthur Bestor, *State Sovereignty and Slavery: A Reinterpretation of Proslavery Constitutional Doctrine, 1846–1860,* 54 J. Ill. St. Hist. Soc'y 117, 130 (1961).

133. *Ex parte Simmons,* 22 F. Cas. 151, 152 (C.C.E.D. Pa. 1823) (No. 12, 863).

134. *In the Matter of Jane, A Woman of Color,* 5 W. L.J. at 205.

135. *See, e.g., In the matter of Ralph (a colored man) on Habeas Corpus,* 1 Iowa 1 (1839).

136. *Thomas, f.w.c. v. Generis,* 16 La. 483 (1840); *see also Smith v. Smith,* 13 La. 441 (1839); *Maria Louise, f.w.c. v. Marot,* 9 La. 475 (1835).

137. *Vincent, a man of color v. Duncan,* 2 Mo. 214, 216 (1830); *see also Julia, a woman of color v. McKinney,* 3 Mo. 270 (1833); *Winny, a free woman held in slavery v. Whitesides,* 1 Mo. 472 (1824). The Missouri Supreme Court subsequently overturned its pro-freedom precedents in Dred Scott's state court lawsuit, which preceded his federal lawsuit. *Scott v. Emerson,* 15 Mo. 576 (1852); Dennis K. Boman, *The Dred Scott Case Reconsidered: The Legal and Political Context in Missouri,* 44 Am. J. Legal Hist. 405, 422–28 (2000); Paul Finkelman, An Imperfect Union: Slavery, Federalism, and Comity 222–28 (1981).

138. B. Cozzens to Henry Eddy (Jan. 30, 1831), Box 1, Folder 1831, Henry Eddy Papers, Abraham Lincoln Presidential Library & Museum, Springfield, Illinois.

139. Sangamon County Commissioner's Court Records (1833–1840), Sept. 4, 1838 (typescript), Illinois Regional Archives Depository, University of Illinois–Springfield, Springfield, Illinois.

140. [Chicago] WESTERN CITIZEN at 2 (Nov. 16, 1847).

141. [Chicago] WESTERN CITIZEN at 2 (Dec. 28, 1847).

142. COLEMAN, ABRAHAM LINCOLN AND COLES COUNTY, ILLINOIS at 104; Chroust, *Abraham Lincoln Argues a Pro-Slavery Case*, 5 AM. J. LEGAL HIST. at 299–300; DUFF, A. LINCOLN: PRAIRIE LAWYER at 131; GARRISON, THE LINCOLN NO ONE KNOWS at 35; NEELY, THE ABRAHAM LINCOLN ENCYCLOPEDIA 207–08; [Neely], *Some New Light on the Matson Slave Case*, LINCOLN LORE no. 1705 at 3; Weik, *Lincoln and the Matson Negroes*, 17 ARENA MAG. at 753; *but see* Finkelman, *Slavery, the "More Perfect Union," and the Prairie State*, 80 ILL. HIST. J. 248, 256.

143. *In the Matter of Jane, A Woman of Color*, 5 W. L.J. at 203; *see also* McIntyre, *Lincoln and the Matson Slave Case*, 1 ILL. L. REV. at 386. An account of the case in the *Coles County Globe* also said that Matson brought Jane and her children into Illinois in August 1845 and that they had remained on his farm until September 1847. The Chicago-based *Western Citizen* reprinted the *Coles County Globe* article in its Nov. 16, 1847, issue. The article was also reprinted in the *Illinois State Register* in its Dec. 1, 1847, edition. Decision in Slave Case, *Illinois State Register* (Dec. 10, 1847) [124490], *In re Bryant* case file [L00714], LPAL.

144. THOMAS, ABRAHAM LINCOLN at 114.

145. Remarks and Resolution Introduced in United States House of Representatives Concerning Abolition of Slavery in the District of Columbia (Jan. 10, 1849), CW 2:20–22; *see generally* PAUL FINDLEY, A. LINCOLN: THE CRUCIBLE OF CONGRESS 122–43 (1979).

146. 1 BEVERIDGE, ABRAHAM LINCOLN at 482; New York Tribune 2 (Sept. 22, 1849), *quoted in* Paul H. Verduin, *Partners for Emancipation: New Light on Lincoln, Joshua Giddings, and the Push to End Slavery in the District of Columbia, 1848–49*, *in* PAPERS FROM THE THIRTEENTH AND FOURTEENTH ANNUAL LINCOLN COLLOQUIA 68 (n.d.).

147. Protest in Illinois Legislature on Slavery (Mar. 3,1837), CW 1:74–75. *Id.*

148. FINDLEY, A. LINCOLN: THE CRUCIBLE OF CONGRESS at 140; Remarks and Resolution Introduced in United States House of Representatives Concerning Abolition of Slavery in the District of Columbia (Jan. 10, 1849), CW 2:222 n.4.; DONALD, LINCOLN at 137.

149. Basler, *James Quay Howard's Notes on Lincoln*, 4 ABRAHAM LINCOLN Q. at 395.

150. Docket entry, *Matson v. Rutherford*, May Term 1848, Docket entry, *Matson v. Ashmore*, May Term 1848 [36865], *Matson for the use of Coles County, Illinois v. Rutherford* [L00715] case file, LPAL.

151. Dr. Hiram Rutherford to John J. Bowman (Oct. 25, 1847), *in* COLEMAN, ABRAHAM LINCOLN AND COLES COUNTY, ILLINOIS at 109–10.

152. COLEMAN, ABRAHAM LINCOLN AND COLES COUNTY, ILLINOIS at 109.

153. Docket entry, *Matson v. Rutherford*, May Term 1848, Docket entry, *Matson v. Ashmore*, May Term 1848 [36865], *Matson for the use of Coles County, Illinois v. Rutherford* [L00715] case file, LPAL.

154. Execution Docket, dated July 3, 1848 [36863], *In re Bryant* [L00714] case file, LPAL.

155. Dr. Hiram Rutherford to John J. Bowman (Oct. 25, 1847), *in* COLEMAN, ABRAHAM LINCOLN AND COLES COUNTY, ILLINOIS at 109; Bill of Costs (n.d.), Matson case, Herndon-Weik Collection, Library of Congress.

156. COLEMAN, ABRAHAM LINCOLN AND COLES COUNTY, ILLINOIS at 109 n.13.

157. Illinois Statewide Marriage Index, 1763–1900, <www.cyberdriveillinois.com/GenealogyMWeb/marrsrch.html>.

158. 1850 United States Census, Fulton County, Kentucky 134.

159. Matson Family Cemetery, Fulton County, Kentucky, USGenWeb Archives, <http://www.rootsweb.com/~kyfulton/Cemeteries/matson.htmll>.

160. WINKLE, THE YOUNG EAGLE: THE RISE OF ABRAHAM LINCOLN at 255–56; GEORGE M. FREDRICKSON, THE BLACK IMAGE IN THE WHITE MIND: THE DEBATE ON AFRO-AMERICAN CHARACTER AND DESTINY 1817–1914, at 1–27 (1971); Annual Message to Congress (Dec. 1, 1862), CW 5:520; THOMAS, ABRAHAM LINCOLN at 363.

161. JAMES BREWER STEWART, HOLY WARRIORS: THE ABOLITIONISTS AND AMERICAN SLAVERY 30 (rev. ed. 1997); WINKLE, THE YOUNG EAGLE: THE RISE OF ABRAHAM LINCOLN at 255; *Quoted in* Paul M. Angle, *Aftermath of the Matson Slave Case*, 3 ABRAHAM LINCOLN Q. 146, 148 (1944).

162. *See, e.g.,* Notes for Speeches at Columbus and Cincinnati, Ohio (Sept. 16, 17, 1859), CW 3:435; *see generally* Phillip S. Paludan, *Lincoln's Pre-War Constitutional Vision*, 15 J. ABRAHAM LINCOLN ASS'N 1, 11–14 (1994); FEHRENBACHER & FEHRENBACHER, RECOLLECTED WORDS OF ABRAHAM LINCOLN at 61.

163. *See generally* Michael Burlingame, *The 1837 Lincoln-Stone Protest Against Slavery Reconsidered, in* PAPERS FROM THE THIRTEENTH AND FOURTEENTH ANNUAL LINCOLN COLLOQUIA 57–62 (n.d.)

164. For background on northern antiabolitionism in the 1830s, *see generally* Ratner, *Northern Concern for Social Order as Cause for Rejecting Anti-Slavery*, 28 HISTORIAN 1; RICHARDS, "GENTLEMEN OF PROPERTY AND STANDING": ANTI-ABOLITION MOBS IN JACKSONIAN AMERICA.

165. 1 BEVERIDGE, ABRAHAM LINCOLN at 190–93.

166. Protest in Illinois Legislature on Slavery (Mar. 3,1837), CW 1:74–75.

167. Autobiography Written for John L. Scripps (c. June 1860), CW 4:65.

168. *See, e.g.,* Peter B. Knupfer, *Henry Clay's Constitutional Unionism*, 89 REG. KY. HIST. SOC'Y 32, 48 (1991); MATTHEWS, RUFUS CHOATE at 202–03; WILLIAM E. GIENAPP, THE ORIGINS OF THE REPUBLICAN PARTY 1852–1856, at 18 (1987); Brooks D. Simpson, *Daniel Webster and the Cult of the Constitution*, 15 J. AM. CULTURE 15, 19 (1992). Both Story and Shaw exaggerated the importance of the fugitive slave clause in the making of the Constitution, according to modern historians. *See* Barbara Holden-Smith, *Lords of Lash, Loom, and Law: Justice Story, Slavery, and Prigg v. Pennsylvania*, 78 CORNELL L. REV. 1086, 1129–31 (1993); William M. Wiecek, *The Witch at the Christening: Slavery and the Constitution's Origins, in* THE FRAMING AND RATIFICATION OF THE CONSTITUTION 181–82 (Leonard W. Levy & Dennis J. Mahoney eds., 1987).

169. *Prigg v. Pennsylvania*, 41 U.S. (16 Pet.) 539, 611 (1842); R. KENT NEWMEYER, SUPREME COURT JUSTICE JOSEPH STORY: STATESMAN OF THE OLD REPUBLIC 370–78 (1985).

170. *Commonwealth v. Aves*, 35 Mass. (18 Pick.) at 221.

171. *In Re Sims*, 61 Mass. (7 Cush.) 285 (1851); LEVY, THE LAW OF THE COMMONWEALTH AND CHIEF JUSTICE SHAW at 99–101.

172. ADDRESSES AND ORATIONS OF RUFUS CHOATE 407–08 (Boston, Little Brown & Co. 1878).

173. Holden-Smith, *Lords of Lash, Loom, and Law: Justice Story, Slavery, and Prigg v. Pennsylvania*, 78 CORNELL L. REV. at 1138–46.

174. *Commonwealth v. Aves*, 35 Mass. (18 Pick.) at 196; 1 MEMOIR OF BENJAMIN ROBBINS CURTIS 86–89 (Benjamin R. Curtis ed., Boston, Little, Brown, & Co. 1879); 2 MEMOIR OF BENJAMIN ROBBINS CURTIS at 89.

175. THEODORE PARKER, THE TRIAL OF THEODORE PARKER, FOR THE "MISDEMEANOR" OF A SPEECH IN FANEUIL HALL AGAINST KIDNAPPING 167 (Boston, Published For The Author 1855).

176. 1 MEMOIR OF BENJAMIN ROBBINS CURTIS at 72; SWISHER, THE TANEY PERIOD 1836–64, at 238–40.

177. 1 MEMOIR OF BENJAMIN ROBBINS CURTIS at 122, 124.

178. *Id.* at 134–35; COVER, JUSTICE ACCUSED: ANTISLAVERY AND THE JUDICIAL PROCESS at 222.

179. MATTHEWS, RUFUS CHOATE at 68; M. Paul Holsinger, *Timothy Walker*, 84 OHIO HIST. 145, 156 (1975); *see generally* STANLEY W. CAMPBELL, THE SLAVE CATCHERS: ENFORCE-MENT OF THE FUGITIVE SLAVE LAW, 1850–1860, at 3–25 (1968). Ohio lawyer Salmon P. Chase, on the other hand, had abandoned the Whig Party in 1841, convinced that the Whigs were completely subservient toward the South on the *"vital* question of slavery." FREDERICK J. BLUE, SALMON P. CHASE: A LIFE IN POLITICS 43 (1987).

180. *People v. Pond* [L00335] case file, LPAL.

181. Steiner, *Abolitionists and Escaped Slaves in Jacksonville*, 89 ILL. HIST. J. at 227.

182. Docket entry, dated Nov. 3, 1845 [15043], *People v. Pond* [L00335] case file, LPAL.

183. *People v. George Kern* [L01267], *People v. James Kern, People v. Scott* [L00335] case files, LPAL. The editors of the Law Practice of Abraham Lincoln note that the refer-ence work Lincoln Day by Day is the only source that associates Lincoln with these cases. It states that the cases were dismissed on Apr. 15, 1847, after Lincoln argued "lack of proof that Negro in case was slave." WILLIAM E. BARINGER, LINCOLN DAY BY DAY, VOL. I: 1809–1848, at 287 (1960). It is likely that the documents that once supported concluding that Lincoln was involved have since been stolen or misplaced.

184. MAURICE G. BAXTER, ONE AND INSEPARABLE: DANIEL WEBSTER AND THE UNION 407–27 (1984); DAVID M. POTTER, THE IMPENDING CRISIS 1848–1861, at 90–120 (Don E. Fehrenbacher ed., 1976); Act of Sept. 18, 1850, Ch. 60, 9 Stat. 462 (1850); CAMPBELL, THE SLAVE CATCHERS: ENFORCEMENT OF THE FUGITIVE SLAVE LAW, at 3–25.

185. Interview with John H. Bunn (Oct. 15, 1914), Jesse Weik Papers, Box 1, Folder 11, Abraham Lincoln Presidential Library & Museum, Springfield, Illinois.

186. On Lincoln's support of the Compromise of 1850 see 2 BEVERIDGE, ABRAHAM LINCOLN, at 126–31. On Lincoln's admiration of Webster and Clay see Mark E. Neely, Jr., *American Nationalism in the Image of Henry Clay: Abraham Lincoln's Eulogy on Henry Clay in Context*, 73 REG. KY. HIST. SOC'Y 31 (1975); Richard N. Current, *Lincoln and Daniel Webster*, 48 J. ILL. ST. HIST. SOC'Y 307 (1955).

187. Seventh and Last Debate with Stephen A. Douglas at Alton, Illinois (Oct. 15, 1858), CW 3:317.

188. AL to Joshua F. Speed (Aug. 24, 1855), CW 2:320.

189. First Inaugural Address (Mar. 4, 1861), CW 4:251.

190. DONALD, LINCOLN'S HERNDON 106, 134.

191. *Fugitive Slave Case, Hiram McElroy, Claimant vs. Frederick Clements, a Negro*, ILL. ST. J. (Aug. 1, 1857) [135800]; *Fugitive Slave Case, Decision of the Commissioner*, ILL. ST. J. (Aug. 3, 1857) [125427], *reprinted in McElroy v. Clements* [L05897] case file, LPAL.

192. *Kinney v. Cook*, 4 Ill. (3 Scam.) at 232; *Bailey v. Cromwell*, 4 Ill. at 73.

193. *Rendition of a Fugitive Slave*, ILL. ST. J. (Feb. 10, 1860) [135807], *reprinted in Dickinson v. Canton* [L05898] case file, LPAL.

194. *Gone South*, ILL. ST. J. (Feb. 14, 1860) [135808], *reprinted in Dickinson v. Can-ton* [L05898] case file, LPAL.

195. *Fugitive Poetry*, ILL. ST. J. (Mar. 16, 1860) [135814], *reprinted in Dickinson v. Canton* [L05898] case file, LPAL.

196. *Quoted in* Weik, *Lincoln and the Matson Negroes*, 17 ARENA MAG. at 755.

197. William M. Wiecek, *Latimer: Lawyers, Abolitionists, and the Problem of Unjust Laws, in* ANTISLAVERY RECONSIDERED: NEW PERSPECTIVES ON THE ABOLITIONISTS 228–29 (Lewis

Perry & Michael Fellman eds., 1979); *Case of George Latimer—Boston Slavehunting Ground—Outrageous Conduct of the City Marshall and City Police*, 12 THE LIBERATOR 171 (Oct. 28, 1842).

198. Wiecek, *Latimer: Lawyers, Abolitionists, and the Problem of Unjust Laws*, in AN-TISLAVERY RECONSIDERED: NEW PERSPECTIVES ON THE ABOLITIONISTS at 228–29; *The Latimer Case*, 12 THE LIBERATOR 186 (Nov. 25, 1842).

199. *See* FINKELMAN, AN IMPERFECT UNION at 149 n.8.

200. John Niven, *Lincoln and Chase, A Reappraisal*, 12 J. ABRAHAM LINCOLN ASS'N 1, 4–5 (1991); *see also* Salmon P. Chase, *Union and Freedom, Without Compromise*, Cong. Globe, 31st Cong., 1st Sess. 470 (1850).

201. AL to Salmon P. Chase (June 9, 1859), CW 3:384; Salmon P. Chase to AL (June 13, 1859), *available at* Abraham Lincoln Papers at the Library of Congress, <memory.loc.gov/ammem/alhtml/malhome.html>, Select: Search by Keyword, Enter: Chase 1859, Select: Item 5.

202. 5 Eugene Wambaugh, *Salmon Portland Chase*, in GREAT AMERICAN LAWYERS 351 (William Draper Lewis ed., 1908).

203. Stephen Middleton, *Antislavery Litigation in Ohio: The Chase-Trowbridge Letters*, 70 MID-AMERICA 105, 107 (1988).

204. *Quoted in* BLUE, SALMON P. CHASE: A LIFE IN POLITICS at 31.

205. THE LINCOLN-DOUGLAS DEBATES OF 1858, at 260 (Robert W. Johannsen ed., 1965).

206. STEPHEN MIDDLETON, OHIO AND THE ANTISLAVERY ACTIVITIES OF ATTORNEY SALMON PORTLAND CHASE 1830–1849, at 114–15 (1990); James Turner, *Use of the Courts in the Movement to Abolish American Slavery*, 31 OHIO ST. L.J. 305 (1970); COVER, JUSTICE AC-CUSED: ANTISLAVERY AND THE JUDICIAL PROCESS at 161.

207. *Quoted in* ROBERT B. WARDEN, AN ACCOUNT OF THE PRIVATE LIFE AND PUBLIC SER-VICES OF SALMON PORTLAND CHASE (Cincinnati, Wilstach, Baldwin & Co. 1874).

208. 1 FREDERIC B. CROSSLEY, COURTS AND LAWYERS OF ILLINOIS 187–91 (1916). *Eells v. People*, 5 Ill. (4 Scam.) 498 (1843); *Willard v. People*, 5 Ill. (4 Scam.) 461 (1843); THE HIS-TORY OF WILL COUNTY, ILLINOIS 263–64 (Chicago, Wm Le Baron, Jr. & Co. 1878); ISAAC N. ARNOLD, REMINISCENCES OF THE ILLINOIS-BAR FORTY YEARS AGO 138–40 (Chicago, Fergus Printing Co. 1881) (Fergus Historical Series no. 14). For cases where Lincoln and Collins were opposing lawyers, *see, e.g., Anderson v. Lawrence* [L05073], *Chauncey v. Jackson* [L02354], *Ripley v. Morris* [L02482] case files, LPAL.

209. DONALD, LINCOLN'S HERNDON at 106, 134.

210. DONALD, LINCOLN 103–04 (1999); THOMAS, ABRAHAM LINCOLN at 112; OATES, WITH MALICE TOWARD NONE at 110; *Bailey v. Cromwell*, 4 Ill. (3 Scam.) 71 (1841).

211. Declaration, filed Sept. 4, 1838 [45563], *Bailey v. Cromwell* [L01213] case file, LPAL.

212. Declaration, filed Sept. 4, 1838 [45563], Amended Plea, filed Sept. Term 1839 [45569], *Bailey v. Cromwell* [L01213] case file, LPAL; *Kinney v. Cook*, 4 Ill. (3 Scam.) 232 (1841); *Bailey v. Cromwell*, 4 Ill. (3 Scam.) 71, 73 (1841); ILL. REV. STAT. ch. 74 (1845).

213. Leonard W. Levy, *Sims' Case: The Fugitive Slave Law in Boston in 1851*, 35 J. NEGRO HIST. 39, 44 (1950).

214. PERRY MILLER, LIFE OF THE MIND IN AMERICA: FROM THE REVOLUTION TO THE CIVIL WAR 104, 188, 203 (1965); *see also* Fannie M. Farmer, *Legal Practice and Ethics in North Carolina 1820–1860*, 30 N.C. HIST. REV. 329 (1953).

215. EDWARD BONNEY, THE BANDITTI OF THE PRAIRIES OR, THE MURDERER'S DOOM!! A TALE OF THE MISSISSIPPI VALLEY 164–65 (1963) (1850).

216. *The Abuses of Law Courts*, 21 U.S. MAG. & DEM. REV. 305, 305–06 (1847); *see*

also Legerdemain of Law-Craft (pts 1 & 2), 22 U.S. MAG. & DEM. REV. 529 (1848), 23 U.S. MAG. & DEM. REV. 134 (1849).

217. MICHAEL SCHUDSON, ORIGINS OF THE IDEAL OF OBJECTIVITY IN THE PROFESSIONS: STUDIES IN THE HISTORY OF AMERICAN JOURNALISM AND AMERICAN LAW, 1830–1940, at 313 (1990). For examples of this defensiveness *see The American Bar,* 28 U.S. MAG. & DEM. REV. at 195, 197; *The Legal Profession in the United States,* 10 AM. L.J. 470, 475–76 (1851); *The Morals and Utility of Lawyers,* 7 W. L.J. 1, 10 (1849); J.F. Jackson, *Law and Lawyers: Is the Profession of the Advocate Consistent with Perfect Integrity?,* 28 KNICKERBOCKER 377, 377 (1846).

218. The literature on antebellum legal ethics is growing. *See, e.g.,* M.H. Hoeflich, *Legal Ethics in the Nineteenth Century: The Other Tradition,* 47 U. KAN. L. REV. 793 (1999); Russell G. Pearce, *Rediscovering the Republican Origins of the Legal Ethics Codes,* 6 GEO. J. LEGAL ETHICS 241 (1992); Norman W. Spaulding, *The Myth of Civic Republicanism: Interrogating the Ideology of Antebellum Legal Ethics,* 71 FORDHAM L. REV. 1397 (2003).

219. Livingston, *Livingston's Law Register for 1852,* at 2; *see also* ALLEN, AN ADDRESS DELIVERED BEFORE THE GRADUATING CLASS OF THE LAW DEPARTMENT OF HAMILTON COLLEGE 30–31.

220. WALKER, AN INTRODUCTION TO AMERICAN LAW 661.

221. THOMAS L. SHAFFER, AMERICAN LEGAL ETHICS 59 (1985); 2 DAVID HOFFMAN, A COURSE OF LEGAL STUDY 765, 754–56 (2d ed. Baltimore, Joseph Neal 1836); *see also* Maxwell Bloomfield, *David Hoffman and the Shaping of a Republican Legal Culture,* 38 MD. L. REV. 673, 684–85 (1979).

222. GREENLEAF, A DISCOURSE PRONOUNCED AT THE INAUGURATION OF THE AUTHOR AS ROYALL PROFESSOR OF LAW IN HARVARD UNIVERSITY at 16–17.

223. *See generally* Bloomfield, *David Hoffman and the Shaping of a Republican Legal Culture,* 38 MD. L. REV. at 673; Gordon, *Lawyers as the American Aristocracy,* 20 STAN. LAW. 2, 3–6; Daniel R. Ernst, *Legal Positivism, Abolitionist Litigation, and the New Jersey Slave Case of 1845,* 4 LAW & HIST. REV. 337, 339 (1986).

224. SHAFFER, AMERICAN LEGAL ETHICS at 176; BLOOMFIELD, *Law and Lawyers in American Popular Culture, in* LAW AND AMERICAN LITERATURE at 137–38; Pearce, *Rediscovering the Republican Origins of the Legal Ethics Codes,* 6 GEO. J. LEGAL ETHICS at 241; Spaulding, *The Myth of Civic Republicanism: Interrogating the Ideology of Antebellum Legal Ethics,* 71 FORDHAM L. REV. 1397.

225. GEORGE SHARSWOOD, A COMPEND OF LECTURES ON THE AIMS AND DUTIES OF THE PROFESSION OF LAW 26 (Philadelphia, T. & J.W. Johnson 1854); *see also Sharswood's Professional Ethics,* 3 AM. L. REV. 193 (1855).

226. J.F. Jackson, *Law and Lawyers,* 28 KNICKERBOCKER 377, 379 (1846); *see also* JOSEPH HOPKINSON, AN ADDRESS DELIVERED BEFORE THE LAW ACADEMY OF PHILADELPHIA 15–16 (Philadelphia, Law Academy 1826).

227. Timothy Walker, *Advice to Law Students,* 1 W. L.J. 481, 483 (1844).

228. ROBERTSON, SCRAP BOOK ON LAW AND POLITICS, MEN AND TIMES at 239; *see also The Legal Profession in the United States,* 10 AM. L.J. at 476; *The Practice of the Bar,* 9 L. REP. 241, 242 (1846).

229. *Legal Morality,* 5 L. REP. 529, 531 (1843).

230. MORETTA, WILLIAM PITT BALLINGER: TEXAS LAWYER, SOUTHERN STATESMAN at 35–36.

231. The murder trial is summarized in ANNUAL REGISTER, OR A VIEW OF THE HISTORY AND POLITICS, OF THE YEAR 1840, at 229–41 (London, J.G.F. & J. Rivington 1841).

232. *See generally* DAVID MELLINKOFF, THE CONSCIENCE OF A LAWYER 142 (1973).

233. A series of articles in the popular magazine *Littell's Living Age* shows the importance of the case in the United States. *See Lawyers, Clients, Witnesses, and the Public;*

or, the Examiner and Mr. Phillips, 24 LITTELL'S LIVING AGE 179 (Jan. 26, 1850); *The Examiner and Mr. Phillips,* 24 LITTELL'S LIVING AGE 230 (Feb. 2, 1850); *Lawyers, Clients &c,* 24 LITTELL'S LIVING AGE 306 (Feb. 16, 1850); *The Practice of Advocacy.—Mr. Charles Phillips, and his Defence of Courvoisier,* 25 LITTELL'S LIVING AGE 289 (May 18, 1850).

234. *Professional Ethics,* 9 AM. L.J. 477–78 (1850); *see also* RICHARD B. KIMBALL, THE LAWYER: THE DIGNITY, DUTIES, AND RESPONSIBILITIES OF HIS PROFESSION 23–27 (New York, George P. Putnam & Co. 1853); Charles P. James, *Lawyers and Their Traits,* 9 W. L.J. 49, 65 (1851).

235. GEOFFREY C. HAZARD, JR., ETHICS IN THE PRACTICE OF LAW 150 (1978); SHARSWOOD, A COMPEND OF LECTURES ON THE AIMS AND DUTIES OF THE PROFESSION OF LAW at 40–41, 107–19.

236. *The Practice of the Bar,* 9 L. REP. at 241; *Professional Conduct.—The Courvoisier Case,* 12 MONTHLY L. REP. 433 (1850); *Mr. Charles Phillips's Defence of Courvoisier,* 12 MONTHLY L. REP. 536 (1850); *Mr. Phillips and the Courvoisier Case,* 12 MONTHLY L. REP. 481 (1850); *Mr. Charles Phillips and the Courvoisier Case,* 12 MONTHLY L. REP. 553 (1850).

237. *The Practice of the Bar,* 9 L. REP. at 242, 242–43, 249.

238. CHARLES W. WOLFRAM, MODERN LEGAL ETHICS 571–72 (1986).

239. [David Dudley Field], *The Study and Practice of the Law,* 14 U.S. MAG. & DEM. REV. at 345, 347–48 (1844).

240. *The Practice of the Bar,* 9 L. REP. at 242.

241. SHARSWOOD, A COMPEND OF LECTURES ON THE AIMS AND DUTIES OF THE PROFESSION OF LAW at 26–27.

242. Fragment: Notes for a Law Lecture, CW 10:20.

243. Plea, filed Jan. 24, 1860 [64487]; Judgment, dated June 29, 1860 [64501], *Rice v. Blakeman* case file [L02198], LPAL.

244. Plea, filed May 29, 1854 [3769]; Order of Dismissal, dated Oct. 25, 1856 [60588], *McFarland v. Layton* case file [L01971], LPAL.

245. *Maus v. Worthing,* 4 Ill. (3 Scam.) 26, 26 (1841).

246. *Id.* at 26–27 (Breese, J., dissenting).

247. Order, dated Dec. 17, 1841 [69238], *Dow v. Averill* [L01229] case file, LPAL.

248. DENNIS K. BOMAN, THE LIFE OF ABIEL LEONARD: EMINENT JURIST AND PASSIONATE UNIONIST 44–45 (1998) (Ph.D. dissertation, University of Missouri).

249. [Field], *The Study and Practice of the Law,* 14 U.S. MAG. & DEM. REV. at 348; *see also The Abuses of Law Courts,* 21 U.S. MAG. & DEM. REV. at 306–07.

250. Teresa Stanton Collett, *The Common Good and the Duty to Represent: Must the Last Lawyer in Town Take Any Case?,* 40 S. TEX. L. REV. 137 (1999).

251. JOHN T. NOONAN, JR., PERSONS AND MASKS OF THE LAW 19–20 (1976).

6—Working for the Railroad

1. GORE VIDAL, LINCOLN: A NOVEL 8, 29, 146, 156, 177, 197 (1984).

2. *See, e.g.,* DONALD, LINCOLN 155–56, 196–97 (1995); GIENAPP, ABRAHAM LINCOLN AND CIVIL WAR AMERICA at 45; OATES, WITH MALICE TOWARD NONE at 113, 148; THOMAS, ABRAHAM LINCOLN at 157.

3. DAVIS, FRONTIER ILLINOIS at 18, 364–65, 372.

4. GEORGE ROGERS TAYLOR, THE TRANSPORTATION REVOLUTION 1815–1860, at 79 (1951).

5. FARAGHER, SUGAR CREEK: LIFE ON THE ILLINOIS PRAIRIE at 179.

6. FEHRENBACHER, PRELUDE TO GREATNESS: LINCOLN IN THE 1850s, at 7–9.

7. ELY, RAILROADS AND AMERICAN LAW at 1–43; SARAH H. GORDON, PASSAGE TO UNION:

How the Railroads Transformed American Life, 1829–1929, at 56–76 (1997); Leonard W. Levy, *Chief Justice Shaw and the Formative Period of American Railroad Law* (pts. 1 & 2), 51 Colum. L. Rev. 327, 852 (1951); Charles Warren, A History of the American Bar 475 (1966) (1911).

8. Diary of William Pitt Ballinger (June 23, 1860), *quoted in* Moretta, William Pitt Ballinger: Texas Lawyer, Southern Statesman at 230.

9. *Notices of New Books*, 14 L. Rep. 102, 102–03 (1851).

10. W.P. Gregg & Benjamin Pond, The Railroad Laws and Charters of the United States (Boston, Charles C. Little & James Brown 1851).

11. 1 Chauncey Smith & Samuel W. Bates, Cases Relating to the Law of Railways, Decided in the Supreme Court of the United States, And in the Courts of the Several States iii (Boston, Little, Brown & Co. 1854).

12. Pierce, Treatise on American Railroad Law; Redfield, A Practical Treatise Upon the Law of Railways.

13. William H. Herndon to [Edward L.] Pierce (Mar. 4, 1861), Herndon-Weik Collection, Library of Congress.

14. *See* Alfred D. Chandler, Jr., *Patterns of American Railroad Finance, 1830–50*, 28 Bus. Hist. Rev. 248 (1954); Alfred D. Chandler, Jr., *The Railroads: Pioneers in Modern Corporate Management*, 39 Bus. Hist. Rev. 16 (1965).

15. John F. Stover, History of the Illinois Central Railroad 69 (1975).

16. Beard, *Lincoln and the Illinois Central Railroad*, 92 Lincoln Herald at 16; Elmer A. Smith, Abraham Lincoln: An Illinois Central Lawyer (pamph. 1945).

17. Thomas, *The Eighth Judicial Circuit*, Bull. Abraham Lincoln Ass'n at 3, 5; Paul M. Angle, *Abraham Lincoln: Circuit Lawyer*, Lincoln Centennial Ass'n Papers 19–41 (1928); King, Lincoln's Manager, David Davis 70–98; Richard Friend Lufkin, *Mr. Lincoln's Light From Under a Bushel—1853*, 55 Lincoln Herald 2, 9 (Winter 1953); Richard Friend Lufkin, *Mr. Lincoln's Light From Under a Bushel—1854*, 56 Lincoln Herald 3, 17 (Winter 1954).

18. Wayne C. Temple, *Lincoln, Moore and Greene: A New Document*, 93 Lincoln Herald 9, 9–10 (Spring 1991); Henry C. Whitney to William H. Herndon (Aug. 27, 1887), *in* Herndon's Informants: Letters, Interviews, and Statements About Lincoln at 630; Jesse W. Weik, The Real Lincoln: A Portrait 194–95 (1922).

19. Sabin D. Puterbaugh, Puterbaugh's Illinois Pleadings and Practice 246–57, 219–20 (Peoria, Henry Nolte 1864).

20. Levy, *Chief Justice Shaw and the Formative Period of American Railroad Law*, 51 Colum. L. Rev. at 337–38; *see also* Pierce, Treatise on American Railroad Law at 138–214; Redfield, A Practical Treatise Upon the Law of Railways 133–58, 170–84.

21. Pierce, Treatise on American Railroad Law at 406–502; Redfield, A Practical Treatise Upon the Law of Railways at 232–353.

22. Comment, *The Creation of a Common Law Rule*, 132 U. Pa. L. Rev. 579; Alfred S. Konefsky, *"As Best to Subserve Their Own Interests": Lemuel Shaw, Labor Conspiracy, and Fellow Servants*, 7 Law & Hist. Rev. 219 (1989); Redfield, A Practical Treatise Upon the Law of Railways at 386–90; Pierce, Treatise on American Railroad Law at 56–126; Tomlins, *A Mysterious Power: Industrial Accidents and the Legal Construction of Employment Relations in Massachusetts* 6 Law & Hist. Rev. 375.

23. Beard, *"I have labored hard to find the law": Abraham Lincoln and the Alton and Sangamon Railroad*, 85 Ill. Hist. J. 209; *see generally* Pierce, Treatise on American Railroad Law at 56–126.

24. *See, e.g.*, Declaration, filed May 5, 1854 [39365], *Allen v. Illinois Central R.R.* [L00770], *Declaration, filed May 5, 1854 [33260], Carey v. Illinois Central R.R.* [L00531],

Declaration, filed May 5, 1854 [33386], *Dye v. Illinois Central R.R.* [L00545], Agreement, filed Sept. 21, 1855 [5085], *Spencer v. Illinois Central R.R.* [L00657] case files, LPAL.

25. STOVER, HISTORY OF THE ILLINOIS CENTRAL RAILROAD at 26–32; PAUL WALLACE GATES, THE ILLINOIS CENTRAL RAILROAD AND ITS COLONIZATION WORK 78–80 (1934).

26. ELY, RAILROADS AND AMERICAN LAW at 35–39.

27. Levy, *Chief Justice Shaw and the Formative Period of American Railroad Law*, 51 COLUM. L. REV. at 337–38; *see also* ROBERT S. HUNT, LAW AND LOCOMOTIVES: THE IMPACT OF THE RAILROAD ON WISCONSIN LAW IN THE NINETEENTH CENTURY 69 (1958).

28. *Barger v. Illinois Central R.R.* [L00516], *Howser v. Illinois Central R.R.* [L01654], *Illinois Central R.R. v. Hill* [L00608], *McGinnis v. Illinois Central R.R.* [L01374] case files, LPAL.

29. An act to provide for a general system of railroad incorporations, approved Nov. 5, 1849, 15th G.A., Ill. Laws 18–33 (1853); PIERCE, TREATISE ON AMERICAN RAILROAD LAW at 184–203.

30. An Act to Provide for a General System of Railroad Incorporations, approved Nov. 5, 1849, 15th G.A., sec. 22, Ill. Laws 24–28 (1853).

31. An Act to Amend the Law Condemning Right of Way for Purposes of Internal Improvement, approved June 22, 1852, 17th G.A., 2nd sess., Ill. Laws 146–52 (1852).

32. *See, e.g.,* Petition, filed May 5, 1853 [32743], Order, filed May 30, 1853 [32745], Certificate, filed June 11, 1853 [32746], Commissioner's Final Report, filed June 13, 1853 [32747], *Illinois Central R.R. v. Barger* [L00515] case file, LPAL.

33. An Act to Amend the Law Condemning Right of Way for Purposes of Internal Improvement, approved June 22, 1852, 17th G.A., 2nd sess., Ill. Laws at 149.

34. ELY, RAILROADS AND AMERICAN LAW at 38; *but see* KOSTAL, LAW AND ENGLISH RAILWAY CAPITALISM 1825–1875, at 160.

35. *Barger v. Illinois Central R.R.* [L00516], *Howser v. Illinois Central R.R.* [L01654], *Illinois Central R.R. v. Hill* [L00608], *McGinnis v. Illinois Central R.R.* [L01374] case files, LPAL.

36. *Howser v. Illinois Central R.R.* [L01654] case file, LPAL.

37. Judgment, dated Oct. 17, 1853 [32759], *Barger v. Illinois Central R.R.* [L00515] case file, LPAL.

38. *See* Tony Freyer, *Reassessing the Impact of Eminent Domain in Early American Economic Development*, 1981 WIS. L. REV. 1263, 1271.

39. THOMAS, LAWYERING FOR THE RAILROAD: BUSINESS, LAW, AND POWER IN THE NEW SOUTH at 15.

40. Amended petition, filed Apr. 15, 1853 [4978], *Howser v. Illinois Central R.R.* [L01654] case file, LPAL.

41. *Alton & Sangamon R.R. v. Baugh*, 14 Ill. 211, 211–12 (1852).

42. *Alton & Sangamon R.R. v. Carpenter*, 14 Ill. 190 (1852); *Alton & Sangamon R.R. v. Baugh*, 14 Ill. 211 (1852).

43. Judgment, dated Sept. 1, 1852 [83209], *Alton & Sangamon R.R. v. Baugh* [L02615] case file, LPAL; *Alton & Sangamon R.R. v. Baugh*, 14 Ill. at 211–12.

44. *Alton & Sangamon R.R. v. Carpenter*, 14 Ill. at 190.

45. Transcript [4787], *Alton & Sangamon R.R. v. Carpenter* [L02617] case file, LPAL.

46. *See, e.g., M'Intire v. State*, 5 Blackf. 384 (Ind. 1840); *Pennsylvania R.R. v. Heister*, 8 Pa. 445 (1848); *Symonds v. City of Cincinnati*, 14 Ohio 148 (1846); *see also* PIERCE, TREATISE ON AMERICAN RAILROAD LAW at 206–07.

47. JAMES W. ELY, JR., THE GUARDIAN OF EVERY OTHER RIGHT: A CONSTITUTIONAL HISTORY OF PROPERTY RIGHTS 77 (1992); HARRY N. SCHEIBER, OHIO CANAL ERA: A CASE STUDY OF GOVERNMENT AND THE ECONOMY, 1820–1861, at 277–78 (1969).

48. *Alton & Sangamon R.R. v. Carpenter*, 14 Ill. at 190.

49. *Id.* at 191–92. The court cited *M'Intire v. State*, 5 Blackf. 384 (Ind. 1840); *Pennsylvania R.R. v. Heister*, 8 Pa. 445 (1848); and *Symonds v. City of Cincinnati*, 14 Ohio 148 (1846).

50. An Act to Amend the Law Condemning Right of Way for Purposes of Internal Improvement, approved June 22, 1852, 17th G.A. 2nd Sess., Ill. Laws 43 (1852).

51. *Alton & Sangamon R.R. v. Carpenter*, 14 Ill. at 192.

52. *Allen v. Illinois Central R.R.* [L00662], *Allen v. Illinois Central R.R.* [L00663], *Allen v. Illinois Central R.R.* [L00664], *Allen v. Illinois Central R.R.* [L00767], *Allen v. Illinois Central R.R.* [L00768], *Allen v. Illinois Central R.R.* [L00769], *Illinois Central R.R. v. Allen* [L00770] case files, LPAL.

53. Witness Affidavit, dated May 18, 1854, *Barger v. Illinois Central R.R.* [L00515], Witness Affidavit, dated May 19, 1854 [33399], *Cundiff v. Illinois Central R.R.* [L00537], Witness Affidavit, dated May 19, 1854 [33456], *Cundiff v. Illinois Central R.R.* [L00538], Bond for Costs, dated Oct. 17, 1854 [34141], *Lear v. Illinois Central R.R.* [L00575], Bond for Costs, dated May 18, 1854 [34923], *Weaver v. Illinois Central R.R.* [L00614] case files, LPAL.

54. Declaration, filed May 5, 1854 [36420], Jury verdict, dated Oct. 17, 1855 [40220], Agreed judgment, filed Oct. 17, 1855 [36443], *Allen v. Illinois Central R.R.* [L00662] case file LPAL.

55. Summons, dated Sept. 25, 1857 [36433], Demurrer [Mar. 1859] [6849], *Allen v. Illinois Central R.R.* [L00663] case file, LPAL.

56. Declaration, filed Feb. 20, 1857 [36446], Demurrer, filed Mar. 5, 1858 [40959], Plea and Notice, Mar. 12, 1858 [36445], *Allen v. Illinois Central R.R.* [L00664] case file, LPAL.

57. Docket entry, dated Oct. 6, 1857 [36463], *Allen v. Illinois Central R.R.* [L00664] case file, LPAL.

58. Declaration, dated Sept. 23, 1859 [39359], Plea, filed Mar. 12, 1858 [39361], Judgment, Aug. 17, 1863 [39396], *Allen v. Illinois Central R.R.* [L00770] case file, LPAL; *Illinois Central R.R. v. Allen*, 39 Ill. 205, 207–09 (1866); C.H. Moore to AL (Feb. 17, 1860), Abraham Lincoln Papers at the Library of Congress, <memory.loc.gov/ammem/alhtml/malhome.html>, Select: Search by Keyword, Enter: Clifton Moore, Select: Item 1.

59. *Alton & Sangamon R.R. v. Baugh*, 14 Ill. 211, 212 (1852); *see also* Pierce, Treatise on American Railroad Law at 320–32.

60. An Act to Regulate the Duties and Liabilities of Railroad Companies, approved Feb. 14, 1855, 19th G.A., Ill. Laws 173–74 (1855).

61. *See, e.g.,* Declaration, filed Oct. 4, 1855 [40988], *Spencer v. Illinois Central R.R.* [L00638], Declaration, filed Apr. 29, 1854 [127971], *Hill v. Illinois Central R.R.* [L00606], case files, LPAL.

62. Pierce, Treatise on American Railroad Law at 352.

63. *Chicago & Rock Island R.R. v. Ward*, 16 Ill. 522, 530 (1855).

64. AL to Mason Brayman (Mar. 31, 1854) [130031], *Lincoln referred legal client to Stuart* [N05243], LPAL; *see also* Beard, *Lincoln and the Illinois Central Railroad*, 92 Lincoln Herald at 16–17.

65. *Allen v. Illinois Central R.R.* [L00767], *Allen v. Illinois Central R.R.* [L00768], *Barger v. Illinois Central R.R.* [L00516], *Carey v. Illinois Central R.R.* [L00531], *Cushman v. Illinois Central R.R.* [L00539], *Dye v. Illinois Central R.R.* [L00545], *Hill v. Illinois Central R.R.* [L00606], *Hill v. Illinois Central R.R.* [L00607], *Spencer v. Illinois Central R.R.* [L00638] case files, LPAL.

66. Mason Brayman, Report, dated Oct. 31, 1854 [72679], *Weaver v. Illinois Central R.R.* [L00614] case file, LPAL.

67. Decree, dated Aug. 10, 1864 [38018], *Allen v. Illinois Central R.R.* [L00767], Decree, dated Aug. 11, 1864 [39344], *Allen v. Illinois Central R.R.* [L00768], Order of Dismissal, dated May 15, 1854 [32779], *Barger v. Illinois Central R.R.* [L00516], Agreed Judgment, filed Nov. 15, 1854 [40986], *Dye v. Illinois Central R.R.* [L00545], Order of Dismissal, dated May 13, 1856 [34719], *Hill v. Illinois Central R.R.* [L00607], Agreed Order of Dismissal, dated May 12, 1856 [35352], *Spencer v. Illinois Central R.R.* [L00638] case files, LPAL.

68. Mason Brayman, Report, dated Oct. 31, 1854 [72679], *Weaver v. Illinois Central R.R.* [L00614] case file, LPAL.

69. Declaration, filed Oct. 4, 1855 [40988], Order, dated May 12, 1856 [35352], *William Spencer v. Illinois Central* [L00638] case file, LPAL.

70. Declaration, filed Oct. 6, 1854 [40985], Agreed judgment, filed Nov. 15, 1854 [33610], *Dye v. Illinois Central R.R.* [L00545] case file, LPAL.

71. Order, dated May 12, 1856 [32614], *Emery v. Illinois Central R.R.* [L00500] case file, LPAL.

72. Order, dated May 13, 1856 [34719], *Hill v. Illinois Central R.R.* [L00607] case file, LPAL.

73. *See* Judgment, dated May 17, 1855 [34936], *Weaver v. Illinois Central R.R.* [L00614] case file; Jury Verdict [dated Nov. Term 1854] [33384], *Cundiff v. Illinois Central R.R.* [L00537] case files, LPAL.

74. Witness Affidavit, dated May 19, 1854 [33399], *Cundiff v. Illinois Central R.R.* [L00537], Bond for Costs, dated May 18, 1854 [34923], *Weaver v. Illinois Central R.R.* [L00614] case files, LPAL.

75. Declaration, dated May 17, 1854 [34930], Affidavit, dated May 15, 1854 [34922], Bond for Costs, dated May 18, 1854 [34923], Pleas, dated May 19, 1854 [3135], Plea, dated May 19, 1854 [3213], Judgment, dated May 17, 1855 [34936], *Weaver v. Illinois Central R.R.* [L00614] case file.

76. Mason Brayman, Report, dated Oct. 31, 1854 [72679], *Weaver v. Illinois Central R.R.* [L00614] case file, LPAL.

77. *Quoted in* Bruce Collins, *The Lincoln-Douglas Contest of 1858 and Illinois' Electorate*, 20 J. AM. STUD. 391, 412 (1986).

78. Declaration, filed May 5, 1854 [36359], Judgment, dated Nov. 16, 1854 [36373], *William Spencer v. Illinois Central R.R.* [L00657] case file, LPAL.

79. Declaration, filed May 5, 1854 [36315], Judgment, dated May 15, 1855 [36350], *John Spencer v. Illinois Central R.R.* [L00656] case file, LPAL.

80. Declaration, filed Oct. 5, 1854 [34128], Judgment, dated Nov. 16, 1854 [34142], *Lear v. Illinois Central R.R.* [L00575] case file, LPAL.

81. *Carey v. Illinois Central R.R.* [L00531], *Cushman v. Illinois Central R.R.* [L00539], *Hill v. Illinois Central R.R.* [L00606] case files, LPAL.

82. Judgment, dated Nov. 14, 1854 [33280], *Carey v. Illinois Central R.R.* [L00531]; Judgment, dated Nov. 11, 1854 [33493], *Cushman v. Illinois Central R.R.* [L00539]; Judgment, dated May 17, 1855 [34666], *Hill v. Illinois Central R.R.* [L00606]; case files, LPAL.

83. Stipulation, filed Nov. 11, 1854 [40983], Judgment, dated Nov. 11, 1854 [33493], *Cushman v. Illinois Central R.R.* [L00539] case file, LPAL.

84. Declaration, filed May 31, 1855 [3628], *Gatling v. Great Western R.R.* [L00480] case file, LPAL.

85. *See* Declaration, filed Mar. 3, 1854 [5139], *Harris v. Great Western R.R.* [L03753] case file, LPAL.

86. WALTER LICHT, WORKING FOR THE RAILROAD: THE ORGANIZATION OF WORK IN THE NINETEENTH CENTURY 181 (1983); DAVID L. LIGHTNER, LABOR ON THE ILLINOIS CENTRAL RAILROAD 1852–1900, at 120 (1977).

87. HORWITZ, THE TRANSFORMATION OF AMERICAN LAW at 208.

88. LIGHTNER, LABOR ON THE ILLINOIS CENTRAL RAILROAD 1852–1900, at 122–26; *see also* LICHT, WORKING FOR THE RAILROAD at 201–07.

89. LICHT, WORKING FOR THE RAILROAD at 199, 204–05.

90. *Id.* at 199 (workers rationally calculated that the possibilities of winning in court were quite slim).

91. ELY, RAILROADS AND AMERICAN LAW at 213–14; KOSTAL, LAW AND ENGLISH RAILWAY CAPITALISM 1825–1875, at 256–70.

92. KOSTAL, LAW AND ENGLISH RAILWAY CAPITALISM 1825–1875, at 256.

93. John Fabian Witt, Note, *The Transformation of Work and the Law of Workplace Accidents, 1842–1910*, 107 YALE L.J. 1467, 1469 (1998).

94. Comment, *The Creation of a Common Law Rule*, 132 U. PA. L. REV. 579.

95. *Farwell v. Boston & Worchester R.R.*, 45 Mass. (4 Met.) 49 (1842); *see generally* Comment, *The Creation of a Common Law Rule*, 132 U. PA. L. REV. 579; Konefsky, *"As Best to Subserve Their Own Interests,"* 7 LAW & HIST. REV. 219; KOSTAL, LAW AND ENGLISH RAILWAY CAPITALISM 1825–1875, at 268–70; Tomlins, *A Mysterious Power: Industrial Accidents and the Legal Construction of Employment Relations in Massachusetts*, 6 LAW & HIST. REV. at 375.

96. *Honner v. Illinois Central R.R.*, 15 Ill. 550, 551–52 (1854); *see also Illinois Central R.R. v. Cox*, 21 Ill. 20 (1858).

97. REDFIELD, A PRACTICAL TREATISE UPON THE LAW OF RAILWAYS at 386–87.

98. *Aurora Branch R.R. v. Grimes*, 13 Ill. 585, 587 (1852).

99. Engel, *The Oven-Bird's Song: Insiders, Outsiders, and Personal Injuries in an American Community*, 18 LAW & SOC'Y REV. at 559.

100. *See, e.g.*, Opinion, dated Jan. 31, 1859 [131082], *Lincoln provided legal opinion to Bureau County Commissioners* [N05384], LPAL.

101. Opinion on Pre-emption of Public Land (Mar. 6, 1856), CW 2:333–35.

102. 5 Stat. ch. 16 (1841); FRIEDMAN, A HISTORY OF AMERICAN LAW at 170; *see also* PAUL W. GATES, HISTORY OF PUBLIC LAND LAW DEVELOPMENT 219–47 (1968).

103. 5 Stat. ch. 16, § 10 (1841).

104. 10 Stat. ch. 78 (1852).

105. 10 Stat. ch. 143 (1853).

106. Opinion on Pre-emption of Public Land (Mar. 6, 1856), CW 2:335.

107. GATES, HISTORY OF PUBLIC LAND LAW DEVELOPMENT at 216.

108. *Walker v. Jacob*, 18 Ill. 570, 572 (1857).

109. *Illinois Central R.R. v. White*, 18 Ill. 164 (1856).

110. Thomas, *Lincoln and the Courts, 1854–1861*, ABRAHAM LINCOLN ASS'N PAPERS at 84–85.

111. *Illinois Central R.R. v. Cassell*, 17 Ill. 388 (1856); *Illinois Central R.R. v. Downey*, 18 Ill. 259 (1857); *Illinois Central R.R. v. Alexander*, 20 Ill. 23 (1858); *Illinois Central R.R. v. Finnigan*, 21 Ill. 645 (1859); *Illinois Central R.R. v. Palmer*, 24 Ill. 43 (1860); *Illinois Central R.R. v. Taylor*, 24 Ill. 323 (1860).

112. *Illinois Central R.R. v. Morrison*, 19 Ill. 136, 141 (1857).

113. *C. Thompson & Co. v. Illinois Central R.R.* [L01309], *Gatewood & Co. v. Illinois Central R.R.* [L01351], *Brock, Hays & Co. v. Illinois Central R.R.* [L01373], *Morrison & Crabtree v. Illinois Central R.R.* [L00708], *J.C. Johnson & Bro. v. Illinois Central R.R.* [L00569], *Woodward v. Illinois Central R.R.* [L00507] case files, LPAL.

114. REDFIELD, A PRACTICAL TREATISE UPON THE LAW OF RAILWAYS *264.

115. *Illinois Central R.R. v. Morrison*, 19 Ill. at 139.

116. ELY, RAILROADS AND AMERICAN LAW at 183.

117. Robert J. Kaczorowski, *The Common-Law Background of Nineteenth-Century Tort Law*, 51 OHIO ST. L.J. 1127, 1151–52 (1990); REDFIELD, A PRACTICAL TREATISE UPON THE LAW OF RAILWAYS at *268.

118. *Illinois Central R.R. v. Morrison*, 19 Ill. at 141.

119. Judge's Docket, dated Apr. Term 1859 [36778], Judgment Docket, dated Apr. 28, 1859 [36777], *Morrison & Crabtree v. Illinois Central R.R.* [L00708] case file, LPAL.

120. FRIEDMAN, A HISTORY OF AMERICAN LAW at 178.

121. *Radcliff v. Crosby*, 23 Ill. 473 (1860) (Chicago, E.B. Myers 1862). In later editions of the *Illinois Reports*, *Radcliff* is listed in a footnote in *Rogers v. Ward*, 23 Ill. 473 (1860).

122. *Illinois Central R.R. v. Brock, Hays & Co.*, 19 Ill. 166 (1857).

123. ELY, RAILROADS AND AMERICAN LAW at 32.

124. AL to James F. Joy (Jan. 25, 1854), CW 2:209–10.

125. Ill. Const. art. 9, § 5 (1848).

126. *Transcript*, dated Sept. 21, 1853 [70658], *Illinois Central R.R. v. County of McLean* [L01655] case file, LPAL.

127. *Assignment of Errors* [Dec. Term 1853] [4881], *Illinois Central R.R. v. County of McLean* [L01655] case file, LPAL.

128. *Illinois Central R.R. v. County of McLean*, 17 Ill. 291, 291 (1855).

129. Brief of Argument in *Abraham Lincoln vs. Illinois Central Railroad* (June 23, 1857), CW 2:397.

130. Brief (Dec. Term 1853) [3230], *Illinois Central R.R. v. County of McLean* [L01655] case file, LPAL; *Illinois Central R.R. v. County of McLean*, 17 Ill. 291, 295–96 (1855). Four of the cases that the court cited were from an annotation in *American Railway Cases* that Lincoln had referred to his argument. SMITH & BATES, CASES RELATING TO THE LAW OF RAILWAYS, DECIDED IN THE SUPREME COURT OF THE UNITED STATES, AND IN THE COURTS OF THE SEVERAL STATES at 354–55.

131. WEIK, THE REAL LINCOLN: A PORTRAIT at 153.

132. *Illinois Central R.R. v. County of McLean*, 17 Ill. at 292–93.

133. Brief (Dec. Term 1853) [3230], *Illinois Central R.R. v. County of McLean* [L01655] case file, LPAL. Lincoln based this discussion on a note in *American Railway Cases*. *See* 1 SMITH & BATES, CASES RELATING TO THE LAW OF RAILWAYS, DECIDED IN THE SUPREME COURT OF THE UNITED STATES, AND IN THE COURTS OF THE SEVERAL STATES at 354–55.

134. Brief (Dec. Term 1853) [3230], *Illinois Central R.R. v. County of McLean* [L01655] case file, LPAL.

135. *Id.* Lincoln cited "4 Cond. 466–84" and "2 Peters 449." The first reference was to the fourth volume of Condensed Reports of Cases in the Supreme Court by Richard Peters. The case that begins on page 466 is *M'Culloch v. Maryland*, which is also found at 17 U.S. (4 Wheat.) 316 (1819). *Weston v. Charleston* is found at 27 U.S. (2 Pet.) 449 (1829).

136. STOVER, HISTORY OF THE ILLINOIS CENTRAL RAILROAD at 55–56.

137. *Illinois Central R.R. v. County of McLean*, 17 Ill. 291, 297–99 (1855).

138. Brief (Dec. Term 1853) [3230], *Illinois Central R.R. v. County of McLean* [L01655] case file, LPAL.

139. 1 JAMES KENT, COMMENTARIES ON AMERICAN LAW 447–49 (8th ed. New York, William Kent 1854).

140. *Sawyer v. City of Alton*, 4 Ill. (3 Scam.) 127 (1841).

141. *Sawyer v. City of Alton*, 4 Ill. (3 Scam.) 127, 130 (1841).

142. *Illinois Central R.R. v. County of McLean*, 17 Ill. at 295.

143. *Id.* at 295–96. The court cited *State Bank of Illinois v. The People*, 5 Ill. (4 Scam.) 304 (1843); *Mayor v. Baltimore & Ohio R.R.*, 31 Md. (6 Gill.) 288 (1848); *O'Donnell v. Bailey*, 24 Miss. 386 (1852); *Gardner v. State*, 21 N.J.L. (1 Zab.) 557 (1845); *Camden & Amboy R.R. v. Commissioners of Appeal*, 18 N.J.L. (3 Har.) 71 (1840); *Camden & Amboy R.R. v. Commissioners of Appeal*, 18 N.J.L. (3 Har.) 11 (1840); *State v. Berry*, 17 N.J.L. (2 Har.) 80 (1839).

144. *State Bank v. People*, 5 Ill. (4 Scam.) at 305.

145. Brief (Dec. Term 1853) [3230], *Illinois Central R.R. v. County of McLean* [L01655] *case file, LPAL.*

146. *Kirby v. Shaw*, 19 Pa. (7 Har.) 258, 261 (1852).

147. *State Bank v. People*, 5 Ill. (4 Scam.) at 305.

148. Brief (Dec. Term 1853) [3230], *Illinois Central R.R. v. County of McLean* [L01655] case file, LPAL.

149. *Id.*

150. *People ex rel. Stickney v. Marshall*, 6 Ill. (1 Gilm.) 672, 688 (1844).

151. *Illinois Central R.R. v. County of McLean*, 17 Ill. at 291, 295–97.

152. ELY, RAILROADS AND AMERICAN LAW at 34.

153. An Act to Incorporate the Illinois Central Railroad Company, approved Feb. 10, 1851, 17th G.A., Ill. Laws 61, 72–73 (1851).

154. *State of Illinois vs. Illinois Central Railroad Company*, ILL. ST. REG. (Dec. 7, 1858) [131493], *reprinted in People v. Illinois Central R.R.* [L02468] case file, LPAL.

155. Opinion on the Two-Mill Tax (Dec. 1, 1858), CW 10:37–38.

156. G.S. Borit, *A New Lincoln Text: An Opinion on an Illinois Tax*, 75 LINCOLN HERALD 152, 154 (Winter 1973); G.S. Borit, *Another New Lincoln Text: Some Thoughts Concerning an Outrageous Suggestion About Abraham Lincoln "Corporation Lawyer,"* 77 LINCOLN HERALD 27, 27 (Spring 1975); Opinion on the Two-Mill Tax (Dec. 1, 1858), CW 10:37 n.1.

157. Ebenezer Lane to W.H. Osborn (Aug. 12, 1857), Illinois Central Railroad Archives, Newberry Library, Chicago, Illinois.

158. Ebenezer Lane to W.H. Osborn (Aug. 14, 1857), Illinois Central Railroad Archives, Newberry Library, Chicago, Illinois.

159. *Id.*

160. David Stewart to Stephen A. Douglas (Jan. 20, 1859) [74750], *People v. Illinois Central R.R.* [L02468] case file, LPAL.

161. NEELY, THE ABRAHAM LINCOLN ENCYCLOPEDIA at 91–92; Jesse K. Dubois to AL (Nov. 21, 1854), Abraham Lincoln Papers at the Library of Congress, <memory.loc.gov/ammem/alhtml/malhome.html>, Select: Search by Keyword, Enter: Dubois Senate, Select: Item 3.

162. AL to Jesse K. Dubois (Dec. 21, 1857), CW 2:429.

163. Paul M. Angle, *Lincoln Defended Railroad*, ILL. CENT. MAG. at 42 (Feb. 1929).

164. Charles LeRoy Brown, *Abraham Lincoln and the Illinois Central Railroad, 1857–1860*, 36 J. ILL. ST. HIST. SOC'Y at 123, 139–40 (1943).

165. Brown, *Abraham Lincoln and the Illinois Central Railroad, 1857–1860*, 36 J. ILL. ST. HIST. SOC'Y at 147; An Act in relation to assessments of the Illinois Central Railroad Company, approved Feb. 21, 1859, 21st G.A., Ill. Laws 206–07 (1859).

166. David Stewart to Stephen A. Douglas (Jan. 20, 1859) [74750], *People v. Illinois Central R.R.* [L02468] case file, LPAL.

167. An Act in relation to assessments of the Illinois Central Railroad Company, approved Feb. 21, 1859, 21st G.A., Ill. Laws 206–07 (1859).

168. List and Valuation of Assets, dated Oct. 15, 1859 [74752], *People v. Illinois Central R.R.* [L02468] case file, LPAL.

169. The Lincoln Log, The Papers of Abraham Lincoln, <http://www.papersofabrahamlincoln.org/reference.htm>, Select: Browse, Select: 1859, Select: July.

170. List and Valuation of Assets, dated Oct. 15, 1859 [74752], *People v. Illinois Central R.R.* [L02468] case file, LPAL.

171. AL to Jesse K. Dubois (Oct. 10, 1859), CW 3:486.

172. Brown, *Abraham Lincoln and the Illinois Central Railroad, 1857–1860*, 36 J. ILL. ST. HIST. SOC'Y at 154–55. Brown relied on Justice Breese's notes on the case, which are no longer extant.

173. *State v. Illinois Central R.R.*, 27 Ill. 64, 66–67 (1861).

174. Brown, *Abraham Lincoln and the Illinois Central Railroad, 1857–1860*, 36 J. ILL. ST. HIST. SOC'Y at 155.

175. *State v. Illinois Central R.R.*, 27 Ill. at 66–67.

176. James H. Stokes to AL (Jan. 31, 1860) [131138], *People v. Illinois Central R.R.* [L02468] case file, LPAL.

177. Robert L. Nelson, *Practice and Privilege: Social Change and the Structure of Large Law Firms*, 1981 AM. B. FOUND. RES. J. 95, 115.

178. ERSHKOWITZ, THE ORIGIN OF THE WHIG AND DEMOCRATIC PARTIES at 180.

7—A Changing Legal Landscape

1. E.P. Thompson, *Time, Work-Discipline, and Industrial Capitalism*, PAST & PRESENT 56, 56–63 (1967); P.S. ATIYAH, THE RISE AND FALL OF FREEDOM OF CONTRACT 273–74 (1979).

2. WINKLE, THE YOUNG EAGLE: THE RISE OF ABRAHAM LINCOLN at 70.

3. [Field], *The Study and Practice of the Law*, 14 U.S. MAG. & DEM. REV. 345, 345.

4. HERNDON'S LINCOLN at 274–75.

5. *Id.* at 261–62.

6. AL to Richard J. Thomas (June 27, 1850), CW 2:80. Herndon wrote "this hat of Lincoln's—a silk plug—was an extraordinary receptacle. It was his desk and memorandum-book. In it he carried his bank book and the bulk of his letters." HERNDON'S LINCOLN at 263.

7. Henry C. Whitney, Statement (Nov. 1866), *in* HERNDON'S INFORMANTS: LETTERS, INTERVIEWS, AND STATEMENTS ABOUT LINCOLN at 405.

8. The Illinois statute of limitations for a suit on a note was sixteen years. An Act to Amend the Several Laws Concerning Limitations of Actions, approved Nov. 5, 1849, 16th G.A., 2nd Sess., Ill. Laws 44 (1849).

9. AL to Blatchford, Seward & Griswold (Apr. 19, 1858) (original owned by Cravath, Swaine & Moore, New York City.)

10. Blatchford, Seward & Griswold to AL (Dec. 9, 1858), *available at* Abraham Lincoln Papers at the Library of Congress, <memory.loc.gov/ammem/alhtml/malhome.html>, Select: Search by Keyword, Enter: Blatchford, Select: Item 3.

11. AL to Blatchford, Seward & Griswold (Dec. 14, 1858) (original owned by Cravath, Swaine & Moore, New York City); *see also* 1 ROBERT T. SWAINE, THE CRAVATH FIRM AND ITS PREDECESSORS 1819–1947, at 163–64 (1946).

12. *See, e.g., S.C. Davis & Co. v. Allen* [L02267]; *S.C. Davis & Co. v. Hillabrant* [L02271]; *S.C. Davis & Co. v. Lowry & Randle* [L02274]; *S.C. Davis & Co. v. Monical & Son* [L02278]; *S.C. Davis & Co. v. Whitney* [L02263] case files, LPAL.

13. *See, e.g., S.C. Davis & Co. v. Allen* ($3,000) [L02267]; *S.C. Davis & Co. v. Dwyer* ($10,000) [L02269]; *S.C. Davis & Co. v. Lowry & Randle* ($1,000) [L02274]; *S.C. Davis &*

Co. v. Sanders ($7,000) [L02256]; *S.C. Davis & Co. v. Wilborn* ($1,500) [L02264]; *S.C. Davis & Co. v. Williams & Hillabrant* ($2,000) [L02265] case files, LPAL.

14. Bill to Foreclose Mortgage, filed Dec. 8, 1857 [65218], *S.C. Davis & Co. v. Campbell & Hundley* [L02268]; Bill to Foreclose Mortgage, filed Dec. 8, 1857 [65242], *S.C. Davis & Co. v. Gibson* [L02270]; Bill to Foreclose Mortgage, filed Dec. 8, 1857 [65287], *S.C. Davis & Co. v. Kinney* [L02273] case files, LPAL.

15. Declaration, filed May 26, 1858 [65372], *S.C. Davis & Co. v. Monical & Son* [L02278] case file, LPAL.

16. Order, dated Jan. 5, 1859 [65377], *S.C. Davis & Co. v. Monical & Son* [L02278] case file, LPAL.

17. *S.C. Davis & Co. v. Dwyer* [L02269] and *S.C. Davis & Co. v. Mace* [L02276] apparently settled as both cases were dismissed. The third case went to trial before the judge, and S.C. Davis received a $2,886.25 judgment. Order, dated Jan. 28, 1858 [65203], *S.C. Davis & Co. v. Allen* [L02267] case file, LPAL.

18. *S.C. Davis & Co. v. Lowry & Randle*, $832.87 [L02274]; *S.C. Davis & Co. v. Sanders*, $699.60 [L02255]; *S.C. Davis & Co. v. Sanders*, $5,372.48 [L02256]; *S.C. Davis & Co. v. Sanders & Sanders*, $666.70 [L02257]; *S.C. Davis & Co. v. Warner*, $744.99 [L02261]; *S.C. Davis & Co. v. Watkins*, $2,433.30 [L02262]; *S.C. Davis & Co. v. Wilborn*, $1,124.38 [L02264]; and *S.C. Davis & Co. v. Williams & Hillabrant*, $1,572.57 [L02265], LPAL.

19. *S.C. Davis & Co. v. Campbell & Hundley* [L02268]; *S.C. Davis & Co. v. Gibson* [L02270]; *S.C. Davis & Co. v. Kinney* [L02273] case files, LPAL.

20. AL to Samuel C. Davis and Company (Feb. 23, 1858), CW 2:434–35.

21. AL to Samuel C. Davis and Company (Nov. 17, 1858), CW 3:338.

22. AL to S.C. Davis & Co. (Nov. 20, 1858), CW 10:35.

23. AL to Samuel C. Davis and Company (Nov. 30, 1858), CW 3:342–43.

24. AL to William M. Fishback (Dec. 19, 1858), CW 3:346.

25. Lincoln reprises the history of the case in an 1859 letter. AL to Samuel Galloway (July 27, 1859), CW 3:393–94.

26. Declaration, filed Dec. 9, 1858 [63073], *Ambos v. James A. Barret & Co.* [L02101] case file, LPAL.

27. Bill to Foreclose Mortgage, filed Dec. 9, 1858 [63055], *Ambos v. Barret* [L02100] case file, LPAL.

28. *See, e.g.,* Peter Ambos to AL (Jan. 5, 1859), *available at* Abraham Lincoln Papers at the Library of Congress, <memory.loc.gov/ammem/alhtml/malhome.html>, Select: Search by Keyword, Enter: Ambos, Select: Item 3.

29. Peter Ambos to AL (Feb. 17, 1859), *available at* Abraham Lincoln Papers at the Library of Congress, <memory.loc.gov/ammem/alhtml/malhome.html>, Select: Search by Keyword, Enter: Ambos, Select: Item 7.

30. Chas. Ambos to AL (Apr. 20, 1859), *available at* Abraham Lincoln Papers at the Library of Congress, <memory.loc.gov/ammem/alhtml/malhome.html>, Select: Search by Keyword, Enter: Ambos, Select: Item 1.

31. AL to Charles Ambos (June 21, 1859), CW 3:386–87.

32. AL to Samuel Galloway (July 27, 1859), CW 3:393–94.

33. *Id.*

34. *Banet v. Alton & Sangamon R.R.*, 13 Ill. 504 (1851); Declaration, filed Jan. 2, 1858 [63829], *Emmitt v. Barret* [L02143] case file, LPAL.

35. Peter Ambos to AL (Jan. 14, 1860), *available at* Abraham Lincoln Papers at the Library of Congress, <memory.loc.gov/ammem/alhtml/malhome.html>, Select: Search by Keyword, Enter: Ambos, Select: Item 2.

36. Peter Ambos to AL (Jan. 21, 1860), *available at* Abraham Lincoln Papers at the Library of Congress, <memory.loc.gov/ammem/alhtml/malhome.html>, Select: Search by Keyword, Enter: Ambos, Select: Item 10.

37. Peter Ambos to AL (Feb. 2, 1860), *available at* Abraham Lincoln Papers at the Library of Congress, <memory.loc.gov/ammem/alhtml/malhome.html>, Select: Search by Keyword, Enter: Ambos, Select: Item 5.

38. Peter Ambos to AL (Feb. 8, 1860), *available at* Abraham Lincoln Papers at the Library of Congress, <memory.loc.gov/ammem/alhtml/malhome.html>, Select: Search by Keyword, Enter: Ambos, Select: Item 9.

39. Peter Ambos to James A. Barret (Feb. 15, 1860), *available at* Abraham Lincoln Papers at the Library of Congress, <memory.loc.gov/ammem/alhtml/malhome.html>, Select: Search by Keyword, Enter: Ambos, Select: Item 8.

40. David Davis, Interview (Sept. 20, 1866), *in* HERNDON'S INFORMANTS: LETTERS, INTERVIEWS, AND STATEMENTS ABOUT LINCOLN at 349.

41. Major J.B. Merwin, *Lincoln in 1860 Declined to Come to New York*, N.Y. EVENING SUN, Feb. 12, 1917, at 9.

42. Speech at Carthage, Illinois (Oct. 22, 1858), CW 3:331. On the political dimensions of Lincoln's representation of the Illinois Central *see* Boritt, *Was Lincoln a Vulnerable Candidate in 1860?*, 27 CIVIL WAR HIST. 32; Collins, *The Lincoln-Douglas Contest of 1858 and Illinois' Electorate*, 20 J. AM. STUD. 391.

43. Speech at Monmouth, Illinois (Oct. 11, 1858), CW 3:244. The reporter for this speech noted that Lincoln "didn't deny the charge that he was then or is now the attorney of the railroad." *Id.*

44. Statement of Anthony Thornton, *quoted in The Story of the Illinois Central Lines during the Civil Conflict 1861–5*, ILL. CENT. MAG. 15 (June 1913).

45. *Quoted in* SMITH, ABRAHAM LINCOLN: AN ILLINOIS CENTRAL LAWYER 5.

46. PRATT, THE PERSONAL FINANCES OF ABRAHAM LINCOLN at 48.

47. AL to William Martin (Feb. 19, 1851), CW 2:98.

48. FEHRENBACHER & FEHRENBACHER, RECOLLECTED WORDS OF ABRAHAM LINCOLN at 374–75 (unlikely that Lincoln lobbied against railroad); THOMAS, ABRAHAM LINCOLN at 156 (Lincoln lobbied for railroad); OATES, WITH MALICE TOWARD NONE at 113 (no evidence Lincoln lobbied for railroad).

49. Stuart & Edwards to Martin L. Bishop (Mar. 12, 1855) [4213], *Bishop v. Illinois Central R.R.* [L01628] case file, LPAL.

50. Declaration, filed Mar. 10, 1854 [4724], Judgment, dated Apr. 20, 1854 [53053], *Bishop v. Illinois Central R.R.* [L01627] case file, LPAL.

51. Judgment, dated Apr. 20, 1854 [53053], *Bishop v. Illinois Central R.R.* [L01627], Order of Dismissal, dated Sept. 9, 1856 [53062], *Bishop v. Illinois Central R.R.* [L01628] case files, LPAL.

52. *Howser v. Illinois Central R.R.* [L01654] case file, LPAL.

53. *Illinois Central R.R. v. McGinnis* [L01374] case file, LPAL.

54. *Barger v. Illinois Central R.R.* [L00515] case file, LPAL.

55. AL to Mason Brayman (Mar. 31, 1854) [130031], *Lincoln referred legal client to Stuart* [N05243], LPAL; *see also* William D. Beard, *Lincoln and the Illinois Central Railroad*, 92 LINCOLN HERALD 16–17 (Spring 1990).

56. AL to Thompson R. Webber (Sept. 12, 1853), CW 2:202.

57. STARR, LINCOLN AND THE RAILROADS 60–61 (1927).

58. AL to Mason Brayman (Oct. 3, 1853), CW 2:205.

59. Mason Brayman to AL (Oct. 7, 1853), Mason Brayman Papers, Chicago Historical Society, Chicago, Illinois.

60. AL to James F. Joy (Sept. 19, 1855), CW 2:326.

61. Frederick Trevor Hill, *Lincoln the Lawyer*, 71 CENTURY MAG. 939, 950 n.1 (Apr. 1906).

62. AL to Mason Brayman (Sept. 23, 1854), CW 2:234.

63. John T. Stuart & AL to Martin L. Bishop (Nov. 10, 1853) [4216], Declaration, filed Mar. 10, 1854 [4724], *Bishop v. Illinois Central R.R.* [L01627] case file, LPAL.

64. Docket entry, dated Apr. 20, 1854 [53053], Docket entry, dated Apr. 11, 1855 [53055], Docket entry, dated Apr. 16, 1856 [53057], *Bishop v. Illinois Central R.R.* [L01627] case file, LPAL.

65. AL to E. Lane (July 25, 1856), CW 11:12; Declaration, filed Apr. Term 1857 [4533], *Lincoln v. Illinois Central R.R.* [L01660] case file, LPAL.

66. CHICAGO J., Oct. 5, 1858, *reprinted in* THE LINCOLN-DOUGLAS DEBATES OF 1858, at 553 (Edwin Erle Sparks ed., 1908) (Collections of the Illinois State Historical Library, vol. 3).

67. Speech at Carthage, Illinois (Oct. 22, 1858), CW 3:331.

68. *Analysis of the Character of Abraham Lincoln: A Lecture by William H. Herndon, reprinted in* 1 ABRAHAM LINCOLN Q. 403, 429 (1941).

69. HERNDON'S LINCOLN at 288.

70. STARR, LINCOLN AND THE RAILROADS at 75–76.

71. The railroad has published several brochures and articles that promote its relationship with Lincoln. *See, e.g.,* ABRAHAM LINCOLN AS ATTORNEY FOR THE ILLINOIS CENTRAL RAILROAD COMPANY (n.d.); *Abraham Lincoln,* 1 ILL. CENT. MAG. 15 (May 1913); *Lincoln and the Illinois Central,* ILL. CENT. MAG. 5 (Feb. 1927); SMITH, ABRAHAM LINCOLN: AN ILLINOIS CENTRAL LAWYER; EDWIN S. SUNDERLAND, ABRAHAM LINCOLN AND THE ILLINOIS CENTRAL RAILROAD (1955); *see also* Angle, *Lincoln Defended Railroad,* ILL. CENT. MAG. 40.

72. ABRAHAM LINCOLN AS ATTORNEY FOR THE ILLINOIS CENTRAL RAILROAD COMPANY; SUNDERLAND, ABRAHAM LINCOLN AND THE ILLINOIS CENTRAL RAILROAD at 19. Albert Beveridge closely followed the Illinois Central's version of its lawsuit with Lincoln in his biography of Lincoln. 1 BEVERIDGE, ABRAHAM LINCOLN at 588–92.

73. PRATT, THE PERSONAL FINANCES OF ABRAHAM LINCOLN 52–53; Sutton, *Lincoln and the Railroads of Illinois, in* LINCOLN IMAGES: AUGUSTANA COLLEGE CENTENNIAL ESSAYS 53–54; Brown, *Abraham Lincoln and the Illinois Central Railroad, 1857–1860,* 36 J. ILL. ST. HIST. SOC'Y at 137–38.

74. Ebenezer Lane to W.H. Osborn, dated Aug. 14, 1857 [86546], *Lincoln v. Illinois Central R.R.* [L01660] case file, LPAL.

75. AL to James Steele and Charles Summers (Feb. 12, 1857), CW 2:389.

76. Ebenezer Lane to W.H. Osborn, dated Aug. 14, 1857 [86546], *Lincoln v. Illinois Central R.R.* [L01660] case file, LPAL.

77. Charles L. Capen to John G. Drennan (Apr. 6, 1906), *quoted in* 1 BEVERIDGE, ABRAHAM LINCOLN at 589.

78. STARR, LINCOLN AND THE RAILROADS at 76.

79. Henry C. Whitney to William H. Herndon (Aug. 27, 1887), *in* HERNDON'S INFORMANTS: LETTERS, INTERVIEWS, AND STATEMENTS ABOUT LINCOLN at 633.

80. STOVER, HISTORY OF THE ILLINOIS CENTRAL RAILROAD at 81, 83.

81. AL to James F. Joy (Sept. 14, 1855), CW 2:325.

82. AL to James F. Joy (Sept. 19, 1855), CW 2:326.

83. Brief of Argument in *Abraham Lincoln v. Illinois Central Railroad* (June 23, 1857), CW 2:397–98.

84. Notice to Take Deposition [filed Apr. Term 1857] [4537], *Lincoln v. Illinois Central R.R.* [L01660] case file, LPAL.

85. Harry E. Pratt, *Abraham Lincoln in Bloomington, Illinois*, 29 J. Ill. St. Hist. Soc'y 42, 51 (1936).

86. King, Lincoln's Manager, David Davis at 91.

87. Judgment, dated June 18, 1857 [53255], *Lincoln v. Illinois Central R.R.* [L01660] case file, LPAL.

88. Judgment, dated June 18, 1857 [53255], Judgment, *dated June 23, 1857* [53256], *Lincoln v. Illinois Central R.R.* [L01660] case file, LPAL.

89. Hill, *Lincoln the Lawyer*, 71 Century Mag. at 950.

90. John G. Drennan to Stuyvesant Fish (Apr. 7, 1906), Illinois Central Railroad Archives, Newberry Library, Chicago, Illinois.

91. Statement of James S. Ewing, dated Apr. 5, 1906, Illinois Central Railroad Archives, Newberry Library, Chicago, Illinois.

92. Statement of James S. Ewing, dated Apr. 5, 1906; Statement of Adlai E. Stevenson, dated Apr. 6, 1906, Illinois Central Railroad Archives, Newberry Library, Chicago, Illinois.

93. Statement of James S. Ewing, dated Apr. 5, 1906, Illinois Central Railroad Archives, Newberry Library, Chicago, Illinois.

94. *Id.*

95. Statement of Adlai E. Stevenson, dated Apr. 6, 1906, Illinois Central Railroad Archives, Newberry Library, Chicago, Illinois.

96. Ezra M. Prince to John G. Drennan (Apr. 5, 1906), Illinois Central Railroad Archives, Newberry Library, Chicago, Illinois.

97. *Id.*

98. Chicago Press and Tribune, Sept. 27, 1858.

99. Henry C. Whitney to William H. Herndon (Aug. 27, 1887), *in* Herndon's Informants: Letters, Interviews, and Statements About Lincoln at 633.

100. 1 Beveridge, Abraham Lincoln at 590.

101. *Dunn v. Keegin*, 4 Ill. (3 Scam.) 292, 297 (1841).

102. Baringer, Lincoln Day By Day, Vol. II: 1849–1860, at 198; Pratt, The Personal Finances of Abraham Lincoln at 54; Bank draft, dated Aug. 31, 1857 [127837], *Lincoln v. Illinois Central R.R.* [L01660] case file, LPAL; Paul M. Angle, Lincoln in the Year 1857, at 40 (1939).

103. Weik, The Real Lincoln: A Portrait at 155.

104. *See generally* Gordon, *Lawyers as the American Aristocracy*, 20 Stan. Law. 2.

105. Lincoln on the Eve of '61: A Journalist's Story by Henry Villard 37 (Harold G. & Oswald Garrison Villard eds., 1941).

Select Bibliography

Published Primary Sources

Abstract of the Arguments of the Hon. Rufus Choate and William D. Northend, Esq. For the Petitioners . . . for a Railroad from Danvers to Malden, Before the Committee on Railways and Canals of the Massachusetts Legislature . . . Session 1847 (Boston, S.N. Dickinson & Co. 1847).

The Abuses of Law Courts, 21 U.S. Mag. & Dem. Rev. 305 (1847).

Addresses and Orations of Rufus Choate (Boston, Little Brown & Co. 1878).

Allen, William F. An Address Delivered Before the Graduating Class of the Law Department of Hamilton College, July 15, 1857 (Utica, Roberts 1857).

The American Bar, 28 U.S. Mag. & Dem. Rev. 195 (1851).

American Law, 1 Sw. L.J. & Rep. 112 (1844).

American Law Books. Story on Sales, 5 W. L.J. 118 (1847).

Analysis of the Character of Abraham Lincoln: a Lecture by William H. Herndon, reprinted in 1 Abraham Lincoln Q. 403 (1941).

Annual Register, or a View of the History and Politics, of the Year 1840 (London, J.G.F. & J. Rivington 1841).

Baldwin, Joseph. The Flush Times of Alabama and Mississippi (1987) (1853).

Basler, Roy P., ed. *James Quay Howard's Notes on Lincoln,* 4 Abraham Lincoln Q. 387 (1947).

Bonney, Edward. The Banditti of the Prairies or, The Murderer's Doom!! A Tale of the Mississippi Valley (1963) (1850).

Bouvier, John. A Law Dictionary Adapted to the Constitutions and Laws of the United States of America (Philadelphia, T. & J.W. Johnson 1839).

Carey, H.C. The Past, The Present, and The Future (Philadelphia, H.C. Baird 1859).

Carpenter, F.B. Six Months at the White House (New York, Hurd & Houghton 1866).

Case of George Latimer—Boston Slavehunting Ground—Outrageous Conduct of the City Marshall and City Police, 12 The Liberator 171 (Oct. 28, 1842).

Caton, John Dean. Early Bench and Bar of Illinois (Chicago, Chicago Legal News Co. 1893).

Chitty, Joseph. A Practical Treatise on Pleading; and on the Parties to Actions, and the Forms of Actions; With a Second Volume Containing Precedents of Headings (New York, Robert M'Dermut 1809).

Cincinnati Law School, 1 W. L.J. 522 (1844).

Clerke, Thomas W. *An Introductory Discourse, on the Study of the Law, Delivered Before the New York Law School, in the City Hall, in the City of New York, on the 23d. Nov. 1840, in* Rudiments of American Law and Practice, on the Plan of Blackstone; Prepared for the Use of Students at Law, and Adapted to Schools and Colleges (New York, Gould, Banks & Co. 1842).

The Collected Works of Abraham Lincoln (Roy P. Basler ed., 11 vols. 1953–1990).

Colton, Calvin. The Junius Tracts and the Rights of Labor (1974) (1844).

Conkling, James C. *Recollections of the Bench and Bar of Central Illinois* in Chicago Bar Association Lectures (Chicago, Fergus Printing 1882).

The Constitutional Debates of 1847 (Arthur C. Cole ed., 1919) (Collections of the Illinois State Historical Library, vol. 14).

Critical Notice, 2 Am. L. Mag. 247 (1843).

Critical Notices, 6 Am. L. Mag. 471 (1846).

Curran, William Henry. The Life of the Right Honorable John Philpot Curran (London, Archibald Constable & Co. 1819).

Diary of George Templeton Strong (Allan Nevins & Milton H. Thomas eds., 1952).

The Elective Principle as Applied to the Judiciary, 5 W. L.J. 127 (1847).

Eloquence of the Bar. Grattan—Curran, 3 W. L.J. 241 (1846).

Mr. & Mrs. Ralph Emerson's Personal Recollections of Abraham Lincoln (1909).

Examination of Attorneys, 5 W. L.J. 480 (1848).

Examination of Students, 3 N.Y. Legal Observer 395 (1845).

The Examiner and Mr. Phillips, 24 Littell's Living Age 230 (Feb. 2, 1850).

"F." The Profession of the Law, 7 W. L.J. 97 (1849).

Ficklin, O.B. A Pioneer Lawyer, Tuscola [Illinois] Review, Sept. 7, 1922.

[Field, David Dudley]. *The Study and Practice of the Law*, 14 U.S. Mag. & Dem. Rev. 345 (1844).

Freeman, Norman L. The "Illinois Digest:" Being a Full and Complete Digest and Compilation of all the Decisions of the Supreme Court (Cincinnati, Moore, Wilstach, Keys & Co. 1856).

Gilman, Charles. *Debtor and Creditor in Illinois*, 5 Hunt's Merchants' Mag. 446 (1841).

Greenleaf, Simon. A Discourse Pronounced at the Inauguration of the Author as Royall Professor of Law in Harvard University, August 26, 1834 (Cambridge, James Munroe & Co. 1837).

———. Treatise on the Law of Evidence (3 vols. Boston, Charles C. Little & James Brown 1842).

Gregg, W.P. & Benjamin Pond. The Railroad Laws and Charters of the United States (Boston, Charles C. Little & James Brown 1851).

Hare, J.I. Clark & H.B. Wallace. Select Decisions of American Courts (Philadelphia, T. & J.W. Johnson 1848).

Herndon's Informants: Letters, Interviews, and Statements About Lincoln (Douglas L. Wilson & Rodney O. Davis eds., 1998).

Herndon's Life of Lincoln: The History and Personal Recollections of Abraham Lincoln as Originally Written by William H. Herndon and Jesse W. Weik (Paul M. Angle ed., 1961).

The Hidden Lincoln: From the Letters and Papers of William H. Herndon (Emanuel Hertz ed., 1940).

Hilliard, Francis. The Elements of Law; Being a Comprehensive Summary of American Jurisprudence (2d ed. New York, John S. Voorhies 1848).

Hoffman, David. A Course of Legal Study (2d ed. Baltimore, Joseph Neal 1836).

Holland, J.G. Life of Abraham Lincoln (Springfield, Mass., G. Bill 1866).

Hopkinson, Joseph. An Address Delivered Before the Law Academy of Philadelphia (Philadelphia, Law Academy 1826).

Howard, J.Q. The Life of Abraham Lincoln with Extracts From His Speeches (Cincinnati, Anderson, Gates & Wright 1860).

Howells, W.D. Life of Abraham Lincoln (1938) (1860).

Humphreys, Charles. Compendium of the Common Law in Force in Kentucky (Lexington, W.G. Hunt 1822).

Hurd, John Codman. The Law of Freedom and Bondage in the United States (Boston, Little, Brown & Co. 1862).

In the Matter of Jane, A Woman of Color, 5 W. L.J. 202 (1848).

Jackson, J.F. *Law and Lawyers*, 28 Knickerbocker 377 (1846).

James, Charles P. *Lawyers and Their Traits*, 9 W. L.J. 49 (1851).

Jefferson, Thomas. Writings (1984).

Kennedy, John Pendelton. Swallow Barn: or, A Sojourn in the Old Dominion (Rev. ed. Philadelphia, J.B. Lippincott & Co. 1860).

Kent, James. Commentaries on American Law (New York, O. Halstead 4 vols. 1826–1830).

———. Commentaries on American Law (8th ed. New York, William Kent 1854).

Kimball, Richard B. The Lawyer: The Dignity, Duties, and Responsibilities of his Profession (New York, George P. Putnam & Co. 1853).

Kinne, Asa. Questions and Answers on Law: Alphabetically Arranged, With References to the Most Approved Authorities 691 (New York, John F. Trow 1850).

The Latimer Case, 12 The Liberator 186 (Nov. 25, 1842).

The Law Practice of Abraham Lincoln: Complete Documentary Edition (Martha L. Benner & Cullom Davis eds., 2000).

Law Relative to Debtor and Creditor, No. 1 Means of Enforcing Debts Against Citizens of the State of Maine, 2 Hunt's Merchants' Mag. 329 (1840).

Law Schools. The Law Department of the Indiana University, at Bloomington, 1 W. L.J. 92 (1843).

Law Studies, 9 L. Rep. 142 (1846).

Lawyers, Clients &c, 24 Littell's Living Age 306 (Feb. 16, 1850).

Lawyers, Clients, Witnesses, and the Public; or, the Examiner and Mr. Phillips, 24 Littell's Living Age 179 (Jan. 26, 1850).

Legal Morality, 5 L. Rep. 529 (1843).

The Legal Profession, Ancient and Modern, 4 Am. Rev. 242 (1846).

The Legal Profession in the United States, 10 Am. L.J. 470 (1851).

Legerdemain of Law-Craft (pts. 1 & 2), 22 U.S. Mag. & Dem. Rev. 529 (1848), 23 U.S. Mag. & Dem. Rev. 134 (1849).

The Letters of Stephen A. Douglas (Robert W. Johannsen ed., 1961).

Lieber, Francis. *On Political Hermeneutics—Precedents*, 18 Am. Jurist 282 (1838).

Life of Abe Lincoln, of Illinois (Printed for the Publishers 1860).

The Lincoln-Douglas Debates of 1858 (Edwin Erle Sparks ed., 1908) (Collections of the Illinois State Historical Library, vol. 3).

The Lincoln-Douglas Debates of 1858 (Robert W. Johannsen ed., 1965).

Lincoln on the Eve of '61: A Journalist's Story by Henry Villard (Harold G. Villard & Oswald Garrison eds., 1941).

Linder, Usher F. Reminiscences of the Early Bench and Bar of Illinois (Chicago, Chicago Legal News Co. 1879).

Livingston, John. Livingston's Law Register (New York, Monthly Law Mag. 1851).

———. Livingston's Law Register for 1852 (New York, U.S. Law Mag. 1852).

———. Livingston's United States Law Register (New York, John A. Gray 1860).

Lomax, John Taylor. Digest of the Laws Respecting Real Property, Generally Adopted and in Use in the United States (Philadelphia, J.S. Littell 1839).

Marvin, J.G. Legal Bibliography (Philadelphia, T. & J.W. Johnson 1847).

Memoir of Benjamin Robbins Curtis (Benjamin R. Curtis ed., Boston, Little, Brown, & Co. 1879).

Memoirs of Gustave Koerner 1809–1896 (Thomas J. McCormack ed., 1909).

Memorials of the Life and Character of Stephen T. Logan 17 (Springfield, Ill., H.W. Rokker 1882).

Metcalf, Theron & Jonathan C. Perkins. Digest of the Decisions of the Courts of Common Law and Admiralty in the United States (Boston, Hilliard, Gray & Co. 1840).

The Morals and Utility of Lawyers, 7 W. L.J. 1 (1849).

Mr. Charles Phillips and the Courvoisier Case, 12 Monthly L. Rep. 553 (1850).

Mr. Charles Phillips's Defence of Courvoisier, 12 Monthly L. Rep. 536 (1850).

Mr. Phillips and the Courvoisier Case, 12 Monthly L. Rep. 481 (1850).

The New Constitution of Illinois, 5 W. L.J. 64 (1847).

New Decisions, 3 W. L.J. 15 (1845).

Notices of New Books, 14 L. Rep. 102 (1851).

The Only Authentic Life of Abraham Lincoln, Alias "Old Abe." (American News Co. n.d.).

O'Regan, William. Memoirs of the Legal, Literary, and Political Life of the Late the Right Honorable John Philpot Curran (London, James Harper 1817).

Parker, Theodore. The Trial of Theodore Parker, For the "Misdemeanor" of a Speech in Faneuil Hall Against Kidnapping (Boston, Published For The Author 1855).

Pierce, Edward L. Treatise on American Railroad Law (New York, John S. Voorhies 1857).

Pitts, John W. Eleven Numbers Against Lawyer Legislation and Fees at the Bar, Written and Printed Expressly for the Benefit of the People (n.p. 1843).

Poe, Edgar Allan. *Magazine Literature*, The Weekly Mirror 299 (Feb. 15, 1845).

The Practice of Advocacy.—Mr. Charles Phillips, and his Defence of Courvoisier, 25 Littell's Living Age 289 (May 18, 1850).

The Practice of the Bar, 9 L. Rep. 241 (1846).

Professional Conduct—The Courvoisier Case, 12 Monthly L. Rep. 433 (1850).

Professional Ethics, 9 Am. L.J. 477 (1850).

Purple, N.H. A Compilation of the Statutes of the State of Illinois (Chicago, Keen & Lee 1856).

Puterbaugh, Sabin D. Puterbaugh's Illinois Pleadings and Practice (Peoria, Henry Nolte 1864).

Putnam, John Phelps. A Supplement to the United States Digest (Boston, Charles C. Little & James Brown 1847).

Records of the Federal Convention of 1787 (Max Farrand ed., 1937).

Redfield, Isaac F. A Practical Treatise Upon the Law of Railways (2d ed. Boston, Little, Brown & Co. 1858).

Reeve, Tapping. The Law of Baron and Femme (3d ed. 1862).

Report of the Trial of Archibald Hamilton Rowan (New York, Tiebout & O'Brien 1794).

Rights of the Slave-Holding States and of the Owners of Slave Property Under the Constitution of the United States, 23 Am. Jurist 23 (1840).

Robertson, George W. Scrap Book on Law and Politics, Men and Times (Lexington, A.W. Elder 1855).

Saxe, John G. *A Legal Ballad*, 24 Knickerbocker 265 (Sept. 1844).

Sedgwick, Theodore. A Treatise on the Measure of Damages (New York, John S. Voorhies 1847).

Sharswood, George. A Compend of Lectures on the Aims and Duties of the Profession of Law (Philadelphia, T. & J.W. Johnson 1854).

Sharswood's Professional Ethics, 3 Am. L. Reg. 193 (1855).

Sherman, William T. Memoirs of General William T. Sherman (New York, D. Appleton & Co. 1875).

Smith, Chauncey & Samuel W. Bates. Cases Relating to the Law of Railways, Decided in the Supreme Court of the United States, And in the Courts of the Several States (Boston, Little, Brown and Co. 1854).

Speech of Hon. Rufus Choate Before the Joint Legislative Rail Road Committee, Boston, Feb. 28, 1851, Application of the Salem and Lowell Rail Road Company For A Parallel and Competing Rail Road From Salem to Danvers 4 (Boston, J.M. Hewes & Co. 1851).

Speeches of the Right Honorable John Philpott Curran (4th ed. London, Hurst, Rees, Orme, & Brown 1815).

Speed, Joshua Fry. Reminiscences of Abraham Lincoln and Notes of a Visit to California: Two Lectures (Louisville, John P. Morton 1884).

Starkie, Thomas. A Treatise on the Law of Slander and Libel, and Incidentally of Malicious Prosecutions; From the Second English Edition of 1830, With Notes and References to American Cases and to English Decisions Since 1830 (2 vols. Albany, C. Van Benthuysen & Co. 1843).

Stevens, Frank E., ed. *Autobiography of Stephen A. Douglas*, 5 Ill. St. Hist. Soc'y J. 330 (1912).

Storer, Bellamy. The Legal Profession: An Address Delivered Before the Law Department of the University of Louisville, Kentucky, February 20, 1856 (Cincinnati, C. Clark 1856).

Story, Joseph. Commentaries on Equity Jurisprudence as Administered in England and America (Boston, Hilliard, Gray & Co. 1836).

———. Commentaries on Equity Pleadings, and the Incidents Thereto, According to the Practice of the Courts of Equity of England and America (Boston, C.C. Little & J. Brown 1838).

———. *Digests of the Common Law, in* Miscellaneous Writings of Joseph Story (William W. Story ed., 1972) (1852).

[Story, Joseph]. *Hoffman's Course of Legal Study*, 6 N. Am. Rev. 45 (Nov. 1817).

Sugden, Edward. A Practical Treatise of the Law of Vendors and Purchasers of Estates (Brookfield, Mass., E. & L. Merriam 1836).

Tocqueville, Alexis de. Democracy in America (P. Bradley ed., H. Reeve trans., 1980) (1835).

Trollope, Anthony. North America (1968) (1862).

Tucker, St. George. Blackstone's Commentaries: With Notes of Reference to the Constitution and Laws, of the Federal Government of the United States and of the Commonwealth of Virginia (1969) (1803).

United States Digest, 3 W. L.J. 239 (1846).

Walker, Samuel. The Moral, Social, and Professional Duties of Attorneys and Solicitors (New York, Harper & Brothers 1849).

Walker, Timothy. *Advice to Law Students*, 1 W. L.J. 481 (1844).

———. An Introduction to American Law, Designed as a First Book For Students (Philadelphia, P.H. Nicklin & T. Johnson 1837).

———. *Ways and Means of Professional Success: Being the Substance of a Valedictory Address to the Graduates of the Law Class, in the Cincinnati College*, 1 W. L.J. 543 (1844).

Walker's Introduction, 1 W. Literary J. & Monthly Rev. 107 (Dec. 1844).

Walker's Introduction to American Law, 45 No. Am. Rev. 485 (1837).

Warden, Robert B. An Account of the Private Life and Public Services of Salmon Portland Chase (Cincinnati, Wilstach, Baldwin & Co. 1874).

Webster, Noah. The American Spelling Book; Containing the Rudiments of the English Language (Concord, H. Hill & Co., 1823).

Whitney, Henry Clay. Life on the Circuit with Lincoln (1940) (1892).

Secondary Sources

Abel, Richard. American Lawyers (1989).

Abraham Lincoln, 1 Ill. Cent. Mag. 15 (May 1913).

Abraham Lincoln as Attorney for the Illinois Central Railroad Company (n.d.).

Altschuler, Glenn C. & Stuart M. Blumin. Rude Republic: Americans and Their Politics in the Nineteenth Century (2000).

Angle, Paul M. *Abraham Lincoln: Circuit Lawyer*, Abraham Lincoln Ass'n Papers (1928).

———. *Aftermath of the Matson Slave Case*, 3 Abraham Lincoln Q. 146 (1944).

———. "Here I have Lived": A History of Lincoln's Springfield, 1821–1865 (1935).

———. *Lincoln Defended Railroad*, Ill. Cent. Mag. 40 (Feb. 1929).

———. Lincoln in the Year 1857 (1939).

———. One Hundred Years of Law: An Account of the Law Office which John T. Stuart Founded in Springfield, Illinois, A Century Ago (1928).

———. A Shelf of Lincoln Books (1946).

Arno, Andrew R. *Ritual Reconciliation and Conflict Management in Fiji*, 47 Oceania 49 (1976).

Atiyah, P.S. Rise and Fall of Freedom of Contract (1979).

Auerbach, Jerold. Unequal Justice: Lawyers and Social Change in Modern America (1976).

Baker, Donald G. *The Lawyer in Popular Fiction*, 3 J. Pop. Culture 493 (1969).

Balleisen, Edward J. Navigating Failure: Bankruptcy and Commercial Society in Antebellum America (2001).

Baringer, William E. Lincoln Day by Day: 1849–1860 (1960).

Barondess, Benjamin. *The Adventure of the Missing Briefs*, 8 Manuscripts 20 (1955).

Bartlett, Irving. Wendell and Ann Phillips: The Community of Reform 1840–1880 (1979).

Barton, Keith C. *"Good Cooks and Washers": Slave Hiring, Domestic Labor, and the Market in Bourbon County, Kentucky*, 84 J. Am. Hist. 436 (Sept. 1997).

Basler, Roy P. The Lincoln Legend: A Study in Changing Conceptions (1935).

Baxter, Maurice G. Orville H. Browning: Lincoln's Friend and Critic (1957).

Beard, William D. Dalby *Revisited: A New Look at Lincoln's "Most Far-reaching Case" in the Illinois Supreme Court*, 20 J. Abraham Lincoln Ass'n 1 (Summer 1999).

———. *"I have labored hard to find the law": Abraham Lincoln for the Alton and Sangamon Railroad*, 85 Ill. Hist. J. 209 (1992).

———. *Lincoln and the Illinois Central Railroad*, 92 Lincoln Herald 16 (Spring 1990).

Beardsley, Arthur Sydney. Legal Bibliography and the Use of Law Books (1937).

Bestor, Arthur. *State Sovereignty and Slavery: A Reinterpretation of Proslavery Constitutional Doctrine, 1846–1860*, J. Ill. St. Hist. Soc'y 117 (1961).

Beveridge, Albert J. Abraham Lincoln, 1809–1858 (4 vols. 1928).

Blair, Harry C. & Rebecca Tarshis. Colonel Edward D. Baker: Lincoln's Constant Ally (1960).

Blau, Joseph, ed. Social Theories of Jacksonian Democracy (1954).

Bloomfield, Maxwell. American Lawyers in a Changing Society, 1776–1876 (1976).

———. *David Hoffman and the Shaping of a Republican Legal Culture*, 38 Md. L. Rev. 161 (1979).

————. *Law: The Development of a Profession, in* Professions in American History (Nathan O. Hatch ed., 1988).

————. *Law and Lawyers in American Popular Culture, in* Law and American Literature: A Collection of Essays 125 (Carl S. Smith et al. eds., 1983).

————. *Law vs. Politics: The Self-Image of the American Bar 1830–1860*, 12 Am. J. Legal Hist. 306 (1968).

Blue, Frederick J. Salmon P. Chase: A Life in Politics (1987).

Bogue, Allan G. et al. *Members of the House of Representatives and the Processes of Modernization, 1789–1960*, 63 J. Am. Hist. 275 (1976).

Boman, Dennis K. *The Dred Scott Case Reconsidered: The Legal and Political Context in Missouri*, 44 Am. J. Legal Hist. 405 (2000).

————. The Life of Abiel Leonard: Eminent Jurist and Passionate Unionist (1998) (Ph.D. dissertation, University of Missouri).

Borit, G.S. *A New Lincoln Text: An Opinion on an Illinois Tax*, 75 Lincoln Herald 152 (Winter 1973).

————. *Another New Lincoln Text: Some Thoughts Concerning an Outrageous Suggestion About Abraham Lincoln "Corporation Lawyer,"* 77 Lincoln Herald 27 (Spring 1975).

Boritt, G.S. Lincoln and the Economics of the American Dream (1978).

————. *Was Lincoln a Vulnerable Candidate in 1860?*, 27 Civil War Hist. 32 (1981).

Bradford, M.E. *Against Lincoln: An Address at Gettyburg, in* The Historian's Lincoln: Pseudohistory, Psychohistory, and History (Gabor Boritt ed., 1988).

Brown, Charles LeRoy. *Abraham Lincoln and the Illinois Central Railroad, 1857–1860*, 36 J. Ill. St. Hist. Soc'y 121 (1943).

Brown, R. Ben. *Judging in the Days of the Early Republic: A Critique of Judge Richard Arnold's Use of History in Anastasoff v. United States*, 3 J. App. Prac. & Process 355 (2001).

Bryant, A. Christopher. *Reading the Law in the Office of Calvin Fletcher: The Apprenticeship System and the Practice of Law in Frontier Indiana*, 1 Nev. L.J. 19 (2001).

Bryson, W. Hamilton & E. Lee Shepard. Note, *The Winchester Law School, 1824–1831*, 21 Law & Hist. Rev. 393 (2003).

Burlingame, Michael. *The 1837 Lincoln-Stone Protest Against Slavery Reconsidered, in* Papers From the Thirteenth and Fourteenth Annual Lincoln Colloquia 57–62 (n.d.).

Campbell, Stanley W. The Slave Catchers: Enforcement of the Fugitive Slave Law, 1850–1860 (1968).

Chandler, Alfred D., Jr. *Patterns of American Railroad Finance, 1830–50*, 28 Bus. Hist. Rev. 248 (1954).

————. *The Railroads: Pioneers in Modern Corporate Management*, 39 Bus. Hist. Rev. 16 (1965).

Chroust, Anton-Hermann. *Abraham Lincoln Argues a Pro-Slavery Case*, 5 Am. J. Legal Hist. 299 (1961).

Cohen, Morris L. et al. How to Find the Law (9th ed. 1989).

Coleman, Charles H. Abraham Lincoln and Coles County, Illinois (1955).

Collett, Teresa Stanton. *The Common Good and the Duty to Represent: Must the Last Lawyer in Town Take Any Case?*, 40 S. Tex. L. Rev. 137 (1999).

Collins, Lewis. History of Kentucky (Covington, Ky., Collins & Co. 1874).

Comment, *The Creation of a Common Law Rule: The Fellow Servant Rule, 1837–1860*, 132 U. Pa. L. Rev. 579 (1984).

Cover, Robert. *Book Review*, 70 Colum. L. Rev. 1475 (1975).

————. Justice Accused: Antislavery and the Judicial Process (1975).

Curry, Richard O. *Conscious or Subconscious Caesarism: A Critique of Recent Scholarly Attempts to Put Abraham Lincoln on the Analyst's Couch*, 77 J. Ill. St. Hist. Soc'y 67 (1984).

Dalley, Paula J. *The Law of Deceit, 1790–1860: Continuity Amidst Change*, 39 Am. J. Legal Hist. 405 (1995).

Davis, Cullom. *Abraham Lincoln, Esq.: The Symbiosis of Law and Politics, in* Abraham Lincoln and the Political Process: Papers from the Seventh Annual Lincoln Colloquium (1992).

———. *Law and Politics: The Two Careers of Abraham Lincoln*, 17 Q.J. Ideology 61 (June 1994).

Davis, James E. Frontier Illinois (1998).

De Ville, Kenneth Allen. Medical Malpractice in Nineteenth-Century America (1990).

Dillon, Merton L. The Abolitionists: The Growth of a Dissenting Minority (1974).

Donald, David Herbert. *Billy, You're Too Rampant*, 3 Abraham Lincoln Q. 375 (1945).

———. Lincoln (1999).

———. Lincoln Reconsidered: Essays on the Civil War Era (2d ed. 1961).

———. Lincoln's Herndon: A Biography (1948).

———. "We Are Lincoln Men": Abraham Lincoln and His Friends (2003).

Duff, John J. A. Lincoln, Prairie Lawyer (1960).

———. *This Was A Lawyer*, 52 J. Ill St. Hist. Soc'y 146 (1959).

Dunn, Jesse K. *Lincoln, the Lawyer*, 4 Okla. L.J. 249 (1906).

Eller, Cathrine Spicer. The William Blackstone Collection in the Yale Law Library (Yale Law Library Publications No. 6, June 1938).

Ely, James W., Jr. The Guardian of Every Other Right: A Constitutional History of Property Rights (1992).

———. Railroads and American Law (2001).

Engel, David M. *The Oven-Bird's Song: Insiders, Outsiders, and Personal Injuries in an American Community*, 18 Law & Soc'y Rev. 551 (1984).

Ernst, Daniel R. *Legal Positivism, Abolitionist Litigation, and the New Jersey Slave Case of 1845*, 4 Law & Hist. Rev. 337 (1986).

Ershkowitz, Herbert. The Origin of the Whig and Democratic Parties: New Jersey Politics, 1820–1837 (1982).

Etcheson, Nicole. The Emerging Midwest: Upland Southerners and the Political Culture of the Old Northwest, 1787–1861 (1996).

Faragher, John Mack. *History from the Inside-Out: Writing the History of Women in Rural America*, 33 Am. Q. 537 (1981).

———. Sugar Creek: Life on the Illinois Prairie (1986).

———. Women and Men on the Overland Trail (1979).

Fehrenbacher, Don E. Lincoln in Text and Context: Collected Essays (1987).

———. The Dred Scott Case: Its Significance in American Law and Politics (1978).

———. Prelude to Greatness: Lincoln in the 1850s (1962).

———. The Slaveholding Republic: An Account of the United States Government's Relations to Slavery (1999).

Fehrenbacher, Don E. & Virginia Fehrenbacher. Recollected Words of Abraham Lincoln (1996).

Ferguson, Robert A. Law and Letters in American Culture (1986).

Fidler, Ann. *"Till You Understand Them in Their Principal Features": Observations on Form and Function in Nineteenth-Century American Law Books*, 92 Papers of the Bibliographical Society of America 427 (Dec. 1998).

Finkelman, Paul. An Imperfect Union: Slavery, Federalism, and Comity (1981).

———. Slavery and the Founders: Race and Liberty in the Age of Jefferson (2d ed. 2001).

———. *Slavery, the "More Perfect Union," and the Prairie State*, 80 Ill. Hist. J. 248 (1987).

Fishman, Joel. *The Digests of Pennsylvania*, 90 Law Libr. J. 481 (1998).

———. *An Early Pennsylvania Legal Periodical: The Pennsylvania Law Journal, 1842–1848*, 45 Am. J. Legal Hist. 22 (2001).

Folsom, Burton E. *The Politics of Elites: Prominence and Party in Davidson County, Tennessee, 1835–1861*, 39 J. S. Hist. 359 (1973).

Foner, Eric. Free Soil, Free Labor, Free Men: The Ideology of the Republican Party Before The Civil War (1970).

Formisano, Robert. The Transformation of Political Culture: Massachusetts Parties, 1790s–1840s (1983).

Fox, Edward J. *The Influence of the Law in the Life of Abraham Lincoln, in* Report of the Thirty-first Annual Meeting of the Pennsylvania Bar Association (1925).

Frank, John P. Lincoln as a Lawyer (1961).

Fraysse, Olivier. Lincoln, Land, and Labor, 1809–60 (Sylvia Neely trans., 1994).

Fredrickson, George. The Black Image in the White Mind: The Debate on Afro-American Character and Destiny 1817–1914 (1971).

———. *The Search for Order and Community, in* The Public and Private Lincoln (G. Cullom Davis et al. eds., 1979).

Freedman, Monroe H. Understanding Lawyers' Ethics (1990).

Freyer, Tony. *Reassessing the Impact of Eminent Domain in Early American Economic Development*, 1981 Wis. L. Rev. 1263.

Friedman, Lawrence. A History of American Law (3rd ed. 2005).

Friedman, Lawrence M. et al. *State Supreme Courts: A Century of Style and Citation*, 33 Stan. L. Rev. 733 (1981).

Galanter, Marc. *Why the "Haves" Come Out Ahead: Speculations on the Limits of Legal Change*, 9 Law & Soc'y Rev. 95 (1974).

Gates, Arnold. *John J. Duff, 1902–1961*, 54 J. Ill. St. Hist. Soc'y 419 (1961).

Gates, Paul W. History of Public Land Law Development (1968).

Gates, Paul Wallace. The Illinois Central Railroad and Its Colonization Work (1934).

Gawalt, Gerald W. *Sources of Anti-Lawyer Sentiment in Massachusetts, 1740–1840*, 14 Am. J. Legal Hist. 283 (1970).

Gertz, Elmer. *The Black Laws of Illinois*, 56 Ill. St. Hist. Soc'y J. 454 (1963).

Gienapp, William E. Abraham Lincoln and Civil War America: A Biography (2002).

———. *The Myth of Class in Jacksonian America*, 6 J. Pol'y Hist. 232 (1994).

———. The Origins of the Republican Party 1852–1856 (1987).

Gilmore, Grant. The Ages of American Law (1977).

Glendinning, Glen V. The Chicago & Alton Railroad: The Only Way (2002).

Goff, John S. Robert Todd Lincoln: A Man in His Own Right (1969).

Gordon, James Wice. Lawyers in Politics: Mid-Nineteenth Century Kentucky as a Case Study (1981) (Ph.D. dissertation, University of Kentucky).

Gordon, Robert W. *The Devil and Daniel Webster*, 94 Yale L.J. 445 (1984).

———. *The Elusive Transformation*, 6 Yale J.L. & Human. 137 (1994).

———. *Lawyers as the American Aristocracy*, 20 Stan. Law. 2 (Fall 1985).

———. *Morton Horwitz and His Critics: A Conflict of Narratives*, 37 Tulsa L. Rev. 915 (2002).

Gordon, Sarah H. Passage to Union: How the Railroads Transformed American Life, 1829–1929 (1997).

Gorn, Elliot J. *"Gouge and Bite, Pull Hair and Scratch": The Social Significance of Fighting in the Southern Backcountry*, 90 Am. Hist. Rev. 18 (1985).

Gowing, Laura. Domestic Dangers: Women, Words, and Sex in Early Modern London (1998).

Granfors, Mark W. & Terence C. Halliday. Professional Passages: Caste, Class and Education in the 19th Century Legal Profession (American Bar Foundation Working Paper 1987).

Green, Thomas M. & William D. Pederson. *The Behavior of Lawyer-Presidents*, 15 Pres. Stud. Q. 343 (1985).

Greenhouse, Carol J. *Courting Difference: Issues of Interpretation and Comparison in the Study of Legal Ideologies*, 22 Law & Soc'y Rev. (1988).

Grimsted, David. *Rioting in Its Jacksonian Setting*, 77 Am. Hist. Rev. 361 (1972).

Haines, Deborah. City Doctor, City Lawyer: The Learned Professions in Frontier Chicago, 1833–1860 (1986) (Ph.D. dissertation, University of Chicago).

Hall, Kermit L. *The Judiciary on Trial: State Constitutional Reform and the Rise of an Elected Judiciary, 1846–1860*, 45 Historian 337 (1983).

Harris, Michael H. *The Frontier Lawyer's Library; Southern Indiana, 1800–1850, as a Test Case*, 26 Am. J. Legal Hist. 239 (1972).

Hartog, Hendrik. *Pigs and Positivism*, 1985 Wis. L. Rev. 899.

Hazard, Geoffrey C., Jr. Ethics in the Practice of Law (1978).

Heiple, James D. *Legal Education and Admission to the Bar: The Illinois Experience*, 12 S. Ill. U. L.J. 123 (1987).

Hertz, Emanuel. Abraham Lincoln: A New Portrait (1931).

Higham, John. History: Professional Scholarship in America (1989).

Hill, Frederick Trevor. Lincoln the Lawyer (1906).

———. *Lincoln the Lawyer*, 71 Century Mag. 939 (Apr. 1906).

Hoeflich, M.H. *John Livingston and the Business of Law in Nineteenth-Century America*, 44 Am. J. Legal Hist. 347 (2000).

———. *Law in the Republican Classroom*, 43 U. Kan. L. Rev. 711 (1995)

———. *The Lawyer as Pragmatic Reader: The History of Legal Common-Placing*, 55 Ark. L. Rev. 87 (2002).

———. *Legal Ethics in the Nineteenth Century: The Other Tradition*, 47 U. Kan. L. Rev. 793 (1999).

Hofstadter, Richard. The American Political Tradition (1974) (1948).

Holsinger, M. Paul. *Timothy Walker*, 84 Ohio Hist. 145 (1975).

Horwitz, Morton. The Transformation of American Law: 1780–1860 (1977).

Howe, Daniel Walker. The Political Culture of the American Whigs (1979).

———. *Why Abraham Lincoln Was a Whig*, 16 J. Abraham Lincoln Ass'n 27 (1995)

Hunt, Gaillard. Israel, Elihu and Cadwallader Washburn (1925).

Hunt, Robert S. Law and Locomotives: The Impact of the Railroad on Wisconsin Law in the Nineteenth Century (1958).

Hurst, James Willard. The Growth of American Law: The Law Makers (1950).

Hyman, Harold M. *A Man out of Manuscripts: Edward M. Stanton at the McCormick Reaper Trial*, 12 Manuscripts 35 (1960).

Hyman, Harold M. & William M. Wiecek. Equal Justice Under Law: Constitutional Development 1835–1875 (1982).

Johannsen, Robert W. *In Search of the Real Lincoln, Or Lincoln at the Crossroads*, 61 J. Ill. St. Hist. Soc'y 229 (1968).

Johnson, William R. *Education and Professional Life Styles: Law and Medicine in the Nineteenth Century*, 14 Hist. Ed. Q. 185 (1974).

Kaczorowski, Robert J. *The Common-Law Background of Nineteenth-Century Tort Law*, 51 Ohio St. L.J. 1127 (1990).

Karachuk, Robert Feikema. *A Workman's Tools: The Law Library of Henry Adams Bullard*, 42 Am. J. Legal Hist. 160 (1998).

Karsten, Peter. *"Bottomed on Justice": A Reappraisal of Critical Legal Studies Scholarship Concerning Breaches of Labor Contracts by Quitting or Firing in Britain and the U.S., 1630–1880*, 34 Am. J. Legal Hist. 213 (1990).

———. *Cows in the Corn, Pigs in the Garden, and "the Problem of Social Costs": "High" and "Low" Legal Cultures of the British Diaspora Lands in the 17th, 18th, and 19th Centuries*, 32 Law & Soc'y Rev. 63 (1998).

———. Heart versus Head: Judge-Made Law in Nineteenth-Century America (1997).

Kelley, Robert. The Cultural Pattern in American Politics (1979).

Kempin, Frederick G., Jr. *Precedent and Stare Decisis: The Critical Years, 1800–1850*, 3 Am. J. Legal Hist. 28 (1959).

King, Andrew J. *Constructing Gender: Sexual Slander in Nineteenth-Century America*, 13 Law & Hist. Rev. 63 (1995).

———. *The Law of Slander in Early Antebellum America*, 35 Am. J. Legal Hist. 1 (1991).

King, Willard L. Lincoln's Manager, David Davis (1960).

———. *Review*, 55 J. Ill. St. Hist. Soc'y 96 (1962).

———. *Riding the Circuit with Lincoln*, 6 Am. Heritage 48 (Feb. 1955).

Klafter, Craig Evan. *The Influence of Vocational Law Schools on the Origins of American Legal Thought, 1779–1829*, 37 Am. J. Legal Hist. 307 (1993).

Knupfer, Peter B. *Henry Clay's Constitutional Unionism*, 89 Reg. Ky. Hist. Soc'y 32 (1991).

Koch, Klaus-Friedrich et al. *Social Structure, Ritual Reconciliation, and the Obviation of Grievances: A Comparative Essay in the Anthropology of Law*, 16 Ethnology 269 (1979).

Koenig, Thomas & Michael Rustad. *The Challenge to Hierarchy in Legal Education: Suffolk and the Night Law School Movement*, 7 Res. In Law, Deviance & Soc. Control 189 (1984).

Kohl, Lawrence. The Politics of Individualism: Parties and the American Character in the Jacksonian Era (1989).

Konefsky, Alfred S. *"As Best to Subserve Their Own Interests": Lemuel Shaw, Labor Conspiracy, and Fellow Servants*, 7 Law & Hist. Rev. 219 (1989).

Konig, David Thomas. Law and Society in Puritan Massachusetts: Essex County, 1629–1692 (1979).

Kostal, R.W. Law and English Railway Capitalism 1825–1875 (1994).

Krause, Susan. *Abraham Lincoln and Joshua Speed, Attorney and Client*, 89 Ill. Hist. J. 35 (Spring 1996).

Landon, Donald M. *Clients, Colleagues, and Community: The Shaping of Zealous Advocacy in Country Law Practice*, 1985 Am. B. Found. Res. J. 81.

———. *Lawyers and Localities: The Interaction of Community Context and Professionalism*, 1982 Am. B. Found. Res. J. 81.

Langbein, John H. *Historical Foundations of the Law of Evidence: A View From the Ryder Sources*, 96 Colum. L. Rev. 1168 (1996).

Larkin, Jack. The Reshaping of Everyday Life 1790–1840 (1988).

Laughlin, Bonnie E. *"Endangering the Peace of Society": Abolitionist Agitation and Mob Reform in St. Louis and Alton, 1836–1838*, 95 Mo. Hist. Rev. 1 (2000).

Lerner, Renee Lettow. *The Transformation of the American Civil Trial: The Silent Judge*, 42 Wm. & Mary L. Rev. 195 (2000).

Levy, Leonard W. *Chief Justice Shaw and the Formative Period of American Railroad Law* (pts. 1 & 2), 51 Colum. L. Rev. 327, 852 (1951).

———. The Law of the Commonwealth and Chief Justice Shaw (1957).

————. *Sims' Case: The Fugitive Slave Law in Boston in 1851*, 35 J. Negro Hist. 39 (1950).

Licht, Walter. Working for the Railroad: The Organization of Work in the Nineteenth Century (1983).

Lipartito, Kenneth. *What Have Lawyers Done for American Business? The Case of Baker & Botts of Houston*, 64 Bus. Hist. Rev. 489 (1990).

Lipartito, Kenneth & Joseph A. Pratt. Baker & Botts in the Development of Modern Houston (1991).

Lightner, David L. Labor on the Illinois Central Railroad 1852–1900 (1977).

Lincoln and the Illinois Central, Ill. Cent. Mag. 5 (Feb. 1927).

Luban, David, ed. The Good Lawyer: Lawyers' Roles and Lawyers' Ethics (1983).

Lucas, Marion B. A History of Blacks in Kentucky: From Slavery to Segregation, 1760–1891 (2d ed. 2003).

Lueckenhoff, Sandra K. Comment, *A. Lincoln, a Corporate Attorney and the Illinois Central Railroad*, 61 Mo. L. Rev. 393 (1996).

Lufkin, Richard Friend. *Mr. Lincoln's Light From Under a Bushel—1853*, 55 Lincoln Herald 2 (Winter 1953).

————. *Mr. Lincoln's Light From Under a Bushel—1854*, 56 Lincoln Herald 3 (Winter 1954).

Lupton, John A. *A. Lincoln, Esq.: The Evolution of a Lawyer, in* Allen D. Spiegel, A. Lincoln, Esquire: A Shrewd, Sophisticated Lawyer in His Time 18 (2002).

————. *Abraham Lincoln and His Informal Partners on the Eighth Judicial Circuit, in* Papers From the Thirteenth and Fourteenth Annual Lincoln Colloquia 96–99 (n.d.).

————. *Basement Barrister: Abraham Lincoln's Practice Before the Illinois Supreme Court*, 101 Lincoln Herald 47 (Summer 1999).

Martile, Roger. *John Frink and Martin Walker: Stagecoach Kings of the Old Northwest*, 95 J. Ill. St. Hist. Soc'y 119 (Summer 2002).

Masters, Edgar Lee. Lincoln the Man (1931).

Matthews, Donald R. *United States Senators and the Class Structure*, 18 Public Opinion Q. 5 (1954).

Matthews, Jean V. Rufus Choate: The Law and Civic Virtue (1980).

McIntyre, Duncan T. *Lincoln and the Matson Slave Case*, 1 Ill. L. Rev. (NW. U.) 386 (1906).

McMurtry, R. Gerald. *Centre College, John Todd Stuart and Abraham Lincoln*, 33 Filson Club Hist. Q. 117 (1959).

Mearns, David C. *Mr. Lincoln and the Books He Read, in* Three Presidents and Their Books (Arthur Bestor et al. eds., 1955).

Mellinkoff, David. The Conscience of a Lawyer (1973).

————. The Language of the Law (1963).

Metzmeier, Kurt X. *Blazing Trails in a New Kentucky Wilderness: Early Kentucky Case Law Digests*, 93 Law Libr. J. 93 (2001).

Middleton, Stephen. *Antislavery Litigation in Ohio: The Chase-Trowbridge Letters*, 70 Mid-America 105 (1988).

————. The Black Laws in the Old Northwest: A Documentary History (1993).

————. Ohio and the Antislavery Activities of Attorney Salmon Portland Chase 1830–1849 (1990).

Miller, Perry. The Life of the Mind in America, from the Revolution to the Civil War (1965).

Miller, Perry, ed. The Legal Mind in America: From Independence to the Civil War (1962).

Milsom, S.F.C. *The Nature of Blackstone's Achievement*, 1 Oxford J. Legal Stud. 1 (1981).

Moretta, John Anthony. William Pitt Ballinger: Texas Lawyer, Southern Statesman, 1825–1888 (2000).

Morris, Polly. Defamation and Sexual Reputation in Somerset, 1733–1850 (1985) (Ph.D. dissertation, University of Warwick).

Nash, A.E. Keir. *In Re Radical Interpretations of American Law: The Relation of Law and History*, 82 Mich. L. Rev. 274 (1983).

Neely, Mark E., Jr. The Abraham Lincoln Encyclopedia (1982).

———. *The Lincoln Theme Since Randall's Call*, 1 Papers of the Abraham Lincoln Ass'n 10 (1979).

[Neely, Mark E., Jr.] *Some New Light on the Matson Slave Case*, Lincoln Lore no. 1705, 3 (Mar. 1980).

Nelson, Robert L. *Practice and Privilege: Social Change and the Structure of Large Law Firms*, 1981 Am. B. Found. Res. J. 95.

Nevins, Allan. The Emergence of Lincoln (1950).

The New High Priests: Lawyers in Post–Civil War America (Gerald Gawalt ed., 1984).

Newmeyer, R. Kent. *Daniel Webster and the Modernization of American Law*, 32 Buff. L. Rev. 819 (1983).

———. Supreme Court Justice Joseph Story: Statesman of the Old Republic (1985).

Nicolay, John G. & John Hay. Abraham Lincoln: A History (10 vols. 1909).

Niven, John. *Lincoln and Chase, A Reappraisal*, 12 J. Abraham Lincoln Ass'n 1 (1991).

Nolan, Dennis R. *Sir William Blackstone and the New American Republic: A Study of Intellectual Impact*, 51 N.Y.U. L. Rev. 731 (1976).

Noonan, John T., Jr. Persons and Masks of the Law (1976).

Norton, Mary Beth. *Gender and Defamation in Seventeenth-Century Maryland*, 44 Wm. & Mary Q. 1 (1987).

Nortrup, Jack. *The Education of a Western Lawyer*, 12 Am. J. Legal Hist. 294 (1968).

Note, *As to liability of owners for trespass of cattle*, 22 L.R.A. 55 (1894).

Note, *Incorporating the Republic: The Corporation in Antebellum Political Culture*, 102 Harv. L. Rev. 1883 (1989).

Novak, William J. The People's Welfare: Law and Regulation in Nineteenth-Century America (1996).

Oates, Stephen B. With Malice Toward None: The Life of Abraham Lincoln (1977).

Ogden, James M. *Lincoln's Early Impressions of the Law in Indiana*, 7 Notre Dame L. 325 (1932).

On the Illinois Frontier: Dr. Hiram Rutherford 1840–1848 (Willene Hendrick & George Hendrick eds., 1981).

Paludan, Phillip S. *Lincoln's Pre-War Constitutional Vision*, 15 J. Abraham Lincoln Ass'n 1 (1994).

Page, Elwin L. *The Effie Afton Case*, 58 Lincoln Herald 3 (Fall 1956).

Parrish, Jenni. *Law Books and Legal Publishing in America, 1760–1840*, 72 Law Libr. J. 355 (1979).

Pearce, Russell G. *Rediscovering the Republican Origins of the Legal Ethics Codes*, 6 Geo. J. Legal Ethics 241 (1992).

Pease, William H. & Jane H. Pease. James Louis Petigru: Southern Conservative, Southern Dissenter (1995).

Peck, George R. *Abraham Lincoln as a Lawyer*, Report of the Annual Meeting of the Wisconsin State Bar Ass'n Held in the City of Madison, February 12 and 13, 1900.

Pessen, Edward. The Log Cabin Myth: The Social Backgrounds of the Presidents (1984).

Peterson, Merrill D. Lincoln in American Memory (1994).

Pollitt, Daniel H. *Counsel For the Unpopular Cause*, 43 N.C. L. Rev. 9 (1964).

Post, Robert C. *On the Popular Image of the Lawyer: Reflections in a Dark Glass*, 75 Cal. L. Rev. 379 (1987).

Potter, David M. The South and the Sectional Conflict (1968).

Pound, Roscoe. The Formative Era of American Law (1938).

Pratt, Harry E. *Abraham Lincoln in Bloomington, Illinois*, 29 J. Ill. St. Hist. Soc'y 42 (1936).

———. *A Beginner on the Old Eighth Judicial Circuit*, 44 J. Ill. St. Hist. Soc'y 241 (1951).

———. *David Davis, 1815–1886*, Ill. St. Hist. Soc'y Trans. 157 (1930).

———. *The Genesis of Lincoln the Lawyer*, Bull. Abraham Lincoln Ass'n (Sept. 1939).

———. Lincoln 1809–1839 (1941).

———. *Lincolniana: The Famous "Chicken Bone" Case*, 45 J. Ill. St. Hist. Soc'y 164 (1952).

———. *Lincoln's Supreme Court Cases*, 32 Ill. B.J. 23 (1943).

———. The Personal Finances of Abraham Lincoln (1943).

Randall, J.G. *Has the Lincoln Theme Been Exhausted?*, 41 Am. Hist. Rev. 270 (1936).

———. Lincoln the President: Springfield to Gettysburg (2 vols. 1946).

Reed, Alfred Zantzinger. Training for the Public Profession of the Law (1921).

Rehnquist, William H. *Daniel Webster and the Oratorical Tradition, in* Yearbook 1989, Sup. Ct. Hist. Soc'y 6 (1989).

Review, 6 Am. J. Legal Hist. 86 (1962).

Richards, John T. Abraham Lincoln: The Lawyer-Statesman (1916).

Richards, Leonard L. "Gentlemen of Property and Standing": Anti-Abolition Mobs in Jacksonian America (1970).

Riddle, Donald W. Congressman Abraham Lincoln (1957).

Russell, Thomas D. *The Antebellum Courthouse as Creditors' Domain: Trial-Court Activity in South Carolina and the Concomitance of Lending and Litigation*, 40 Am. J. Legal Hist. 331 (1996).

———. *Articles Sell Best Singly: The Disruption of Slave Families at Court Sales*, 1996 Utah L. Rev. 1161 (1996).

———. *Historical Study of Personal Injury Litigation: A Comment on Method*, 1 Ga. J. S. Legal Hist. 109 (1991).

———. *A New Image of the Slave Auction: An Empirical Look at the Role of Law in Slave Sales and a Conceptual Reevaluation of the Nature of Slave Property*, 18 Cardozo L. Rev. 473 (1996).

Scheiber, Harry N. Ohio Canal Era: A Case Study of Government and the Economy, 1820–1861 (1969).

Schlegel, John Henry. *The Line Between History and Casenote*, 22 Law & Soc'y Rev. 969 (1988).

Schlesinger, Arthur M., Jr. The Age of Jackson (1945).

Schluter, Herman. Lincoln, Labor and Slavery (1965) (1913).

Schnell, Christopher A. *At the Bar and on the Stump: Douglas and Lincoln's Legal Relationship, in* Papers From the Thirteenth and Fourteenth Annual Lincoln Colloquia 99–106 (n.d.).

Schudson, Michael. Origins of the Ideal of Objectivity in the Professions: Studies in the History of American Journalism and American Law, 1830–1940 (1990).

Schwartz, Thomas F. *The Springfield Lyceums and Lincoln's 1838 Speech*, 83 Ill. Hist. J. 45 (1990).

Sellers, Charles. The Market Revolution: Jacksonian America 1815–1846 (1991).

Sellers, Charles Grier, Jr. *Who Were the Southern Whigs?* 59 Am. Hist. Rev. 335 (1954).

Shaffer, Thomas L. American Legal Ethics (1985).

Shepherd, E. Lee. *Breaking into the Profession: Establishing a Law Practice in Antebellum Virginia*, 48 J. S. Hist. 393 (1982).

Siegel, Andrew M. Note, *"To Learn and Make Respectable Hereafter": The Litchfield Law School in Cultural Context*, 73 N.Y.U. L. Rev. 1978 (1998).

Silbey, Joel H. *"Always a Whig in Politics": The Partisan Life of Abraham Lincoln*, 7 Papers of the Abraham Lincoln Ass'n 21 (1986).

Simeone, James. Democracy and Slavery in Frontier Illinois: The Bottomland Republic (2000).

Simpson, Brooks D. *Daniel Webster and the Cult of the Constitution*, 15 J. Am. Culture 15 (1992).

Smith, Elmer A. Abraham Lincoln: An Illinois Central Lawyer (pamph. 1945).

Spaulding, Norman W. *The Myth of Civic Republicanism: Interrogating the Ideology of Antebellum Legal Ethics*, 71 Fordham L. Rev. 1397 (2003).

Spencer, Omar C. *Abraham Lincoln, The Lawyer, in* Thirty-Sixth Annual Convention Report of the Proceedings of the Washington State Bar Ass'n 133 (1924).

Sprecher, Robert A. *Admission to Practice Law in Illinois*, 46 Ill. L. Rev. (Nw. U.) 811 (1952).

Stampp, Kenneth. The Era of Reconstruction (1965).

Starr, John W., Jr. Lincoln and the Railroads (1927).

Steiner, Mark E. *Abolitionists and Escaped Slaves in Jacksonville: Samuel Willard's My First Adventure With a Fugitive Slave: The Story of It and How It Failed*, 89 Ill. Hist. J. 213 (1996).

———. *General Catalogue of Law Books, Alphabetically Classified by Subjects (1859)*, 18 Legal Ref. Servs. Q. 47 (1999).

Stephen T. Logan Talks About Lincoln, Bull. Lincoln Centennial Ass'n 3 (Sept. 1, 1928).

Stevenson, James A. *Abraham Lincoln on Labor and Capital*, 38 Civil War Hist. 197 (1992).

Stover, John F. History of the Illinois Central Railroad (1975).

Stowell, Daniel W., ed. In Tender Consideration: Women, Families, and the Law in Abraham Lincoln's Illinois (2002).

Strickland, Arvarh E. *The Illinois Background of Lincoln's Attitude Toward Slavery and the Negro*, 56 Ill. St. Hist. Soc'y J. 474 (1963).

Strozier, Charles B. Lincoln's Quest for Union: Public and Private Meanings (1982).

———. *The Lives of William Herndon*, 14 J. Abraham Lincoln Ass'n 1 (1993).

Sunderland, Edwin S. Abraham Lincoln and the Illinois Central Railroad (1955).

Surrency, Erwin C. A History of American Law Publishing (1990).

———. *Law Reports in the United States*, 25 Am. J. Legal Hist. (1981).

Sutton, Robert M. *Lincoln and the Railroads of Illinois, in* Lincoln Images: Augusta College Centennial Essays (O. Fritiof Ander ed., 1960).

Swaine, Robert T. The Cravath Firm and Its Predecessors 1819–1947 (1946).

Swisher, Carl B. The Taney Period 1836–1864 (1974).

Taylor, George Rogers. The Transportation Revolution 1815–1860 (1951).

Temple, Wayne C. *Lincoln, Moore and Greene: A New Document*, 93 Lincoln Herald 9 (Spring 1991).

Thomas, Benjamin P. *Abe Lincoln, Country Lawyer*, 193 Atlantic Monthly 57 (Feb. 1954).

———. Abraham Lincoln: A Biography (1952).

———. *The Eighth Judicial Circuit*, Bull. Abraham Lincoln Ass'n (Sept. 1935).

———. *Lincoln and the Courts, 1854–1861*, Abraham Lincoln Ass'n Papers (1933).

———. *Lincoln's Earlier Practice in the Federal Courts 1839–1854*, Bull. Abraham Lincoln Ass'n (June 1935).

———. Portrait for Posterity: Lincoln and His Biographers (1947).

Thomas, William G. Lawyering for the Railroad: Business, Law, and Power in the New South (1999).

Thompson, Charles Manfred. The Illinois Whigs Before 1846 (1915).

Thompson, E.P. *Time, Work-Discipline, and Industrial Capitalism*, Past & Present 56 (1967).

Thornton, J. Mills. Politics and Power in a Slave Society: Alabama, 1800–1860 (1978).

Tomlins, Christopher L. *A Mysterious Power: Industrial Accidents and the Legal Construction of Employment Relations in Massachusetts, 1800–1850*, 6 Law & Hist. Rev. 375 (1988).

Townsend, William H. *Lincoln on the Circuit*, 12 A.B.A. J. 91 (1926).

———. *Lincoln's Law Books*, 15 A.B.A. J. 125 (1929).

Turner, James. *Use of the Courts in the Movement to Abolish American Slavery*, 31 Ohio St. L.J. 305 (1970).

Vandervelde, Lea & Sandhya Subramanian. *Mrs. Dred Scott*, 106 Yale L.J. 1033 (1997).

Verduin, Paul H. *A New Lincoln Discovery: Rebecca Thomas, His 'Revolutionary War Widow,'* 98 Lincoln Herald 3 (Spring 1996).

———. *Partners for Emancipation: New Light on Lincoln, Joshua Giddings, and the Push to End Slavery in the District of Columbia, 1848–49*, in Papers from the Thirteenth and Fourteenth Annual Lincoln Colloquia 67–86 (n.d.).

Vidal, Gore. Lincoln: A Novel (1984).

Wambaugh, Eugene. *Salmon Portland Chase, in* Great American Lawyers (William Draper Lewis ed., 1908).

Warren, Charles. A History of the American Bar (1966) (1911).

Warren, Louis A. *Herndon's Contribution to Lincoln Mythology*, 41 Ind. Mag. Hist. 221 (1945).

———. *Lincoln's Law Library*, Lincoln Lore, no. 619 (Feb. 17, 1941).

Weik, Jesse W. *A Law Student's Recollection of Abraham Lincoln*, 97 Outlook 311 (1911).

———. *Lincoln and the Matson Negroes*, 17 Arena Mag. 752 (Apr. 1897).

———. *Lincoln as a Lawyer: With an Account of his First Case*, 68 Century Mag. 279 (June 1904).

———. The Real Lincoln: A Portrait (1922).

White, G. Edward. The Marshall Court and Cultural Change, 1815–35 (1988).

Wiebe, Robert H. The Opening of American Society (1984).

Wiecek, William M. *Latimer: Lawyers, Abolitionists, and the Problem of Unjust Laws, in* Antislavery Reconsidered: New Perspectives on the Abolitionists (Lewis Perry & Michael Fellman eds., 1979).

———. The Sources of Antislavery Constitutionalism in America, 1760–1848 (1977).

———. *The Witch at the Christening: Slavery and the Constitution's Origins, in* The Framing and Ratification of the Constitution (Leonard W. Levy & Dennis J. Mahoney eds., 1987).

Wills, Garry. Lincoln at Gettysburg (1992).

Wilson, Douglas L. Honor's Voice: The Transformation of Abraham Lincoln (1998).

———. Lincoln Before Washington: New Perspectives on the Illinois Years (1997).

———. *William H. Herndon and His Lincoln Informants*, 14 J. Abraham Lincoln Ass'n 15 (1993).

Wilson, Edmund. Patriotic Gore (1987) (1962).

Wilson, Major L. *Lincoln and Van Buren in the Steps of the Fathers: Another Look at the Lyceum Address*, 29 Civil War Hist. 197 (1983).

Wilson, Terry. *The Business of a Midwestern Trial Court: Knox County, Illinois, 1841–1850*, 84 Ill. Hist. J. 249 (1991).

Winkle, Kenneth J. The Young Eagle: The Rise of Abraham Lincoln (2001).

Witt, John Fabian. Note, *The Transformation of Work and the Law of Workplace Accidents, 1842–1910*, 107 Yale L.J. 1467 (1998).

Woldman, Albert A. Lawyer Lincoln (1936).

Wolfram, Charles W. Modern Legal Ethics (1986).

Index of Cases

General Index

Herndon's Lincoln: The True Story of a Great Life, 5, 7–10, 12, 19, 22–23, 27, 40–41, 160–61

Herndon's Lincoln: The True Story of a Great Life (Herndon and Weik), 5, 7–10, 12, 19, 22–23, 27, 40–41, 160–61

Hewett, Josephus, 79

Hickox, Virgil, 86

Hill, Frederick Trevor, 174; *The Care of Estates,* 21; *Lincoln the Lawyer,* 21–22

Hill, George L., 144–45

Hilliard, Francis, *Elements of Law: Being A Comprehensive Summary of American Jurisprudence,* 36

Hines, Robert, 94

historiography of Lincoln's law practice: and biographers, early, 5, 10–12; and biographers, modern, 5, 13–18; canonical cases, 5–6, 14, 18; and circuit riding, 10; and cultural image of lawyers, 5–7, 10–12; and cultural image of Lincoln, 5, 7–8, 10; documentary problems, 8–9, 17; and folklore Lincoln, 7, 8, 11, 13; and avoiding law practice, 5, 17–18; lawyers appropriate Lincoln's image, 18–24; and Lincoln Legal Papers, 9, 17; memoirs by contemporaries, 5, 7–10; and professionalization of history, 17

Hoeflich, M. H., 41

Hoffman, David, *Course of Legal Study,* 132–33, 135

Hoffman, Murray, *A Treatise upon the Practice of the Court of Chancery,* 47(t)

Hofstadter, Richard, 11

Holland, Josiah Gilbert, 12, 103

Honor's Voice: The Transformation of Abraham Lincoln (Wilson), 18, 33

Horwitz, Morton J., 194n3

Hotchkiss, Henry, 102

Howard, James Quay, 33

Howells, William Dean, 33

Howland, Thomas A., 71

Hoyt, Charles, 42

Hughes, Matthew, 106

Hughes, Otto, 106

Humphreys, Charles, *Compendium of the Common Law in Force in Kentucky,* 36

Hurd, John S., 69

Hurst, James Willard, 7

Hutchason, L. R., 110

Illinois Black Code, 110–12, 114, 124

Illinois Central Railroad, 4, 6, 11–12, 18, 64, 72, 113, 137–40, 142–43, 145–52, 154–59, 167–74, 176

Illinois Constitution of 1818, 110, 114, 119, 152–53

Illinois Constitution of 1848, 150, 152–53

Illinois Digest (Freeman), 50

Illinois Historic Preservation Agency, 17

Illinois railroad incorporation Act, 139

Illinois Reports, 150

Illinois River, 64

Illinois Supreme Court, 15, 37–38, 48, 50, 52–53, 59, 61–62, 64, 66–67, 71, 77, 79, 81–82, 86, 88–89, 92–93, 98, 114–15, 117–18, 130–31, 135, 137, 140–43, 145, 147–48, 150–58

indentured servitude, 110, 114–15, 122

instrumentalism, 55, 60, 63

insurance, 69

An Introduction to American Law (Walker), 29–30, 34–35

Irwin, James S., 71

Jackson, J. F., 133

Jacobus, Mary Ann, 97

Jefferson, Thomas, 34, 37, 41

Jennings, James F., 84

John Frink & Co., 69

Johnson, Andrew, 28

Johnson, Samuel, 84

Johnson, William, *A Digest of the Cases,* 51(t)

Jones, Albert, 40

Jones, John, 84

Joy, James F., 138, 151, 169, 172–73, 175

Judd, Norman, 98, 173

judges, election of, 60

juries, 58, 83–84, 87, 89–91, 93–94, 97–99, 101, 159, 173–74; as fact finder, 59; as judges of law and fact, 59; instructions for, 59, 81–82, 94, 141–42; and railroad cases, 144–45

Keeling, Haden, 86

Kennedy, John Pendleton, *Swallow Barn,* 30

Kent, James, 43; *Commentaries on American Law,* 30, 44(t), 77, 152

Ketcham, Christopher, 82

Ketcham, Josephus, 82

King, George A., 62